SLOW

Cheshire

Local, characterful guides to Britain's special places

Kate Simon & Suzanne King

EDITION 1
Bradt Travel Guides Ltd, UK
The Globe Pequot Press Inc, USA

TAKING IT SLOW IN

Cheshire

A SNAPSHOT OF THE REGION

Take things Slow in Cheshire and you'll discover just how diverse and diverting a county it is, its lush green pastures and forests criss-crossed by tranquil canals, studded with handsome stately homes and gardens and enlivened with a generous dollop of quirky character.

ROY CONCHIE/A

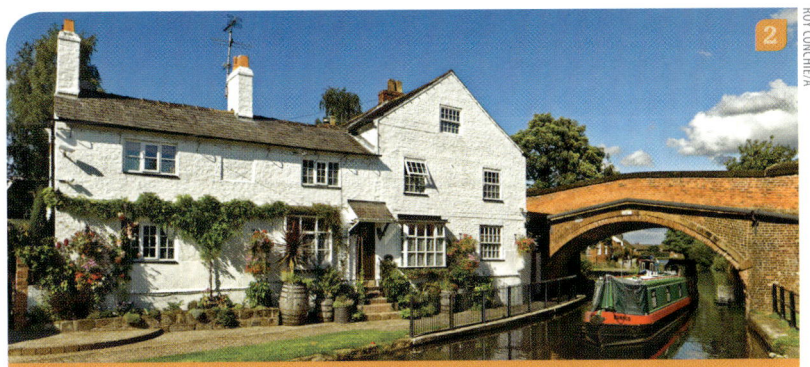

1 Two of Cheshire's three highest peaks in one shot: the view from Shining Tor towards Shutlingsloe. 2 The Bridgewater Canal, arguably Britain's first canal, at Lymm. 3 The quaint cottages at Beeston were built by Lord Tollemache for the workers on his estate. 4 The cheese world descends on Nantwich each year for the world-famous International Cheese Show. 5 Delamere Forest is a remnant of the ancient forests of Mara and Mondrem.

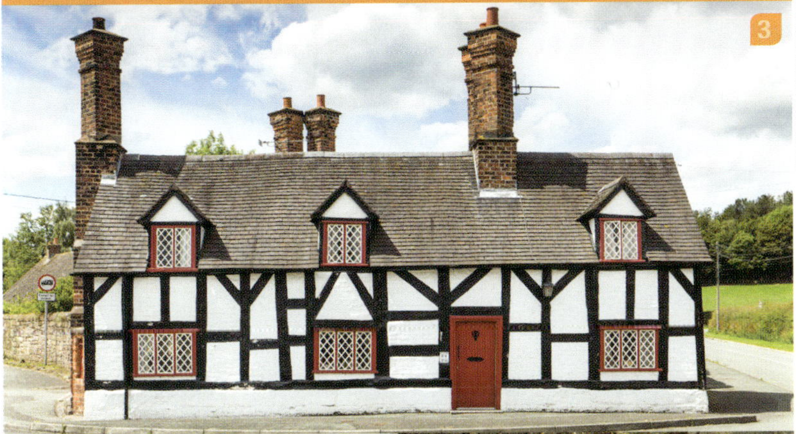

JOE WAINWRIGHT PHOTOGRAPHY

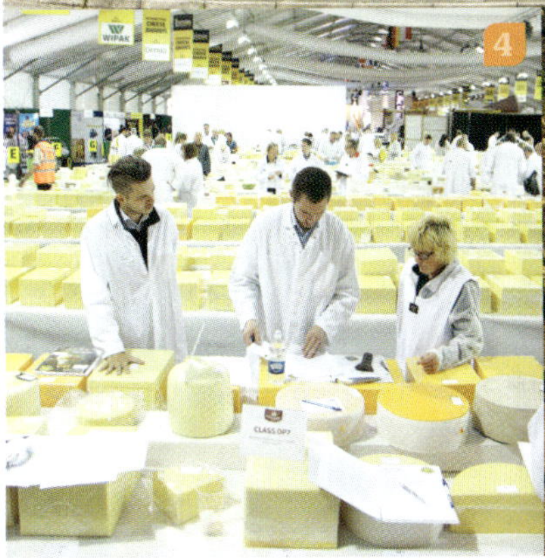

TIM JERVIS PHOTOGRAPHY

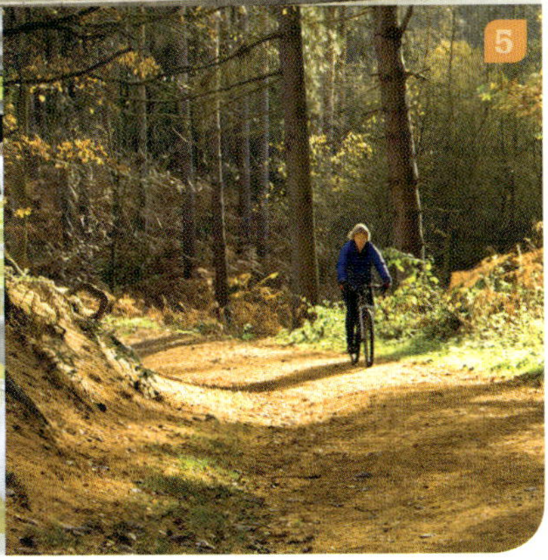

ALAN NOVELLI/A

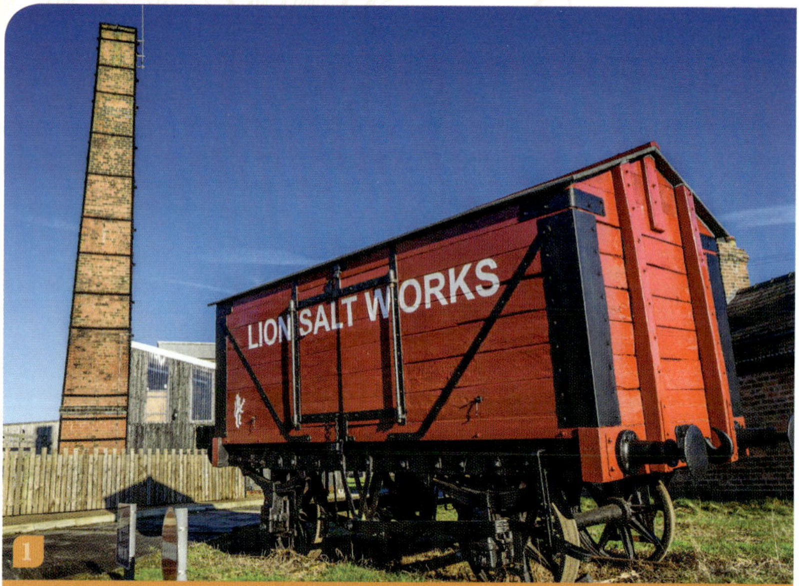

HISTORY & HERITAGE

Over the centuries, many have left their mark on the local landscape. Viking influences are easy to find on the Wirral peninsula; the Romans began the salt industry that played a big part in the county's history; and Victorian industrialists left a rich legacy of handsome mills, model villages and impressive feats of engineering.

1 Learn all about Cheshire salt at Lion Salt Works. 2 The Anderton Boat Lift showcases Victorian engineering at its most ingenious. 3 Quarry Bank offers an insight into the lives of mill workers in the 18th and 19th centuries. 4 The National Waterways Museum in Ellesmere Port. 5 Port Sunlight village was created by William Hesketh Lever for his workers. 6 The railway transformed Crewe into an industrial town. 7 The Lovell Telescope keeps an eye on the sky at Jodrell Bank. 8 Hack Green Secret Nuclear Bunker is hidden in the countryside near Nantwich.

THE GREAT & THE GRAND

Cheshire is blessed when it comes to impressive stately homes, picturesque ruins and glorious gardens. Scattered across the county you'll find everything from the remains of ancient castles and abbeys to photogenic Victorian follies and magnificent Georgian halls. And if you love a timber-framed mansion, you're in for a treat – in Little Moreton Hall and Bramall Hall, Cheshire has two of the best in England.

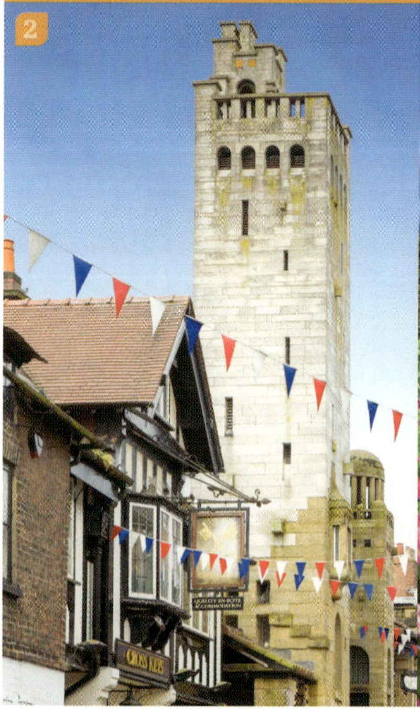

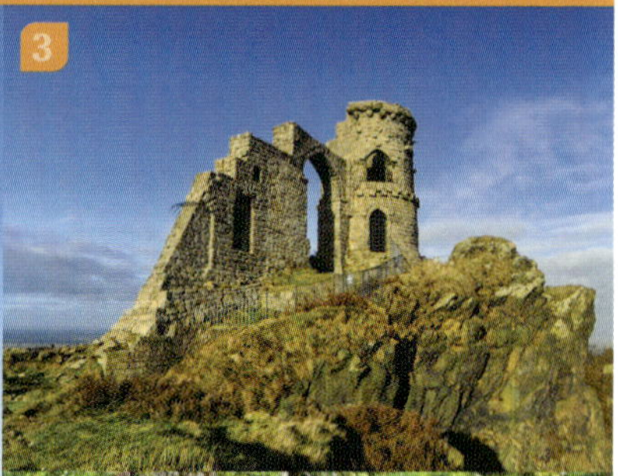

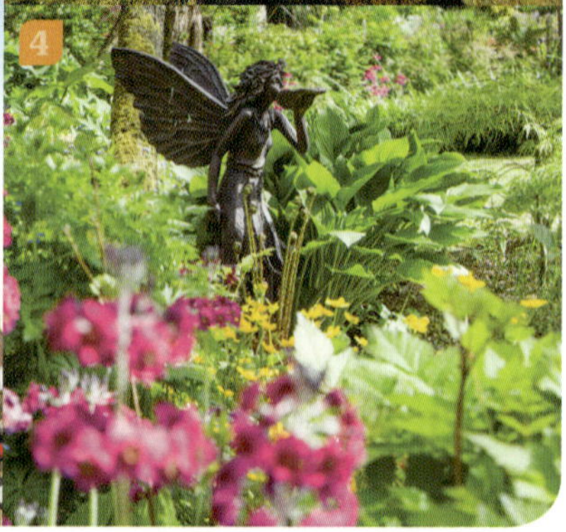

C.J.WILLIAMSON/S

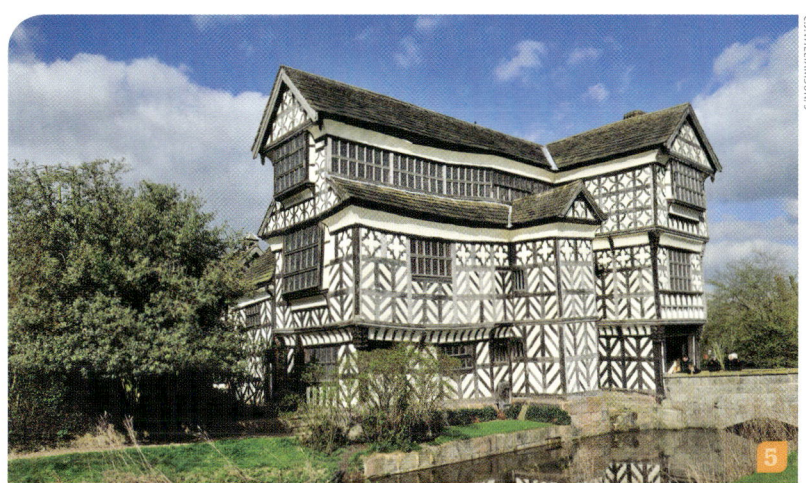

1 Lyme Park played Pemberley in the 1995 BBC series of *Pride and Prejudice*. 2 The Gaskell Memorial Tower is a tribute to former Knutsford resident Elizabeth Gaskell. 3 Mow Cop masquerades as castle ruins but is a Victorian folly. 4 Children can go on the trail of fairies at Stonyford Cottage Gardens. 5 Little Moreton Hall is an extraordinary legacy from Tudor times. 6 At Mount Pleasant Gardens there are sculptures as well as shrubs to admire. 7 Romantic Cholmondeley Castle is surrounded by one of Cheshire's finest gardens.

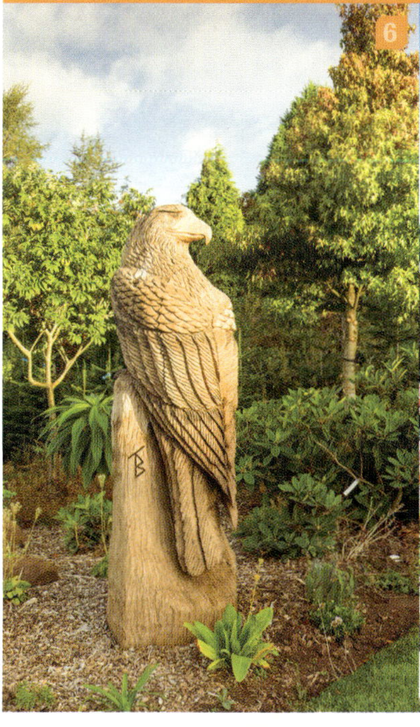

JOE WAINWRIGHT PHOTOGRAPHY

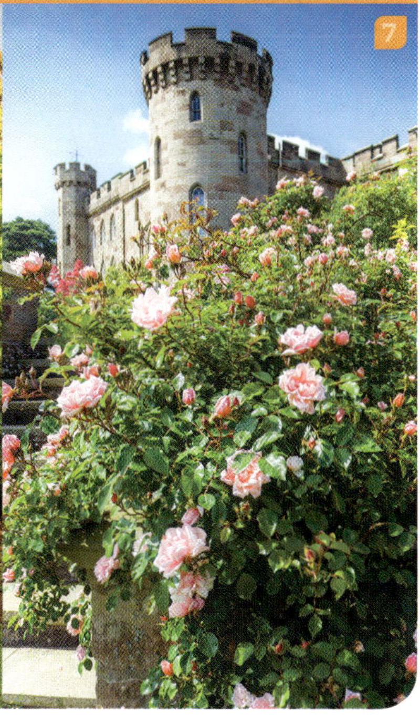

JOE WAINWRIGHT PHOTOGRAPHY

JOE WAINWRIGHT PHOTOGRAPHY

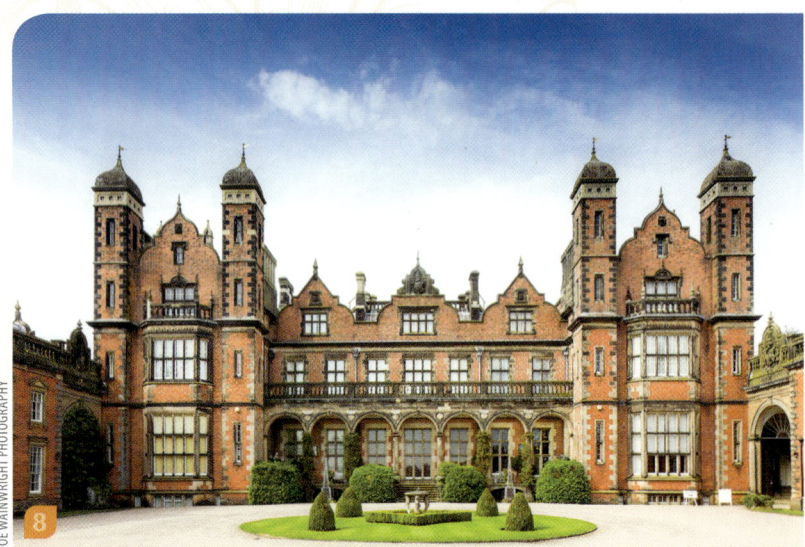

8 The Elizabethan-style turrets and gables of Capesthorne Hall provide a photogenic backdrop for summer events including music festivals and classic car shows. 9 Allow plenty of time to wander round the grounds of Arley Hall, where the rich variety of horticultural landscapes is sheer joy for garden-lovers.

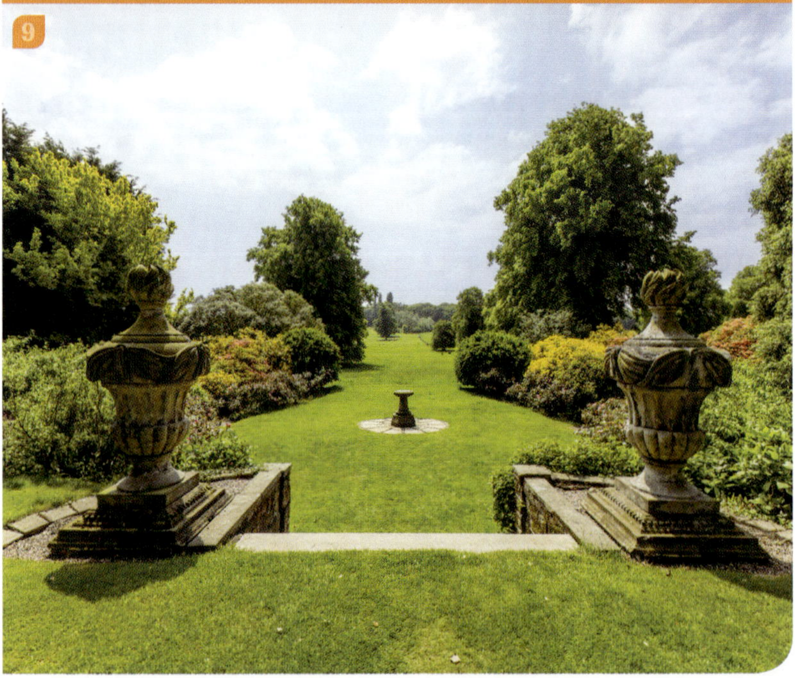

DEBUSSY/S

AUTHORS

Kate Simon has been a writer and editor for more than 30 years. She is a former Travel Editor of the *Independent on Sunday* and has written for national newspapers and magazines including *The Independent*, *Daily Telegraph*, *The Guardian* and *National Geographic Traveller*.

Suzanne King has worked in journalism for 30 years and is now a freelance travel writer and editor. Her work has appeared in titles as diverse as *The Guardian* and *Grazia*, *Condé Nast Traveller* and *Cosmopolitan*, and she regularly reviews hotels (including many in Cheshire) for *Telegraph Travel*.

AUTHORS' STORIES

Cheshire is where I (Kate) grew up, first in Alsager and later in Nantwich. When I moved to London to pursue a career in journalism, I kept strong links with friends and family in the area but it was an invitation from Visit Cheshire in 2010 to write a food and drink trail for them that marked the beginning of my rediscovery of my home turf. A new view opened up to me as I travelled across the Plain to the foothills of the Peak District in one direction and the shores of Wirral in the other, seeking out the county's best food and drink producers and providers. It sparked a desire to tell more stories about this often disregarded county and led directly to this book, for which I persuaded my co-author to join me.

Suzanne, too, grew up in Cheshire (in Poynton, Cheadle Hulme and Alderley Edge) and since returning ten years ago to her northwest roots, she has been relishing the 'Slower' pace of life it offers. For both of us, co-authoring this guide provided the perfect chance to revisit old haunts and discover new ones as we walked the county's hills and towpaths, explored its gardens and stately homes, and stocked our cupboards with fine local produce from the many excellent farm shops.

First edition published June 2018
Bradt Travel Guides Ltd
IDC House, The Vale, Chalfont St Peter, Bucks SL9 9RZ, England
www.bradtguides.com
Print edition published in the USA by The Globe Pequot Press Inc,
PO Box 480, Guilford, Connecticut 06437-0480

Text copyright © 2018 Kate Simon & Suzanne King
Maps copyright © 2018 Bradt Travel Guides Ltd; includes map data © OpenStreetMap contributors
Photographs copyright © 2018 Individual photographers (see below)
Project Managers: Laura Pidgley & Anne-Marie McLeman
Cover research: Pepi Bluck, Perfect Picture

The author and publisher have made every effort to ensure the accuracy of the information in this book at the time of going to press. However, they cannot accept any responsibility for any loss, injury or inconvenience resulting from the use of information contained in this guide. All rights reserved. No part of this publication may be reproduced, stored in a retrieval system, or transmitted in any form or by any means, electronic, mechanical, photocopying, recording or otherwise without the prior consent of the publisher. Requests for permission should be addressed to Bradt Travel Guides Ltd in the UK (print and digital editions), or to The Globe Pequot Press Inc in North and South America (print edition only).

ISBN: 978 1 78477 082 2 (print)
e-ISBN: 978 1 78477 553 7 (e-pub)
e-ISBN: 978 1 78477 454 7 (mobi)

British Library Cataloguing in Publication Data
A catalogue record for this book is available from the British Library

Photographs
Photos © individual photographers and organisations credited beside images & also from picture libraries credited as follows: Alamy.com (A), Cheshire Wildlife Trust (CWT), Dreamstime.com (D), Shutterstock.com (S), SuperStock.com (SS)

Front cover Beeston Castle (Alan Novelli/A)
Back cover View across Tegg's Nose Country Park (www.markhelliwell.com)
Title page Bollington (Stanth/S)

Maps David McCutcheon FBCart.S

Typeset by Ian Spick, Bradt Travel Guides
Production managed by Jellyfish Print Solutions; printed in the UK
Digital conversion by www.dataworks.co.in

ACKNOWLEDGEMENTS

We have been overwhelmed by the generosity of the many people who have helped out during the research for this book. Our thanks go to the locals who showed us around their communities, to the volunteers and staff in various attractions who took the time to share their knowledge and enthusiasm, and to all the people in pubs, cafés and shops who found themselves being grilled about the local area and were patient enough to answer our many questions. Although there isn't room to mention everyone by name, we're hugely grateful to you all. We also must thank everyone on the team at Bradt for their support and hard work throughout the project.

KATE SIMON
Special thanks to the Marketing Cheshire team, to Rebecca Wainwright and Katie Bentley for their orientating tours, to Arnold and Simon Forrester for knitting a hole in a walk after I was thwarted by the weather, and to Rachel Graham for joining me for part of my journey armed with her camera. I couldn't have written the book without the support of my business partner at Traveltappers, Simone Kane, and my mum, Violet 'Sted' Simon, who provided five-star bed, board and companionship during the months of research. Special thanks go to my husband Dean and son Quincy, who have fuelled me with tea and often taken my turn to walk Diggle the dog.

SUZANNE KING
Big thanks to the friends and family who went the extra mile to help out when help was needed. Anne King, Robert and Sharon King, Laura and Stuart Roberts, John Anderson, Angela Jarvis and Amanda Stone – all supported in different ways, all much appreciated. Extra big thanks go to Simon Jarvis, who joined me on all my explorations, fearlessly road-tested pies, cakes and ales, provided invaluable IT support and stayed remarkably good-humoured as our lives became dominated by all things Cheshire.

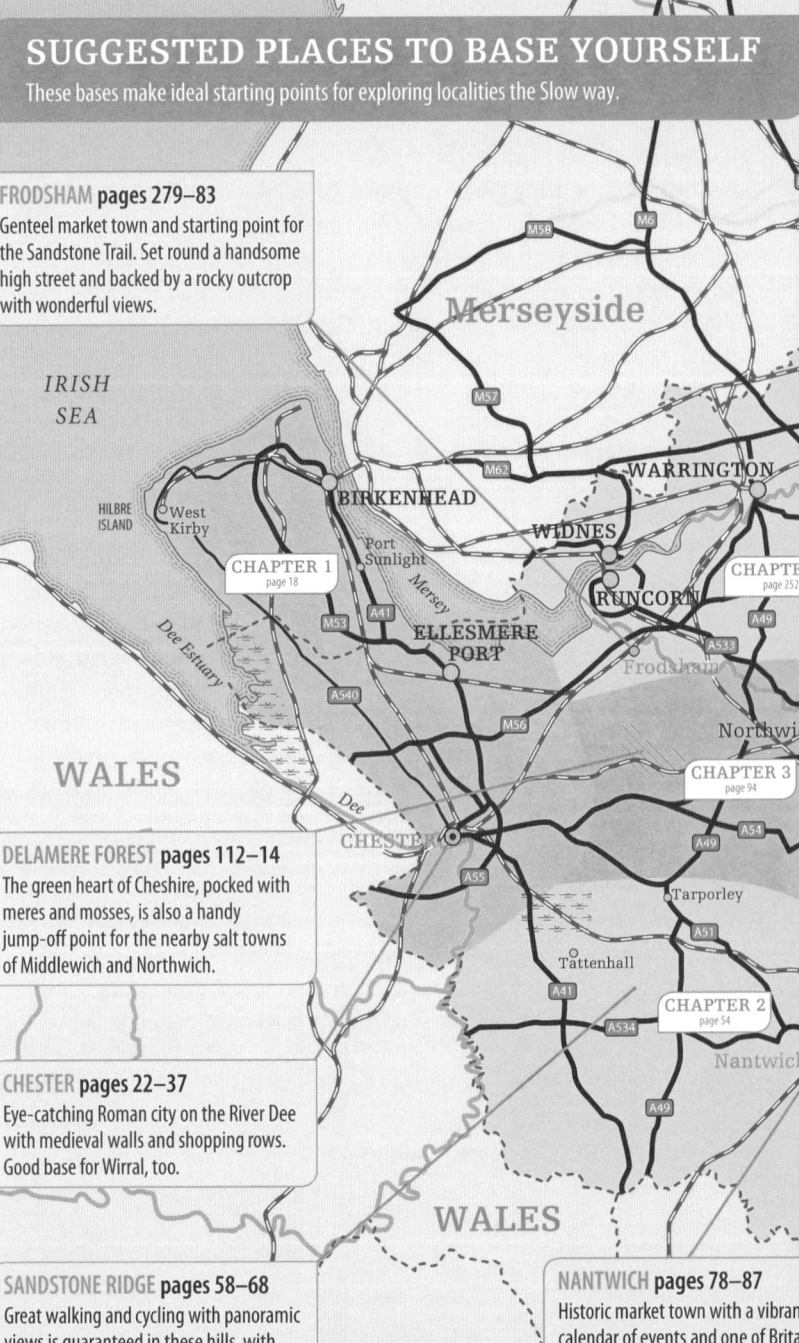

SUGGESTED PLACES TO BASE YOURSELF

These bases make ideal starting points for exploring localities the Slow way.

FRODSHAM pages 279–83
Genteel market town and starting point for the Sandstone Trail. Set round a handsome high street and backed by a rocky outcrop with wonderful views.

DELAMERE FOREST pages 112–14
The green heart of Cheshire, pocked with meres and mosses, is also a handy jump-off point for the nearby salt towns of Middlewich and Northwich.

CHESTER pages 22–37
Eye-catching Roman city on the River Dee with medieval walls and shopping rows. Good base for Wirral, too.

SANDSTONE RIDGE pages 58–68
Great walking and cycling with panoramic views is guaranteed in these hills, with forts and ancient villages to explore.

NANTWICH pages 78–87
Historic market town with a vibrant calendar of events and one of Britain's finest churches.

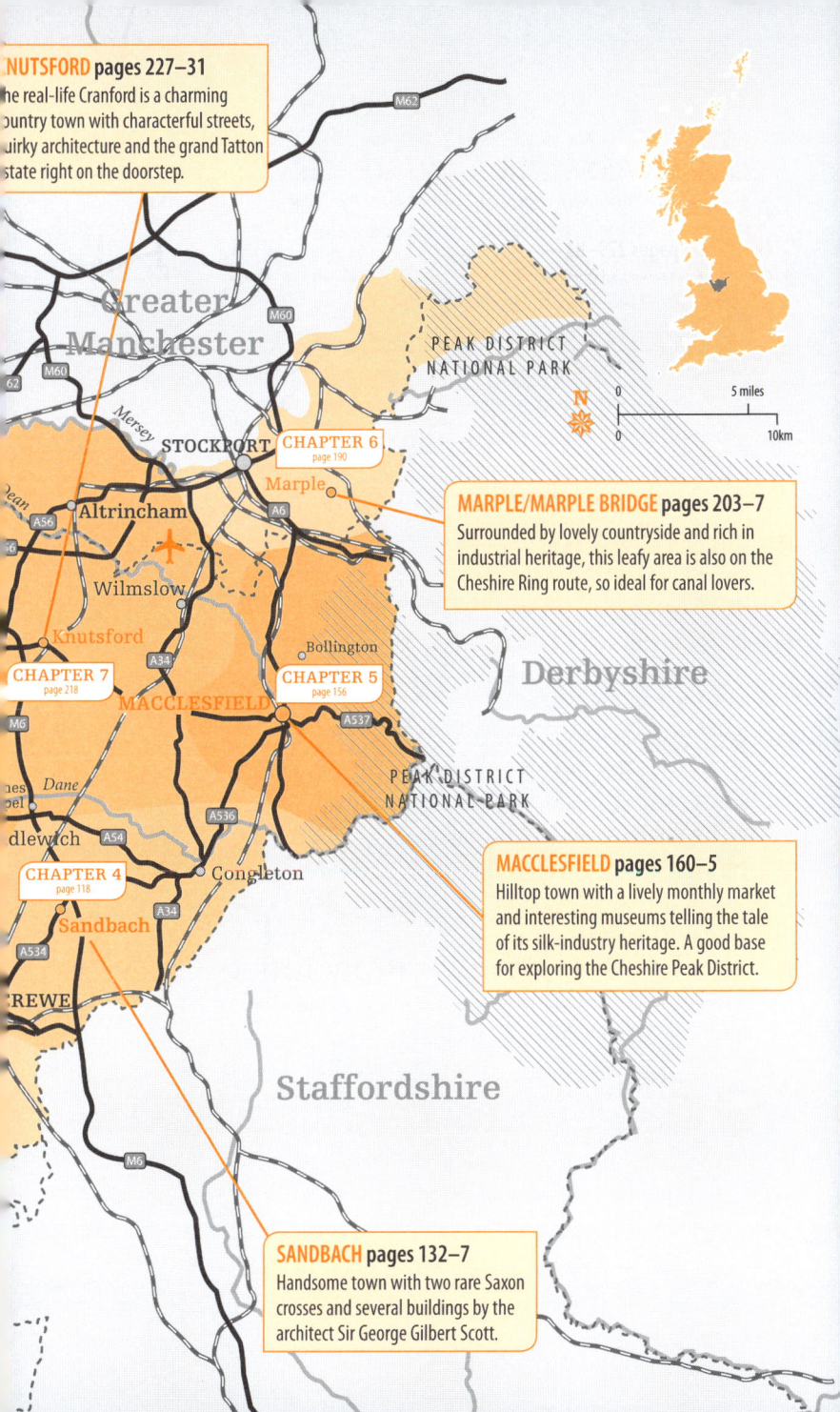

CONTENTS

GOING SLOW IN CHESHIRE 7
A taste of Cheshire **9**, Architecture **10**, Arts & culture **11**, Gardens **11**, Getting there & around **12**, How this book is arranged **15**

1 CHESTER & WIRRAL 19
Getting there & around **20**, Chester & around **22**, Wirral **40**

2 SOUTH CHESHIRE 55
Getting there & around **56**, The islands on the Cheshire Plain & around **58**, The Welsh & Shropshire borderlands **68**, Nantwich & around **78**

3 THE HEART OF THE PLAIN 95
Getting there & around **96**, Northwich to Middlewich & around **98**, Delamere Forest & around **111**

4 CREWE & THE STAFFORDSHIRE BORDERS........................... 119
Getting there & around **120**, Crewe to Alsager **121**, Sandbach, Congleton & around **132**

5 MACCLESFIELD & THE PEAK DISTRICT 157
Getting there & around **158**, Macclesfield & around **160**, North of Macclesfield **171**, Peak District National Park **179**

6 STOCKPORT & THE CHESHIRE PANHANDLE 191
Getting there & around **192**, Stockport & around **193**, Marple & around **203**, Werneth Low to Longdendale **212**

7 NORTHEAST CHESHIRE 219
Getting there & around **220**, Trafford **222**, Knutsford to Holmes Chapel **226**, Styal to Marton **241**

8 MERSEY & NORTHWEST CHESHIRE............. 253
Getting there & around **254**, Warrington & around **256**, Halton & around **265**, Lymm to Great Budworth **284**

ACCOMMODATION.. 291
INDEX 299

GOING SLOW IN
CHESHIRE

Cheshire is a county that confounds expectations. Visitors who come expecting it to be totally flat (most have heard of the Cheshire Plain) find instead that it has a wide variety of landscapes. Yes, there is indeed a central plain, but beyond that the land rolls and rises to the hills and moors of the Pennines and Peak District in the east and to surprisingly dramatic sandstone ridges in the west. Those who expect Cheshire to be landlocked are forgetting the Wirral peninsula, flanked by the major estuaries of the rivers Mersey and Dee, flowing into the Irish Sea.

Most people have heard of the county's famous dairy industry, so are unsurprised to find a largely rural landscape: Cheshire fields are filled with not just grazing cattle but also flocks of sheep and crops of grain – three golden wheatsheaves feature on the county's coat of arms. Less familiar, perhaps, is the industrial and scientific heritage, ranging from Bronze Age mining sites to the internationally important astronomical observatory at Jodrell Bank, the UK's nominee for UNESCO World Heritage Site status in 2019.

Those who come expecting bling (the county has become known for its multi-millionaire footballers, WAGs and *Real Housewives*) can certainly find it in the many affluent villages where the super wealthy have made their homes, but they'll also discover this is a part of the country with much to offer lovers of Slow travel. It's a land of market towns, meres and marshes, farm shops, forests and falconries, a place where people are happy to stop and chat to strangers and where you can easily find a deserted corner of woodland or moorland to yourself, or pick up flowers and fresh-laid eggs from a country-lane honesty stall.

The county town of Chester has a fascinating history, unique double-decker shopping arcades that date back to the Middle Ages and the most complete Roman and medieval city walls in Britain. Elsewhere, there are the ruins of ancient castles and reminders of the salt and silk industries that helped shape the county's fortunes. Some of the UK's loveliest gardens are here (home to several National Collections), as are many of the finest black-and-white mansions. You could make a literary pilgrimage around sites associated with local authors such as Lewis Carroll, Elizabeth Gaskell and Alan Garner, or follow in the musical footsteps of artists as diverse as Handel and Harry Styles. You can visit unique museums housing quirky collections and experience equally eccentric customs, from the world worm-charming championships at Willaston to fig pie rolling at Wybunbury.

Local legends abound, too, from the mermaid that appears in one of the county's many meres every Easter and the ghost of Britain's last

THE SLOW MINDSET
Hilary Bradt, Founder, Bradt Travel Guides

> We shall not cease from exploration
> And the end of all our exploring
> Will be to arrive where we started
> And know the place for the first time.
>
> T S Eliot, 'Little Gidding', *Four Quartets*

This series evolved, slowly, from a Bradt editorial meeting when we started to explore ideas for guides to our favourite country – Great Britain. We wanted to get away from the usual 'top sights' formula and encourage our authors to bring out the nuances and local differences that make up a sense of place – such things as food, building styles, nature, geology, or local people and what makes them tick. Our aim was to create a series that celebrates the present, focusing on sustainable tourism, rather than taking a nostalgic wallow in the past.

So without our realising it at the time, we had defined 'Slow Travel', or at least our concept of it. For the beauty of the Slow movement is that there is no fixed definition; we adapt the philosophy to fit our individual needs and aspirations. Thus Carl Honoré, author of *In Praise of Slow*, writes: 'The Slow Movement is a cultural revolution against the notion that faster is always better. It's not about doing everything at a snail's pace, it's about seeking to do everything at the right speed. Savouring the hours and minutes rather than just counting them. Doing everything as well as possible, instead of as fast as possible. It's about quality over quantity in everything from work to food to parenting.' And travel.

So take time to explore. Don't rush it, get to know an area – and the people who live there – and you'll be as delighted as the authors by what you find.

professional jester dancing along country lanes to the sleeping knights and their milk-white steeds who lie beneath the Cheshire countryside, ready to wake and save England in her hour of greatest need.

These are the kind of things you discover when you travel round Cheshire the Slow way. It's not simply about abandoning the car wherever possible in favour of more sustainable modes of transport (though it's certainly true that travelling around by bus, train, bike, boat or on foot is a better way to get beneath the county's skin). It's also about abandoning any preconceptions and expectations and travelling with an open mind, not just admiring Cheshire's obvious beauties but taking the time to head off the beaten track, unearthing treasures in unexpected places as well. There are plenty to find.

A TASTE OF CHESHIRE

Ask people what food they associate with Cheshire and they'll invariably say cheese. The familiar variety – crumbly, creamy and deliciously salty – is one of the country's oldest named cheeses, and was long its most popular. But traditional Cheshire is no longer the only local cheese; the ranks of the established cheesemakers are now being joined by small artisan producers, creating interesting new cheeses that have proceeded to win medals and awards around the globe – including at the International Cheese awards, held in Nantwich (see box, page 83). And if you fancy pulling your own pint of raw milk, there are handy self-service vending machines at Peckforton Farm Dairy (Peckforton Hall Ln, CW6 9TH), Chance Hall Farm at Rode Heath (Chance Hall Ln, CW12 4TL) and Street Farm Dairy near Kelsall (Street Farm Rd, CH3 8NR).

There's more to Cheshire dining than dairy foods, though. The county's lush pastures play their part in bringing high-quality lamb, beef and pork to the table (goat, too), and the River Dane contributes fresh trout to local restaurant menus. If you're lucky, they'll be accompanied by some of Cheshire's wonderful potatoes – look out for roadside signs in spring so you can stock up on new season spuds fresh from the farm. In summer you'll find pick-your-own fruit farms and gooseberry shows, while autumn brings an abundance of excellent apples and punnets of famous Cheshire damsons. Places to pick them – enough for a pie is the courteous thing to do – include the wild orchard by Lock 11 of the Bosley flight on the Macclesfield Canal and Marbury Orchard near Northwich.

To drink with your dinner? Try one of the new Cheshire gins being produced by small-batch distillers, including Forest Gin (⌀ forestgin.com) from Macclesfield Forest, Second Son (⌀ secondson.co.uk) on the edge of Delamere Forest, The Wirral Distillery near Spital (page 51) and Cheshire Gin in Wallasey (page 49) – the latter two you can visit for gin tastings. Alternatively, seek out craft ales from the wave of microbreweries and their taps, which continue to pop up around the county; you'll find details of these within individual chapters.

For those with a sweet tooth, the ace up Cheshire's foodie sleeve is its excellent ice cream. The area is now home to some fantastic ice-cream farms, from small family concerns to one of the largest parlours in the country. At the time of writing, one even comes with a giant statue of Peter Rabbit pulling a 10-foot carrot out of the fertile Cheshire soil …

A good starting point for foodie explorations is to visit the Taste Cheshire website (⌀ tastecheshire.com), where you'll find a directory of local food and drink producers, as well as independent restaurants, bars and shops.

ARCHITECTURE

Given Cheshire's pastoral image, you probably wouldn't expect to find much in the way of cutting-edge modern architecture – and you'd be right. What the county excels at is beautiful historic buildings. There are grand castles, such as those at Peckforton and Cholmondeley, and stately homes, including Adlington Hall and Lyme Park. A true Tudor beauty embellishes the countryside at Little Moreton Hall near Congleton, while the black-and-white revival of the 19th century is well represented in many market towns. There are reminders of the age of cotton in the conserved mills of Bollington and Macclesfield, and the more progressive attitudes of some employers reflected in model workers' villages such as Port Sunlight and Styal and the rural communities on the Grosvenor Estate. Some of Britain's finest churches can be found within the county boundaries - not just the mighty cathedral at Chester, but parish churches such as St Mary's at Astbury are particularly prized. There is also a starry cast list of architects to follow around Cheshire: the handiwork of Sir George Gilbert Scott, designer of the Albert Memorial, can be detected almost everywhere; Alfred Waterhouse, who built the Natural History

Museum, also makes appearances; as does Edward Blore, renowned for his work on Buckingham Palace.

ARTS & CULTURE

Cheshire punches above its weight when it comes to arts and culture. In 2017, Chester saw the opening of Storyhouse, comprising a theatre with its own repertory company – an unusual feature in this day and age – a cinema and a public library, confirming the county's commitment to the arts. Cultural venues, temporary and permanent, appear all over the place and in many different formats, from exhibitions at the Lady Lever Art Gallery in Wirral to concerts in the gardens of Gawsworth Hall. There is also a high-profile calendar of events to which folk flock from across the nation, including the family-friendly Just So Festival at Rode Hall (see box, page 153), and bluedot at Jodrell Bank (page 238), where music and science meet, with both international musicians and renowned scientists headlining. If you want to find out what's on during your visit, go to ⌗ visitcheshire.com and look at the 'Slant' programme.

GARDENS

One of Cheshire's biggest claims to fame is its gardens, both big and small, from the high-maintenance formal planting schemes created as show-off settings for grand stately homes to the pocket parks of Congleton. Keen gardeners could easily build a whole holiday around the county's horticultural highlights, which would have to include Ness Botanic Gardens, whose founder was responsible for introducing hundreds of new plants to the UK (including rhododendrons and camellias), and Tatton Park, which every July plays host to one of the RHS Flower Shows. Then there's Arley Hall, with glorious herbaceous borders that have been acclaimed as some of the finest in the world; Dunham Massey, where thousands of bulbs create carpets of colour in Britain's largest winter garden; and the Lovell Quinta Arboretum, home to more than 800 distinct species of trees and shrubs. There are ancient woodlands and walled gardens, National Collections and, at Combermere Abbey, the world's only maze made from fruit trees. Plus there is the chance to follow in the footsteps of some eminent designers including Lancelot 'Capability' Brown, Humphry Repton and Edward

Kemp, and discover the story of the herbalist John Gerard, a man so inspired by the natural landscape of the county of his birth that he wrote the first encyclopedia of plants.

GETTING THERE & AROUND

Cheshire is a mixed bag for the Slow traveller. In truth, unless you are on a cycling or long-distance walking holiday, some areas are tricky to access without a car, especially in the south and northeast of the county. That's not to say, though, that an entirely car-free holiday isn't possible; it will just require more planning. And it will be worth it – it's far more rewarding to experience the Cheshire countryside from the window seat of a train or bus than via its motorways.

Much of the county is covered by a comprehensive bus network (though evenings might be light on services), and you'll find more details about the main hubs and information sources in individual chapters. There are also good rail connections crossing from Crewe towards Liverpool and Manchester, as well as the Mid-Cheshire Line, which shuttles passengers across the Cheshire Plain northeast–southwest between Manchester and Chester, providing good jump-off points in some rural backwaters. Another useful rail link is the Wirral Line, which runs from Chester along the east coast of the peninsula to Liverpool, with a quick change enabling access to stations along the north coast, and round to West Kirby.

Cheshire's strong rail links also make it easy to get here from other parts of the country. There are fast trains from London Euston to Chester, Stockport, Macclesfield, Wilmslow, Runcorn, Warrington and Crewe. The latter, being an historic railway hub, also connects to the east

> **FEEDBACK REQUEST AND UPDATES WEBSITE**
>
> At Bradt Travel Guides we're aware that guidebooks start to go out of date on the day they're published – and that you, our readers, are out there in the field doing research of your own. You'll find out before us when a fine new family-run hotel opens or a favourite restaurant changes hands and goes downhill. So why not write and tell us about your experiences? Contact us on 01753 893444 or info@bradtguides.com. We will forward emails to the author who may post updates on the Bradt website at bradtupdates.com/cheshire. Alternatively, you can add a review of the book to bradtguides.com or Amazon.

and west. Use these lines not only to get here but to aid your movement around the county.

When you need to resort to car travel, major roads include the M6, M53 and M56, and the past 40 years has seen a steady upgrade in the local road network, striping Cheshire with fast highways. See the box on page 14 for a list of useful websites to help plan your journeys. Alternatively, individual journeys can be plotted using Traveline (traveline.info).

WALKING

For a county that most people think of as flat, there is a surprising mix of terrain to cover by foot. Certainly, there are a lot of paths on the level, but head to the Sandstone Ridge and the foothills of the Peak District and you'll find plenty of opportunities to work up a sweat with magnificent panoramas of the county and its neighbours as your reward. There's also a varied landscape in which to rejoice, enhanced by the changing seasons, with the patchwork of fields giving way to the wild fringes of waterways, plus opportunities to dip beneath forest canopies and even stride out on barren heaths.

Several notable long-distance paths run through Cheshire. Among the best are two ridge walks: the **Sandstone Trail**, from Whitchurch to Frodsham; and the **Gritstone Trail**, which arrives in Cheshire at Mow Cop and has Disley as its northern trailhead. The 70-mile **North Cheshire Way**, from Hooton on Wirral to Disley in the Peak District, and 34-mile **South Cheshire Way**, from the Shropshire border to Mow Cop, are also useful waymarked routes, as is the **Trans Pennine Trail**, which traces the north of the county from the Peaks to Runcorn. But there are also shorter routes and accessible greenway tracks to follow, details of which you'll find in the individual chapters. Don't forget, too, the extensive network of towpaths around the many canals, with the **Cheshire Ring Canal Walk** providing a neat circuit of their banks.

Cheshire has two '**Walkers are Welcome**' towns (walkersarewelcome. org.uk) – Bollington (pages 173–5) and Disley (pages 181–3) – both part of a national initiative to promote going by foot by offering information on local routes and ensuring footpaths and signposts are well maintained.

For more information on walking in Cheshire, check out the Mid-Cheshire Footpath Society (mcfs.org.uk) and The Long Distance Walkers Association (ldwa.org.uk). Other useful resources include

John Harris' Walking in England (⌁ walkingincheshire.co.uk/groups) and, for canal walks, the Canal & River Trust (⌁ canalrivertrust.org.uk).

CYCLING

There's cycling to suit everyone in Cheshire because while much of it is on the flat there are also hillier stretches for more serious cyclists. Families with young children will enjoy pootling around the safe, broad, traffic-free paths that have been laid where trains once travelled, such as the **Whitegate Way** (see box, page 106), while road cyclists will enjoy the scenic long-distance routes, with the steep ascents of the **Sandstone** and **Gritstone ridges** providing enticing challenges – even off-road cyclists can get their fix in the bike skills area at Delamere Forest. The cross-county **Cheshire Cycleway** (⌁ cheshirecycleway.co.uk) makes a 176-mile loop of the area – details of individual sections are given in relevant chapters. In Chester, a 'tube map' has been devised to show the best ways to get around the city on two wheels, and if you fancy following a refreshing route around the coast, the **Wirral Circular Trail** offers the opportunity to do just that.

CANALS

Slow travellers will adore the fact that Cheshire is criss-crossed by canals. Once used to take salt, ceramics and other goods towards the Mersey ports – and bring cargo such as clay and cotton inland – they now provide scenic routes to follow by bike, on foot and, of course, by narrowboat, with canalside beer gardens providing pleasant places to pause and contemplate how these serene waters were the expressways of their day. Six major canals weave their way around Cheshire, opening up a variety of landscapes to today's visitor, a point exploited by the clever marketeers who devised the cruising route The Cheshire Ring in

USEFUL WEBSITES

Visit Cheshire ⌁ visitcheshire.com; see ad, 4th colour section
Cheshire East ⌁ cheshireeast.gov.uk
Cheshire West & Chester ⌁ cheshirewestandchester.gov.uk
Cheshire Wildlife Trust ⌁ cheshirewildlifetrust.org.uk
Travel Cheshire ⌁ travelcheshire.co.uk
Your West Cheshire ⌁ yourwestcheshire.co.uk

the 1960s. They include the ground-breaking Bridgewater, considered the first modern British canal, which was created by the pioneering engineer James Brindley. His work can also be seen on the Trent and Mersey, the site of the Anderton Boat Lift, an admirable example of high Victorian engineering dubbed the 'Cathedral of the Canals'. The work of another giant of the canal age, Thomas Telford, can be appreciated along the Shropshire Union and at the canal hub he created at Ellesmere Port, now one of the two National Waterways Museums. Other manmade waterways include the Peak Forest, Macclesfield and Manchester Ship canals. There are marinas across the county and the widespread nature of the canals and how they interlink means that you can jump on at different points, though Middlewich and around is a particularly good central spot, offering the option of all points of the compass. Narrowboat operators are recommended in the introductions of the different chapters.

HOW THIS BOOK IS ARRANGED

When it came to writing a guidebook about Cheshire there was one big hurdle to overcome before we even started: how to define it. If ever a county had cause to be confused about its boundaries, it's this one, its borders messed about with so much over recent decades that even those who live here aren't always entirely sure where they lie. Once upon a time, the county had a particularly distinctive shape, described by some as looking like a teapot or Aladdin's lamp, though John Speed, a mapmaker and historian at the turn of the 17th century, had a more poetic turn of phrase, comparing it to an eagle's wing outstretched from Wirral to Yorkshire. In 1974 the eagle's wing was clipped (and the teapot/lamp lost both handle and spout) when large chunks of east and west were lopped off and handed over to other authorities, and the northern border shuffled in and out. The most recent tweak in a long history of border-bending came in 2009, when what remained was split into two separate administrative areas: Cheshire West and Chester, and Cheshire East, curling into each other like a yin and yang symbol.

After much deliberation, we opted for an all-inclusive approach, welcoming into the guide anywhere that's ever been considered part of this moveable feast of a county, and breaking it down into areas that felt like natural divisions. With two of us writing, we divided them between us based on the areas we know best, which roughly works out as south and west for Kate (chapters 1 to 4) and north and east for Suzanne (chapters 5 to 8). Given the limitations of space, this can't be an exhaustive guide to every corner of the county; instead we've tried to cherry-pick its highlights. Some are famous attractions – you can't write about Cheshire without including its big stately homes and glorious gardens – others are barely known, even within their local area. As with other Slow guides, it's a very personal take on the county, featuring the kind of little, easily overlooked details we find interesting, or trying to answer the kind of questions we'd ask visiting another county for the first time.

We haven't gone into exhaustive detail about every building's architecture or every family's history, fascinating though they might be, purely because there are others, specialists in their fields, who are more qualified to do that. Most of the big-ticket attractions have in-depth guides that will give you far more detail than we have space to go into here, and throughout this book we've tried to direct you towards other information sources that might be useful for those keen to learn more about a particular place or subject.

ACCOMMODATION, FOOD & DRINK

In the final chapter of this book, we've listed a selection of places to stay. Some we've stayed at ourselves; others have been recommended by people in the know. Hotels, B&Bs and pubs with rooms are indicated by 🏠 under the town or village headings, while self-catering options are indicated by 🏡 and campsites by ▲. For full descriptions of these listings, visit ⊘ bradtguides.com/cheshiresleeps.

Throughout the guide we've suggested some of our favourite restaurants, bars and shops, picking out places that fit with the 'Slow Travel' approach. That might mean a shop that specialises in local or organic produce, a bar that gives you a real sense of place, or a restaurant with an extra helping of character, quirkiness or cosiness.

MAPS

On pages 4–5 you'll find an overall map of Cheshire, with suggested places to base yourself. At the start of each chapter is a more detailed map of that particular area, marked with numbers that correspond to numbered headings in the text. A 📍 symbol on these maps indicates that there is a walk in that area, sometimes accompanied by a simple route map. The OS Explorer maps that cover Cheshire include: 266 Wirral & Chester, 267 Northwich & Delamere Forest, 257 Crewe & Nantwich, 268 Wilmslow, Macclesfield & Congleton, 275 Liverpool, St Helen's, Widnes & Runcorn, and 276 Bolton Central, Wigan & Warrington, OL1 Peak District (Dark Peak area) and OL24 Peak District (White Peak area).

ACCESSIBILITY

As well as being home to one of Europe's most accessible cities (see box, page 24), the county has several greenways with wide well-made paths that are suitable for wheelchair users, such as at Astbury Mere. Some heritage sites are also making concerted efforts to improve access; for example, at the time of writing, Quarry Bank Mill was installing a new lift and reorganising its galleries to make the whole building fully wheelchair accessible. Cheshire East (⌁ cheshireeast. gov.uk) has an accessible transport guide on its public transport pages, while accessibility information for Cheshire West and Chester can be found at ⌁ disabledgo.com. For another useful source, check out ⌁ accessiblecountryside.org.uk/cheshire.

FOLLOW US

Use **#cheshire** to share your adventures using this guide with us – we'd love to hear from you.

- Bradt Travel Guides
- @bradtguides (#cheshire)
- youtube.com/bradtguides
- @BradtGuides & @Traveltappers (#cheshire)
- pinterest.com/bradtguides

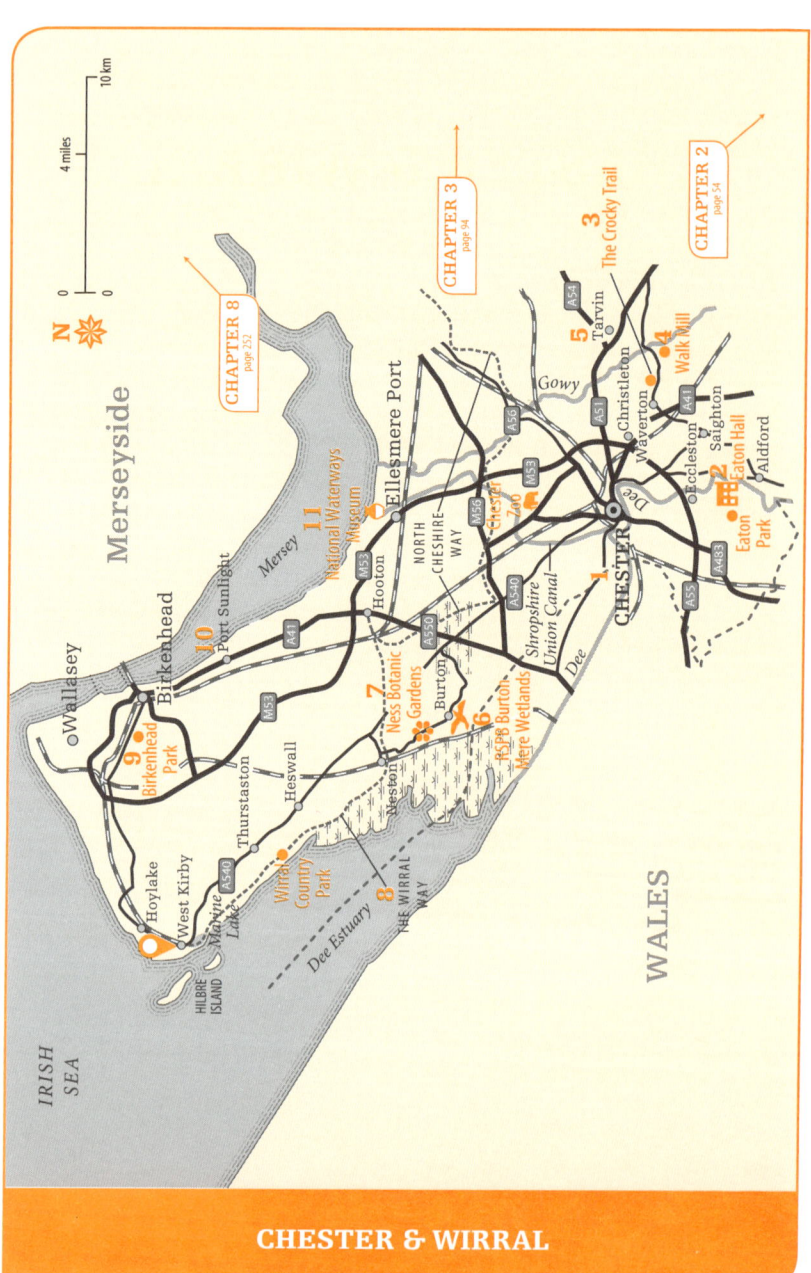

CHESTER & WIRRAL

1
CHESTER & WIRRAL

Chester may be small compared with many other British cities, but it has had a big impact locally and nationally down the centuries. The largest of the Roman forts in Britain, on the frontline of Wales, Chester, say some historians, was meant to become the capital of Britannia. The Danes, Saxons and Normans capitalised on this strategic position, which was also bitterly fought over during the English Civil War. As peace descended on Chester, the Georgians and Victorians embellished its streets, imposing an air of elegance, with 20th- and 21st-century architects and town planners applying their own brush strokes (and provoking varied reactions). Chester was an important trading hub in the Middle Ages, a port of more importance than Liverpool, providing an entry point for goods including linen from Ireland. But by the 18th century, the city had been eclipsed by its northern neighbour due to the silting of the Dee. The 'Cestrians' (as the locals are called) were known for their leatherwork – boots, shoes, saddles and gloves – and for silver, of which there is a fine collection in the Grosvenor Museum (page 33). The Industrial Revolution left its mark with the railway station (of which there were once two) and the Chester Canal, part of the Shropshire Union Canal (over which the 18th-century Steam Mill still looms), with its spur that once delivered narrowboats onto the waters of the River Dee for a smooth and efficient transfer of freight.

"Chester may be small, but it has had a big impact locally and nationally."

 Yet Chester isn't stuck in the past. The presence of the university and the city's appeal to young families, with its gentle mix of the urban and rural, maintains a youthful atmosphere, where new trends quickly reach its shops, bars and restaurants. There's a thriving cultural scene: the city has its own orchestra, the Chester Philharmonic, an open-air theatre, and a new arts centre, Storyhouse, with a theatre, cinema and library.

CHESTER & WIRRAL

An impressive amount of world-class exhibitions call by here and the lack of a major art gallery has fostered a creative approach where buildings such as the cathedral are put to work as innovative art spaces.

To the northwest of the city lies the Wirral peninsula, adding a perhaps unexpected coastal aspect to the county. In this first edition, we are taking a selective approach to our coverage of this area, winding the clock back to the days of the Vikings, whose influence echoes down the years, the medieval monks who rowed the first ferry across the Mersey, the industrialists who built model workers' towns at Port Sunlight and Bromborough Pool, and the canal engineers who connected the industrialists of Shropshire to a global market. The peninsula is also home to the world's first public park and Britain's first country park, an exotic garden, an RSPB reserve teeming with wildfowl, the historic shorefront communities of the River Dee, and the most unexpected of Cheshire's pleasures: its very own islands.

GETTING THERE & AROUND
PUBLIC TRANSPORT

This area is well connected by public transport, with fast direct **trains** between Chester and London on the West Coast Line. There's a regular rail service on the North Wales Coast Line between Crewe and Holyhead that stops at Chester, while the Chester–Manchester Line and Mid-Cheshire Line serve the likes of Frodsham, Warrington, Runcorn, Northwich, Knutsford and Stockport. Going northwest, Merseyrail's Wirral Line to Liverpool connects Chester with all stations on the peninsula, wih a change at Birkenhead's Hamilton Square for the line to West Kirby.

Chester station is half a mile from the city centre, but there are frequent shuttle buses between the two. Alternatively, walk along City Road (directly opposite the station entrance) and then drop down to the canal, turn right and follow the towpath to the Lock Keeper pub where a short path connects to Frodsham Street.

Useful **buses** for this chapter include the 1 and X8 to Chester Zoo and Ellesmere Port, the 2 to Birkenhead, the 22 to West Kirby, the 41 to Waverton and Tattenhall, the C56 to Saighton and Aldford, the 82 to Tarvin and Kelsall and the 84 to Nantwich and Crewe. Check out ⌁ cheshirewestandchester.gov.uk.

GETTING THERE & AROUND

 TOURIST INFORMATION

Chester Visitor Information Centre Town Hall, Northgate St, CH1 2HJ ⌔ 01244 405340 ⊙ Mar–Oct 09.00–17.30 Mon–Sat, 10.00–17.00 Sun, Nov–Feb 09.30–16.30 Mon–Fri, 09.00–17.00 Sat, 10.00–16.00 Sun

WALKING

Chester is a compact city and partly pedestrianised, with most of what you would wish to see around the city walls. These ancient walkways also lead to many of the sights. For longer treks, Chester is the gateway to a variety of routes out to the countryside. Long-distance walks include the 127-mile **Dee Way**, which calls at Chester on its way from North to Mid Wales, as well as the daddy of them all in this part of the world, the 861-mile **Wales Coast Path**, of which the outskirts of Chester are the most northerly point. The **Two Saints Way** (⌔ twosaintsway.org.uk) is a 92-mile pilgrimage route between Chester and Lichfield cathedrals in honour of two Saxon saints, Chad and Werburgh, who brought Christianity to ancient Mercia. The 13-mile **Baker Way** connects Chester and Delamere railway stations via the pretty villages of Christleton and Tarvin, while the 12-mile **Longster Trail** runs between Piper's Ash on the outskirts of Chester and Helsby Hill. Routes for the latter three walks are available on the Mid-Cheshire Footpath Society website (⌔ mcfs.org.uk), which has also created the 70-mile **North Cheshire Way** that skirts Chester's northern suburbs on its way from Hooton to Helsby. The 37-mile **Wirral Circular Trail** is just one of a number of walks on Wirral; for more information go to ⌔ visitwirral.com. OS Explorer 266 Wirral & Chester is the most useful map for this area.

CYCLING

The Chester Cycle Network Tube Map is available to download at ⌔ chestercyclecity.org, which illustrates the best ways to explore the city on two wheels and suggests routes for family bike rides, such as the **River Dee Round**, a traffic-free 15-mile loop from Chester city centre to Hawarden Bridge and back along the banks of the Dee. National Cycle Network routes 5, 45, 56, 71, 89 and 568 pass through this chapter, as well as the **Cheshire Cycleway**, which, in this area, threads its way through

Waverton, Chester, Burton, Neston and Parkgate before crossing west to Ellesmere Port and heading south and west again towards Mouldsworth. The **Wirral Circular Trail**, which traces the coast of the peninsula, is also a favourite with cyclists.

BIKE HIRE & REPAIRS

Bikes and Boards 170 Banks Rd, West Kirby CH48 0RH ⌁ 0151 625 5533 ⌁ bikeshopwestkirby.co.uk
Chester Cycle Hire 38 Hoole Rd, CH2 3NL ⌁ 01244 351305 ⌁ chestercyclehire.com
KCycles 1186 New Chester Rd, Eastham CH62 9AE ⌁ 0151 327 1594 ⌁ kcycles.com
Tracs Station Rd, Thurstaston CH61 0HN ⌁ 01606 881802 ⌁ thurstastonbikes.co.uk

CHESTER & AROUND

Think Chester, think Romans. Yet, they were not the only contributors to the creation of one of Britain's prettiest cities, enhanced by its setting on the banks of the River Dee. The visible layers of Chester's history – Roman, medieval, Tudor, Georgian, Victorian – provide a charming place to wander down the ages, best done on the ancient walls that clasp its heart. But there is more to the city than just its history: there is lots to do here amid the bustling streets, with plenty of shops, restaurants, pubs and cafés, and a lively arts scene. Heading east from the city, Chester's suburbs soon give way to countryside. Among the highlights for the Slow traveller are the estate of one of Britain's most influential aristocratic families, cradled by a collection of quintessential English hamlets, and countryside fun for outdoorsy kids (and adults).

1 CHESTER

🏠 **80 Watergate Street** (page 291), 🏠 **The Boathouse and Riverside Rooms** (page 291), 🏠 **The Chester Grosvenor** (page 291), 🏠 **Edgar House** (page 291), 🏠 **Oddfellows Hotel** (page 291), 🏕 **Heritage View** (page 291), 🏕 **The Little Tin Chapel** (page 291)

The most compelling reason to visit Chester is to enjoy its attractive historic backdrop. Established by the Romans around AD75, Deva Victrix, their westernmost fort, became one of the most important of the occupation, home of the celebrated XX Valeria Victrix legion. The site was chosen for its strong strategic position on a hill near the border of Wales, at a bridgeable point of the River Dee, with access to the river and the sea beyond via a large natural harbour (now occupied by the Roodee racecourse). The fort mushroomed, attracting a substantial civilian settlement, too, and the recovered fragments of its buildings, which included a headquarters, palace, houses, barracks, granaries, baths and an amphitheatre, give us a rare physical link back to these distant times. The settlement's next era of influence was under the Saxons, who established the spiritual site still occupied by Chester's first cathedral, St John the Baptist. Next came the Normans, with Hugh d'Avranches (aka Hugh 'the wolf' Lupus), a cousin of William the Conqueror, presiding as the ruthless first Earl of Chester. Under the Normans, Cheshire became a palatinate – to this day the earldom is conferred on the Prince of Wales – and they built the castle above the Dee, a later stone version of which sits on the original motte, and established the

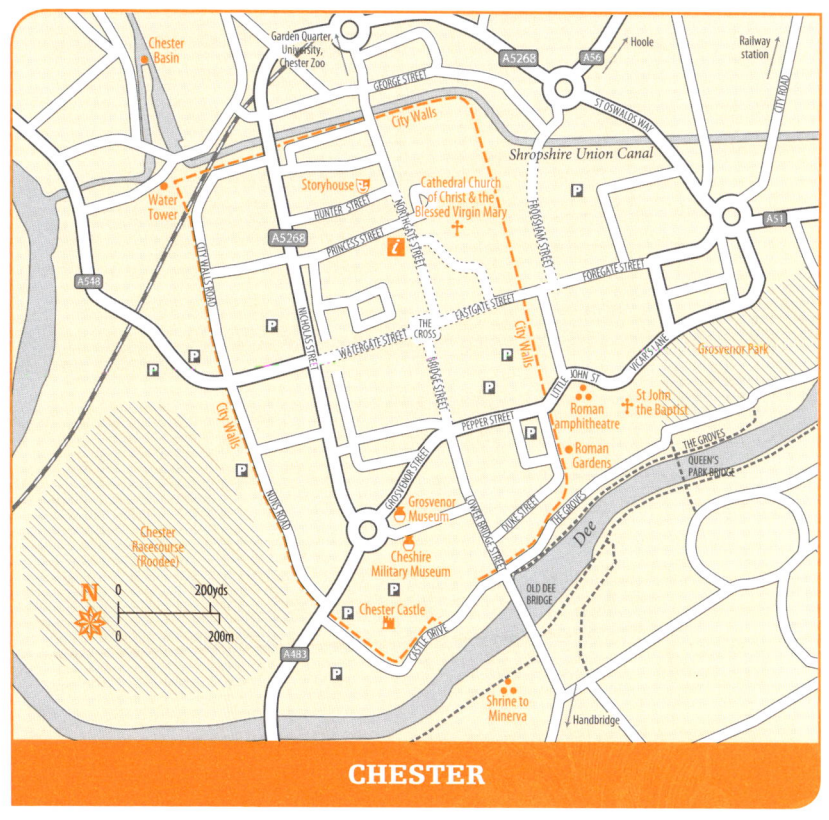

ACCESSIBLE CHESTER

In 2016, Chester was named the most accessible city in Europe, beating off 42 rivals to win the European Commission's Access City Award. It may come as a surprise: after all, this multi-storey landscape, with its ancient walls and two-level shopping arcade, doesn't look like the kind of place where people with limited mobility can get around easily. Yet Chester won the accolade for its 'efforts to make its historical and cultural heritage fit for persons with disabilities' and was deemed to 'deserve the highest praise'. The free 'Chester City Centre Access' guide is available to download at ⊘ visitchester.com.

Benedictine monastery that became today's cathedral. The stronghold built by these earlier generations provided a base for Edward I during his campaigns against the Welsh in the late 13th century, enabling the construction of castles from Conwy to Harlech. It was also a garrison for the Royalists during the English Civil War, the subject of a year-long siege until the surrender in 1646 to the forces of Sir William Brereton, the Parliamentarian commander in these parts, following the defeat of Charles I at Rowton Heath.

The Georgians repaired Chester and added many fine buildings to the architectural mix, some of the best by the 18th-century architect Thomas Harrison, including the Neoclassical castle. In Victorian times, the vogue was mock-Tudor as well as buildings constructed from red Ruabon brick, which were enhanced by shading, diapering and pressed mouldings that gave the effect of carvings. It was the Victorians, too, who were the first to tamper with the Romans' original urban plan with the introduction of Grosvenor Street, but the underlying design, on an east–west axis, has survived for the best part of two millennia.

Today, this is a lovely setting for a city that has lots to offer on top of exploring its history, with boat rides on the Dee, a good selection of independent shops to browse, some great places to eat and drink, one of the country's newest arts centres, and a packed calendar of events and festivals. The following guide to this multi-layered city will inevitably scratch its surface, yet we've strived to pick out the most important elements for the Slow traveller.

The city walls

Chester is defined by its city walls, the most complete Roman and medieval walls in the UK. Once, they ensured protection for those who dwelt within; today, properties inside this ring of stone are Chester's most desirable addresses. Beautiful in themselves, the walls also provide visitors with the perfect elevated overview of the city; from the ramparts, you can orientate yourself quickly and easily, circumnavigating the historic centre and passing many landmarks along the way.

The original walls are thought to have been built from turf in about AD75 but were soon replaced with a stone version, the earliest section of which can be seen from Northgate, looking east. At some point the Romans did a repair job using gravestones, which were uncovered in the 19th century and now provide the most impressive display in the Grosvenor Museum (page 33). It's thought that the Anglo-Saxon queen Aethelflaed (see box, page 26) extended some sections, which were further improved by the Normans and enhanced by the Georgians, who repaired much of the damage sustained during the English Civil War. The Georgians were more interested in the walls for their recreational qualities than as defences, using them as a place to promenade and even widening parts to enable couples to stroll side by side (think of the size of women's skirts in those days). They also transformed the main gates into archways so that coaches could pass through. The Victorians removed sections to connect a road to the Grosvenor Bridge and to enable the passage of the railway, with further adaptations in the 20th century.

> "Beautiful in themselves, the walls also provide visitors with the perfect elevated overview of the city."

Regardless of which gate you choose to start from, the mile-long walls will transport you to almost all the main city highlights, including the cathedral, the Roman gardens and amphitheatre, the Dee and the Roodee racecourse. Meanwhile, you can examine the walls' own sights as you go, including the ornate Eastgate clock, a favourite image for postcards, built for Queen Victoria's Jubilee, and the King Charles Tower from where Charles I is said to have watched his troops retreat from the Battle of Rowton Heath. You'll need to gather some reading matter from the Visitor Information Centre (page 21) for a real insight into the walls' stories and assets, and to understand which parts belong to which eras, or join one of the tours run by the Guild of Chester Tour Guides (chestertours.org.uk). At the time of writing, a new attraction titled 'Within These Walls' was due to open in spring 2018, the work of the innovative organisation Big Heritage (bigheritage.co.uk) that

AETHELFLAED AND THE FOUNDING OF CHESTER

Aethelflaed (870–918), the eldest daughter of Alfred the Great, was an Anglo-Saxon general who, like her father, spent much of her energy on expelling Vikings. The Lady of the Mercians was an extraordinary woman, unusually a female ruler, and her achievements included building the Saxon 'burh' of Chester, as well as rebuilding and extending the Roman city walls to the edge of the River Dee around AD907.

is breathing fresh life into history-themed tourism. It will be based in the 14th-century Water Tower in the walls' northwest corner and, if Big Heritage's previous projects are anything to go by, it should live up to its promise of offering an interactive exploration of how the walls were built and maintained and the impact they had on the city and its people, past and present. St Michael's Church, on the corner of Bridge and Pepper streets, which was until recently occupied by Chester History & Heritage until it relocated to the Grosvenor Museum, is also due to be transformed by Big Heritage. See ⌘ bradtupdates.com/cheshire for news on these projects.

The Rows & city centre

Chester's unique **Rows** provide a very different perspective to your usual shopping centre. The city's four main streets – Eastgate, Watergate, Bridge and Northgate – all have walkways at the first-floor level and open on one side to the street. The Rows are reached via flights of stairs, while the premises beneath them are lower than street level and generally entered down a few steps. Embellished in Tudor times with half-timbered structures, a style amplified by the Victorians, the Rows provide one of the prettiest aspects of the city, especially if you've come here just to shop. The layers of architecture also constitute a treasure hunt; the Guild of Chester Tour Guides runs a 'Rows Revealed' tour (⊙ currently 14.00 last Sun of the month) that uncovers some astonishing remains, including pillars from the Roman fort in Pret a Manger and a Tudor plasterwork trail in Sofa Workshop that suggests Catherine of Aragon once visited the city.

Beyond the Rows, these four main streets, pedestrianised in part, are where you're most likely to browse. The main shopping avenue is **Eastgate Street**, which is also the location of two high-class establishments: the venerable Chester Grosvenor Hotel and its Michelin-star restaurant (page 36) and the department store Browns of Chester (now part of Debenhams), which was regarded as so posh that some people would dress up to go shopping in its hallowed halls. **Watergate Street** has an array of independent shops and is the address of Booth Mansion, a magnificent Grade I-listed Georgian property that became the assembly rooms of the period and is now home to an art gallery and tea room. The corner of Eastgate Street and **Bridge Street** is a much-snapped example of the 19th-century black-and-white revival architecture found throughout the city, while **Northgate Street** is the home of the Town Hall, a triumph of the Gothic revival style. All four streets pivot on **The Cross**, a former marketplace with a medieval High Cross at its centre (the Roman headquarters was also hereabouts). The town crier makes a daily proclamation from here during summer. In fact, Chester has two town criers, husband-and-wife team David and Julie Mitchell, who celebrated their 20th anniversary in the post in 2018.

Chester's cathedrals

Just outside Newgate, next to the Roman amphitheatre, is Chester's original cathedral, **St John the Baptist** (Vicar's Ln, CH1 1SN ⌂ parishofchester.com ⊙ 10.00–16.00 daily). A religious site is thought to have existed here since the days of Aethelred, King of Mercia in AD689, but today's sandstone edifice became the city's cathedral in the 11th century, a status it retained until the dissolution of the monasteries in 1541. The church's exterior is a mix of medieval and Victorian architecture and the ruins of the chapels at its east end are a romantic vision, a lovely introduction if you're arriving in the city along the adjacent main road. Pass through the huge archway of the north porch to discover what is truly special

"Pass through the huge archway of the north porch to discover what is truly special about this church: its grand Norman interior."

about this church: its grand Norman interior. There is a lot of detail to unpick in this structure, particularly the beautiful clerestory, and there are helpful notes available to borrow. As you wander, look out for the fragments of ancient gravestones and a 14th-century wall painting on a pillar in the north aisle that shows St John holding a book, on which rests a lamb, with a pastoral scene as a backdrop. The church has a claim to fame in that its organ was played at Queen Victoria's coronation in Westminster Abbey before being installed here.

St John the Baptist was superseded as the seat of the bishop by the **Cathedral Church of Christ and the Blessed Virgin Mary** (St Werburgh St, CH1 2HU ⌁ 01244 500979 ⌁ chestercathedral.com ⊙ 09.00–18.00 Mon–Sat, 13.00–16.00 Sun). The Grade I-listed sandstone complex, found behind Northgate and Eastgate streets, is medieval even though it looks more Victorian thanks to a major restoration project carried out in the 1800s. Based on a cruciform design with a central tower, the shape is varied not least by the monastic quarter to the north, which you can view from the city walls along its north and eastern edges. (If you are lucky, you might catch the sight of falcons on the wing at the same time – the cathedral's falconry (⌁ 01244 699053) operates daily displays out of the Dean's Field). The relics of St Werburgh were brought here in 875 (they are kept in a shrine in the Lady Chapel) and the church became the abbey of a Benedictine monastery in 1092, continuing to expand in size and influence until it gained cathedral status. Among the cathedral's many stories is the tale of how Handel's *Messiah* first came to be performed here in 1742. The composer was due to debut the new work in Dublin but his departure from Parkgate on Wirral was delayed by rough seas, so he rehearsed his great oratorio in the cathedral with local musicians.

"Among the cathedral's many stories is the tale of how Handel's Messiah *first came to be performed here in 1742."*

The cathedral fell into disrepair over the centuries until its restoration by the Victorians, including Thomas Harrison and, later, Sir George Gilbert Scott, the celebrated Victorian architect best known for designing the Albert Memorial in London. The freestanding bell tower was added in 1975, an 85-foot-high structure that is officially called the Addleshaw Tower but also known as 'The Chester Rocket' because of its appearance. The tower, clad in Bethesda slate with a sandstone base, was the final work of the ecclesiastical architect George Pace and is meant to echo the detached bell towers of medieval days – in fact, it was the first to have been built since the 15th century.

There is much to admire, all of which is explained on the guided tours and also documented in guides available in the shop. I'm allowing myself to choose just two of my favourite elements: the 14th-century quire stalls, with their spikey canopies and intriguing carvings on the bench-

CHESTER'S GHOSTS

Any self-respecting historic city has its fair share of ghost stories and Chester is no different. The Guild of Chester Tour Guides runs a ghost tour at 19.30 on Saturdays if you want to find out about more of the city's apparitions, but here are three of the best.

A **Roman legionnaire**, who was killed by a mob for abandoning his post to see his secret Celtic love and leaving the fort open to attack, is said to haunt the Roman amphitheatre and walls at Newgate.

In a former public house called The Hand and Snake on Watergate Street, where young boys were given the deadly task of cleaning aristocrats' powdered wigs with a substance including arsenic, the ghost of a **little boy** can sometimes be heard sobbing.

When her Royalist love was killed at Rowton Heath in the English Civil War, a maiden called **Henrietta**, waiting at the first-floor window of The Bluebell on Northgate Street for his return, retreated to the cellar to commit suicide. She still traces her steps back up to the window.

---

ends, such as the elephant carrying a castle; and the cool walkways of the cloisters, with their stone rib-vaulted ceilings and intricate carvings. Make sure you pop into the café (⊙ 09.30–16.30 Mon–Sat, noon–16.00 Sun), a magnificent space appropriately set in the monks' refectory. The cathedral often hosts world-class art exhibitions within its walls – check out what's on during your visit. For one of the best views in the city, join one of the daily 'Cathedral at Height' tours and climb the spiral staircase to the top of the tower.

Roman Chester

It took until the early 20th century to unearth Chester's Roman **amphitheatre** (Little St John St, CH1 1RE ⊙ daylight hours ⚭ English Heritage), hidden beneath buildings between St John the Baptist Church and Newgate for 2,000 years. Only a portion has been uncovered, about two-fifths of what is thought to be the largest amphitheatre in Britain, dating from the 1st century AD. In its heyday, this was a place for military training, executions and entertainment, hosting everything from bear baiting to gladiator fights, with the capacity for about 7,000 spectators, and today it's possible to get a sense of the amphitheatre as it must have been. The locations of two of the original four entrances are visible (the main north entrance and the one in the east), the slopes from which have enabled archaeologists to estimate the depth of the oval-shaped arena floor. Modern concrete slabs filled with sandstone suggest the thickness of the outer wall, and replicas here include a shrine to the goddess Nemesis and a chain block on the arena floor to which animals and possibly humans would have been tethered. Much of the amphitheatre is covered by listed buildings, so a 50-foot-wide *trompe l'œil* mural has been painted on the wall of the southern walkway that skirts the site to suggest what the whole structure would have looked like, right down to the historical detail of the red-brown colouring of the arena wall.

Around the corner is the **Roman Gardens** (Pepper St, CH1 1QQ), a small open-air gallery containing an assortment of fragments of the fortress that have been found in Chester since Victorian times, and which also celebrates the Romans' role in developing gardening as a pastime. Sitting in the shadow of Newgate and the city walls, from where it can also be admired, this green corridor doubles as both a pretty and handy cut-through from Pepper Street to the River Dee. The gardens first opened in 1949 but were extended and redesigned in 2000 in the shape of the symbol of Aesculapius, Roman god of medicine, which, in case you don't know, is a rod coiled by a serpent, so one of the two paths is straight, and the other winding. Here you'll find columns from the headquarters building and the exercise hall of the bathhouse, a reconstructed hypocaust, and three specially commissioned mosaics, one a replica of an image of a mythological creature, a design found in the city's bathhouse. The ancient columns are deftly reflected in the cypress trees planted here, and the benches from which you can take in the scene are suggestive of the seating that might have been sat on by a toga-clad frequenter of the caldarium. There is also a plaque commemorating the dead from the siege of Chester in the English Civil War, close to a part of the city walls that was breached when the Parliamentarians pounded it with cannon, the repairs for which are clear to see. The gardens are also the venue for the annual summertime open-air cinema screenings, **Moonlight Flicks** (moonlightflicks.co.uk).

River Dee & around

A walk along **The Groves** on the north bank of the River Dee is a must-do on a trip to Chester. The elegant promenade is bookended by two quite different yet equally lovely bridges. To the west is the **Old Dee Bridge**, a red sandstone span built in the 14th century on the spot of an earlier Roman bridge, while to the east is the **Queen's Park Bridge**, a graceful suspension bridge built in 1923. There are benches on which to linger and swans to watch gliding around the water – you can even listen to the *oompah* of the brass bands that sometimes play on the bandstand. This is also the place to embark on a cruise along the river, possibly as far as the Eaton Estate with Chester Boat (⌀ chesterboat.co.uk), or hire a motor, paddle or row boat from Chester Boat Hire (⌀ chesterboathire.co.uk).

In Edgar's Field, on the southwest bank by the Old Dee Bridge, you'll find the **Roman shrine to Minerva**. Carved into a sandstone outcrop, the weathered image of the goddess is the only one of its kind to survive in situ. On the north bank behind The Groves is **Grosvenor Park** (⌀ grosvenorparkchester.co.uk), on land given to the city by the second Marquess of Westminster and designed by his favourite architect, John Douglas, alongside the influential 19th-century landscape architect, Edward Kemp, who helped design the world's first publicly funded park at Birkenhead (pages 46–9). Corporation minutes from 5 October 1867 record that the park was given as a gift to the citizens of Chester 'hoping it may afford health and recreation to themselves and their families for many years to come'.

"There are benches on which to linger and you can even listen to the oompah *of the brass bands that sometimes play."*

And so it has. But while the Marquess sanctioned music being played here, it seems dancing was 'forbidden'. The 20 acres of lawns, framed by trees, paths and ornamental flowerbeds, feature a lodge (spot the carvings of William the Conqueror and seven Norman earls of Chester on the upper storey), a well, medieval arches gathered from around the city, and, of course, a marble statue of the benefactor. In summer, plays by Shakespeare and other playwrights are performed at the **Grosvenor Park Open Air Theatre** (⌀ grosvenorparkopenairtheatre.co.uk).

It's possible to follow the river northeast along the south bank to loop round to the green spaces of the **Chester Meadows**, or head westwards, around the racecourse, to connect with the **Chester Basin**, the historic link between the river and the Chester Canal, part of the Shropshire Union Canal. This is a pleasant place to pause and take

WELSHMEN, BEWARE!

Watch your step in Chester after dark if you come from Wales – you could risk decapitation. It's still legal to chop off the head of a Welshman if found inside the city walls between dusk and dawn, according to a 15th-century law yet to be repealed.

a close look at the Northgate Locks, cut from sandstone and the deepest in the UK – there were once five locks here that lowered the narrowboats onto the river. Continue along the Dee branch of the canal back into Chester, where regenerated warehouses have been put to modern use as bars and suchlike, or head northwards out of the city towards Ellesmere Port.

Chester Castle
Castle Dr, CH1 2DN ⌖ English Heritage ⊙ currently Apr–Oct by guided tour only

Chester has such a strong story as a Roman fortress that its Norman castle does not enjoy the profile it might elsewhere. Yet, William the Conqueror established a motte and bailey castle here on the banks of the Dee in 1070 (probably where Aethelflaed sited a fort in the previous century) and it became the nerve centre of the powerful Earls of Chester. Later, Henry III and Edward I also used it as military headquarters during their campaigns against the Welsh, and the city's Royalist governor, Lord John Byron, based himself here during the English Civil War. The Agricola Tower is the main survivor of the first stone fort built in the 12th century, a gateway to the inner bailey containing the chapel of St Mary de Castro, in which there are some rare medieval wall paintings. The fort on view today was designed by Thomas Harrison at the turn of the 19th century, a well-regarded transformation with a sequence of buildings and columns in abundance, including the Shire Hall, barracks and armoury and a monumental Propylaeum, with a huge gateway and two pavilions colonnaded to the front and rear. Today, the county court and **Cheshire Military Museum** (The Castle, CH1 2DN ✆ 01244 327617 ⌖ cheshiremilitarymuseum.co.uk ⊙ 10.00–17.00 daily, closed Wed in winter & Christmas period) can be found among these buildings, the latter charting four centuries of the Cheshire Regiment's history.

MINE'S A PINT – OR TWO
There are so many pubs to recommend in Chester, whether for the atmosphere of their ancient quarters or the fine pints pulled at their pumps. So thank goodness for the Chester Ale Trail (⌖ chesteraletrail.co.uk), now available as a free app, that links 25 of the city's best pubs, from the Albion Inn to the Town Crier. Collect the free tokens as you go and, with every ten, you'll earn a free pint.

Grosvenor Museum

27 Grosvenor St, CH1 2DD ⌲ 01244 972197 ⌲ grosvenormuseum.westcheshiremuseums.co.uk ⌲ 10.30–17.00 Mon–Sat, 13.00–16.00 Sun

This may be the most important archive in the county, but the Grosvenor Museum is quite old school in how it presents the natural and cultural history of the area. Still, there is much to ponder in its varied collection, from fine art to fossils, and the temporary exhibitions it puts on. The most interesting exhibits are the rare Roman tombstones discovered by the Victorians in the city walls, where they had been used for repairs, which are fascinating not only for their age, but the implicit stories of the lives of the individuals commemorated as told through their carvings. There is also a Period House at the back of the museum with different rooms depicting the style of different ages, from the 17th century to the 1920s; a fun insight into the changes in fashion, technology and expectations of living standards.

Chester Racecourse

CH1 2LY ⌲ 01244 304600 ⌲ chester-races.co.uk

Chester's Roman harbour, long since silted up, has been the city's racecourse since the mayor, Sir Henry Gee, granted permission to race horses here in 1539 (can you guess where 'gee-gees', the slang term for horses, comes from?). The oldest working racecourse in the UK, it draws the crowds for flat racing and polo between May and September. Spot the stone cross, the 'rood', amid the turf – some say it marks the spot where an icon of the Virgin Mary is buried. Top tip: you can watch the races for free from the city walls.

Storyhouse

Hunter St, CH1 2AR ⌲ 01244 409113 ⌲ storyhouse.com ⌲ 08.00–23.00 Mon–Sat, 09.00–23.00 Sun & bank hols

The old Chester Odeon gained a new lease of life in 2017 when it was transformed into one of the UK's newest art centres, home to a very rare thing: a resident professional theatre company. Now called Storyhouse, the Art Deco building has been redesigned to integrate a theatre, cinema and adult and children's libraries (apparently, local children formed a bookworm to bring some of the books here from the old library, just along the road). Storyhouse's programme strikes a balance between mainstream tastes (touring comedians and regional

GHOULS & GOSPELS

One of the most exciting nights of the year in Chester is the December evening on which **The Winter Watch** and **Saturnalia** parades take place. The Winter Watch dates from medieval times when the city leaders would hand over the keys to the city watch, and it is enhanced today by the sight of 'soldiers of the XX Legion' marching through the streets in full military dress, bearing torches. In the mix is Saturnalia, when the Lord of Misrule is unleashed and a procession of fire breathers and ghoulish creatures (think devils, skeletons and mad cooks bearing a head on a platter) dance around the streets to beating drums. Make sure you grab a good place on one of the Eastgate Rows for the best views. A summer version, The Midsummer Watch Parade (midsummerwatch.co.uk), takes place in June.

Chester also hosts the **Mystery Plays** (chestermysteryplays.com) every five years, honouring the 13th-century tradition of biblical storytelling, over which are laid contemporary themes, to celebrate the feast of Corpus Christi. Performed by a mixture of professionals and locals, the latest were held in June 2018.

---

panto) and more high-brow fodder (contemporary dance and opera), and there is lots for young ones to get involved in here during the school holidays. Adults will find respite in the rooftop Garret Bar, while on the ground floor is The Kitchen (thekitchenstoryhouse.co.uk), an open-plan restaurant where Middle Eastern dishes are served on large shared tables, encouraging a friendly atmosphere.

Chester Zoo
Upton-by-Chester CH2 1LH 01244 380280 chesterzoo.org daily

Whatever your take on zoos, there's no ignoring the fact that Chester has one of the biggest in Britain or that it's recognised as a leading conservation centre. The 125-acre grounds are home to more than 21,000 animals and 500 species, from polar bears to komodo dragons, as well as a nature reserve, and recent developments include a revamped Penguin Island, with a bigger pool and larger windows through which to view the creatures. If it all seems a bit overwhelming and you're not sure where to start, there is a handy map that splits the zoo into four manageable zones, with animals to see, activities to take part in and refreshment stops along the way. There's lots to see and do, from informative talks about particular animals to, well, puddle-jumping for the seriously distracted juniors in your party. The story of the zoo itself has recently been in the spotlight. The quest of the founder, George

Mottershead, to set up a 'zoo without bars' is the subject of a book and the BBC TV series *Our Zoo*, and Channel 4's *The Secret Life of the Zoo* focuses on staff as well as the animals. Outside the zoo gates is a nature reserve, which was substantially expanded in 2018.

FOOD & DRINK

The Architect 54 Nicholas St, CH1 2NX ⌂ 01244 353070. Our first encounter in this guide with a Brunning & Price pub – a local group that will become familiar in these pages – is this hostelry in the Georgian former home of the architect, Thomas Harrison. The style is spacious rooms decorated with antique pieces, where drinkers and diners gather around polished wood tables to drink beer from local brewers (as well as fine wines and spirits, including, of course, gins) and eat freshly produced modern British fare, with some further-flung influences.

The Brewery Tap Ale House 52–54 Lower Bridge St, CH1 1RU ⌂ 01299 340999 ⌂ the-tap.co.uk. The Jacobean great hall, Gamul House, is the extraordinary and well-preserved setting for the tap of Chester's Spitting Feathers Brewery. Sample its beer as well as food prepared from fresh, seasonal ingredients, with Cheshire Farm Ice Cream in Tattenhall (page 63) and Born and Bread in Wirral among the suppliers. If you like the beer, take a tour of where it's made in nearby Waverton (⌂ spittingfeathers.org).

The Chef's Table Music Hall Passage, CH1 2EU ⌂ 01244 403040 ⌂ chefstablechester.co.uk. Book ahead if you want to get a table at this very popular restaurant. It works with local growers such as The Natural Veg Men in Malpas (⌂ vegmen.co.uk), which cultivates crops in one of the oldest organic fields in England. The interesting menu features the likes of jerk-spiced kid goat loin with curds, wheyonaise, Cumberland sauce and beetroot.

Commonhall St Social 10 Commonhall St, CH1 2BJ ⌂ 01244 313258 ⌂ commonhall.co.uk. This spacious and relaxed venue keeps it quirky, mixing drinking and dining (local producers feature) with soul-music nights and edifying Spanish and tapas workshops.

Corks Out 21 Watergate St, CH1 2LB ⌂ 01244 310455 ⌂ corksout.com. Here's your chance to try a glass of expensive wine without having to fork out for a bottle. Fill your glass from the wines available to dispense using an optic and take a seat beneath the stone-vaulted ceilings in this beautiful medieval cellar, set up by the adjacent wine merchants. Tasty sharing boards are also available.

ExSqueeze Me 13 Handbridge, CH4 7JE ⌂ 07864 186125. Hybrid shops are all the rage and there's synergy to this one in Handbridge, a greengrocer using some of the produce to whiz up smoothies and juices, such as 'Celebrity Clean' (celery, apple, kale, parsley and lime).

Goat & Munch 52 Garden Ln, CH1 4EW ⌂ 07807 198267 ⌂ goatandmunch.com. Small is beautiful when it comes to this micro-pub in the Garden Quarter, especially if you like craft beer (though prosecco is available, too).

The Jaunty Goat 57 Bridge St, CH1 1NG 01244 421492 jauntygoatcoffee.co.uk. Freshly roasted coffee from traceable sources is served at this small independent café. There's a tempting choice of cakes and pastries, as well as snacks and soups.

Joseph Benjamin 140 Northgate St, CH1 2HT 01244 344295 josephbenjamin.co.uk. The seasons dictate what appears on the creative menu at this award-winning restaurant – smoked eel Waldorf salad with pickled grapes and tarragon mayonnaise is a typical example. Brothers Joe and Ben recently opened Porta next door, serving superb, authentic Spanish tapas.

Meltdown 14 Queen's Park View, CH4 7BU 01244 659528 meltdown-chester. business.site. They like their cheese at this café in Handbridge dedicated to the gourmet toastie. The Nuclear Meltdown – a blend of three cheeses with bird's eye chilli – should give you a flavour of what to expect.

Simon Radley at the Chester Grosvenor Eastgate, CH1 1LT 01244 324024. The eponymous chef has kept the dining room of Cheshire's premier hotel at the top of the national restaurant tables since the 1990s. His Michelin-star fare is for seriously special occasions – even veggies get their own tasting menu.

Sticky Walnut 11 Charles St, CH2 3AZ 01244 400400 stickywalnut.net. This small dining room in Hoole (one of the city's trendiest suburbs, known as Notting Hoole) should be on every discerning diner's list to try. You'll be spoilt for choice with tempting dishes including butter-roasted skate wing and braised feather blade.

Telford's Warehouse Canal Basin, Tower Wharf, CH1 4EZ 01244 390090 telfordswarehousechester.com. This former canal warehouse has been transformed into a music venue, where you can tap your foot while supping beers including local Weetwood Cheshire Cat (weetwoodales.co.uk).

SHOPPING
Shops

The Cheese Shop 116 Northgate St, CH1 2HT 01244 346240 chestercheeseshop. co.uk. Cheese fans will love this wonderful little shop, which stocks a wide selection of cheese, hosts tastings, and always has a bowl of water by the door for passing dogs.

The Hat Place 70–72 Northgate St, CH1 2HT 01244 409283 thehatplace.com. From fedoras to fascinators, this store is stacked with headgear and is the place to purchase something to top off your look. Get expert advice, too, on everything from folding a panama to measuring your head.

Lily Vintage 45 Bridge St, CH1 1NG 01244 324896. Retro fans will love scouring the racks of this clothes and accessories store, which updates its on-trend stock weekly.

Turmeaus 28–34 Watergate St, CH1 2LA 01244 403022 turmeaus.co.uk. Amid the stone arches in this medieval warren of rooms, Turmeaus sells premium cigars and fine

EVENTS CALENDAR
Find out more at ⌀ visitcheshire.com/chester.

Feb Chester International Film Festival ⌀ festival.chesterfilmfans.co.uk
Apr Chester Food, Drink & Lifestyle Festival ⌀ chesterfoodanddrink.co.uk
May Chester Folk Festival ⌀ chesterfolk.org.uk
Jun Chester Live, The Midsummer Watch (see box, page 34), Chester Heritage Festival
Nov Chester Literature Festival
Dec The Winter Watch & Saturnalia (see box, page 34)

whiskies as well as smokers' paraphernalia, and has its own humidor and bar serving whisky flights. It's worth a peep inside even if you're a teetotal non-smoker.
Watergate Street Gallery 60 Watergate St, CH1 2LA ⌀ 01244 345698 ⌀ watergatestreetgallery.co.uk. The mission of this gallery is to supply 'new, fresh, different yet affordable art' from artists based locally and beyond. Exhibitions and meet-the-artist events are also hosted.
Weasel and The Bug 19 Watergate St, CH1 2LB ⌀ 01244 348176 ⌀ weaselandthebug. com. Got young kids in tow? Keep them entertained with a new toy from this shop where the shelves are filled with fun that is 'powered by children not by batteries'.

Markets
Chester Market is found in the Forum Shopping Centre on Northgate Street (⊙ 08.00–17.00 Mon–Sat except bank hols). The **Taste Cheshire Farmers Market** is held outside the Old Library on the third Saturday of the month (⊙ 09.30–16.30), and there is a **Christmas Market** in December outside the Town Hall.

2 EATON HALL & THE GROSVENOR VILLAGES
Of all the great families of Cheshire, the Grosvenors reign supreme. **Eaton Hall** (Eccleston CH4 9ET ⌀ 01244 684400 ⌀ eatonestate. co.uk), on the outskirts of Chester, is the home of the seventh Duke of Westminster, Hugh Grosvenor, ninth-richest man in Britain, the wealthiest aristocrat in the country (including the Queen) and the owner of much of Belgravia and Mayfair in London, as well as the city of Chester (you'll discover many shared place names). The hall has been through five transformations of the original 17th-century structure, and involved architects including Alfred Waterhouse, who built London's Natural History Museum and whose clock tower,

courtyard and chapel remain here. The boldest attempt at the hall was surely in the 1970s, when it was wrapped in white travertine for a sleek modern look, but the most recent modifications, from the turn of the 1990s, have toned down the styling to a gentler evocation of a chateaux in pink stone. The ornamental Golden Gates, parts of which date back to when the original hall was built, is a lavish marker of the Grosvenors' lands, which include 800 acres of grounds, with a deer park and 88 acres of formal gardens. The latter, like the house, have changed many times, but some gems are preserved; the handiwork of Sir Edwin Lutyens can be seen in the gardens, while there is also evidence of the work of the Capability Brown in the wider park. The gardens are the only part of the hall that open to the public, just four times a year. If you visit, be sure to take in the Lioness and Kudu Pond, named after the contemporary sculpture of the animals on the water, showing a lioness in hot pursuit. You will also be able to view the Grosvenors' fine collection of Victorian carriages and ride the re-laid tracks of the Victorian light railway that once connected to the Shrewsbury–Chester line at Balderton, three miles away. Once used to haul, variously, coal, visitors to the hall, and local schoolchildren, today a replica steam engine, *Katie*, pulls passengers back to yesteryear.

"It would be easy to spend a day rambling around these elegant communities, taking in their trim farms and dwellings, embellished here and there with thatched roofs and patterned brickwork."

The Grosvenor seat is in **Eccleston**, the finest of the villages on the family's estate, which hugs the Welsh border and outskirts of Chester. Eccleston's church, St Mary, commissioned by the 1st Duke of Westminster in 1897, is a handsome red ashlar sandstone affair, with luxurious furnishings such as the oak pulpit with its green marble base. But the joy of the surrounding villages, which also include lovely **Saighton** (where the remnants of a medieval abbey are sadly hidden on private land) and **Aldford**, is about the general landscape. It would be easy to spend a few hours rambling or cycling around these elegant communities – you can walk out of Chester along the River Dee to this pastoral enclave in an hour – taking in their trim farms and dwellings, churches, village shops, schools and community halls, embellished here and there with thatched roofs, half-timbering, decorative chimney stacks and diapered and patterned brickwork.

CHESTER & AROUND

FOOD & DRINK

The Grosvenor Arms Chester Rd, Aldford CH3 6HJ ☏ 01244 620228 🌐 brunningandprice.co.uk/grosvenorarms. Our second encounter in this book with a Brunning & Price pub is a typically elegant yet spacious hostelry serving good food and classy pub fare, with a conservatory and a lovely beer garden for warmer days.

3 THE CROCKY TRAIL

Cotton Abbotts, Waverton CH3 7PH ☏ 01244 336084 🌐 crockytrail.co.uk ⊙ Easter–Oct 09.00–17.00 daily

Active families who don't mind the odd bump and bruise will love this giant adventure playground. The mile-long route throws up plenty of fun challenges – steep slides, spinning discs, rotating tunnels, high beams, wobbly bridges, slippery walls and moving obstacle runs. Your ticket entitles you to stay all day, so bring a picnic (there's a café, too).

FOOD & DRINK

Ring O'Bells Village Rd, Christleton CH3 7AS ☏ 01244 335422 🌐 ringobellschester.co.uk. Christleton is easy on the eye, with a hotch-potch of historic houses and a large pond frequented by birds. It is also where you'll find this pub, which prides itself on serving fresh local food, right down to the bread in the sandwiches from Wallis The Bakers at Saltney. Some of the menu prices include donations to local homeless charities.

4 WALK MILL

Walk Mill Ln, Waverton CH3 7RZ ☏ 01829 749373 🌐 walkmillflour.co.uk
⊙ 10.00–17.00 Tue–Sun

A mill has stood here on the banks of the River Gowy since 1200, but the one you can visit today was constructed in the early 2000s, with historic bits and pieces discovered along the way providing decorative references, such as a date stone engraved 'RW 1668' (perhaps for one of the Wilbrahams, a local landed family?) above the fireplace in the cafe. The new Walk Mill is still powered in the traditional way; its waterwheel is a soothing sight outside, while inside the entrance, on the ground and first floors, you can take a look at the mechanics, including the gears that turn the French burrstones. Today, wheat from the surrounding fields is turned into wholemeal, white and malted flour and used in the bread and cakes made in the on-site bakery that are sold in the café, The Miller's Kitchen, which was recently extended to include a conservatory with views across the fields. You can also buy bags of flour for your own baking day.

5 TARVIN

🏠 **Inglenook Cottage** (page 291), 🏠 **The Outbuilding** (page 291)

Tarvin, a pocket of land caught in a pincer of the A51 and A54, could be easily bypassed. But follow the signs to the old village and you'll be rewarded with a handsome high street, with a pleasing mix of Tudor, Georgian and Victorian buildings. The hub of the village is the junction of High Street and Church Street, the location of two pubs and a shopping parade with the appeal of bygone times. **St Andrew's Church**, off Church Street, approached through an 18th-century gate and along an avenue of lime trees, features many influences in its appearance, from as far back as the 14th century. **Church House**, the half-timbered building by the gate, dates from around 1600, and has some grand twins from the Georgian era for neighbours in the shape of **The Flaggs** and **Hamilton House**. Just outside town, off Platts Lane, are the **Hockenhull Platts**. These three sandstone packhorse bridges, which span the River Gowy and its watery banks, one after the other, were on the road from London to Holyhead in medieval times, although the current structures are thought to date from the 18th century. The surrounding area is a nature reserve where otters might be spotted. A self-guided walk of the area is available to download on the Cheshire Wildlife Trust's website.

Budding wilderness explorers might want to visit **Broomheath Plantation Bushcraft Academy** (Broomheath Ln, Stapleford CH3 8HE ⌀ broomheath.academy ⊙ various dates) set in lowland oak woods around a mile south of Tarvin, where adults as well as children can learn skills such as foraging, fire-making and building shelters.

🍴 FOOD & DRINK

Cornichon at the Gunnery 71 High St, CH3 8JA ⌀ 01829 741391 ⌀ cornichonrestaurant. co.uk. This newcomer to the Cheshire food scene is set in a former grocery, with the original fittings providing the distinctive décor. Cornichon is gaining a lot of attention for its interesting flavours from Europe and beyond, with local sources including meat from H E Coward in Frodsham.

WIRRAL

A jut of land 15 miles long and 7 miles wide, bounded by the Mersey and Dee estuaries and the Irish Sea, the Wirral peninsula is the westernmost reach of this book. Add in a fourth waterway, the Shropshire Union

Canal, cutting another border from Chester to Ellesmere Port, and Wirral could almost be described as an island. With so much shoreline, this area is like nothing else in the rest of the county, and there's more to discover inland, too. Only the southern third of Wirral remains within the formal boundary of Cheshire, the rest now being part of Merseyside. It's a point we're ignoring, though for this first edition we are skipping across the peninsula, cherry picking the highlights. Our exploration begins on the south coast at Ness and travels around its shoreline to Ellesmere Port on the north coast.

6 RSPB BURTON MERE WETLANDS

Puddington Ln, Burton CH64 5SF ⌀ 0151 353 8478 ⌀ rspb.org.uk/burtonmerewetlands ⊙ 09.00–21.00 daily, except Christmas Day

It's all about sound as well as sight at RSPB Burton Mere. Mid-chat with a friendly volunteer in the visitor centre, the point of entry to these wetlands, we had to break off our conversation as a squadron of pink-footed geese descended from the skies, to open the door so that we could hear them honk their approach. On a cold November day, such as the one on which I visited, this modish wooden box with a glass window is very inviting, enabling front-row views of the passing wildfowl and the benefit of the warmth of the woodburner. But the point here is to get outside on the marshes bordering the River Dee to see and hear the birds by following the boardwalks around the pools, grasslands, fens and reed beds, where hides provide opportunities for close-ups. Some paths lead into the woods that fringe the shores, where tree-lovers such as snipe can be spotted, and across farmland, where flocks of finches gorge on seeds. During my visit, a healthy list of birds was being chalked up on the board – teal and shoveler ducks, black-tailed godwit, little and cattle egrets, lapwing, marsh and hen harriers, peregrine falcon, ruff and kingfisher had all been duly noted. Guided walks are available and children can hire 'Wildlife Explorers' backpacks at reception to keep the educational element fun, plus there are special events during school holidays.

7 NESS BOTANIC GARDENS

Neston Rd, Ness CH64 4AY ⌀ 0151 795 6399 ⌀ nessgardens.org.uk ⊙ 1 Mar–31 Oct 10.00–dusk daily, 1 Nov–28 Feb 10.00–16.30 daily

These wonderful gardens are a must-see, both because of their importance as a horticultural laboratory for the botanist Arthur

Kilpin Bulley and the promise of an exotic enclave amid the horizontal marshes of the Dee Estuary. Bulley, from New Brighton, worked as a cotton broker for the family business, a job that took him around the world, but he became obsessed about how species from the Far East, in particular, could bloom in England. In 1898, he bought a sheltered 60-acre plot on the west bank of the Dee Estuary where he propagated seeds from the Himalayas and China, gathered for him by renowned plant collectors including George Forrest and Frank Kingdon-Ward, and also set up the seed company, Bees. In short, we have Bulley to thank for the rhododendrons and camellias that grace the borders of Britain's gardens.

Now run by Liverpool University, Ness has been open to the public since its inception and remains so, as stipulated in Bulley's will. Today, you must pass through a modern visitor centre (with café) to emerge at the gardens' highest point, on the sandstone promontory of Mickwell Brow, where Bulley's handsome Ruabon brick villa stands, looking over the Dee towards Snowdonia. *Stachys byzantine*, *Stipa tenuissima*, *Verbena rigida* … the meticulous signage detailing the Latin names of each plant begins in the borders that scallop the edges of the lawn here. Nearby is a viewpoint, reached via a short double flight of stone steps, offering a preview of what you might see on your wanderings. From here you can also gain a sense of how this garden was divided up in the 1950s, after Bulley's death – apparently, much has changed since his lifetime. There is a visitor map to pop in your pocket, but it isn't essential, because the fingerposts will point you to the different landscapes – Rock Garden, Mediterranean Bank, Spinney Wilderness (the national

THE WIRRAL VIKINGS

If Chester is all about the Romans, in Wirral it's the Vikings who make their presence felt. They settled here in the 1st century AD and their legacy shows in many place names – the ending '-by' (as in Irby and Frankby) derives from the Danish word for a settlement. Entering the village of Thingwall, you'll find bilingual signs giving the name in Old Norse as well as English explaining that it means 'assembly field'. Viking remains have been found around the peninsula and in a genetic test of long established families in the area, it was found that around half of them had Norse ancestry. Even the local football team, Tranmere Rovers, has Viking links – Tranmere comes from the Old Norse for 'crane [as in the birds] sandbank', and the team has a supporters' club in Norway.

collection of Sorbus is here, too). Or you can be guided by your natural curiosity to study a plant or tree that commands your attention – your fellow visitors are certain to be engrossed in scrutinising leaves and having a good sniff of the blossoms. You can't lose your way because there are well-made paths looping the site, off which run occasional tracks to hidden spots, sometimes set with a bench. There are plenty of delightful scenes to savour, such as one just below the sandstone terraces of the Rock Garden that overlooks a tree-fringed pool. Guided walks are available, and the adventure playground, with a tractor play park for tiny tots, confirms that children are very welcome at Ness.

"There are plenty of delightful scenes to savour, such as one just below the sandstone terraces of the Rock Garden."

8 THE WIRRAL WAY

⌂ **42 Caldy Road** (page 291), ⌂ **The Ship** (page 291)

Following a disused railway line for 12 miles from Hooton to West Kirby, this broad, level path is popular with walkers, cyclists and horseriders alike. There are plenty of opportunities *en route* to nip off and explore some of the area's other attractions, many of which are covered in turn below. Your first detour should certainly be **Parkgate**, a pretty village on the Dee Estuary, where you can take a stroll along The Parade, the seafront promenade. At least, it was a seafront promenade once, in the days when ferries to Ireland used to leave from here and the supposedly curative powers of its sea air and water made it a popular bathing resort. Celebrity visitors included Lady Emma Hamilton, who stayed here in 1784, hoping to cure a skin complaint. Today though, the shore has silted up, but it's still a great place to come for ice cream or fish and chips, ideally eaten as you sit on the seawall, gazing across to the Welsh mountains and watching the odd kestrel hovering above the saltmarsh, picking out its prey.

Continuing along the path northwest brings you to **Heswall**, where the moody foreshore offers plenty of scope for photographers to capture the perfect arty shot of old boats scattered across the marshes. Nip off to the other side of the path here instead, and you can take a stroll through **Heswall Dales**, an area of lowland heath with views across the Dee Estuary. There are more good views a little further along, too, at **Thurstaston Beach**, where high cliffs drop down on to a long sand and pebble beach below, and great flocks of turnstones and redshanks scuttle around at low tide. Just off the old station platform here is **Thurstaston Visitor Centre** with leaflets and info on Wirral attractions, and plenty of picnicking space for families who can trust their children not to go plummeting off the cliff edge. Here, too, is **Wirral Country Park**, opened in 1973 as the first country park in Britain.

Turn your back on the beach and head up Station Road, you come to **Thurstaston** village, where the graves in St Bartholomew's churchyard include the family tomb of Thomas Henry Ismay, founder of the White Star Line, the company that launched the RMS *Titanic* in 1912. Until his death in 1899, he lived in the village and paid a fortune to have the main A540 road diverted through a sandstone cutting so it wouldn't run quite so close to the family mansion. Behind St Bartholomew's is **Church Farm** (Church Ln, CH61 0HW ⌁ 0151 648 7838 ⌁ churchfarm.org. uk ⊙ times vary; see website), a 60-acre organic farm with assorted animals to meet (including miniature ponies and pygmy goats), various activities and, in summer, a lavender maze. There's also an on-site farm shop and café.

From here, it's not far up Telegraph Road to **Thurstaston Common**, a woodland and heathland area laced with footpaths, where you can soak up the great views from **Thurstaston Hill** and check out the sandstone outcrop of **Thor's Stone**. In 2001, a Norwegian newspaper reported, possibly not entirely seriously, that this was the hammer of Thor and should be returned, but a visiting delegation from Trondheim decided it was fine where it was.

Heading back down to the Wirral Way and turning right leads to the end of the path at **West Kirby**, home to some quaint shopping parades, a huge, manmade marine lake (a popular place for learning to windsurf, sail and kayak), and the starting point for a walk to Hilbre Island (see box, pages 46–7).

FOOD & DRINK

Benty Farm Tea Rooms 3a School Ln, Thurstaston CH61 0HH ⌁ 0151 648 2746 ⌁ bentyfarmtearooms.co.uk. The location of the tea rooms, hidden away on Thurstaton Common, means you can only reach them on foot. Once there, you'll find great cakes, scones, toasties and afternoon teas, to be enjoyed indoors by the log burner or at one of the trestle tables outside.

Burnt Truffle 106 Telegraph Rd, Heswall CH60 0AQ ℘ 0151 342 1111 ⌂ burnttruffle.net. Local diners helped crowdfund this Heswall bistro, the second opening from Gary Usher of Sticky Walnut (page 36) fame. Canny move: they've got themselves an excellent little restaurant, with consistently good food. For meat eaters, the signature feather blade always gets a thumbs up, but they do good fish and veggie options, too.

Julian's Restaurant 20 Birkenhead Rd, Hoylake CH47 3BW ℘ 0151 632 6241 ⌂ juliansrestaurant.co.uk. This family-run bistro features an imaginative menu that's mainly inspired by British fare but looks as far afield as north Africa. Lamb from over the Welsh border is a stalwart of the menu and vegetarian and vegan options change daily. Chef Julian also hosts masterclasses.

The Little Teahouse The Parade, Parkgate CH64 6SA ℘ 0151 538 7934 ⌂ thelittleteahouseparkgate.com. It's the cakes that grab the headlines at this vintage-style tea room, but they also serve sandwiches, brunches and afternoon teas.

Parkgate Fish & Chips The Parade, Parkgate CH64 6SB ℘ 0151 336 8811. Excellent fish and chips is served in generous portions here – just what the doctor ordered. If it's sunny, take them out to eat on the sea wall opposite, but if it's rainy, grab yourself one of the inside tables instead.

The Viking Black Horse Hill, West Kirby CH48 6DS ℘ 0151 601 1888 ⌂ thevikingpub.co.uk. This pub and bakehouse is part-owned by TV chef Simon Rimmer, who often cooks in the kitchen. As the name suggests, there are definite Scandi influences in evidence, from the décor (lots of natural wood and door handles in the shape of horns) to the children's play things (a wooden ship in the garden and dressing-up helmets and shields indoors). The menu, too, has Nordic touches (smörgåsbord tasting platters and a selection of *akvavits*) but much of the produce is local, including Cheshire beef and pork.

Whitmore & White 124a Telegraph Rd, Heswall CH60 0AQ ℘ 0151 342 7799 ⌂ whitmoreandwhite.co.uk ⊙ closed Sun. Of the three Whitmore & White outposts Heswall was the first, though it recently moved from its original Pensby Road premises to this new location practically next door to Burnt Truffle. Like its siblings in Frodsham (page 282) and West Kirby (3 Banks Rd, CH48 4HD ℘ 0151 625 8460), it's a smart little food hall and wine merchant that stocks a tempting range of continental deli foods but sources items from local suppliers as well.

SHOPPING

Linghams Booksellers 248 Telegraph Rd, Heswall CH60 7SG ℘ 0151 342 7290 ⌂ linghams.co.uk ⊙ 09.00–17.00 Mon–Sat. There's a wide range of titles on offer at this independent bookshop, including a good section on local subjects and authors. It also lays on plenty of events, including poetry evenings, a book club and author talks from big-name writers.

CHESTER & WIRRAL

West Kirby to Hilbre Island

Produced with the kind permission of The Friends of Hilbre (deeestuary.co.uk/hilbre)

🏠 **Hillbark Hotel & Spa** (page 291)
✳ OS Explorer 266; start: Dee Lane Slipway 📍 SJ2186; 4 miles; easy, flat sands & some rocky terrain

The prospect of a walk across the sands to an island is an unexpected pleasure in Cheshire. It is made more exciting by the fact that this is a tidal landscape, yet that also means the walk should be approached with caution. Hilbre (pronounced hill-bree) is one of three rocky outcrops at the mouth of the Dee Estuary, along with Little Eye and Middle Eye (the latter also known as Little Hilbre), and is a two-mile walk from West Kirby. The destination, a Local Nature Reserve, is an intriguing one, with plants and birdlife to appreciate, and evidence, too, of human inhabitants, which down the years have included Benedictine monks from Chester Abbey and the innkeepers of a public house that served the crews of passing ships.

A word of **warning**: do not be tempted to set out from Hoylake or to cross direct to Hilbre. The following route is the safest, yet it comes with caveats. The islands are cut off from the mainland by the tide for about 5 hours out of every 12, so don't set out without first checking the tide tables, which are posted on the information board at the slipway or you can seek advice from the rangers at Wirral Country Park (🕾 0151 648 4371). Find out the time of high water – it will be safe to leave West Kirby for Hilbre 3 hours after this time. For large tides of more than 9m, increase timings to 3½ hours. Return from Hilbre at least 3 hours before the next high tide. Don't set out unless you are sure of your calculations, and never in the dark or poor weather. The crossing itself takes an hour to complete, unless you're a slow walker. Wear strong footwear and warm, waterproof clothing. There are no shops or fresh water on the islands and little shelter, so pack some provisions, plus sun cream in spring and summer. There are, however, composting toilets.

9 BIRKENHEAD PARK

Park Dr, Birkenhead CH41 4HY 🕾 0151 652 5197 🌐 birkenheadpark1847.com 🕙 dawn–dusk daily; Visitor Centre 09.00–16.30 daily except Christmas Day, Boxing Day & New Year's Day

The thriving seaport that was 19th-century Birkenhead became a town of firsts. This is the site of the first tunnel to be built beneath a tidal estuary, the location of Britain's first street tramway, and the place that opened the world's first publicly funded park. The latter is a revelation in a once model town that has seen better days. Step through the ostentatious

1 Start at **Dee Lane Slipway**, adjacent to the Marine Lake in West Kirby.
2 Walk towards **Little Eye**, the smallest of the three islands, keeping it on your right. A landmark once stood here, guiding ships through the sandbanks to Wales, but only its concrete base remains.
3 As soon as you pass Little Eye, turn right and continue on the sand, passing **Little Hilbre** on your left. The island was used as a decoy during the Second World War, illuminated to confuse German bombers heading for Liverpool.
4 Between Little Hilbre and **Hilbre**, take the rough track over the rocks towards the south end of the island and join a path. Today, Hilbre's only permanent inhabitant is nature, particularly birds, including oystercatchers and purple sandpipers, robins and chaffinches. This is also one of the best places in the UK to see Leach's storm petrel, and where shelducks, meadow pipits and linnets breed. Hermit crabs, mussels, whelks, winkles and different seaweeds populate the shores, while Atlantic grey seals reside on a nearby sandbank – up to 500 of them in summer. Voles are the only mammals you're likely to encounter on land, where plant life is more prolific, including rock sea lavender, which is found at only four other sites in the world. Among the structures to explore is the Telegraph Station, which dates from 1841, one of a chain from Holyhead to Liverpool relaying information to the port and the ships at sea. It is now a Visitor Centre run by The Friends of Hilbre and manned on occasion. The former homes of the telegraph keeper and buoymaster are still standing – some suggest a section of these buildings may have been part of the Seagull Inn and that beneath these foundations might lie those of the monks' chapel.
5 Retrace your steps on the return walk to West Kirby.

Grand Entrance at the park's eastern corner, a triple-arched confection with Ionic columns and balustraded parapets linking two gatehouses, to discover more than 100 acres of meadows, playing fields, lakes, gardens and woodland, adorned by ornate lodges and romantic structures, and laced with paths through the park's Upper and Lower sections.

Designed by the architect Joseph Paxton, best known for creating The Crystal Palace for the Great Exhibition of 1851, the park was publicly funded and its purpose was to provide a green oasis for everyone to enjoy, awfully democratic for its age. Paxton's plan was implemented by Edward Kemp, who became the superintendent when it opened in 1847 – a job he kept, alongside his private work, for almost 50 years. The total effect, especially the novel aspect of being open to the public, made such an impression on the American landscape architect Frederick Law Olmsted, who visited twice in the 1850s, that he drew on the park as inspiration for New York's Central Park.

Anyone who has visited both parks will see certain similarities in these naturalistic landscapes, especially the way the paths display different facets of the landscape at each turn and deliver the visitor from open lawns to tranquil spaces, capturing a rural peace far removed from the bustle of urban life just beyond the railings. One such spot is concealed by trees along a path across the road from the Visitor Centre, which is a strikingly modern structure that somehow melds with the scene. The path leads to the Lower Lake, a languid pool, fringed by trees, including two unusual specimens, the black mulberry and a cucumber tree. By the water sits the Roman Boathouse, which was originally meant to be a bandstand, an arcaded cube with pyramid roof set on a base with a semi-circular arch at its centre through which boats could conceivably enter. Here, too, is The Swiss Bridge, an ornate covered timber span painted bright red with a black tiled roof. It would have been a tranquil scene if I hadn't been harrassed by over-familiar squirrels and pigeons.

"The paths display different facets of the landscape, capturing a rural peace far removed from the bustle of urban life."

If you feel like doing more than just strolling around the park, volunteers are always sought to help with tasks such as picking up litter, packing bird food and even weeding. Just pop in to the Visitor Centre between 10.00 and 15.00, or join the ranger-led activities between 10.00

FERRY 'CROSS THE MERSEY

The first ferries crossed the Mersey sometime around 1150, when monks from the Benedictine Priory on the eastern banks of Wirral would row passengers across the estuary for a fee. Over the years, sailing ships, paddle steamers and today's diesel-powered vessels have plied the waters. Though the development of road transport has seen ferry services decline, you can still take a boat across the river to Liverpool from Woodside and Seacombe (merseyferries.co.uk) – humming Gerry and The Pacemakers' hit *Ferry 'Cross the Mersey* as you go is, of course, obligatory.

and noon on Wednesdays and the first Saturday of the month. A weekly Park Run departs the Park Drive entrance at 09.00 on Saturdays.

FOOD & DRINK

Caffe Cream Visitor's Centre, CH41 4HD ⌁ caffecream.co.uk. This outpost of the New Brighton café is a good choice for a snack, with an outdoor terrace for sunny days. The treat to try is the homemade Italian ice cream (vegan versions are also on the menu).

The Cheshire Cheese & Cheshire Gin Garden 2 Wallasey Village, Wallasey CH44 2DH ⌁ 0151 630 3641 ⌁ thecheshirecheesewallasey. Gin devotees should pop over to this pub in Wallasey with its own gin garden, selling specialist gins including Cheshire Gin, which is made on the premises.

Fraiche 11 Rose Mount, Oxton CH43 5SG ⌁ 0151 652 2914 ⌁ restaurantfraiche.com. Plan well ahead and keep your fingers crossed if you want to eat at Fraiche. This highly rated restaurant in the attractive Birkenhead suburb of Oxton has limited opening hours and just a handful of tables, reservations for which are snapped up months in advance. The *Good Food Guide* included it in the country's top 20 restaurants for 2018 and the lucky few who manage to get a booking rave about the no-choice tasting menu, which is accompanied by a kind of *son et lumière* experience reflecting the relevant season. The exact menu changes regularly, but the mix of classic technique and inventive twists is consistent – if you see a 'tree' on the menu, there's every chance you'll get a tree-shaped sculpture, hung with edible 'leaves' that you pick off and eat.

10 PORT SUNLIGHT

The Book Keeper's Cottage (page 291)

Travel along the New Chester Road just southeast of New Ferry and your attention is sure to be caught by a sudden change in the quality of the architecture. This is the gateway to Port Sunlight, an industrial garden village established in the 1880s by the soap tycoon William Hesketh Lever, later Lord Leverhulme, for the workers in his adjoining factory. The son of a wholesale grocer who grew up in Bolton, Lever built his fortune manufacturing soap from vegetable oil rather than tallow, which he innovatively packaged and branded with his Sunlight logo. Port Sunlight was an expression of Lever's progressive attitudes, what he called 'prosperity sharing', with rents set at just enough to cover the rates and maintenance of the properties, which were attached to employees' earnings. Yet this benevolence came with an agenda; villagers were also expected to follow rules about how they lived their lives and to engage in healthy and edifying pursuits.

The legacy is a 140-acre estate, navigated via 20-plus roads, around which cluster about 1,000 houses, with front gardens and allotments to the rear, interlaced with green spaces and public buildings. The main two-storey dwellings, arranged as superblocks yet designed to look like terraces, were either 'kitchen cottages', if they contained a kitchen, scullery and three bedrooms, or 'parlour cottages' where the extra benefits of a living room and a fourth bedroom were afforded.

"More than 30 architects were engaged to create this romantic vision, playing freely with shapes and features from past eras."

Such uniformity was confined to the interiors. Port Sunlight displays an array of architectural influences and is a manifestation of the anti-industrial principles of the Arts and Crafts Movement. More than 30 architects (one of whom was Sir Edwin Lutyens, one of Britain's greatest architects) were engaged to create this romantic vision, playing freely with shapes and features from past eras. The result is a mix of half-timbered, red-brick and pebbledash façades, with shaped and diapered brick, mullions and quoins, jetties, bays and bows, porches and verandas, gabled, pitched and hipped roofs, turrets and twisted chimney stacks.

The grand plan that visitors see today evolved over a number of years. Early public buildings include the Gladstone Theatre, once a recreation hall, and the Bridge Inn, which first opened as a temperance hotel, both of which still stand. You can glimpse the original landscape, before most of the tidal creeks of this former marshland were filled in, at The Dell, a grassy tree-lined channel with a path at its base, over which arcs a sandstone bridge with seated refuges from where the surrounding scene could be admired. The centre of village life is The Diamond, a large lozenge of grass with a double promenade, flanked by broad avenues and crowned by the **Lady Lever Art Gallery** (⌁ 0151 478 4136 ⌁ liverpoolmuseums.org.uk ⌁ 10.00–17.00 daily, except 24, 25, 26, 31 Dec & 1 Jan). A memorial to the Viscount's wife, Elizabeth, this imposing Beaux Arts building is clad in Portland stone, with porticoes and domes – quite a contrast to the surrounding rustic cottages. Inside is a collection of the 20,000 pieces of art, sculpture, antiquities and furniture that Lever amassed during his lifetime, including fine Wedgwood Jasperware and Pre-Raphaelite paintings. Across the road, in the former Girls' Club, is the **Port Sunlight Museum** (⌁ 0151 644

> ### WIRRAL'S FIRST MODEL VILLAGE
> While Port Sunlight is renowned as Wirral's model village, it wasn't the first to be built on the peninsula. Price's Village, aka Bromborough Pool, about a mile southeast, was constructed in the 1850s for workers at Price's Candles (prices-candles.co.uk), a community of 142 houses served by a church, school, institute, library and shop.

4818 portsunlightvillage.com Mar–Sep 10.00–17.00 daily, Oct–Feb 10.00–16.30 daily), a small but interesting exploration of Lever the man, his empire and the model village he built, as well as the lives of the residents, the 'Sunlighters'. Among the exhibits is a quiz about familiar brands belonging to the company's latest incarnation, Unilever. Answer this: How many Pot Noodles do you reckon are made in Crumlin, South Wales, per week? A) 1 million B) 3.3 million or C) 10,000? Don't know? You'll have to visit to find out the answer. There is also a small section on The Beatles, who played four times at Hulme Hall in the village, including Ringo's debut on 18 August 1962. The museum has a shop that will satisfy nostalgia-hunters with its array of gifts and souvenirs heavy on brands from the not-too-distant past. The entrance fee also includes a chance to look around a nearby cottage, decorated in Edwardian style. Guided tours of the village are available or you can pick up a free self-guided trail from the museum shop.

FOOD & DRINK

Claremont Farm Old Clatterbridge Rd, Bebington CH63 4JB 0151 334 1133 claremontfarm.co.uk. This is so much more than your average farm shop. The Pimbley family have created a place where you can buy great local produce, dine on it in the café and celebrate it at the food and drink festivals they host. There's a cookery school here, too, offering workshops on everything from Spanish tapas to wild foraging. Pick your own fruit here in summer.

The Wirral Distillery The Old Shippon, Poulton Rd, Spital CH63 9LN 0151 334 9784 wirraldistillery.com. Home of Wirral Gin, this artisan distillery also champions other small-batch makers from around Cheshire and the northwest and holds regular tasting events.

11 NATIONAL WATERWAYS MUSEUM
South Pier Rd, Ellesmere Port CH65 4FW 0151 355 5017 canalrivertrust.org.uk/places-to-visit/national-waterways-museum 10.00–16.00 Tue–Sun

A historic complex of locks, basins and warehouses, where the Shropshire Union Canal, Manchester Ship Canal and River Mersey meet, provides impressive premises for the National Waterways Museum. Most of the buildings on the seven-acre site are Victorian, but the locks and basins date from 1795, built by Thomas Telford and William Jessop, who created a link from Shropshire to the River Mersey. Over the following century, the junction boomed into a major hub, with huge warehouses built to store china clay, grain and other freight, supported by a foundry, stables, offices, power hall and pump house. Most of these have now been put to use as exhibition spaces, where visitors can find out about the lives of those who built and worked on the canals, from the engineers to the humble navvies, the role this junction played in the region's industrial fortunes, and the development of the town of Ellesmere Port and its community. The museum also unpicks the detail of how and where boats were made, the different boat-building trades and associated crafts, and even looks at canal art and the reasons behind the choice of names for vessels. One elucidating display reveals that a Mr John Smith of Tunstall paid £154 for a boat in July 1814, with the costings detailed right down to the price of a foot of two-inch elm for the bottom of the vessel. Others may find the firing up of the collection of engines in The Power Hall on the first Sunday of the month a little more thrilling.

> *"One elucidating display reveals that a Mr John Smith of Tunstall paid £154 for a boat in July 1814, with the costings detailed right down to the price of a foot of two-inch elm."*

Moored in the museum's Upper Basin and alongside the Exhibition Hall is a collection of historic boats that show the range used on inland waterways, including narrowboats (one of which you can explore), barges, tugs and ice breakers. There's a working boatyard on the site where you can watch (and even learn) traditional boatbuilding skills and techniques, and the resident smithy in the foundry offers workshops. Beyond the Upper Basin is Porters Row, a terrace of four houses, each decorated from different eras, where you can step back in time to the 1830s, 1900s, 1930s and 1950s. Visit on a Sunday and you'll see costumed actors re-enact aspects of the daily life of a dock worker and his family. It's also possible to take a ride on the museum's narrowboat, *Centaur*.

FOOD & DRINK

Backford Belles Acres Farm, Chester Rd, Backford CH1 6PE ⌀ 01244 851374 ⌀ backfordbelles.com. Ice cream made from the milk of the farm's herd of Jersey cows is sold at this ice-cream parlour and coffee shop. There's a small children's playground, a mini maize trail in autumn and a few animals to see.

SEND US YOUR SNAPS!

We'd love to follow your adventures using our *Slow Travel Cheshire* guide – why not send us your photos and stories via Twitter (🐦 @BradtGuides) and Instagram (📷 @bradtguides) using the hashtag #cheshire. Alternatively, you can upload your photos directly to the gallery on the Cheshire destination page via our website (⌀ bradtguides.com/cheshire).

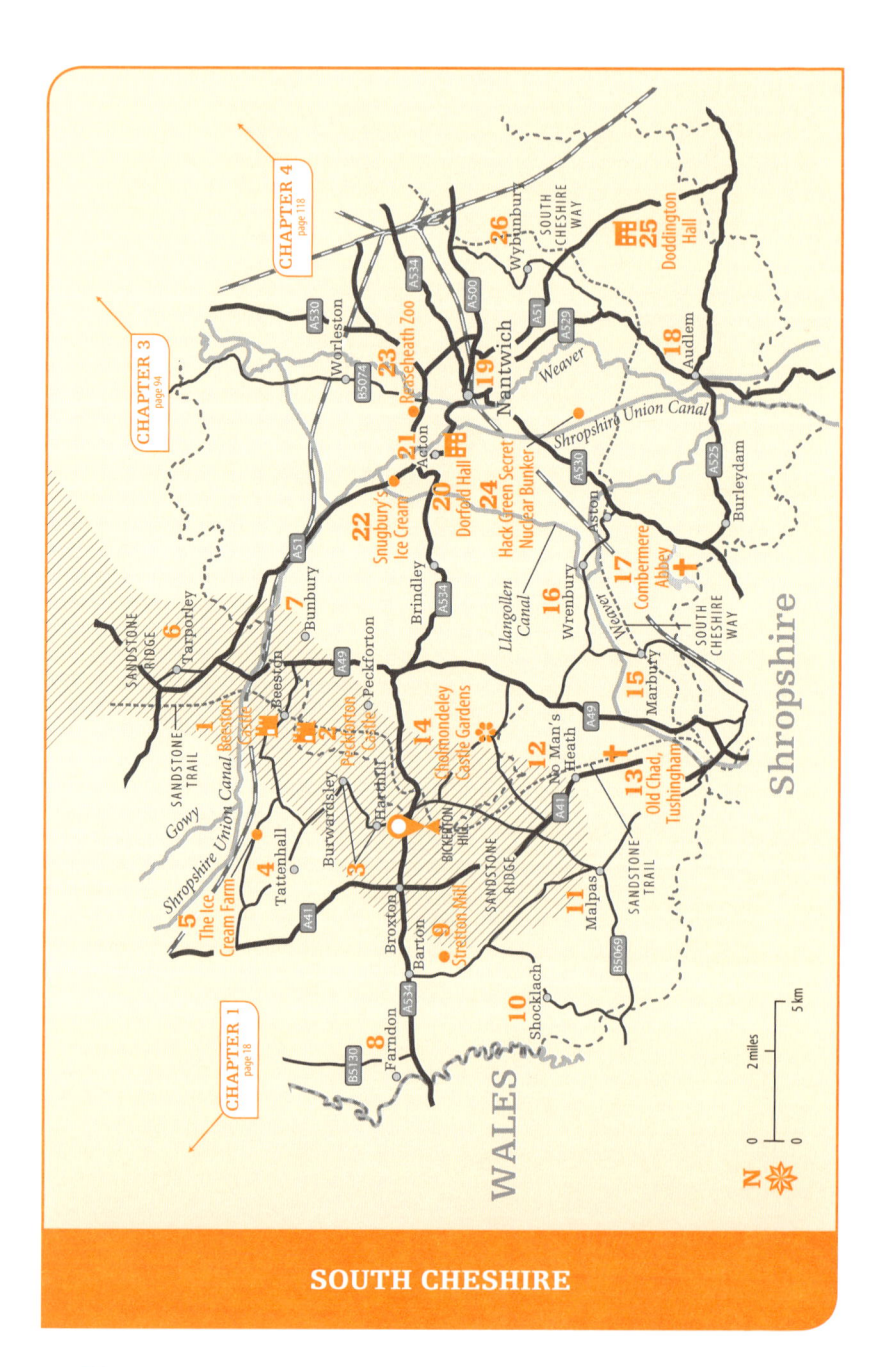

SOUTH CHESHIRE

2
SOUTH CHESHIRE

This chapter travels from the outskirts of Chester to Nantwich, via the borders of Wales and Shropshire and the southern folds of the Sandstone Ridge. It is a swathe of the county that bears few of the scars of industry, despite salt-making and tanning taking place here and there. Instead, its fertile pastures have long been favoured by dairy and wheat farming. Through the fields and meadows of South Cheshire course rivers that once propelled the waterwheels of long-gone mills and canals that carried goods to and from Shropshire and north Wales, their banks and towpaths now providing pleasant places for peaceful walks.

In this area, you'll begin to sense the power of the Norman Earls of Chester, who presided over the county, as well as the influence of the great Cheshire families who established themselves after the dissolution of the monasteries or from the spoils of the English Civil War. Malbank, Tollemache, Grosvenor, Cholmondeley, Wilbraham and Cotton are among the names you will constantly come across in these parts. They left their mark in the shape of castles, country houses and churches, which subsequent generations have constantly tinkered with, creating irresistible puzzles for history-lovers. Though quiet today, the border with Wales reveals remnants of age-old defences, such as at Malpas, a reminder that this was once a heavily patrolled frontline, while the turmoil of the English Civil War is evidenced in places, from an annual re-enactment of a battle at Nantwich to the ruination of the castle on Beeston Crag. The latter is one of two showstopping castles on the Sandstone Ridge, which rises abruptly from the plain to offer some of the county's best walking, through woods and heaths, emerging on outcrops from which not only Cheshire but surrounding counties can be surveyed. Down in the valley,

"In this area, you'll begin to sense the power of the Norman Earls of Chester, who presided over the county."

the villages and market towns provide more historic eye candy, yet there is plenty of contemporary interest here, too, with busy calendars of events and attractions to satisfy young and old, plus recommendable places to eat and drink.

GETTING THERE & AROUND
PUBLIC TRANSPORT
Chester and Crewe are the **rail** gateways to this part of Cheshire. Otherwise, the only railway to pass through this area is the Welsh Marches Line, part of the Wales & Borders Railway run by Arriva Trains Wales (arrivatrainswales.co.uk), which travels between Crewe and Carmarthen, calling at Nantwich and Wrenbury. You'll have better (if limited) luck linking the western and eastern reaches of this chapter by **bus**. Useful routes include the 41 from Chester to Whitchurch via Tattenhall and Malpas, the 70 which follows a circular route from Nantwich calling at Bunbury, the 72 from Nantwich to Marbury via Wrenbury, the 73 from Nantwich to Whitchurch via Audlem, the 84 linking Nantwich and Chester, and the 85 from Nantwich to Hanley via Crewe.

WALKING
The best walking in this part of the county is along the 34-mile **Sandstone Trail** (sandstonetrail.co.uk), which heads north from the Shropshire border rising along the escarpment to Peckforton and Beeston, then passes west of Tarporley towards Delamere Forest on its way to Frodsham. The **South Cheshire Way** also starts its 34-mile journey in this chapter, climbing northeast from Grindley Brook to Wrenbury then heads east to Wybunbury before turning northeast towards Mow Cop. The 218-mile **Marches Way** heads south from Chester along the Dee then goes via Malpas over the Shropshire border, and you can also join the 17-mile-long **Eddisbury Way** at Burwardsley headed for Frodsham (see ldwa.org.uk for details of these three routes). The **Bishop Bennet Way**, named after an 18th-century clergyman, is a 34-mile multi-user route looping west and south of Beeston, along the Welsh border then skirting the Shropshire border around Whitchurch. Although primarily a bridleway, it's a pleasant walking route and a free leaflet of the route is available to download at visitcheshire.com. The 40-mile **Weaver Way** starts in Audlem bound for Frodsham; check out the Mid-Cheshire

GETTING THERE & AROUND

> **TOURIST INFORMATION**
>
> **Nantwich Information Centre** Civic Hall, Market St, CW5 5DG ✆ 01270 303150/628633
> ⏲ 09.00–13.00 Tue, 09.00–15.00 Thu, 09.00–16.00 Sat

Footpath Society (⌂ mcfs.org.uk) for more details. The **Two Saints Way** (page 21) passes through this area, close to Wybunbury, Nantwich, Bunbury and Beeston. This area is covered by OS Explorer 257 Crewe & Nantwich and OS Explorer 267 Northwich & Delamere Forest.

CYCLING

Quiet rural lanes amid rolling fields and some thigh-burning ascents up the slopes of the Sandstone Ridge await cyclists in south Cheshire. National Cycling Routes in the area include 45, 71 and 451, while the **Cheshire Cycleway** covers quite a lot of territory here, zig-zagging its way right across this chapter looping south from Beeston to Malpas and then east through to Wybunbury.

BIKE HIRE & REPAIRS

For bicycle hire, see page 97. The following offer repairs:

Audlem Cyclesport 16 The Square, Audlem CW3 0AD ✆ 01270 811333
⌂ audlemcyclesport.co.uk
One More Bicycle Unit 7, Gate Farm Enterprise Pk, Wettenhall Rd, Poole, Nantwich CW5 6AL
✆ 01270 626997 ⌂ onemorebicycle.co.uk. Offers bike sales and repairs, but also has a café.
Rock Garden Cycles 58 High St, Tarporley CW6 0AG ✆ 01829 730699
⌂ rockgardencycles.co.uk

CANAL-BOAT HIRE

Chas Hardern Boats Beeston Castle Wharf, Beeston CW6 9NH ✆ 01829 732595
⌂ chashardern.co.uk. Long-established operator who lives on-site. Boat holidays offered all year round.
Cheshire Cat Narrowboats Overwater Marina, Coole Ln, Newhall CW5 8AY ✆ 07867 790195 ⌂ cheshirecatnarrowboats.co.uk. Short breaks and day-boat hire are available from this narrowboat fleet.
Floating Dreams Nantwich Marina, Nantwich CW5 8LB ✆ 01270 382025
⌂ floatingdreams.co.uk. Cruise the Shropshire Union and beyond on one of this operator's Nantwich-based narrowboats.

SOUTH CHESHIRE

THE ISLANDS ON THE CHESHIRE PLAIN & AROUND

South Cheshire is the high point of our travels on the plain, literally, for the following section includes one of the most picturesque stretches of the Sandstone Ridge that flows across Cheshire's flatlands for some 34 miles, rising here in two distinctive humps divided by the Beeston Gap, looking like islands sitting on the plain. On the wooded slopes are some of the county's prettiest villages, and the ancient paths that lace the escarpment offer exceptional walking, often emerging at a rocky platform for a spectacular panorama, views also commanded from the two quite different castles at their summits, Peckforton and Beeston. For more information about these hills, the Sandstone Ridge Trust (⌂ sandstoneridge.org.uk) is a great resource.

1 BEESTON CASTLE

Chapel Ln, Beeston CW6 9TX ⌂ 01829 260464 ⌂ English Heritage ⌂ 1 Apr–30 Sep 10.00–18.00 daily, 1–31 Oct 10.00–16.00 daily, 1 Dec–31 Mar 10.00–16.00 w/ends, closed Christmas Day & Boxing Day, open various days Feb half-term holidays

Take the train from Crewe to Chester and one of the highlights *en route* is Beeston Castle, sitting on its crag high above the plain (it will appear on your left if you sit forward-facing in the direction of Chester). From wherever you choose to appreciate Beeston Castle, it is an impressive site, a tumble of ruins clinging to a rock. Ranulf, Earl of Chester, built this castle in the sky in the 1220s. But the discovery of flint arrowheads from the Neolithic period suggests prehistoric man was the first to spot this vantage point, plus there's evidence of a Bronze Age community and an Iron Age hill fort, the latter being used as a foundation for the outer bailey walls of the 13th-century castle. The ruins are reached via a modern bridge, which spans a deep ditch that once repelled invaders, to deliver visitors into the mouth of the huge gatehouse from where it's possible to explore the remaining towers and embattled curtain wall, and see one of England's deepest castle wells, with a 370-foot drop. Beeston's vantage point on the crag, with sheer cliffs on three sides, made it a formidable stronghold, commanding stupendous views from the Pennines to the Welsh mountains that visitors still enjoy today. The castle suffered a torrid history from its inception. Just 17 years after its construction it was seized by Henry III, and was later besieged by the

> **WATCH THE BIRDIES**
>
> A pretty back garden on the Tollemache estate, in the shadow of Beeston Crag, is ground control for the peregrine falcons that breed in the rocks above. From April to June, Janet Blinkhorn keeps a beady eye on these birds of prey, with the support of the police, to ensure thieves don't disturb the birds, their nest, or, worse, steal their precious eggs.
>
> Local volunteers, and those recruited through the RSPB, call by to help with the round-the-clock surveillance from Janet's comfortable summer house, which is supplied with blankets, an electric fire and, just outside, that all-important telescope trained on the crag. To find out more, go to RSPB.org.uk/groups/chester.

Parliamentarians in the English Civil War. In 1646, Beeston was partly demolished to prevent it from ever being used as a fort again. Now stewarded by English Heritage, the castle has a permanent exhibition about its history, the 'Castle of the Rock', and also hosts a lively programme of fort-themed events, plus an annual fete on August Bank Holiday. There are also 40 acres of woodlands in which to gambol here.

FOOD & DRINK

Lockgate Coffee House Whitchurch Rd, Beeston CW6 9NJ 01829 730592 lockgatecoffee.co.uk. This café is the real deal, monitoring its carbon footprint, powered by solar panels and recycling down to the last coffee ground; there's even a parking area for bicycles (and repair kits). The freshly made cakes are raved about, too.

SHOPPING

Beeston Reclamation The Old Coal Yd, Whitchurch Rd, Beeston CW6 9NJ 01829 260299 beestonreclamation.co.uk. Prepare to lose some time to picking through the goodies in this vast yard, stuffed full of antiques and curios, garden furniture and antique flooring.
Cheshire Grandfather Clocks The Gables, Beeston Brook, Tiverton CW6 9NH 01829 733028 cheshiregrandfatherclocks.com. If you're in the market for a grandfather clock, there are more than 40 fully restored pieces on display here, but you must make an appointment to browse these beauties.

2 PECKFORTON CASTLE

Peckforton Castle (page 292)
Stone House Ln, Peckforton CW6 9TN 01829 260930 peckfortoncastle.co.uk
This 19th-century castle is impressively deceptive as a Gothic fort. Built between 1842 and 1851, the faux-medieval stronghold was the dream

home of John, 1st Lord Tollemache, who also invested in the pretty farmhouses and cottages you will see around Peckforton and Beeston for his tenants. The castle's successful execution lies not only in its construction but also in its position on top of the ridge in a perpetual challenge to the fort at Beeston. A gatehouse marks the entrance to the long drive, climbing through woods to the castle, which emerges through the trees. It's massive, in the true sense of the word, huge and heavy. Visitors pass through a giant embattled arch into an irregular courtyard bounded by a sequence of huge red sandstone buildings – service quarters, a chapel, the hall itself – with arches, towers, battlements and arrow slits completing the picture. The castle continues to play the part inside, with a suite of traditional rooms, including a long gallery, encased in stone, with embellishments including ornate wood carvings, coffered ceilings, grand staircases and huge fireplaces. Unsurprisingly, this vast atmospheric mansion has been turned into a luxury hotel, which does a swift business in weddings and conferences. It has sumptuous rooms and suites, a three AA Rosette restaurant called 1851 and a brasserie called 2010, as well as a spa and upscale activities such as archery, shooting and a Land Rover experience.

Tollemache's estate also included Beeston Castle and the attractive surrounding villages of Beeston and Peckforton, which are a joy to amble about. Check out the elephant with a castle on its back, carved in sandstone, in the front garden of one of the Peckforton cottages on Stone House Lane.

3 BURWARDSLEY & HARTHILL

The Pheasant Inn Higher Burwardsley (page 292)

Among the villages on the ridge, these two have more to offer the visitor than bucolic winding lanes scattered with cottages. Following

SANDSTONE RIDGE FESTIVAL

Sandstone Trail Cottages (page 292)

The villages on the Sandstone Ridge make a virtue of their location in a natural beauty spot during a festival in May, which debuted in 2017 (sandstoneridgefestival.co.uk). Music, theatre, art, author talks, poetry, walks and tours are at the heart of the event, with different villages taking part, including Bickley, Cholmondeley, Bickerton, Bunbury, Peckforton, Malpas, Harthill, Burwardsley and Tattenhall.

the road upwards, you'll arrive first in the small community of Harthill, climbing higher to reach Burwardsley, with, at every twist and turn, views to stop and gawp at as you ascend. Quiet Harthill is the setting for chef Brian Mellor's **Harthill Cookery School** (The Green, CH3 9LQ ♪ 01829 782097 ♂ harthillcookeryschool.co.uk), in the Victorian former village schoolrooms, with day-long sessions available in a variety of subjects, from breadmaking to Thai street food. Just outside the centre of Burwardsley is the location of **The Cheshire Art Hub** (Mikerloo Barn, CH3 9NU ♪ 01829 771993 ♂ ladylonghorn.co.uk/cheshire-art-hub), which is home to the Lady Longhorn Gallery, set up by two sisters to exhibit and sell original work by national and local artists as well as workshops hosted by artists. Higher still you'll reach the high street for Burwardsley, where you'll find the **Village Store** (Harthill Rd, CH3 9NU ♪ 01829 770359). Pop inside – it doesn't just sell groceries (many of which are sourced from local producers) and provide the community with a post office, but also has a mini *brocante* in the back room selling vintage bric-a-brac. Follow the road along the side of the store to reach Higher Burwardsley, the location of one of the county's best pubs (see below), and over the crossroads is the **Cheshire Workshops** (Barracks Ln, CH3 9PF ♪ 01829 770401 ♂ cheshireworkshops.co.uk), which runs family-friendly candle-making and other craft sessions.

FOOD & DRINK

The Pheasant Inn Pennsylvania Ln, Higher Burwardsley CH3 9PF ♪ 01829 770434 ♂ thepheasantinn.co.uk. Run by local group Nelson Hotels, this is one of my favourite pubs in the book. A cosy place with open fires and fantastic views over the plain from the terrace and beer garden, the pub is a very popular watering hole for walkers and their dogs (pick up a leaflet detailing some walks from its door), who drop off the Sandstone Trail here for a pint of local ale and recommendable food made from local produce. You can stay the night here, too (page 292).

4 TATTENHALL

Allium by Mark Ellis (page 292), **Newton Hall Shepherd's Hut** (page 292), **Broad Oak Farm** (page 292)

Tattenhall is focused on a busy high street along which a grand and handsome mix of homes and shops clamour for attention. Once served by the Chester canal and two railway stations, Tattenhall's links are now confined to road transport, but it remains well connected, just eight miles from Chester. The place has the air of a well-to-do backwater, perhaps confirmed by the presence of one of the county's top restaurants, Allium by Mark Ellis (see below). The town has a terrace of houses designed by the architect Clough Williams-Ellis in the 1920s for the Barbour family, local textile magnates. Williams-Ellis is best known for the Italianate village of Portmeirion, the surreal backdrop for the 1960s' TV show *The Prisoner*, so his brick cottages on **Rosemary Row**, off Frog Lane, might disappoint; they're quite unremarkable, except for the pediments over pairs of neighbouring front doors. **Rose Corner**, where Frog Lane meets Rocky Lane, is a little more diverting, with its large columned portico. Williams-Ellis also remodelled nearby **Bolesworth Castle** (⌕ bolesworth.com), the Barbours' residence, moving the entrance of the 19th-century property from the south to the east, onto which he added an iron and glass canopy, and giving the interiors a classical makeover. The house isn't open to the public, unfortunately, but it does provide a dramatic backdrop for the big events held here, including CarFest North and the Bolesworth International Horse Show.

If you're travelling with young children, take full advantage of the inviting green space with children's playground on Tattenhall Road to tire out little legs. For more information about the village and its events, go to ⌕ tattenhallpc.co.uk.

FOOD & DRINK

Alison's Country Kitchen Jupiter Hs, High St, CH3 9PX ✆ 01829 771330
⌕ alisonscountrykitchen.co.uk. This coffee shop is renowned for the cakes from its bakery and its special bistro nights. Look out, too, for Alison's Vintage Kitchen, a pop-up tea room, at local outdoor events.
Allium by Mark Ellis Lynedale Hs, High St, CH3 9PX ✆ 01829 771477 ⌕ theallium.co.uk. The eponymous chef of this top-class restaurant is a northwest star of the British cookery scene, familiar from the BBC's *Great British Menu*. Dishes here draw on the flavours in the kitchen garden and the adventurous menu features names that get straight to the point, such as Pig, a plate featuring tenderloin, sticky cheek, celeriac and quince caramel.
Applegates Milton Green CH3 9DR ✆ 01829 770941 ⌕ applegatesfarmshop.co.uk.
This farm shop just north of Tattenhall, off the A41 near Milton Green, had just changed management during the writing of this guide, but plans to add a working smokehouse had been announced.

5 THE ICE CREAM FARM
⚑ Cheshire Farm Yurts (page 292)
Newton Ln, Tattenhall CH3 9NE ✆ 0800 133 7000 ⌕ theicecreamfarm.co.uk ⏱ 10.00–17.00 daily, closed Christmas Day, Boxing Day & New Year's Day

A theme park dedicated to ice cream – it's a no-brainer in Cheshire, where the lush grass nourishes the local dairy herds. The Ice Cream Farm sells more than 50 flavours of its Cheshire Farm Ice Cream, from vanilla to Cointreau and orange (there are even gluten-free cones), which are served in the world's largest purpose-built parlour. It's perhaps advisable to treat the kids to an ice cream after they have enjoyed the rides in the farm's play park, which has attractions with lip-smacking names such as Strawberry Falls and Honeycomb Canyon, and promises rollicking good fun with indoor sand and water play, climbing frames, inflatable slides, battery-powered quad bikes and the like.

6 TARPORLEY
⌂ 32 by The Hollies (page 292), **⌂ Victoria Apartments** (page 292)

Tarporley is an attractive village, based around a high road with a hotchpotch of historic houses, many now containing upmarket boutiques, restaurants, bars and cafés. The best place to start exploring is in the **Old Fire Station**. Now the home of a chocolate shop and coffee house, this is where you can pick up a free copy of *Guide to Tarporley and a history of Tarporley and surrounding areas*. This informative booklet was written by

WILFRED OWEN AT BROXTON

Wilfred Owen may be remembered for his poems about the horrors of the First World War, but were the hills of Cheshire what really awakened the poet within him? So said his brother, Harold, who recalled in his autobiography, *Journey from Obscurity*, the impact a holiday with his mother to Broxton in 1907 had on Owen. Harold wrote: 'It was in Broxton among the ferns and bracken and the little hills, secure in the safety and understanding love that my mother wrapped about him … that the poetry in Wilfred, with gentle pushings, without hurt, began to bud, and not on the battlefields of France.'

Indeed, an unfinished poem by Owen himself reads:

Even the weeks at Broxton, by the Hill
Where first I felt my boyhood fill
With uncontainable movements; there was born My Poethood.

the shop's owner, Charles Hardy, a champion of Tarporley and Cheshire in general, and it tells visitors not only what to see in and around the village but fills in a little background, too. The main road through the village has always been key to Tarporley's fortunes, a major trading hub not only because it was on the main thoroughfare from London to Chester, but also because it became the location of the market after a charter was granted in 1281. It's also where you'll find **St Helen's**, the 14th century parish church. There is a row of cottages in Forest Road known as the Wagon Houses, which were once the site of stables and a waggoner's house, revealing Tarporley's importance as a staging post and transfer point for local goods bound for destinations such as Manchester. The **Swan Hotel** (⌀ 01829 733838 theswantarporley.co.uk), a coaching inn dating from 1769 that still offers hospitality today, is the meeting place of England's oldest hunt club, founded in 1772, which was also responsible for organising the village races until their demise in 1939. The Georgian Hunt Room on the first floor of the inn is hung with portraits of the masters of the hounds and lists of the names of the club's presidents are displayed on wooden panels, reading like a who's who of the county's wealthiest families – Baker-Wilbraham, Cotton, Cholmondeley, Egerton, Grosvenor and so on. Less controversial is the village's claim to have one of the first fire stations in England run by the volunteer fire service, dating from 1866, which can be found on Park Road. It has been a museum in the past, but isn't currently open.

FOOD & DRINK

32 By The Hollies 32 High St, CW6 0DY 32bythehollies.co.uk. At the time of writing, a new hotel, bar and restaurant was due to open in the village in 2018 by the Cowap family of The Hollies Farm Shop at nearby Little Budworth (pages 114–15).
Little Tap 69 High St, CW6 0DP ⌀ 01829 730101. Take your pick from ten beers on tap and others available by the bottle, including Cheshire brews, to wash down a modern British menu of small plates created with local produce. A selection of wine and 50 gins are alternative tipples.
Take Me Home 76 High St, CW6 0AT ⌀ 01829 733733. This butcher and baker is particularly known for its pork pies, but fish, cakes and even local honey are also available at the small shop.

MARKETS

Tarporley Country Market is held around Chestnut Court and the road to the Manor House on the first Saturday of the month (⊙ 09.30–13.30).

7 BUNBURY
🏠 **Garden Cottage** (page 292)

It may be a small village, but Bunbury has some good reasons to visit. The first two relate to its industrial heritage: the **staircase locks** on the Shropshire Union Canal, a mile north of the village, are a pleasant place to watch the intricacies of narrowboat navigation as they pass through two locks here. **Bunbury Mill** (Bowes Gate Rd, CW6 9PP 🕿 01829 733244 🌐 bunburymill.com ⊙ 25 Mar–31 Oct 13.00–17.00 Sun & bank hols), a mid-18th-century grain mill on a pond, is now a museum, where you can explore the building and its history on a guided tour and be put to work weighing grain, starting the wheel and such-like. After all your hard work, have a snack in the café or just enjoy the idyllic surroundings; this spot attracts birdlife including herons and kingfishers, as well as butterflies and dragonflies.

Another reason to visit Bunbury is the fact that it has one of Cheshire's most admired churches, 14th-century **St Boniface**. This Grade I-listed red sandstone structure, bounded by a walled churchyard, dominates the top of the village. Apart from its sheer volume, the church is striking for its high west tower, which bears a crown of battlements and crocketed pinnacles, and the attractive sweep of large arched windows with stone tracing along its aisle walls (the finer example is on the north side). Inside, features to seek out include the alabaster chest tomb of Sir Hugh Calveley, the church's benefactor, surrounded by the original 'hearse', spiked railings on which candles would once

BUNBURY AT WAR

Bunbury is also known as Great Paxford, at least in fictional terms. The village was chosen as the picturesque setting for ITV drama *Home Fires*, starring Francesca Annis and Samantha Bond, which hit our screens between 2014 and 2016. The story of a country community during the Second World War was inspired by Julie Summers' book *Jambusters*, and much of the action takes place around Vicarage Lane at the heart of Bunbury, with St Boniface and the village hall enjoying starring roles and many of the locals playing walk-on parts. R F Burrows & Sons became Brindsley's Butchers and The Village Chippy was turned into a service station. Unfortunately, Bunbury also played a role in the real Second World War, when it was attacked by a German aircraft, which dropped surplus bombs on the return from a night raid on Liverpool.

have been placed. There are also fragments of murals of biblical scenes that date from before the Reformation. In the south aisle, there is a painted medieval altarpiece, which, though faint, shows Christ rising from the tomb attended by the two Marys and two bishops, one perhaps St Boniface.

Bickerton Hill walk

OS Explorer 257; start: National Trust car park, SJ50315303; 2½ miles; moderate

A favourite hike from my younger days, this is a variation on a walk plotted by the Sandstone Ridge Trust (sandstoneridge.org.uk), which is available on the site; free leaflets are sometimes posted at information boards at the main entry points to Bickerton Hill, too. This route quickly ascends to offer fabulous views of the countryside below, the surrounding counties and even the Welsh mountains, taking you across heath, into woods and down the side of the escarpment before a steep climb rewards you with more panoramas.

1 Pass through the wooden gate at the end of the car park and follow the sandy track that gently climbs through broom, gorse and heather. Bilberries thrive on this heath in August and September; pack a little box to collect some for later, but watch out for the thorns. John Gerard, the 16th-century botanist (see box, page 85), noted that 'the people of Cheshire do eate the black whortles in creame and milke'.

2 Within a few minutes you will reach a fork; continue forward, bearing left, and cross an intersecting path to reach a flight of sandstone steps. You'll need a little burst of energy here to make the short ascent (fitness fans like to run up and down them) and just as you reach the summit you'll find there's a second flight to conquer, albeit a shorter and shallower one. Already puffed out? Don't worry, there's a log bench where you can pause and take in the marvellous views towards the Dee Valley and Welsh hills.

3 Continue along the path for a few minutes, tracing the edge of the escarpment, to reach Maiden Castle, one of Cheshire's Iron Age hill forts, built between 900BC and 400BC. Here the views open up to Rawhead in the north, the highest point of the Sandstone Ridge, and Shropshire in the south. Follow the path around the earthworks and down a few steps – look out for an information panel, on your left, which offers a detailed explanation about the fort.

4 Ignore the steep slope to one side of the base of the fort. Instead, follow the path across the centre of the heath to a gate, which will take you into birch woods. Follow the path round to

Bunbury's lanes are also a pleasure to walk around (the high luxury-car count should tell you this is a desirable place to live). There are some pretty houses at the roadsides, including 17th-century **Chapel Cottage** on Bunbury Lane, and, next to St Boniface's, **Church Bank Cottage**, from the 1800s, and the 19th-century **Church Cottages**.

the right, passing through the trees, and within a few minutes you will need to bear left at the edge of the slope.

5 You are now entering one of the prettiest sections of this walk. The undulating path begins to make its way down the side of the escarpment, passing a gallery of sandstone outcrops shaped by time that are tempting to explore with your hands as well as your camera. Take a moment to listen to the birds singing in this cool quiet enclave; greater spotted woodpecker, redstarts and pied flycatchers are among the species found here.

6 The path makes a sharp right turn to switchback along the slope on a path lined at foot level by tree trunks, passing through woods of oaks, holly, rowan and birch, where badgers, bats and tawny owls live.

7 At the foot of the slope bear right and follow the path into a small field. Cross the base of the field towards an information panel and turn right up the track, which ascends sharply. Pass through the wooden gate and continue uphill to a wooden fingerpost.

8 Turn left and climb the short slope to Cuckoo Rock for more views, then return to the fingerpost continuing forward, in the direction of Maiden Castle, bearing left. The path climbs sharply up the side of the hill, with tree branches and bits of sandstone providing footholds, emerging at Maiden Castle once again. Retrace your earlier route, this time ascending the few short steps and skirting the top of the fort, passing the log bench and descending the two flights of sandstone steps, admiring the views as you go.

9 At the bottom of the sandstone steps go forward, crossing the top of the path to the car park, which you walked up earlier, to reach a wooden waymarker pole. Continue forward along a sandy cutting, up some more natural sandstone steps, to a fingerpost. Take a sharp left and follow the path to the edge of the plateau to Kitty's Stone, a large piece of rock bearing a dedication to the late wife of a man whose bequest enabled the National Trust to complete the purchase of Bickerton Hill in 1991.

10 After you've had your fill of the views, return to the fingerpost, turn right through the cutting, and take a left down the slope to Pool Lane car park.

SOUTH CHESHIRE

🍴 FOOD & DRINK

The Dysart Arms Bowes Gate Rd, CW6 9PH ☎ 01829 260183 🔗 brunningandprice.co.uk/dysart. Great quality food and drink and lovely views of the village church from the beer garden make this pub a place people head to from the surrounding area for lunch or dinner.
Tilly's Coffee Shop Bunbury Ln, CW6 9QS ☎ 01829 261591 ⏰ 09.00–16.00 Mon, Tue & Sat, 09.00–17.00 Wed–Fri, 10.00–15.30 Sun. Spacious café with a cosy touch of yesteryear serving breakfast, lunch and snacks using local produce. It's particularly popular with cyclists and also puts on special events, from kids' activities in the school holidays to author talks.
The Yew Tree Long Ln, CW6 9RD ☎ 01829 262518 🔗 yewtreeinnbunbury.co.uk. This pub at the southern edge of the village changed management recently, but is already giving The Dysart a run for its money for turning locally sourced produce into delicious and inspired menu choices.

THE WELSH & SHROPSHIRE BORDERLANDS

At its southernmost edge, Cheshire not only meets another county, but also another country. At one time, the Welsh and Shropshire borderlands were part of The Marches and the rich farming pastures of this area were jealously guarded, the scene of frequent clashes with the Welsh. Today, you are likely to be blissfully unaware that you are crossing a once-fraught divide as you pass along some of the county's quietest country lanes, bordered by farmland, where only the occasional dwelling interrupts the view.

8 FARNDON

Farndon is one of the places that marks the end of Cheshire and start of Wales. The high street at its heart is certainly lined with some pretty historic buildings, but the real reason to come here is to follow that road to its end to the banks of the River Dee and discover the bridge to Wales. The sandstone span was built in 1345 by the monks from St Werburgh's Abbey in Chester and was later the scene of a skirmish in the English Civil War. But never mind the history, an atmospheric photo of its arches and the water flowing through them is what you're here to snap, and perhaps another of the sign announcing to travellers heading northeast that they are entering not only Cheshire but England. Royal-watchers will do a double-take at the name of Farndon's florist, **Paul**

Burrell on High Street, which is owned and run by the former butler to the late Princess of Wales. If you're interested in ceramics, check out the studio and gallery **Top Farm Pottery** (High St, CH3 6PT ⌁ 01829 271571 ⌁ williepotter.wixsite.com/pottery).

9 STRETTON MILL
⌁ **Barton Bank Cottage** Barton (page 292)
Mill Ln, Stretton SY14 7JA ⌁ 01606 271640 ⌁ strettonwatermill.westcheshiremuseums.co.uk ⌁ Apr & Sep 13.00–17.00 w/ends, May–Aug 13.00–17.00 Tue–Sun

Along a quiet country lane near the hamlet of Barton, a pastoral snapshot of the olden days is offered at this old mill on a pond. Once the waterwheel here (in fact there are two, one within its walls) cranked into action to grind corn. Now it serves to entertain visitors who want to find out why a mill has stood here since 1630 (or possibly earlier), how it functioned, and why the 19th-century one that remains was still hard at work in the 1950s. A small exhibition on the first floor of the adjacent Victorian stable explains the mill's history and tells the story of local landowners the Leche family, several generations of which lived at neighbouring Carden Hall. A modern hotel now stands on the site of the hall, which was destroyed by fire in 1912.

10 SHOCKLACH
The curious name of this little village might prove compelling enough to draw you here. In fact, the origin of the peculiar word Shocklach is simple: it was the name of the local Norman lord, Thomas de Shocklach, who had a castle nearby. He also built the church of **St Edith's** (⌁ tilstonandshocklachchurch.co.uk ⌁ during services), given Grade I-listed status for its simple Norman work. The church sits at the end of a lane, a mile north of the centre of the village and is easily found off the B5069. But on

"The curious name of this little village might prove compelling enough to draw you here."

31 October 1756, a Robert Aldersley was inspired to scratch a message on the east window explaining that his journey was anything but straightforward: 'The roads were so bad we were in danger of our lives', he opined. This example of olden-day vandalism is now preserved in a box on the wall. If you attend a service here, cast your eyes to the rear of the church before proceedings begin, to see the bell ringer in action.

FOOD & DRINK

The Bull Worthenbury Rd, SY14 7BL ⌕ 01829 250335 ⌕ thebullatshocklach.co.uk. This elegant country pub is a good reason to visit Shocklach in itself. It's attractive and cosy, and the multi-coloured tiles around the bar are a nice touch. A good choice of beers, wines and spirits are served, and I've returned more than once for the cracking food.

11 MALPAS

The most rudimentary French speaker will recognise the foreboding nature of the word Malpas, a name given by the Normans that means 'bad road'. After all, this village in The Marches, on the border of England and Wales, was tasked with repelling the marauding Welsh down the centuries, from Roman times when the road from Hadrian's Wall to Richborough in Kent ran through here. Today, Malpas is a peaceful place, but reminders of less settled times are present for the visitor to explore, starting with the hummock behind the church. This is the remains of a Norman motte and bailey **castle** – it is on private property, so you can't climb to the top, but there are hopes that public access might be established in the future. Those of us lucky enough to have been allowed to clamber to its summit find it easy to appreciate why Malpas was part of a surveillance network, along with nearby Oldcastle and Shocklach, for preventing raids on the surrounding fertile farmlands, because the views into Wales are far-reaching. It is quite shocking to discover that in the 1830s this historic plot was dug into and used as a reservoir to supply the community with piped water.

The adjacent church of **St Oswald's** dates from the late 1300s but was significantly remodelled in the 15th century, when the stained glass and clerestory were added. Its impressive battlements, buttresses and tower (the latter, it is thought, was originally meant to support a spire) are complemented by some interesting assets within. Seek out the alabaster tombs of Sir Randle and Lady Eleanor Brereton (1522) and Sir Hugh and Lady Mary Cholmondeley (1605) in the respective family chapels – note the difference in the fashions of the ages. One of the children carved on the Brereton tomb is their son, William, who was falsely accused of adultery with Anne Boleyn and executed on Tower Hill in May 1536. The scenes on the east window depict the life of Reginald Heber, a bishop and missionary born in 1783 in the Higher Rectory, who wrote many well-known hymns, two of which are still sung frequently – *Holy, Holy, Holy* and *Brightest and best of the sons of* *the morning*. Another must-see is the camber-beam ceiling in the nave, the full glory of which can now be enjoyed thanks to a fairly recent restoration including re-painting and re-gilding its bosses and angels. St Oswald's also played a minor role in the English Civil War, providing refuge one night for Parliamentarian troops, who destroyed the local salt works at Higher and Lower Wych and wrested control of nearby Cholmondeley Castle from the Royalists.

Malpas revolves around its High Street and has a pretty mix of architecture, including black-and-white houses, notably **Bank Cottage**, **The Nest** and **Tudor Cottage** on Old Hall Street, and, from Georgian times, the **Old Printing House** on Church Street and **Woodville** in Tilston Road. **Market House** on Church Street, also Georgian, is especially eye-catching because of its colonnaded veranda; this is where the old butter market was held. **The Red Lion Inn** on Old Hall Street, closed at the time of writing, was once the refreshment stop for passengers travelling by stagecoach, revealing Malpas to be a staging post on the roads to Chester, Shrewsbury and London. Close by, on the corner of Church Street and High Street, is a stepped plinth bearing a Victorian memorial. This was the site of the original cross and the livestock market, a charter for which was granted in the late 1200s, a benefit probably conferred due to Malpas's important strategic position.

More about the history of the village can be found in David Hayns' two booklets, available locally: *Malpas, Cheshire's Town in the Marches* and *A Malpas Miscellany*. Call by Malpas on the second weekend after August Bank Holiday to catch the **Yesteryear Rally** at Hampton Heath,

THE VILLAGE WITH TWO RECTORS

From 1285 to 1885, Malpas had two rectors, the Higher and the Lower, and theories for this curious situation abound. One says that the custom for having two was not uncommon in Wales, and because this large parish straddled the border, it is unsurprising it occurred here, too. Another contests that this anomaly was a consequence of the heirless Norman lord Fitz Hugh leaving his barony to his two daughters. But the best explanation is surely as follows. When King John visited the village incognito in the 13th century, he was said to be so unimpressed by the poor hospitality he received from the rector of the time that he gave half the job to the curate. Both rectories, the Higher near the church, the Lower further down Church Street, still stand today but are now private properties.

northeast of the village, a transport festival featuring everything from military vehicles to heavy horses. Further events taking place in and around the village can be found at ⌀ malpasonline.org.

FOOD & DRINK
The Old Fire Station Café and Bar High St, SY14 8NR ⌀ 01948 860989. After all that pavement pounding, take a snack break in the 1930s fire station, now transformed into a café serving snacks and meals.

12 NO MAN'S HEATH
Millmoor Farm Cottages (page 292)

If you pass through No Man's Heath, just east of Malpas, seek out the Celia Fiennes Waymark on the corner of Back Lane and the old A41. The Monument, as locals call it, was commissioned in 1998 to mark the 300th anniversary of this adventurous woman's travels on horseback around Britain at the turn of the 18th century. In 1698, Fiennes (an ancestor of the explorer Ranulph and the film stars Ralph and Joseph) journeyed from Cornwall to Newcastle, calling by this spot *en route* to Whitchurch. It was the only point at which she was threatened by highwaymen, according to her diaries (now kept at Broughton Castle in Oxfordshire, the Fiennes' family home). The sculpture, by Chester-based Jeff Aldridge, shows Fiennes on her horse, the highwaymen and the market-goers, whose increasing numbers on the road near Malpas deterred the thieves.

13 OLD CHAD, TUSHINGHAM
The 17th-century chapel of Old Chad is a lonely sight, cast adrift in farmland southeast of Malpas, reached via Chad Lane (off the A41 Chester Road), with the final approach across a couple of fields. It's a simple church with a nave, gallery and small tower and, inside, furnishings from the 17th century (the writer Nikolaus Pevsner, in his Cheshire volume of *The Buildings of England*, questioned whether its Jacobean font was adapted from a bedpost). Next door is a hearse-house, home to a restored Victorian horse-drawn hearse. Both chapel and hearse-house are only open during services, which take place one Sunday a month between Rogation Day in May and September. The rushbearing festival, when freshly cut rushes are scattered over the floor as a symbol of renewal, is still observed on the first Sunday in August.

A pamphlet titled 'Brief History of Old St Chad Chapel Tushingham' is available at nearby St Chad's Church on Chester Road.

14 CHOLMONDELEY CASTLE GARDENS

The Cholmondeley Arms (page 292), **Manor Farm Holiday Cottages** (page 292) Malpas SY14 8ET 01829 720383 cholmondeleycastle.com Mar–Sep 11.00–17.00 Wed, Thu, Sun & bank hols

Of all Cheshire's great houses, Cholmondeley Castle must win the prize for the most romantic. The pink and buff stone pile, built between 1801 and 1830, has elements straight out of a child's drawing of a castle, with its crenellated towers, turrets, battlements and arched lancet windows. It was built around a previous half-timbered hall, encircled by a moat – a building of some sort is thought to have been present here since the family seat was established in Norman times. Cholmondeley Castle sits on a hill, with lawns rolling away to a compact mosaic of gardens and pools below, which are largely the work of the late Lavinia, Dowager Marchioness, who died in 2015. Unfortunately, the castle isn't open to the public; only St Nicholas Chapel, on the east side of the park, can be entered. The main event is the gardens (you can bring your dog, so long as it stays on the lead), which burst with rhododendron, magnolia and camellia in season. Highlights include the ornate white screen gates by the foremost wrought ironsmith of the 18th century, Robert Bakewell,

> *"The main event is the gardens, which burst with rhododendron, magnolia and camellia in season."*

and the Temple and Folly Gardens, which are dressed with sculptures and arranged around pools of water. There are drifts of bluebells to see in May, a nature trail to follow, and a large mere to walk around while enjoying views of the castle. The path that connects the Temple Garden to the Rose Garden, renamed the Lavinia Walk as a tribute to the late Dowager, has been recently redeveloped with 100m-long double herbaceous borders and Chinese crab apple trees. The gardens also have playgrounds, picnic areas and some tea rooms. Although Cholmondeley formally opens at the end of March, snowdrop walks are held in February; check the website for details. But you'll enjoy it at its best in full bloom.

FOOD & DRINK

The Cholmondeley Arms Wrenbury Rd, SY14 8HN 01829 720300 cholmondeleyarms.co.uk. This Victorian school-turned-pub is a pretty gabled building, where church candles and open fires add a cosy touch. It has a great reputation for its local food and serves beer from nearby micro-breweries, plus there are 300 gins to choose from. Stay the night in suitably named rooms for a former school, such as Mr Chips (page 292).

15 MARBURY

Just to confuse you, there are two Marburys in Cheshire: one near Northwich and the other here, close to the Shropshire border. This is the very picture of an English hamlet, or at least it will be once again when the local inn, The Swan, reopens for business – at the time of writing it was being restored by Jerry Brunning, retired former co-owner of Brunning & Price, whose pubs you will be familiar with in these pages. You can check out how the project is proceeding at ⌀ swanatmarbury.co.uk. For now, you must be satisfied with the other bucolic elements; a village green shaded by a 200-year-old oak tree, two meres, and the 15th-century church of St Michael's. Visit in May for Marbury Merry Days (⌀ marburymerrydays.co.uk), a traditional country fair that takes place in the field next to the church.

"This is the picture of an English hamlet: a village green shaded by a 200-year-old oak tree and a 15th-century church."

16 WRENBURY

Cheshire Boutique Barns (page 292)

The joys of Wrenbury are simple. Sup a drink in the canalside beer garden of the **Dusty Miller** (Cholmondeley Rd, CW5 8HG ⌀ 01270 780537 ⌀ robinsonsbrewery.com/dustymiller), a former corn mill, and watch the narrowboats slink by on the waters of the Llangollen branch of the Shropshire Union Canal. Investigate the three wooden lift bridges over the canal, early works of the engineer Thomas Telford, from the 1790s. Then pop your head in 16th-century **St Margaret's** (⌀ wrenburychurch.org.uk/st-margarets-wrenbury ⊙ daily), on the village green, to see a rare example of a pew once reserved for a dog whipper. This title is really as brutal as it sounds: a vicious version of a dog warden, who would brandish a long whip at any animals – stray or belonging to members of the congregation – causing a commotion in the churchyard during the service. (It's said he was also responsible for keeping the congregation awake during the sermon.) Visit Wrenbury on the first weekend in July to catch the **Scarecrow Trail**, when more than 100 creations, from horses to Grenadier Guards, populate the fields and waysides.

FOOD & DRINK

The Bhurtpore Inn Wrenbury Rd, CW5 8DQ ⌖ 01270 780917 ⌖ bhurtpore.co.uk. A pub since 1720, the Bhurtpore Inn (another spelling of Bharatpur, see below) ticks all the boxes for a well-run country pub, with a cosy atmosphere, real ale and homemade food sourced locally that includes staples such as fish and chips and more unusual choices such as cheese and leek cakes.

ARTS & CRAFTS

The Firs Pottery Sheppenhall Ln, Aston CW5 8DE ⌖ 01270 780345 ⌖ firspottery.co.uk ⌖ most days. A longstanding feature of Aston, just southeast of Wrenbury, this pottery run by Joy Wild showcases the stoneware made on-site, from cooking pots to indoor fountains, and there is a workshop in which regular sessions on designing, creating and glazing pottery are offered.

17 COMBERMERE ABBEY

⌖ **The North Wing** (page 292), ⌖ **Combermere Abbey Cottages** (page 292) Whitchurch SY13 4AJ ⌖ 01948 662880 ⌖ combermereabbey.co.uk ⌖ selected dates – see website for details

Spectacular Combermere Abbey, a 12th-century Cistercian monastery on the shores of a large mere, cuts a dash in the landscape right on the Cheshire–Shropshire border. Yet, the cluster of buildings that you see today owes more to a remodelling of the abbey in the 16th century by Sir Richard Cotton, who took over the land in 1539 following the dissolution of the monasteries. The estate is an historical jigsaw. The Abbot's Lodge, today's Library, is the earliest section, dating from 1503, and Cotton's 16th-century half-timbered version was re-faced in the Gothic style in the early 1800s by Sir Stapleton Cotton, a feted general who fought under Wellington at Salamanca in the Peninsular War and stormed the fort at Bharatpur in India, for which he was made a Viscount. Cotton even added a wing in honour of Wellington's visit to the abbey in 1820, one of a variety of eminent people who have stepped through its doors down the centuries, also including Charles II, William of Orange and Elizabeth, Empress of Austria. The adjacent brick-built service buildings, with their arrow slits, turrets and clock tower, date from the 18th and 19th centuries, and the red-brick Jacobean-style stable block was built in 1837, designed by Edward Blore, who also worked on some of the royal palaces.

Combermere is now the family home of Sarah Callander Beckett, the great-granddaughter of Sir Kenneth Crossley, the industrialist and car manufacturer who bought the estate from the Cotton family in 1919. She has dedicated herself to piecing together the jigsaw in an ongoing restoration project of the property, grounds and gardens (the latter now features the world's only fruit maze), opening luxury holiday cottages in the stable block and a top-end guesthouse in the North Wing of the house itself. With such a romantic aspect, it's no surprise that Combermere is a popular wedding venue. Even if you don't stay the night, the house and gardens are occasionally open to the public for tours, special events, and the annual bluebell walk; check the website for dates.

FOOD & DRINK

The Combermere Arms Burleydam, Whitchurch SY13 4AT ⌀ 01948 871223 ⌀ combermerearms.co.uk ⊙ 11.30–11.00 Mon–Sat, noon–10.30 Sun. This 16th-century country pub from Brunning & Price in the nearby village of Burleydam is worth going out of your way to visit for its excellent food, which you can eat in one of the jumble of rooms around the bar or the beer garden on a sunny day. Dogs welcome – Scooby Snax available for those that deserve a treat.

18 AUDLEM

It's hard to lose your bearings in Audlem on the southern border of the county. Stand at the crossroads of this pretty village and pick your onward direction; Stafford Street for Staffordshire, Whitchurch Road if you're Shropshire-bound, or the self-explanatory Cheshire Street. Even if you don't wish to stray so far, these three highways will lead you to all points of interest (though that shouldn't deter you from wandering at will, especially along byways such as School Lane). The crossroads is a good place to start because it is the location of **St James** (⌀ audlemstjameschurch.org.uk), a church dating from the 13th century with additions from the 1800s. The grand red sandstone ashlar structure has a crenellated and pinnacled 14th-century square tower and an embattled clerestory with 12 arched windows. Yet, it is made even more imposing by its position on a mound. Step inside to see treasures including a 13th-century chest and Victorian stained-glass windows by designer Charles Kempe. Outside the church is what appears to be a grand bus shelter, with eight stone Tuscan columns. But this was originally a market hall or shambles, known locally as the Buttermarket, and is thought to date from the early 1700s.

THE WELSH & SHROPSHIRE BORDERLANDS

PASSPORT TO AUDLEM

In 2008, the good folk of Audlem were so impressed by the benefits of living in Wales that they decided to call a referendum to break away from England. The villagers, who live nine miles from the Welsh border and were attracted by the likes of free hospital parking and prescriptions, held an online poll, sponsored by the parish council, which recorded a 63% vote in favour of the move. Point made, Audlem remains on the English side of the border.

Shropshire Street is the route to Audlem's main highlight, the **Shropshire Union Canal**, a natural centre of activity for visitors. Slip down to the towpath by the Bridge Inn to find Audlem Wharf, where the buildings include an old grain mill transformed into a canal-themed shop, with original hoppers and chutes preserved inside, and a former warehouse that is now the **Shroppie Fly** pub (Audlem Wharf, CW3 0DX ⌕ 01270 812379 ⌕ shroppiefly.com). The curious name is taken from the fly-boats, the express service of the 19th century, that ran between Birmingham and Ellesmere Port carrying perishable goods. The pub's bar is crafted from the hull of an original Shroppie Fly.

For part of the year, it's possible to take to the water briefly on the Audlem Lass (⌕ audlemlass.co.uk ⌕ Apr–Oct 10.00–17.00 w/ends & bank hols), a 15-minute trip between Lock 15, north of the wharf, to Overwater Marina. The motor-boat service (it's not a narrowboat, don't be disappointed) is volunteer-led, with most of your fare going to the RNLI. There is a sister boat service in a wheelchair-friendly Overwater Wheelyboat called Maughan Lass (⌕ 01270 811454). Alternatively, head south along the towpath to find a **ladder of 15 locks**, which was built to allow the canal to descend 93 feet over 1¼ miles and continue its journey north on the Cheshire Plain. The village has an award-winning website (⌕ audlem.org), which tells its history as well as listing events.

¶¶ FOOD & DRINK

Farm Made Tea Rooms 11e Cheshire St, CW3 0AH ⌕ 01270 811488. A recent opening, this airy café with an outdoor terrace serves homemade food throughout the day, including a generous choice of 14 loose-leaf teas, from English Breakfast to Pai Mu Tan, as well as tasty cakes.
Finefoodies Deli 5 Shropshire St, CW3 0AE ⌕ 01270 811554. As the name suggests, this deli will delight foodies who can stock up on posh nosh, some by local producers, and snack on homemade food in the tea room.

SOUTH CHESHIRE

> ### EVENTS CALENDAR
> Find out more at ⌁ audlem.org.
>
> **May** Audlem Music Festival
> **Jul** Historic Boats & Festival of Transport
> **Aug** Beer Festival
> **Sep** RNLI Overwater Festival

The Lord Combermere The Square, CW3 0AQ ⌁ 01270 812277 ⌁ thelordcombermere. co.uk. At the heart of the village is this spacious pub, using local produce to create a mixture of solid pub fare and more unusual choices such as Moroccan-spiced vegetable tagine with mint and dried-fruit couscous. Salopian's Darwin Origin is one of the local brews served.
The Old Priest House 2 Vicarage Ln, CW3 0AA ⌁ 01270 881749. A full English or tea and cake can be enjoyed by the cosy woodburner in this old-fashioned sweet shop that also sells homemade ice cream.
Oxtail & Trotter 11 Cheshire St, CW3 0AH ⌁ 01270 811793 ⌁ oxtailandtrotter.com. Even if you weren't planning to stock up, you'll find it hard not to resist stepping through the door of this attractive village shop to browse the local meat, game and poultry, fresh bread, pies and vegetables.

NANTWICH & AROUND

There's a treat in store on arrival in Nantwich, a town often compared with Chester for its depth of history and impressive architecture, though on a smaller scale. The nickname of the town's church, the 'Cathedral of South Cheshire', is no vain boast, because St Mary's is acknowledged to be one of Britain's finest. The network of streets that emanates from the churchyard offers a similarly rich and revealing guide to the past of this industrious market town, where the English Civil War once raged. Beyond the town's limits, the surrounding pastures and canal towpaths have their own centuries-old tales to tell and traditions to share.

19 NANTWICH

⌂ **The Crown** (page 292), ⌂ **Pillory House Loft Apartment** (page 292),
⌂ **The Snuggery** (page 292)

Nantwich is one of Cheshire's most attractive towns, both in look and character. Its streets are lined with an appealing jumble of historic buildings, many half-timbered, and the lure of its shops, markets, pubs and venues, plus a busy calendar of events, gives it energy. The town's origins lie in salt-making, with the Romans among the first to capitalise on the natural brine springs by the River Weaver, which runs south–north through the town. The industry reached its peak here in the Tudor period, with 216 salt houses recorded in 1563, before migrating to the Northwich area following the discovery of rock salt there in 1670. Nantwich then turned its skills to tanning, shoe-making, clock-making and latterly manufacturing clothes, and its location in the middle of fertile agricultural land also made it an important place for trade down the ages. Oatmarket and Swinemarket are names that hark back to the days of William Malbank, the first Norman lord, and are the place where salt, leather, animals and comestibles, including the prized Cheshire

THE BATTLE OF NANTWICH

A town reeling from siege and repeated attack: this was Nantwich during the English Civil War. In contrast to the rest of the county, the town was on the side of the Parliamentarians, and, in 1643, Sir William Brereton of nearby Brereton Hall, Parliament's commander in Cheshire, made it his headquarters, establishing a garrison of about 1,000 soldiers led by Colonel George Booth. But in September of the same year, Nantwich came under siege from Royalist Lord John Byron and his army of 3,000-plus men on their return from Ireland through the port at Mostyn in neighbouring Flintshire. Parliament ordered Sir Thomas Fairfax to help secure the town and he marched an army of 2,300 foot soldiers, 2,800 cavalry and 500 dragoons to its aid, only to come under attack on the final approach, which forced a confrontation. By the afternoon of 25 January 1644, the two sides were embroiled in a full-scale battle on the fields below Acton, with the larger Parliamentary army emerging victorious. Some 300 were killed and 1,500 Royalists taken prisoner in the church (the pockmarks on one of the exterior walls suggest some succumbed to a firing squad). This was the first clear victory by the Parliamentarians and it left the Royalists' ambitions to take the town and the region in tatters.

There is no need to imagine the scene though, because it is retold each year on the Saturday nearest to 25 January, which is known locally as Holly Holy Day (battleofnantwich.co.uk), a contemporary commemoration and celebration of the end of the siege. As in 1644, locals wear sprigs of holly in their hair and hats and the town comes alive with music and morris dancing, plus there's a re-enactment of the battle (from 14.00) on Mill Island by the Sealed Knot, which descends on Nantwich in full regalia for the first major battle of its annual countrywide calendar.

SOUTH CHESHIRE

A PINT OF BEER – OR A NICE CUP OF COCOA?

Such a busy community surely needed refreshment and Nantwich has always had a surfeit of inns, with more than 100 at the end of the 19th century. The temperance movement was alive and well in Victorian Nantwich and in 1878 The Three Cups Cocoa House opened on Pillory Street as an alternative to the alehouse. Cocoa, tea, coffee and soup were served, reading matter and table games provided, and there was even a separate room for female customers. Within three years, the business had moved across the road into larger premises, at number 21, expanding to include a restaurant, meeting rooms, bedrooms and stables, and, by the early 1900s, had changed its name to the Victoria Temperance Hotel. Cocoa House's premises still stand and a restored cooper's kiln in Cocoa Yard, now a small complex of shops and apartments, is a reminder of its previous incarnation. But as for temperance – there remains a healthy tally of about 20 pubs in and around the town.

cheese, were brought to market. Later, in the 18th century, the Market Hall opened next to the church, a Victorian version of which still serves the community. The town was also strategically important, being the last major settlement before Chester and its port, a day's march away, and also because it was on the road to Ireland, a fact that both brought it wealth and put it in harm's way. Indeed, this now peaceful town has had its fair share of turbulence; it hosted a Norman military stronghold, came under repeated attack from Welsh armies, was consumed by a great fire in the late 1500s, and endured a siege and battle during the English Civil War (see box, page 79).

A wander around town

There are many layers of history to peel away in this town. Start your explorations in **The Square**, the site of the mighty medieval St Mary's Church (pages 82–4), fronted by a former graveyard where some of the victims of the 1849 cholera epidemic lie beneath a blanket of grass (which is why you will see most locals walk around this green). This is the point from which fan the main roads to browse; High Street: Pepper Street, Hospital Street, Pillory Street, Mill Street and Castle Street, beyond which lie Oatmarket, Swinemarket, Beam Street, and, across a stone bridge over the River Weaver, Welsh Row. Just across from The Square are **44** and **46 High Street**, two Elizabethan half-timbered and jettied buildings crowned by gables and bearing an unusual pattern of cusped curving lines. The two houses appear to sag where they touch each other;

one suggestion is that they have been built across the infilled moat of the Norman motte and bailey castle that stood hereabouts (hence Castle Street runs along the side of number 46). The sweeping curve of High Street is said to follow the line of the fort's palisade. Across the road at number 41 High Street is **Queen's Aid House**, a three-storey building capped by a gable and decorated with multiple symbols including chevrons and quatrefoils. Note the sign at its first floor, which reads: 'God grante our ryal queen in England longe to raign for she hath put her helping hand to bild this town again'. The words allude to the fact that this house, like those opposite, was rebuilt following the Great Fire of Nantwich of 1583, which razed to the ground most of what stood east of the River Weaver.

An appeal was launched to restore the town, to which Elizabeth I made the considerable donation of £1,000 plus oak trees, ensuring it was quickly and soundly rebuilt, perhaps an acknowledgement of Nantwich's importance both strategically and as a centre of trading and salt-making.

"An appeal was launched to restore the town, to which Elizabeth I made the considerable donation of £1,000 plus oak trees."

The coaching inn **The Crown** (page 86) is another rebuild, and is notable for the windowed gallery at its third level, which runs the length of the building. Other fine examples of the period include **The Cheshire Cat** (26 Welsh Row), three cottages that were converted into almshouses for widows in the late 1600s by Roger Wilbraham, a Nantwich-born lawyer who once served Elizabeth I as Solicitor-General for Ireland and built Dorfold Hall (pages 87–8). It's said each cottage housed two widows, their areas separated by a marker on the ground floor, an inevitable point of tension. For many years, the building was a popular nightclub, but today it is a bar and restaurant.

However, the best example of Tudor architecture is half-timbered **Churche's Mansion**. Located on the outskirts of the town centre at 150 Hospital Street, it survived the fire, as noted by the carving of the reputedly fireproof salamander tucked in one of the exterior corbels. In the porch, the face of Richard Churche, the wealthy man for whom the house was built in 1577, is portrayed in a gilt carving on a corbel. The rooms in the two-storey house display a beautiful mix of exposed half-timber and oak-panelled walls, with more oak-clad ceilings and floors, as well as leaded windows and a large inglenook. Today, the building houses an antiques shop.

NANTWICH RACES

Nantwich was a prosperous place in Georgian times. A survey of the town (then known as Namptwich), by P P Burdett in 1777 reports '… the buildings are elegant and every street adorned with gentleman's seats. The trade of the town is very considerable, and its inhabitants wealthy and numerous, resulting from the advantage of its situation on the great road to Ireland, and also from the salt and cheese which it produces in great plenty and perfection.' At this time, Nantwich hosted annual horse races on a racecourse near today's Alvaston Hall Hotel and the Middlewich Road. Although no evidence of the track remains, there is a chance it could be the backdrop in a painting of a horse and jockey, 'Mr Walsh's Perdita, with Jockey Up, on Nantwich Racecourse', by Benjamin Killingbeck (1781), which can be seen in the town's museum.

Back in the centre, on Monks Lane, are **Dysart Buildings**, an elegant row of nine Georgian houses built in 1778–79. The Victorian age is well represented, too, particularly by the **Manchester and Liverpool District Bank** (1–3 Churchyardside), now the TSB, which was built by Victorian architect Alfred Waterhouse. Look just below the oriel window on the first floor to discover two shields bearing a ship and a Liver bird from the coats of arms of Manchester and Liverpool respectively. Of the more contemporary buildings, **1 Pillory Street**, where the road meets Hospital Street, is unmissable. Built in 1911 in florid French Baroque style, the curious corner block might seem more appropriate for a coastal town considering the multiple porthole-shaped windows that embroider its mansard roof, yet their swags of fruit and flowers give the clue to its original owner: a grocer.

These recommendations scratch the surface of what to see and the easiest way to scoop all this up for an architectural tour is to get a copy of the *Nantwich Guide and Historical Trail* and the pamphlet *Nantwich, a Brief History and Guide* from the Nantwich Museum (pages 84–5).

St Mary's Church

Church Walk, CW5 5RG ⌀ 01270 625268 ⌀ stmarysnantwich.org.uk ⌀ 09.00–16.30 Mon–Sat & during services

The centrepiece of Nantwich is the town's 14th-century church, which is a commanding red sandstone edifice, designed in the shape of a cross and dominated by a 100-foot-high octagonal crossing tower. Step inside the west entrance and you will understand instantly why

St Mary's has been rated one of the top 100 churches in England most worthy of a visit by the writer Simon Jenkins in his book, *England's Thousand Best Churches*. The vast four-bay nave has three aisles and a clerestory, which floods light onto the sweep of oak pews that lead the eye through the arches of the crossing and the three-bay chancel to the high altar and the east window.

This church may have the wow factor but its glory is in the detail. There is plenty to point out, not least two rare pulpits: one in stone from the 14th century, a rarity in England, and an Elizabethan wooden pulpit from 1601. Echoing this ornate decoration is an octagonal font (where I was christened), by the south aisle, in creamy Caen stone, introduced by Sir George Gilbert Scott. He restored elements of the church in the mid 1800s, though not all his modifications were welcomed, especially his west window, which was swiftly replaced. Some of the 16th-century timbers from the roof of the North Transept have been preserved and are displayed on the north and south walls, one carved with the date

SAY CHEESE: THE NANTWICH SHOW

nantwichshow.co.uk

Nantwich holds a country show to rival the county's own. For one day in July, thousands converge on the fields around Dorfold Hall, on the edge of town, to inspect vintage tractors and state-of-the-art quad bikes, watch gun dog displays and shire-horse parades, and judge for themselves the cattle, chickens, marrows and cabbages competing with their kind for Best In Show. The show is also the home of the **International Cheese Awards** (internationalcheeseawards.co.uk) one of the most important events in the global cheese calendar. In the mega-marquee, the Cheese Pavilion, there are cookery demonstrations by celebrity chefs and a marketplace of cheese producers, who invite visitors to stab a cocktail stick in everything from a creamy Italian *speziato* to a good old chunk of cheddar. One type you must try is the local Cheshire cheese, from the pastures of South Cheshire; the crumbly, semi-hard cheese is mild in taste but has a salty tang and is one of the oldest named cheeses in Britain. Local producers to look out for here and during your travels in the area include H S Bourne at Malpas (hsbourne.co.uk), which has been making the cheese since 1750, Joseph Heler at Hatherton (joseph-heler.co.uk), and, just over the county border, Belton Farm near Whitchurch (beltonfarm.co.uk) and Appleby's Cheese near Shrewsbury (applebyscheese.co.uk). The serious business takes place at the back of the marquee where a sea of truckles, blocks and wheels of cheese (milk and yoghurt, too) compete for award-winning status.

THE DABBERS

Nantwich residents born within the parish boundary are known as Dabbers – yet where that boundary lies and the origins of the word are hotly debated questions. There are lots of theories about the name. Could it be to do with dabbing glue to attach the lining to the upper of the shoes that were made here? Or is it about illiterate farmers making a mark on a deed? Another popular explanation is a corruption of the word 'daubing', as in wattle and daub, used in the construction of timber-framed buildings – were the folk of Nantwich particularly skilled in this?

As to where you must be born to qualify, the point is discussed in full on the interesting website 'A Dabber's Nantwich' (dabbersnantwich.me.uk). Here, too, you can find more out about another unusual town tradition, the Beam Heath Trust. This fund was established in 1823 to pay a fee to residents living around enclosed common ground in lieu of their grazing rights. Almost two centuries later, the residents of the affected properties still receive an annual payment. At the time of writing, it was the princely sum of £35.

(1577) and names including Thomas Clayes, who designed Churche's Mansion (page 81). A modern-day addition is the beautiful collection of colourful tapestry kneelers throughout the church, embroidered with motifs celebrating the town and its people, as well as biblical references. There are more than 550 in the nave alone, all of which have been painstakingly hand-stitched by volunteers, a labour of love that began in 1976.

The chancel has an outstanding 14th-century Lierne-vaulted stone ceiling, its ribs studded with 70 bosses – see them more clearly with the help of the viewing box. But the highlight is likely to be the exquisite 600-year-old choir stalls, with their delicate triple-hooded canopies, like high crowns, to protect the choristers from draughts, and the surprising carvings on the misericords, such as the woman beating her husband with a ladle.

Nantwich Museum

Pillory St, CW5 5BQ ⌀ 01270 627104 ⌀ nantwichmuseum.org.uk ⌀ 10.30–16.30 Tue–Sat

The Victorian architect Thomas Bower's handsome library is now the home of the Nantwich Museum, a well-planned exhibition that walks visitors through the town's timeline, its industries and events, and the social history of the community. One of the most important artefacts found in the town takes pride of place here: a section of a salt ship found on Second Wood Street in 2004. The hollowed-out trunk of an oak tree would have been used to store brine before its evaporation to make salt. There is also a room dedicated to cheesemaking, of which Nantwich is an important centre, set in the middle of dairy pasturelands and close to the salt industry. Fittingly, the town is home to the International Cheese Awards (see box, page 83). Local interest in the past is evident in the shop, where a wealth of pamphlets written by knowledgeable residents about different aspects of their town's history are on sale.

On the waterfronts

The River Weaver, Nantwich Lake and Shropshire Union Canal offer a breath of fresh air close to the town centre and can be united in an easy three-mile hike, the **Nantwich Riverside Loop Walk**, route notes for which are available at the Nantwich Information Centre (page 57) or to download at ⊘ nantwichtowncouncil.gov.uk. Along the way you'll take in the lake, which brims with swans, the Shropshire Union Canal, which was forced to skirt Dorfold Hall, requiring the engineer Thomas Telford to build an embankment, and the black-and-white cast-iron aqueduct, with its elegant balustrade, that arches over the Chester Road. It also includes one of Nantwich's most attractive streets, Welsh Row, named after the Welsh salt merchants who would enter the town here and lined with historic buildings from different eras, and heads to Mill Island, where a mill stood from the 13th century until the last one burnt down in 1970. Head for the north side of Welsh Row's bridge to find a plaque marking the spot of Old Biot, the brine spring that once supplied the

JOHN GERARD

One of the founders of English botany, John Gerard was born in Nantwich in 1545. His fascination with plants began during his childhood here, an interest that was to define his life. Later, a surgeon by profession, he became the herbalist to James I and wrote the first ever compendium of plants, *Catalogus Arborum*, in 1596, a precious record of what was being grown in England at this time. In the following year, Gerard published *The Herball*, or *Generall Historie of Plantes*, an illustrated encyclopaedia of more than 2,000 plants, the first of its kind in the English language and the authority on the subject until the 19th century. The Nantwich Walled Garden Society (⊘ nantwichwalledgarden. org.uk) is currently campaigning to save and restore a walled garden in Welsh Row, which dates from the turn of the 17th century, as a tribute to Gerard.

EVENTS CALENDAR

Find out more at nantwichtowncouncil.gov.uk.

Jan Holly Holy Day & The Battle of Nantwich
Mar/Apr Jazz, Blues & Music Festival
May Classic Car Rally
Jul The Nantwich Show & International Cheese Awards (see box, page 83)
Sep Food Festival
Oct Words & Music Festival

salt-making industry and today feeds the open-air **Brine Pool**, Britain's only inland outdoor swimming pool of its kind, which is open to the public in spring and summer. For details, go to everybody.org.uk and search for Nantwich.

FOOD & DRINK

Barrel & Tap 90–92 Hospital St, CW5 5RP 01270 486076 thebarrelandtap.co.uk. A relative newcomer, this bar serves craft beers and gin cocktails in a stripped-back warren of rooms and a beer garden with comfy booths. On Thursdays and Fridays wood-fired pizzas are on sale to help line the stomach.
The Black Lion 29 Welsh Row, CW5 5ED 01270 628711 blacklion-nantwich.co.uk. This may be one of the oldest pubs in Nantwich, dating from 1664, but within the half-timbered structure's wattle and daub walls they keep up with the latest on the real ale scene, with frequently changing guest beers, and food to suit contemporary tastes, such as lamb two ways.
Chatwins 40 High St, CW5 5AS 01270 625688 chatwins.co.uk. Chatwins is a Cheshire institution, with shops across the county. It all started here in Nantwich in 1913, and the bakery on Market Street still works through the night turning out bread, cakes, pasties and pies. Taste them for yourself at the shops (with café) on High Street or Pepper Street.
Cheerbrook Farm Shop Newcastle Rd, CW5 7EL 01270 666431 cheerbrook.co.uk. On the edge of town, fill up your shopping bag with top-quality local meat, dairy and produce – the butchery is particularly good – and then enjoy a snack or meal in the café.
The Crown High St, CW5 5AS 01270 625283 crownhotelnantwich.com. Recently the subject of a subtle revamp that has enhanced its olde-worlde charm, this independent inn is just the place to enjoy a well-kept pint by the open fire. There's a restaurant and hotel here, too (page 292).

Ginger and Pickles 3a Mill St, CW5 5ST ⌀ 01270 610329 ⌀ gingerandpickles.co.uk. If ever a town deserved a quaint tea room, it's Nantwich. Ginger and Pickles fits the bill, with breakfast, lunch and afternoon tea served beneath the bunting on pretty mismatched china.
Teresa's Ice Cream Parlour 1 Oatmarket, CW5 5AL ⌀ teresasicecreamparlour.co.uk. Choose from 22 flavours of homemade gelato at this family-run ice-cream parlour, from Bakewell tart to Belgian chocolate, including dairy-, sugar- and gluten-free choices.

SHOPPING
Shops
Nantwich Book Shop & Coffee Lounge 46 High St, CW5 5AS ⌀ 01270 611665. Lively independent bookshop that sells a wide variety of reading matter, including a healthy stock of local history and guide books, and doubles as a café, with an outside terrace for warmer days. The shop hosts author's evenings, too.
Peter Wilson Fine Art Auctioneers Victoria Gallery, Market St, CW5 5DG ⌀ 01270 623878 ⌀ peterwilson.co.uk. This auction house will be familiar to fans of BBC's *Bargain Hunt*, on which it often appears. Drop by and watch or even take part in the bidding.

Markets
Nantwich's **town market** is held in and around Market Hall, at the junction of Market Street and Churchyardside (⊙ 09.00–13.00 Tue, 09.00–15.00 Thu & 09.00–16.00 Sat), while **Nantwich Farmers Market** is held on The Square on the last Saturday of the month and the Saturday before Christmas in December (⊙ 09.00–15.00). **Vintage & artisan markets** and **antiques markets** take place in the Civic Hall and on The Square throughout the year.

20 DORFOLD HALL
Redwood Cottage (page 292)
Chester Rd, CW5 8LD ⌀ 01270 625245 ⌀ dorfoldhall.com ⊙ Apr–Oct 13.00–17.00 Tue & bank hols

Head west out of Nantwich, passing beneath Thomas Telford's aqueduct, and you will soon reach the gates of Dorfold Hall. The Grade I-listed Jacobean manor was built by Sir Roger Wilbraham around 1621 to host James I and has pretty much stayed in the family down the centuries. The red brick mansion and the two lodges that flank it are original. Later renovations added a further pair of lodges, creating a courtyard, as well as the carriage house with clock tower and another wing on the east side of the main house. You'll need to join a guided tour to see inside the house, a highlight of which is The Great Chamber, with its tunnel-vaulted

WILLASTON WORLD WORM CHARMING CHAMPIONSHIPS

willastonprimaryacademy.co.uk/worm-charming

Worm charmers young and old do battle every June on the playing field at Willaston Primary Academy, just two miles east of Nantwich. Competitors descend on the 144 neatly marked out 3m² plots for 30 minutes of cajoling the slippery customers from their soily lairs without resorting to digging, an event overseen by the International Federation of Charming Worms and Allied Pastimes, also your go-to body for underwater Ludo and indoor hang-gliding. A variety of techniques are employed; most wiggle a garden fork in the turf to stimulate vibrations said to be similar to rainfall, but brute force is also popular – jumping up and down, bashing the ground – and some worms are even serenaded on musical instruments such as the tuba. When the bell rings, the cacophony ends and the count begins, with trophies awarded for categories including Most Worms, Heaviest Worm and Chief Wormer. Meanwhile, the worms must wait until after dusk, when the birds have gone to their roosts, to safely return home. What's a good trawl, you might ask? Well, the world record for the most worms charmed is 567, unearthed by 10-year-old Sophie Smith in 2009.

ceiling bearing plasterwork with an elaborate geometric design. The gardens, though a small feature of the parkland, include a tree-fringed lake, a pretty dingle with a stream at its heart where drifts of bluebells can be seen in season as well as rhododendron and magnolia, and an ancient chestnut tree, the thick and gnarly trunk of which testifies to it being more than 1,000 years old. One feature you can't miss is 'Chienne et ses petits', a fearsome sculpture in the centre of the courtyard of a chained wolfhound protecting her three puppies, which was bought by Wilbraham Tollemache at the 1862 Salon Exhibition in Paris.

21 ACTON

West of Nantwich, the village of Acton may be small, but its influence on the area has been significant over the centuries. **St Mary's Acton** on Monks Lane (stmarysacton.com) was the mother church of the parish, once under the control of the monks at Combermere Abbey (pages 75–6), and is notable for having the oldest tower in Cheshire, parts of which date from 1180. Inside, there is a mix of architectural influences that stretch back to medieval times and a notable collection of fragments of Norman sculptures, in sandstone and limestone, depicting natural subjects and biblical scenes. Every Sunday, the church hosts **Tea at the Tower** (⊙ 14.30–16.30), when you can climb to its summit.

FOOD & DRINK

Chestnut Meats Long Ln, Brindley CW5 8NF ⌕ 01270 524750 ⌘ chestnutmeats.co.uk/shop-cafe ⊙ 09.00–17.00 Mon–Fri, 09.00–14.00 Sat. This artisan butchery from a Spurstow-based goat farm opened in 2017. Local beef, lamb, pork and seasonal game also feature. At time of writing, the café was due to open in spring 2018.

22 SNUGBURY'S ICE CREAM

Park Farm, Hurleston CW5 6BU ⌕ 01270 624830 ⌘ snugburys.co.uk ⊙ Mar–Oct 09.30–18.00, Oct–Mar 10.00–17.00, daily except Christmas Day & Boxing Day

The ice cream sold at Snugbury's, just north of Acton, licks many of its competitors in this dairy-rich county. Production moved from the farm's kitchen table to its factory some years ago and now the ice-cream parlour sells more than 35 flavours in its signature giant cones as well as take-home tubs. Visitors also drop by to see the giant straw sculptures in Snugbury's field, currently a 38-foot-high Peter Rabbit, with a 10-foot-long carrot, which was built in 2016 to commemorate the 150th anniversary of the birth of Beatrix Potter. He's not the first version – the original was burnt down by arsonists in early 2017, but in true community spirit was rebuilt by local volunteers. You can't miss 'Straw Peter' as you travel along the A51, but a better way to view this eight-ton sculpture is to pick up an ice cream then wander across the field for a closer look. The gigantic bunny's predecessors have included a meerkat, polar bear, Olympic cyclist and a Dalek that could move its eye stalk and utter the immortal words 'Exterminate!'.

23 REASEHEATH ZOO

🏠 **The Badger Inn** Church Minshull (page 292)

Animal Management, Reaseheath College, Main Rd, CW5 6DF ⌕ 01270 613222 ⌘ reaseheath.ac.uk/zoo ⊙ 10.00–16.00 w/ends & college holidays

Avid fans of *The Archers* may be familiar with the word Reaseheath, Helen Archer's alma mater. Yet, while the agricultural college at this historic hall on the northern outskirts of Nantwich is renowned for teaching Britain's farmers – the Cheshire School of Agriculture opened here in 1921 – few realise that it also tutors students in how to look after more exotic animals. Within the college complex is a mini zoo, but don't expect to see lions and tigers; this collection features the likes of lemurs, meerkats and alpaca, with events and experiences for adults and children, including Twilight Nights, Keeper for the Day and Zoo School.

FOOD & DRINK

The Badger Inn Cross Ln, Church Minshull CW5 6DY ⌀ 01270 522348 ⌀ badgerinn.co.uk. Pork pies, risottos and lamb and chorizo shepherd's pie reveals a menu that pushes the bounds of pub grub, with local producers featured, but the quaint setting of this oak-beamed coaching inn should also satisfy appetites for a proper country pub.

J Hulse Baker and Grocer 99 Main Rd, Worleston CW5 6DN ⌀ 01270 625706 ⌀ jhulse.co.uk ⊙ 08.00–17.00 Mon–Fri, 09.00–14.00 Sat. This grocery and bakery in Worleston, just north of Reaseheath, has been in business since 1878 and is now run by the fourth generation of the same family. Stock up on home-baked pies and bread and, on warmer days, enjoy a freshly made sandwich at the table outside.

SHOPPING

Metropolitan Machine Knitting Wettenhall Rd, Poole CW5 6AL ⌀ 01270 628414 ⌀ metropolitanmachineknitting.co.uk ⊙ 10.00–16.00 Mon–Sat, excluding bank hols. I'm not sure what's more surprising about this centre dedicated to machine knitting: that it's up a quiet country lane or that it's heading for its centenary in 2025. Machine knitters can meet the like-minded at the Saturday afternoon club, where speakers are occasionally hosted, or just browse the premises, where patterns and yarns are sold and old knitting machines are exhibited, and enjoy a cuppa in the tea room.

24 HACK GREEN SECRET NUCLEAR BUNKER

French Ln, Hack Green CW5 8AL ⌀ 01270 629219 ⌀ hackgreen.co.uk ⊙ Mar–Oct 10.00–17.00 daily, Oct–Feb daily 10.00–16.00 Wed–Sun

Hidden in the green fields of the Cheshire countryside is a surprising reminder of war in the shape of one of a network of operation centres that was dedicated to protecting Britain from attack in the second half of the 20th century. Hack Green was initially a decoy for the railway junction at Crewe during the Second World War, then an RAF base, before becoming a sophisticated Radar station to counter Soviet attack during the Cold War. The centre was closed in 1966, but 11 years later it was given a new lease of life and substantially extended as the UK's regional government headquarters in the event of a nuclear war, becoming operational in 1984. For the past two decades, Hack Green has been a museum, offering an insight into those nervous times. It's simply presented, yet it holds some significant exhibits, such as one of the largest public collections of decommissioned nuclear weapons in Europe. The café, the NAAFI Canteen, recalls Hack Green's purpose in the 1950s and 1960s, hung with Union Jack bunting and low-flying model fighter aircraft, with Chocolate Rations and Bay of Pigs paninis on the menu.

25 DODDINGTON HALL

London Rd, Bridgemere CW5 7PU ⌀ thedoddingtonestate.co.uk ⊙ grounds only 10.00–14.00 2nd w/end of month

Doddington Hall is currently shut to the public but you can look around the grounds of this fine late-18th-century hall by the architect Samuel Wyatt, where some of the landscaping is credited to Capability Brown. The estate's most intriguing feature is Delves Hall, named after Doddington's owner, Sir John Delves, a crenellated, early-15th-century tower house that was part of the original mansion, but is now marooned in a field. It looks like the top of a great sandstone castle that has been swallowed up by the ground, with its large entrance arch, lancet windows and embattled turrets at the four corners of its roof. Yet, it also has an incongruous addition on its east side, a 17th-century staircase that rises to a landing supported by statues of the Black Prince, Lord Audley and four squires, including Delves, who fought at Poitiers in 1356. The historians are sketchy about Capability Brown's contribution, which is thought to have included the expansion of Doddington Pool.

FOOD & DRINK

The Boar's Head 1 Wybunbury Rd, Walgherton CW5 7LA ⌀ 01270 660111 ⌀ theboarsheadnantwich.co.uk. This attractive inn, with pretty black-and-white gables, had a contemporary makeover in early 2017 but hasn't lost any of its cosy rustic atmosphere. Posh pub classics meet further-flung fare, such as Malaysian coconut curry, on the menu. If you're wondering, the two squat gate lodges across the road mark the original entrance to Doddington Hall.

SHOPPING

Dagfields Crafts & Antique Centre Dagfields Farm, Crewe Rd, Walgherton CW5 7LG ⌀ 01270 841336 ⌀ dagfields.co.uk ⊙ 10.00–17.00 daily, except Christmas Day & Boxing Day. Just outside Walgherton, seven barns have been transformed into huge antiques

SOUTH CHESHIRE

> **JUST OVER THE BORDER**
> **Dorothy Clive Garden** Shropshire TF9 4ET ⊘ dorothyclivegarden.co.uk. A 12-acre hillside garden created in the mid 20th century by Col Harry Clive for his sick wife.
> **Erdigg Hall** Nr Wrexham LL13 0YT ⊘ National Trust. Stately home dating from the 17th century.
> **World's End** Denbighshire LL11 3DE. Steep-sided narrow valley offering walkers and cyclists spectacular views.

emporiums, with more than 260 dealers on site and many more items on sale here, from bird tables to Persian rugs. There's a tea room and restaurant where you can rest your feet and review your booty before diving in again.

26 WYBUNBURY

What does the Cheshire village of Wybunbury (pronounced winberry) have in common with the Italian city of Pisa? They've both got a leaning tower. **Wybunbury Tower** (⊘ wybunbury.org.uk) may not lean quite so dramatically as its Tuscan counterpart – around 18 inches to the vertical, as opposed to the Pisan's lurch of 12 foot – but stand before this 15th-century remnant of a previous church and you'll clearly see the tilt. In fact, the locals have tried to straighten the 96-foot-high tower twice over the centuries, latterly setting it on concrete stools that can be jacked up in future if necessary.

Try to time your visit with the annual **Fig Pie Roll** in June, a fun 19th-century tradition that was revived in 1995 to raise funds for the preservation of the tower. The pies, which must be home-baked to a traditional recipe, are rolled down the hill between the village's two pubs, the Swan Inn and Red Lion, with the owner of the one that rolls the furthest and, crucially, remains intact, winning the title Pie-roller Champion.

Also, while you're here, take a walk around **Wybunbury Moss**, just north of the village. This rare schwingmoor, or quaking bog, surrounded by meadows and woods, is one of the best examples in Britain of a moss with a raft of peat floating on the water-filled basin and is a National Nature Reserve. You won't be able to get too close to the centre of the moss because it's regarded as dangerous and access is by permit only, but a safe walk that offers views of the bog and visits part of it was developed in 2007 by Natural England (a visitor leaflet is available to download at ⊘ gov.uk/natural-england).

Discover the Britain you didn't know existed

By rail, road and everything in between, Bradt's transport guides suggest a personal and relaxed approach to travel. Colourfully written, they are specialist books prepared with connoisseurs in mind.

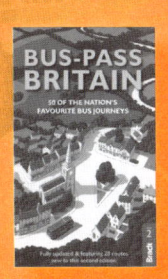

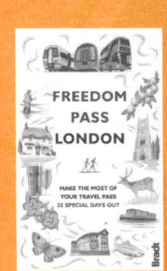

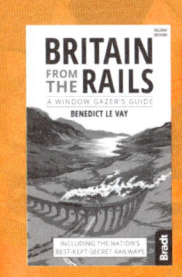

Bradt

Available from bookshops or www.bradtguides.com

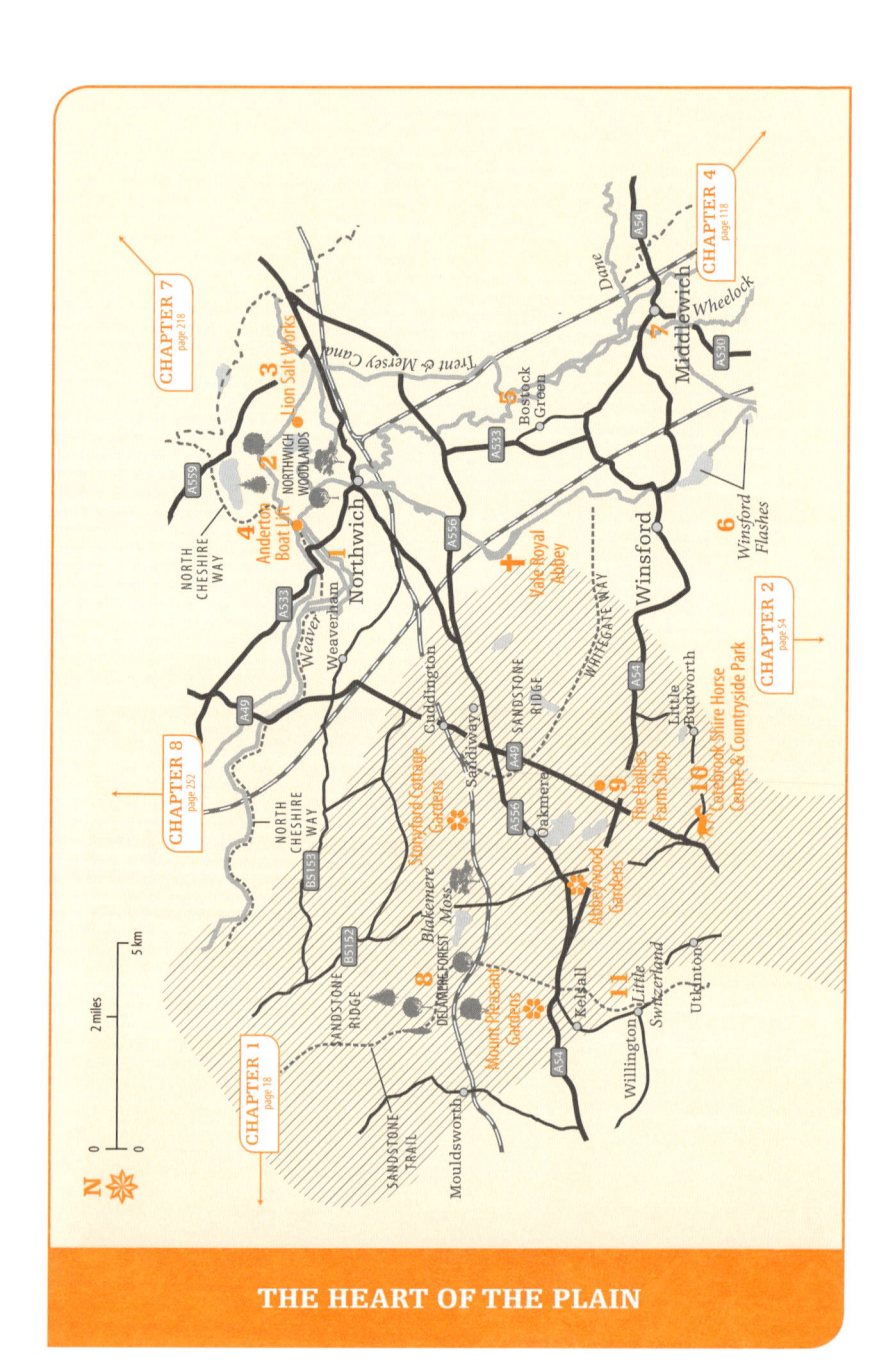

THE HEART OF THE PLAIN

3
THE HEART OF THE PLAIN

The Cheshire Plain has two tales to tell. To the east, it is the story of Britain's salt industry, from its rise during Roman times to its continuing importance for the chemical plants that toil here. Tour this area and you will soon appreciate the effect that the precious mineral has had, good and ill, on the landscape and its people, and how it set the foundations for today's thriving communities, which the rash of modern housing estates and fast roads suggest continue to expand. Northwich and Middlewich were known as Condate and Salinae to the Romans, who built roads and forts and exploited the lakes of brine beneath the soil, an industry that consolidated in this area once rock salt was discovered in the 17th century. Discover salt's role in powering the pioneering transport network on a narrowboat trip along the Trent and Mersey Canal, or on its towpaths, following in the hoof prints of the horses that drew the heavily laden barges. Where the canal meets the Weaver Navigation, get a close-up look at a feat of high Victorian engineering that connected the two waterways with a ride on the Anderton Boat Lift. At the museums at Weaver Hall and Lion Salt Works unpick the details of how salt shaped society and sharply defined the fortunes of the locals, rich and poor. Then follow the newly laid paths around the once weak and poisoned wastelands that are successfully being returned to nature at the Northwich Woodlands and Winsford Flashes.

To the west, the heart of the plain is the story of nature, dominated by the Sandstone Ridge, which ripples through the land on its passage northwest, and Delamere Forest, a great gulp of green pockmarked by meres and mosses created at the dawn of time. Delve into this remnant of the ancient Mara and Mondrem forests to discover where Iron Age man built hill forts, feudal lords hunted for game, and today's conservationists wrestle with maintaining healthy yet relevant ancient woodland so that it can flourish while also providing a place to enjoy being outdoors. Climb on foot or use pedal power to reach its highest point for a show-stopping panorama of the surrounding counties and dip beneath its leafy canopy to discover a quaking bog or go in search of the Gruffalo. At the forest's edges, step through the gates of some of Cheshire's loveliest gardens, such as those at Abbeywood and Stoneyford Cottage, and discover the hidden history of Little Switzerland and its fruit farms.

GETTING THERE & AROUND
PUBLIC TRANSPORT

This area is served by two **railway** lines. The Mid-Cheshire Line (see box, page 104) cuts across the plain, linking Manchester to the northeast, and Chester, to the southwest. A roughly hourly service in each direction, it's a useful train that stops at rural towns and villages including Northwich, Cuddington (check out the gallery of local artist Brian Booth in the old station house; ⌀ bryanbooth.artweb.com), Delamere (10 minutes' walk from the visitor centre around which forest activity revolves) and Mouldsworth. In addition, Winsford and Acton Bridge can be reached on the line between Birmingham and Liverpool, operated by London Midland (⌀ londonmidland.com), which also calls at Crewe for multiple onward connections.

The **bus** network serves town and countryside, although times are restricted, especially in the evening. Useful services for this chapter include the 37 to Winsford, Middlewich, Sandbach and Crewe, and the 82 to Sandiway, Kelsall, Tarvin and Chester.

WALKING

The heart of the plain offers a good variety of walks, the best of which is focused on the Sandstone Ridge and Delamere Forest, with rambles beneath the canopy as well as one of the best panoramas of the county and beyond from its highest point, Old Pale. The **Sandstone Trail** (⌀ sandstonetrail.co.uk) traces the ridge for 34 miles from Whitchurch to Frodsham, for the purposes of this chapter travelling into the heart of Delamere Forest before turning west to Manley and then continuing north. The 21-mile **Delamere Way** between Frodsham and Stockton Heath near Warrington also calls at the forest before heading northeast through Norley and skirting west of Acton Bridge. The **Baker Way** is a 13-mile route connecting Delamere Forest and Chester, while the

70-mile-long **North Cheshire Way** traces the northern boundary of this chapter, closing in on Weaverham before climbing north past the Anderton Boat Lift. The **Weaver Way**, a 40-mile trek from Audlem to Frodsham, snakes north from Winsford to Northwich before heading northwest past Acton Bridge.

Locally focused rambles include the **Northwich Woodlands**, to the north of the town (pages 102–3), where the six-mile network of paths known as the Saltscape Trail (⌀ saltscape.co.uk) link the Anderton Boat Lift and the Lion Salt Works. The **Whitegate Way** (see box, page 106) follows the old railway track that once connected Winsford to Cuddington for six miles through wooded cuttings and open land. Plus, of course, there are extensive towpaths to follow on the Trent and Mersey Canal (⌀ canalrivertrust.org.uk). This area is covered by OS Explorer 267 Northwich & Delamere Forest.

CYCLING

A number of National Cycle Network routes pass through the area, including 5, 71 and 551, as well as the **Cheshire Cycleway** (page 14) which, in this chapter, travels northeast from Mouldsworth through Delamere Forest towards Acton Bridge. The 20-mile **Tatton Trail**, an easy rail and ride route using the Mid-Cheshire Line, starts at Northwich Station and heads past the Anderton Boat Lift towards Tatton Park. Delamere Forest has two easy trails for families to follow, as well as more challenging routes and a bike skills area for those seeking big air. Cyclists are also allowed on the Whitegate Way.

BIKE HIRE & REPAIRS

Cheshire Cycle Hire Blakemere Village, Chester Rd, Sandiway CW8 2EB ⌀ 01606 882223 (choose the option Cheshire Outdoors) ⌀ cheshirecyclehire.co.uk. Bike hire for adults and children.

Delamere Bikes Linmere Visitor Centre, Delamere Forest CW8 2JD ⌀ 01606 881802 ⌀ delamerebikes.co.uk. This outlet rents bicycles mainly for use on the trails in the forest, but also offers a repair service.

CANAL-BOAT HIRE

ABC Boat Hire Anderton Marina, Uplands Rd, Anderton CW9 6AJ ⌀ 0330 333 0590 ⌀ abcboathire.com. This countrywide operator has a base at the marina just north of the Anderton Boat Lift, offering narrowboat holidays.

THE HEART OF THE PLAIN

> **TOURIST INFORMATION**
> **Northwich Customer Service Centre** 1 The Arcade, Northwich CW9 5AS ⌀ 01606 288828 ⊙ 08.30–17.00 Mon–Fri

Andersen Boats Wych House Ln, Middlewich CW10 9BQ ⌀ 01606 833668
⌀ andersenboats.com. Middlewich is a great starting point for canal-boat holidays on the Cheshire Ring, as well as routes towards Chester, north Wales, Staffordshire and the West Midlands. Andersen offers a range of narrowboats, all hand-built at its yard.
Drift Away Uplands Marina, Uplands Rd, Northwich CW9 6AJ ⌀ 0333 335 0005
⌀ driftaway-holidays.co.uk. Small family-run business with three boats available to hire – *Vivien*, *Marilyn* and *Audrey*.

NORTHWICH TO MIDDLEWICH & AROUND

Northwich and Middlewich may seem too ordinary to be tourist hotspots but these towns are gateways to Cheshire's Roman history and the salt industry founded by the conquerors, which endures today. Northwich tells the story of salt best through its curious architecture and at the three museums in and around the town, and while Middlewich may not have such a tangible tourism landscape, its history is just as deep, being the site of a Roman garrison and an important canal junction, stories unlocked by an impressive array of town trails. Beyond both towns' limits, the salt heritage can also be explored enjoyably in green spaces where nature has reclaimed the land.

1 NORTHWICH

Arrive in Northwich on the main road and you might be tempted to exit just as swiftly, when the unattractive modern buildings on Watling Street hove into view. However, this town's architecture is one very good reason why you should stop for a while. Northwich sits on salt beds and for many years was held aloft by deteriorating pillars of the mineral and millions of gallons of brine. In fact, subsidence became such a serious issue for the town in the 19th century that the sight of buildings suddenly slipping into holes in the ground was not unfamiliar to residents. Flooding was another constant problem, requiring the street level in the town centre to be raised more than once. In an attempt to find a solution, from the 1880s all new buildings were constructed using a tightly bolted timber frame infilled with brick and supported by a wood or steel ring beam, pioneering architecture which meant that these structures could be jacked up and even relocated. In the early 1920s, all the new buildings in the town centre were raised in what was dubbed 'the big lift' – and subsequently could only be accessed using steps. Nevertheless, despite these best efforts, flooding and subsidence continued to plague the town into the 21st century. In 2000, the town embarked on the £30 million Mines Stabilisation Project, which steadied the ground by filling the honeycomb of now-abandoned salt beds beneath it with pulverised fuel ash, cement and salt.

Take a walk down **High Street** and **Witton Street**, the main shopping thoroughfare, and you will see many of these unusual buildings between patches of artless modern precinct. From a distance, they seem terraced, but look closer and you will discover that each building is detached. They also appear to be mock-Tudor in style, though on closer inspection the beams look more like strips, latticing the brickwork. That's not to say that mock Tudor flourishes weren't favoured. The old post office, at 110 Witton Street, now a pub aptly named **The Penny Black**, is a case in point. The looming black-and-white building, more than three storeys high, is intricately patterned with diamonds, chevrons and quatrefoils, and has five gables at its roofline and an oriel above the entrance. Another notable building is the **Brunner Library**, also on Witton Street, with two cross-wings with oriels and an arched entrance, and **The Salty Dog** (21–23 High St) has a particularly florid frontage, with its first-floor gables flanked by colourful statuettes of a town crier, night watchman and a past mayor and his wife. Some of the smaller shops, while less visually impressive, are charming – there's a pretty gabled range from

ON THE ART TRAIL

Northwich has a vibrant art scene, including a well-supported annual trail held for a week in July, when shops around the town display works of art. But don't worry if you can't time your visit with this event because there are events throughout the year at various venues. Outside these times, you can see original local art on show at Northwich Art Shop (111 Witton St), the Weaver Hall Museum (pages 100–1), The Red @ The Red Lion (1 Wharton Rd) in nearby Winsford, and the Whitegate Station House Café (see box, page 106). For more details about upcoming events check out visualartscheshire.blogspot.co.uk.

101–111 Witton Street. All are the subject of an ongoing project to restore and conserve their façades.

With such mobile foundations, new development of the town was halted until the completion in the early 2000s of the Mines Stabilisation Project. Now stable, Northwich is embarking on a new era of expansion, as expressed by the vast black modern boxes on **Barons Quay**, which are slowly filling with shops, restaurants, cinemas and the like. These will probably divide opinion, but everyone can surely agree that it is a positive that the town, apparently at its residents' request, is turning at last to look out over the River Weaver, which runs through it. Terraces of steps now provide a pleasant perch from which to gaze over the water here and further south by the marina at **Hayhurst Quay**.

Weaver Hall Museum

162 London Rd, CW9 8AB ✆ 01606 271640 🌐 weaverhall.westcheshiremuseums.co.uk
🕐 10.00–17.00 Tue–Fri, 14.00–17.00 w/ends, 10.00–17.00 bank hols & Mon in school hols except Dec, closed Christmas Eve, Christmas Day, Boxing Day & New Year's Day

The story of Northwich is told in the austere setting of this former workhouse, a long plain two-storey brick building, crowned by a clock tower. Here, the geographic, social and cultural evolution of the town is charted from the time when the Romans used it as a fording point on the River Weaver, through the rise of salt extraction, the formation of friendly societies and trade unions, and the emergence of the chemical industry. The detail is conveyed simply if thoroughly using information boards, models, artefacts and film and one of the cleverer presentations is a sequence of wooden boxes, which, when you lift their flaps, emit smells of the Victorian era – I'd advise quickly inhaling the 'carbolic soap' after the truly unpleasant whiff of the 'privy'.

Another exhibit that stands out – for its shock factor – is a 'scold's bridle'. This metal contraption was used to punish women 'guilty of nagging their husbands or shouting abuse at their neighbours'. The offending 'scold' would be fitted with the barbaric headgear, which had a spiked mouthpiece for holding down the tongue, and led around the town on a lead. Cheshire has the ignominy of being the first and last place in which this misogynistic apparatus was used on women unafraid to speak their mind.

The reconstruction of a Victorian schoolroom will undoubtedly delight young children, like the one I saw who had turned the tables on his mum and was instructing her in the three Rs. Meanwhile, the genteel Red House, the quarters of the master and matron of the workhouse, is an eye-opener, revealing how some lives were well lived within these four walls, just the turn of a door handle from abject poverty. Pick up the telephone in the sitting room to hear a recording of the voice of the last master of the workhouse.

Dock Road Pumping Station

Weir St, CW9 5HL ⊖ enquire about open days at Northwich Customer Service Centre, 1 The Arcade, CW9 5AS (⌀ 0300 123 8123 ⌀ gettinghere.co.uk/the-dock-road-pumping-station ⊖ 08.30–17.00 Mon–Fri)

Just around the corner from Weaver Hall Museum, at the far end of Weir Street, is what looks like a miniature fort but is, in fact, a sewage pump house. This architectural oddity, dating from 1910, is a curious show of civic pride; the squat one-storey building has a crenellated parapet, an arched double doorway and multi-paned windows embellished with quoining. Inside stand the mechanisms that make it a rare example of a gas-powered pumping station for treating sewage, but these inner workings are open only for inspection on occasion.

FOOD & DRINK

The Salthouse NW Bar Hayhurst Quay, London Rd, CW9 5HD ⌀ 01606 624385 ⌀ thesalthousenw.co.uk. Coffee, craft ales, wines and spirits, as well as cakes and deli boards, are served at this café-bar. Pull up a stool at one of the scrubbed wooden tables and deliberate where to go next with the help of the huge map of Northwich on its wall.

MARKETS

Northwich's **town market** is held on Apple Market Street on Tuesday, Friday and Saturday (⊖ 09.00–16.00), while the **Northwich Artisan Market** takes place on Witton Street on the second Saturday of the month (⊖ 09.00–16.00).

EVENTS CALENDAR

Find out more at ⌀ visitnorthwich.co.uk/events.

Mar Easter Extravaganza
Jul Art Trail
Aug River Festival

THE HEART OF THE PLAIN

2 NORTHWICH WOODLANDS

🌐 northwichwoodlands.org.uk ⊙ Apr–Sep 09.00–20.00 daily, Oct–Mar 09.00–17.00 daily

The Northwich Woodlands cover a swathe of countryside and former industrial land between Northwich and Marbury to the north, encompassing open spaces, including Marbury Country Park and Budworth Mere, Furey Woods, Anderton Nature Park, Ashton's and Neumann's Flashes and Dairy House Meadows, as well as the Trent and Mersey Canal and River Weaver. The area has well-maintained paths for walkers, cyclists and horseriders, as well as bird hides and a pond-dipping platform, a play area and an open-air swimming pool at Marbury.

This is the place to spy redshanks and sanderlings, which call by in the summer months, and the kingfisher is a regular sight on the banks of brooks. Where industrial waste was once dumped, lime beds have encouraged the appearance of the rare dingy skipper butterfly and plants such as marsh orchids have set down roots. The elusive great crested newt now dwells in the meadows, while woods of oak, birch, sycamore and crack willow provide shade for eye-catching drifts of bluebell and anemones in spring. The arboretum and avenues of limes in Marbury

A BRIEF GUIDE TO CHESHIRE'S SALT

Cheshire's rich salt deposits formed during the Permian and Triassic periods when this area was the site of an inland sea, creating huge stores layered in the clay beds over time. While the Cornovii tribe were already extracting salt from the brine when the Romans arrived, the latter were the first to exploit the salt on a significant scale, from the 1st to 4th centuries. By the time of the Domesday Book, salt communities had established at Northwich, Middlewich and, further south, at Nantwich ('wich' derives from the Saxon word for salt). It wasn't until 1670 that rock salt was discovered, purely by accident, by the Smith-Barry family at Marbury while they were searching for coal.

Salt mining began, consolidating around the settlements at Northwich, Winsford and Middlewich.

By the 1700s, the construction of the Trent and Mersey Canal and the transformation of a local stretch of the River Weaver into a navigable waterway enabled better transportation of salt to the Mersey Estuary and markets beyond (as well as inbound to the Staffordshire Potteries for use in glazing). Northwich's two swing bridges over the River Weaver – Town and Hayhurst – and an upgrade of the lock system in the 19th century allowed ships to travel upriver, with boatbuilding and repair becoming important activities until the 1970s. Leading

Country Park provide a particularly lovely setting for a walk in what was once a great estate, where a hall once stood which had pretentions to emulate the palace at Fontainebleau in France. Check out the website of the Friends of Anderton and Marbury (FOAM ⌀ foam.merseyforest. org.uk) for walks, talks and other events here.

3 LION SALT WORKS

Ollershaw Ln, Marston CW9 6ES ⌀ 01606 275066 ⌀ lionsaltworks.westcheshiremuseums. co.uk ⊙ Feb–Oct 10.30–17.00 Tue–Sun, Nov–Jan 10.30–16.00 Tue–Sun & bank hols

Once derelict, the Lion Salt Works – the last surviving inland open-pan salt works in England and one of the last in the world – has been transformed into a lively attraction, which deftly tells the story of salt extraction in the area. The tale of how open-pan salt-making was first exploited by the Romans and continued in an unbroken tradition for 2,000 years unfolds across the renovated complex, with visitors making their way through the former stove and pan houses, packing and loading areas. The processes of evaporating, drying, grading, cutting, crushing, storing and transporting the salt and the impact of the industry on the community and landscape is brought to life through objects such as a boatbuilders such as Yarwood and Pimblott eventually served not just the salt industry but the British armed forces as well as other clients in all four corners of the world.

Later, salt was put to use for the chemical industry when Lord Stanley's estate at Winnington, on the edge of Northwich, was chosen by John Brunner and Ludwig Mond as the headquarters for their new company, Brunner Mond. It opened in 1874, becoming a world leader in the alkali industry, which was used for dyeing cloth and making soap and glass, later part of ICI and now Tata Chemicals. (There are ambitions for the statues of Brunner and Mond to be moved from their relative isolation in the grounds of the factory works and put on public show in the Bull Ring in Northwich's town centre.) The location was perfect for bringing together the vital ingredients – local salt and water, coal from Staffordshire and limestone from Derbyshire – and sending the resulting product around the world via the Liverpool docks. Soon the railway became key to moving these goods, which made a strong impression on the landscape, too – if you walk between the town and the Weaver Hall Museum (pages 100–1), you will pass through one of the 48 arches of the mighty 900m-long Northwich Viaduct that dominates the skyline, built from local red sandstone in 1862.

> ### GET ON BOARD THE MID-CHESHIRE LINE
>
> The Mid-Cheshire Line (midcheshirerail.org.uk) doesn't just transport passengers across the plain between Manchester and Chester – the railway doubles as a gateway to the surrounding countryside and even as a venue. Take one of its music trains in summer and be entertained by live bands along the way – you can even follow them on to a local pub to hear more.
>
> The line has also launched the 'Marvellous Days Out' campaign (marvellousdaysout.org.uk) centred on a collection of newly created vintage-style railway posters (available to buy), one for each station on the route, which also feature in a useful free booklet crammed with ideas about what to do at each stop. In 2018, the Amazing Women By Rail trail (amazingwomenbyrail.org.uk) was launched to celebrate the 100th anniversary of women's suffrage. Again accompanied by a free booklet, the route explores the influential women who lived at the destinations along the line, from the writer Elizabeth Gaskell (Knutsford) to the Chartist Mary Fildes (Chester and Manchester). Take a look at the website, too, for its collections of rail walks and rail and ride cycle routes, which are available to download.

crushing machine, automaton, and a 'subsiding house', as well as other entertaining multimedia displays, artefacts and first-hand accounts.

The salt works also features a reconstruction of the pub – the Red Lion Inn – used by workers and bargees from the neighbouring Trent and Mersey Canal, who would put salt in their beer to compensate for how much they'd sweated out during the day. There's a large open pan outside, by the children's industrial-themed playground, a section of the track that connected the works to the nearby railway network, and the Manager's House, where, rather eccentrically, wages were paid in empty sardine tins. The Nodding Donkey and Pump House, topped by a brick chimney, drew brine from the depths of the earth.

Initially called the Alliance Works, the business was run by the Thompson family for six generations until its closure in 1986. The Thompsons employed up to 50 local men and women in its heyday to do the gruelling work. Among them were the 'lumpmen', the most experienced workers, skilled at tending the fires to produce the correct grade of salt (slow heat produced coarse crystals, rapid boiling the finer salt). Nine tons of salt could be produced in a day, with a good lumpman turning out up to 230 lumps in his 8-hour shift, for which he would be paid piecemeal. Pan House 3 brings this to life, with audiovisual effects that plunge the visitor into the claustrophobic atmosphere of a room that could reach 60°C, dominated by a vast steaming pan of brine, boiling on four furnaces within the brick kilns below. Models of men, naked from the waist up, are suspended in animation on the slippery 'hurdles' – wooden platforms on the edge of the pan – engaged in the dangerous business of raking the crystals into heaps, which could result in a fatal scalding.

4 ANDERTON BOAT LIFT

Lift Ln, Anderton CW9 6FW 01606 786777 canalrivertrust.org.uk/enjoy-the-waterways/museums-and-attractions/anderton-boat-lift Feb–Oct 10.30–17.00 Tue–Sun & bank hols, Nov–Jan 10.30–16.00 Tue–Sun & bank hols

To the north of Northwich stands this extraordinary feat of high Victorian engineering that enabled narrowboats to ascend the 50-foot-high gap between the Weaver Navigation and the Trent and Mersey Canal. Opened in 1875, it provided an economic and efficient solution to the problem of moving goods between these two waterways, replacing a long-winded system of sending salt brought by narrowboat down chutes to the flat-bottomed double-ended barges called 'Mersey flats'. The ingenious design, the brainchild of civil engineer Edwin Clark, used hydraulic rams to raise and lower counterbalanced tanks known as 'caissons', operating rather like a pair of traditional scales within a cast- and wrought-iron superstructure. Each caisson can carry two narrowboats, 72 foot long and 15 foot, six inches wide, or a single barge up to 13 foot wide, and a maximum 250 tons in weight. Thirty years after its construction, the lift was upgraded from steam to electric power, with the addition of a control room. Today, it continues to connect the river and the canal but is also a tourist attraction, to which is attached an interesting visitor centre (with appropriately themed children's play area) that delves into the history, engineering and people associated with the lift.

You can follow in the wake of the boats of yesteryear on a guided trip through the lift. Take it from the top and the boat moves gently over an

DID YOU KNOW?

In 1933, Reginald Gibson and Eric Fawcett, two scientists at the Winnington Research Laboratory, were hard at work researching the effect of high pressure on chemical reactions when they accidentally invented polythene. This now familiar household plastic went into commercial production in 1939 in nearby Wallerscote.

> ## THE WHITEGATE WAY
>
> Once freight trains trundled through the countryside between Winsford and Cuddington, carrying salt to the Chester to Manchester railway line from 1870 to 1966. Today, walkers, cyclists and joggers pick up the trail at Bradford Road in Winsford, Waste Lane in Cuddington or Whitegate Station at Marton to travel along the broad six-mile path that has largely replaced the tracks. Now harebells, toadflax, butterflies and dragonflies are among the plants and wildlife residing in the cuttings and embankments, encouraged by keen volunteer conservationists. There was just one station on this old railway, at Whitegate, where the station house has been transformed into a pretty community café (Clay Ln, Marton CW7 2QE ⌀ 01606 889567 ⌀ whitegatestation.org.uk ⊙ 10.00–15.00 Mon–Fri, 10.00–16.00 w/ends & bank hols), also run by volunteers. It is a pleasant midway point to refuel on giant crumpets and traybakes (there are treats for dogs, too) while taking in the gallery of photos of the station from yesteryear and other works of art – afterwards you could hire one of the trikes they rent out. The Oakmere Way, a dedicated bridleway, provides a two-mile link between this greenway and Delamere Forest (see ⌀ midcheshirebridleways.co.uk for more details).

aqueduct that was necessary to span some of the 400 foot horizontal gap between the waterways, and passes into the caisson. Once inside, its watertight gates are closed and the lift slowly descends, providing great views and the quite unusual sensation of floating in a boat in mid-air as the on-board guide offers a light-hearted yet informative commentary, pointing out the features of the lift. At the bottom, a moment is taken for the water levels to match and ensure a smooth transition onto the Weaver Navigation, affording great photo opportunities of the lift as the boat turns and moors on the riverbank. You can alight here and head back into the small museum that provides an interesting explanation of what you've just experienced, or continue on a short boat ride along the river into Northwich for a waterborne view of the town and one of its swing bridges. There's also a café and shop on-site.

5 BOSTOCK GREEN

11 Bostock Green by Tatton Stays (page 292)

The A533 from Northwich to Middlewich passes by a quintessential village green at Bostock. You are unlikely to be alone in your desire to take in this idyllic picture of rural England from one of the tables in the beer garden of The Hayhurst Arms (CW10 9JP ⌀ 01606 541810), a cosy and characterful pub on the green (another Brunning & Price outlet serving excellent food, so you may want to make this a lunch stop). It was created from the former parish and reading rooms and the stables and coach house of the original inn that stood here, just some of the facilities of a model village created and enhanced down the centuries by the France-Hayhursts, owners of nearby Bostock Hall (a private residence, so no chance of a peep inside). As one of the great families of the area, their philanthropic largesse also extended to building the pretty cottages with black-and-white gables and trellised porches that can be seen along the main road. Take a seat on the bench around the trunk of the oak tree opposite the pub and you'll be sitting at the centre of the original County of Chester.

FOOD & DRINK

Define 2 School Ln, Sandiway CW8 2NH ⌕ 01606 882191 ⌕ definefoodandwine.com. Know your cabernet sauvignon from your malbec? Then you will enjoy trawling the shelves of this well-stocked wine (and spirits) merchant, complemented by an upscale deli. Some wines can be sampled from the Enomatic machine – best pair them with one of the platters or dishes served in the restaurant, open for lunch and occasionally for supper.

6 WINSFORD FLASHES

Winsford's urban charms may pale in comparison with other Cheshire towns and villages, yet its rural edges are home to three **flashes** (see box, page 116) – the 'Cheshire Broads'. Two of the flashes on this 200-acre site are used for recreational purposes (one is silted up), including 'Top' flash, which attracts anglers hopeful of catching carp, pike and bream. But 'Bottom' flash is the most popular, for sailing (it is home to Winsford Flash Sailing Club), walking and birdwatching – wildfowl such as great crested grebes and cormorants are common visitors. Nearby, the **Weaver Parkway** has been created from former industrial wasteland, threaded with a broad path that can be reached from Weaver Valley Road, and offers easy walking over a distance of 1½ miles.

7 MIDDLEWICH

⌂ **The White Bear** (page 292)

All Roman roads appear to lead to Middlewich, for this Cheshire town had five roads for the legionnaires to stomp along on their way to Deva (Chester), Condate (Northwich), Macumium (Manchester) and beyond.

VALE ROYAL ABBEY

You'll see mentions of Vale Royal wherever you go in this area because it is the name of the local borough. But where do these words come from? In the late 13th century, Vale Royal was the name of the largest abbey church in England, which stood close to Northwich. Edward I, keen to thank his maker for surviving a storm at sea, gave the lands to the Cistercian monks who settled here. While his original plans were subject to cost cuts, the complex still laid claim to having the longest Cistercian church in Britain, with some 13 chapels at its eastern end.

The once-powerful abbey was eventually pulled down by Thomas Holcroft, Henry VIII's commissioner, during the dissolution of the monasteries during the 16th century. Yet Holcroft, a wily man who made his fortune developing monastic lands, retained the refectory and part of the cloisters, which he turned into his main residence. Today, you can see remnants of these structures amid the more recent development that now houses the Vale Royal Golf Club and an upmarket suite of apartments, that can be viewed from Vale Royal Drive.

No wonder some believe that the town could have been an important military base. Middlewich's position at the confluence of three rivers, the Croco, Dane and Wheelock, its role as a centre of salt production, a site of two Civil War battles, and the junction of three canals – the Trent and Mersey, Shropshire Union and Wardle – has offered up a quality and quantity of artefacts unearthed here down the centuries, underlining its important place on the Cheshire map. Restrain yourself from whizzing through Middlewich on the main road and you will find a town with a tranquil canal at its heart, where a community passionate about the richness of the local history is working hard to share a heritage story that is by and large hidden.

Undeterred by a lack of physical history for visitors to see with their own eyes, the heritage folk here have created a suite of informative self-guided trails and walks, available from the town hall (Victoria Buildings, Lewin St, CW10 9AS ✆ 01606 833434) and the public library (22 Lewin St, CW10 9AS ✆ 01606 288070), and can also be downloaded at ⌂ middlewich-heritage.org.uk. These provide visitors with routes along which they can explore the influence of geology, the Romans, medieval society, the industrial revolution and the waterways, an impressive story that requires the help of a little imagination and carefully sited information boards. The latest trail is themed on salt and features King Street, a major military route to the north during the campaigns against the Brigantes around AD70, and Harbutt's Field, where a fort built to defend the river crossing and the local brine springs was positively identified in 1993. To the naked eye, the King Street Roman Fort is just a grassy knoll on the north bank of the Trent and Mersey, but ongoing investigations have revealed that the 3.5-acre site once contained a timber headquarters, commanding officer's house, granaries and barrack blocks, all enclosed by a turf rampart, timber palisade and defensive ditch, of which there are extensive archaeological remains beneath the ground.

Sadly, only a small selection of the wealth of Roman booty discovered in Middlewich's soil over the centuries is exhibited because the local museum closed its doors some years ago. You'll find the display in the public library, where a rotating exhibition details pre-Roman and Roman history, and features some precious pieces such as samian pottery and a rare soldier's diploma. The aim is to open an accredited museum in the next few years as part of a renovation of **Murgatroyd's Brine Pump**, the last example in England of a hand-dug shaft for wild brine extraction, currently hidden within an industrial estate and only occasionally open to the public. Until that time, Middlewich's treasure is spread across 28 museums and archives around the county. However, the town's savvy heritage folk have harnessed the internet to share this bounty, setting up an online museum (⌕ middlewichvirtualmuseum. co.uk) where a variety of objects, from a workaday Roman amphora to an affecting 17th-century mourning ring, are pictured and described and the place they were found is noted. More photographs of significant finds are being steadily uploaded for all to admire until the time when Middlewich's treasure can return home.

The town's medieval church, **St Michael and All Angels**, has had more luck holding on to its relics. Twenty-four historic pieces of furniture, memorials, windows and aspects of the very fabric of the building, dating from 1150 to 1934, are the subject of a trail that is available as a free app for visitors to use (⌕ heritage.middlewichparishchurch. org.uk). These are not just eye-catching in themselves, but they reveal stories from the past; even the smallest, such as the Poors Box of 1682, to the right of the south door, sitting on a corbel shaped like the top half of a man's head, has a tale to tell. The house-shaped oak box has two iron locks for two different keys and would have been opened only twice a year for its contents to be distributed to the destitute, on

Easter Day and Michaelmas Sunday. The support was sorely needed by the community, which had reeled from the demise of Vale Royal Abbey under the dissolution of the monasteries in the mid 1500s and endured plague and English Civil War, including two skirmishes in the town, during the following century.

The Poors Box is a sign of a rising trend at the time for parish relief, led by influential families in the area. Some of these families' names can be picked out in other elements of the trail, most notably the Venables, the barons of Kinderton, who built the chapel in the northeast corner of the church (where they could keep their distance from the hoi polloi). The tombstones of Peter, the last of the Venables line, and his wife Catherine, are at the east end of the north aisle. Other names that will be familiar from your travels around these parts include the France family of Bostock Hall, whose coat of arms is pictured in the quatrefoil that crowns the Great West Window, and the Breretons of nearby Brereton Hall, one of whom paid for the chancel's hammer-beam roof (the one you can see is a copy, the deathwatch beetle having had their way with the original). Guided tours of the church are available on the day of the Mexon Market (page 111).

Beyond the church, the town's most tangible visitor experience is its three **canals**, with plenty of narrowboat action to enjoy around its three locks: Wardle, King's and Big. It's also possible to walk the complete length of a canal here – this is the site of the shortest canal in the country, the Wardle, which is just 30m long. If you don't mind crowds, one of the liveliest times to visit the town is during the **FAB Festival**, which stands for Folk and Boats, a popular three-day celebration in June of canal life and live music. If your visit doesn't coincide with the festival, open mic nights take place on the first Tuesday of the month at The King's Lock Inn (1 Booth Ln CW10 0JJ ✆ 01606 833537), by the lock of the same name.

AH! BISTO

Middlewich is the home of the Bisto Kids. Freeze-dried gravy granules were invented at the Cerebos plant – the aroma of gravy hung heavy in the air at one time – and Bisto was first manufactured in Middlewich. When the Cerebos building was demolished, the brick sculpture of the cheeky urchins on display in its reception was saved and can now be seen in the town library.

EVENTS CALENDAR
Find out more at ⌀ middlewich.org.uk/events-timetable.

Jun FAB Festival (page 116)
Jul Classic Car & Bike Show
Oct Beer & Cider Festival

FOOD & DRINK
Café Bonbon 41 Wheelock St, CW10 9AB ⌀ 01606 836207. The fancy cakes, fruit tarts and colourful meringues on display are likely to entice you into this neat coffee shop, but they serve savouries, too, from breakfast to afternoon tea, receiving rave reviews from the locals.
Drinks & Bites at No 35 35 Wheelock St, CW10 9AG ⌀ 07926 023114 ⌀ drinksandbites. co.uk. This attractive café does what it says on the sign – light lunches, snacks and drinks – with sofas and chairs to perch on.
The White Bear Wheelock St, CW10 9AG ⌀ 01606 837666 ⌀ thewhitebearmiddlewich. co.uk. One of the town's original coaching inns, dating from 1625, the pub has been spruced up for the 21st century, though it retains a rustic feel with exposed brick walls. It's a pleasant place to peruse the day's papers over a coffee or a pint.

MARKETS
The **Middlewich Mexon Market** is held in Wheelock Street on the third Saturday of the month (⌀ mexonstreetmarket.co.uk ⌀ 09.00–16.00).

DELAMERE FOREST & AROUND

In sharp contrast to the industrious eastern reaches of the county, this part of the plain is dominated by the Sandstone Ridge, as it continues its passage through the heart of the county, and the vast green space of Delamere Forest, which is the remnant of an ancient hunting ground. Today there are quiet pockets of the woods to enjoy but, with active pursuits popular here, it can be a busy place, attracting crowds of day trippers, which swell in numbers according to the vagaries of the weather. A number of walking and cycling routes and bridleways pass through the forest, providing a pleasant way to continue beyond the canopy to explore villages that might not catch your attention otherwise and connect historic sights such as the Iron Age hillforts that march along the ridge.

THE HEART OF THE PLAIN

8 DELAMERE FOREST
▲ Delamere Forest Camping & Caravanning Club Site (page 292)
Linmere Visitor Centre, Delamere CW8 2JD ✆ 0300 067 4340 ⌲ forestry.gov.uk/delamere
⊙ summer 08.00–20.00 daily, winter 08.00–17.00 daily

A remnant of the ancient forests of Mara and Mondrem, Delamere is where the Norman Earls of Chester (and possibly the Saxons before them) hunted wild boar and deer. These 2,400-acre woods, wetlands and heaths dominated the heart of Cheshire in medieval times, stretching from the Mersey in the north to Nantwich in the south, the River Gowy in the west to the banks of the River Weaver in the east. Yet by the 1800s, much of the area had been deforested and turned to arable use, the rest a sandy wasteland covered in gorse and bracken. During the 19th century, significant timber planting began, which stopped and started over the following century, resulting in the current mix of farmland and woods, populated by broadleafs and conifers, including English oak, common beech, sweet chestnut, larch, common beech, silver birch and Scots pine.

The word Delamere, meaning 'forest of the lakes', gives a clue to one of its very special aspects: the area was freckled with more than 100 meres and mosses (see box, page 116). Sadly many of these have been lost over the centuries, drained and planted with timber. A project to restore these wetlands continues, with the rewetting of Blakemore Moss a successful example of efforts to return these areas to their natural state and welcome back inhabitants such as the white-faced darter dragonfly (a metal sculpture of which can be seen in the Old Pale car park), great crested newts, and birds including the woodcock. Black Lake, just south of the railway line near the Linmere Visitor Centre, may look like an unremarkable pool of water to the untrained eye, but its raft of sphagnum moss marks it out as a rare example of a schwingmoor, or quaking bog.

Delamere is managed by the Forestry Commission and is one of the busiest forests in Britain. More than half a million people visit annually (the forest is open year round) to take advantage of the network of walking, cycling, and running trails on the sandstone paths that weave through the trees and up and over the high point, Old Pale hill, which offers sublime views of Cheshire and the surrounding counties. Facilities here include a café, a cycle-hire and repair shop (page 97) and various activities (page 114), including a skills area for off-road biking at Manley Hill. Tucked in the trees near Blakemere Moss is

THE GARDENS OF THE PLAIN

Cheshire's plain positively blooms with gardens, of which these three are outstanding examples. Many in the area, as well as other parts of Cheshire, open their gates on an occasional basis as part of the National Open Garden Scheme (ngs.org.uk).

Abbeywood Gardens
Chester Rd, Delamere CW8 2HS 01606 889477 abbeywoodestate.co.uk
 09.00–17.00 Sun–Thu
A sequence of themed areas – the Exotic, Pool, Chapel and Prairie Gardens – provides a satisfying variety of plants and layouts to contemplate in this 45-acre plot. The evolving arboretum, with species including sequoia, fagus and quercus, will delay tree lovers for a while. There's also a gift shop, florist, café and hotel.

Mount Pleasant Gardens
Yeld Ln, Kelsall CW6 0TB 01829 751592 mountpleasantgardens.co.uk
 1 Apr–30 Sep noon–17.00 Wed, w/ends & bank hols
The lovely terraced gardens at Mount Pleasant offer the dual attraction of close-ups of nature and long views across the Cheshire plain. A sculpture trail adds a further dimension – you can even join in one of resident artist Andrew Worthington's sandstone-carving workshops. There's also a tea room and nursery on-site.

Stonyford Cottage Gardens
Stonyford Ln, Oakmere CW8 2TF 01606 888970 stonyfordcottagegardens.co.uk
 1 Mar–31 Oct 10.00–17.00 Tue–Sat & bank hols, 1 Nov–28 Feb 10.00–16.00 Mon–Fri
The Overland family has transformed this patch of wetlands into a magical water garden, its pool, streams and spring-fed fountain set within a floral frame and shaded by natural woodlands. Follow the boardwalk that loops around the site (children can look out for the 'fairies' and 'pixies' hidden in the undergrowth) – you're sure to do a double-take at the bridge reminiscent of Monet's flower garden at Giverny. The nursery here will wow serious plant enthusiasts with its unusual stock. There is also a tea room, and, from March to October, members of the Caravan Club can hire pitches in an adjacent field.

---

a giant wooden Gruffalo, the subject, over the past few years, of fun trails for young children.

Plans to upgrade facilities and trails at Delamere were the subject of an appeal with the borough council at time of writing. If successful, the forest will develop a new visitor hub, improved and additional trails and bridleways, more play areas, and a complex of Forest Holidays cabins.

For more information on the current trails around the forest, buy a visitor map in the bike shop or download it from the Delamere website.

Delamere hosts events throughout the year, from Hell Up North, the toughest half-marathon in the UK, to pop concerts featuring international stars. If you're a keen runner, there's a free 5km park run every Saturday morning (parkrun.org.uk/delamere 09.00).

FOOD & DRINK

The Goshawk Inn Station Rd, Mouldsworth CH3 8AJ 01928 740900 thegoshawkpub.co.uk. This beautiful old inn serves fresh bistro-style food with roaring log fires or garden views, depending on the time of year. It's popular with walkers from nearby Delamere Forest, so you can be assured a warm welcome for your dog, too.

SHOPPING

Bookstore at Oakmere Chester Rd, Oakmere CW8 2HB 01606 883750. From archaeology to zoology, few subjects are not covered by the books on the shelves of this huge bargain bookshop for readers young and old. There's a café and picnic tables where you can get down to reading straightaway.

ACTIVITIES

Delamere Outdoor Fitness 07968 077180 delamereoutdoorfitness.co.uk. Offers group and personal training indoors and under the treetops.

Go Ape 0333 433 0536 goape.co.uk/days-out/delamere. Zipline and Segway adventures.

9 THE HOLLIES FARM SHOP

The Hollies Forest Lodges (page 292), **Shays Farm Caravan & Camping** (page 292)

Tarporley Rd, Little Budworth CW6 9ES 01829 760414 theholliesfarmshop.co.uk shop 08.00–19.00 Mon–Sat, 08.00–18.00 Sun, café 08.00–17.00 Mon–Sun, restaurant 17.00–23.00 Mon–Sun

The Hollies is one of the best farm shops in Cheshire if not the northwest. What started as a stall on the roadside in 1959 has expanded into a booming business featuring a shop, gift barn, café and the recently added restaurant, 59 at The Hollies. Visitors can even stay in the grounds at a collection of five luxurious lodges, for four to six sharing, each of which comes with an indulgent outdoor jacuzzi. (A hotel, 32 by The Hollies (page 292), is due to open in Tarporley in 2018.) At its heart, The

Hollies, run by the third generation of the Cowap family, offers a top-notch choice of produce from more than 50 local and artisanal suppliers, including fresh fruit and veg, baked goods, a grocery, meat from the in-house butchery, delicatessen fare, and wines and spirits. A good place to fill your picnic hamper or stock up if you're self-catering.

SHOPPING

Reclaimed World Tarporley Rd, Little Budworth CW6 9ES ⌀ 01829 760288 ⌀ reclaimedworld.com. Feast your eyes on three acres of architectural salvage, with vintage collectibles and antiques, too. Flooring is a particular forte, but there are lots of other items to peruse, from fireplaces to carousel horses.

10 COTEBROOK SHIRE HORSE CENTRE & COUNTRYSIDE PARK

Tarporley Rd, Cotebrook CW6 9DS ⌀ 01829 760506 ⌀ cotebrookshirehorses.co.uk
⊙ 10.00–17.00 daily except Christmas Day & Boxing Day

Cotebrook offers the rare chance to take a close look at shire horses, which they've bred here for more than 40 years (if you're lucky, as I was, you might see a gangly-legged newborn foal). There are a number of these impressive beasts dotted around the fields – it's a magnificent sight to see one galloping about. But there are other animals and wildlife to meet (and not just the hens that peck around your feet in the yard), such as Shetland ponies, a Scottish wildcat and the cutest trio of otters. Follow the waymarked nature trail, created in association with the Cheshire Wildlife Trust, to learn more about the plant and animal life in and around the surrounding meadows and ponds, where herons, Canada geese and other wildfowl gather.

FOOD & DRINK

The Fox & Barrel Foxbank, Cotebrook CW6 9DZ ⌀ 01829 760529 ⌀ foxandbarrel.co.uk. Good food, cask ales and fine wines are on offer at this cut-above country inn. When you see items such as homemade black pudding and tandoori tofu on a pub menu, you know you're in for a treat.

11 LITTLE SWITZERLAND

🏠 **The Royal Oak** (page 292)

With the opening of the Manchester–Chester railway line in the 1840s, Cheshire's pastures became accessible to city dwellers in search of a breath

MERES, MOSSES & FLASHES: A DEFINITION

Cheshire is one of Britain's most important wetland areas. Positively sieve-like, there is no comparative area in Europe with so many ponds. You'll read the following three words many times in this guide, so what do they mean?

Cheshire's **meres** were formed as a consequence of the last Ice Age, some 10,000 years ago. When the huge sheet of ice that covered the area retreated as the climate heated up, it left in its wake the glacial drift that formed today's landscape, featuring depressions and hollows known as kettle holes, where large chunks of buried ice had melted away. These subsequently filled with water, pockmarking the county with its distinctive pools known as meres.

A **moss** is a peat bog created over thousands of years by pickled wetland plants, mainly Sphagnum moss. They can be in the shape of a hummock or inhabit a crater, and are sometimes on the move in the case of the deliciously named schwingmoor, a quaking bog. Just like the meres, mosses provide a natural habitat for the likes of the white-faced darter dragonfly, bog bush-cricket, curlew, skylark and Britain's only venomous snake, the adder. They are also important carbon reservoirs, storing up to twice as much as forests, and provide a critical record of the landscape, including the effects of climate change and the activities of man, back in the last Ice Age.

A **flash** is a pool created where the ground has collapsed due to brine extraction and the subsequent depression has filled with water. As with meres, flashes are home to vegetation that is more commonly seen on the coast, such as sea-aster and creeping willow.

of country air. The savvy folk at Willington, a short horse-and-carriage ride from Mouldsworth Station, quickly tapped into this new trend for rural short breaks by branding Willington Hill 'Little Switzerland' and opening up spare rooms to paying guests. Although this Victorian tourism campaign hasn't survived into modern times, it's still pleasant to follow in the footsteps of travellers of that era. It is also a great excuse to first pop into the pretty country pub the Boot Inn (see opposite) for a drink (or lunch), then, when you leave, turn left out of the door and follow the road until it turns into a path, signposted Gooseberry Lane. Continue forward onto a single-file path that gently ascends to another road, from where you can look down across a fruit orchard. During the mid 20th century this area was full of market gardens and orchards, which flourished in the shelter of the hill above – Willington was also renowned for its fruit. From the 1940s, apples, strawberries, rhubarb and Cheshire's famous damsons were among the produce that thrived on these slopes, above the frost line. Sadly, most farms have closed, though **Willington Fruit Farm** (Chapel Ln, Willington CW6 0PH ⌀ 01829 751216 ⌀ willingtonfruitfarm.co.uk ⊙ 10.00–16.00 Tue & Wed), run by the Winsor family since 1950, was still open at the time of writing, and the Eddisbury Fruit Farm, a little further north on Yeld Lane, has recently been acquired by **Ollie's Orchard** (⌀ olliesorchard.co.uk). Although not open to the public, look out for Ollie's Orchard juice at outlets across the county.

If you're visiting at Easter, look across the road as you emerge from Gooseberry Lane – there is likely to be a bush dressed with tiny decorative eggs in the front garden of Rose Cottage, an annual ritual by its owner. Follow the road upwards until you reach the drive to a house, where you'll see a thin path that has been created at the bottom of a wooded slope that climbs above a field to give a beautiful view over Boothsdale and beyond. At the top, pass through a kissing gate to the edge of a field to find an earthwork bank of Kelsborrow Castle, one of the county's Iron Age forts. It may look like a grassy hump but there is a useful information board that explains what might have been seen here in those times.

FOOD & DRINK

The Boot Inn Boothsdale, Willington CW6 0NH ⌀ 01829 751375 ⌀ thebootinnwillington.com. This pretty country pub in a converted row of cottages is a cosy place for a drink, especially by the open fire on cooler days, and offers an imaginative menu. Sitting at the foot of Little Switzerland, it's the obvious place to refresh after a brisk walk.

Rose Farm Shop Utkinton Rd, Utkinton CW6 0LP ⌀ 01829 732978 ⌀ rosefarmshop.co.uk. This farm shop in the nearby village of Utkinton sells beef and pork hand-reared on-site, as well as poultry and lamb from trusted local suppliers. Delicatessen products are also on offer and there is a gift shop and café here, too.

SHOPPING

Morreys Nursery Forest Nursery, Kelsall CW6 0SW ⌀ 01829 751342 ⌀ morreys-nursery.com. A firm local favourite, this nursery on the edge of Delamere Forest has been producing azaleas, rhododendrons, herbaceous alpines and more since 1910 and also offers expert plant advice.

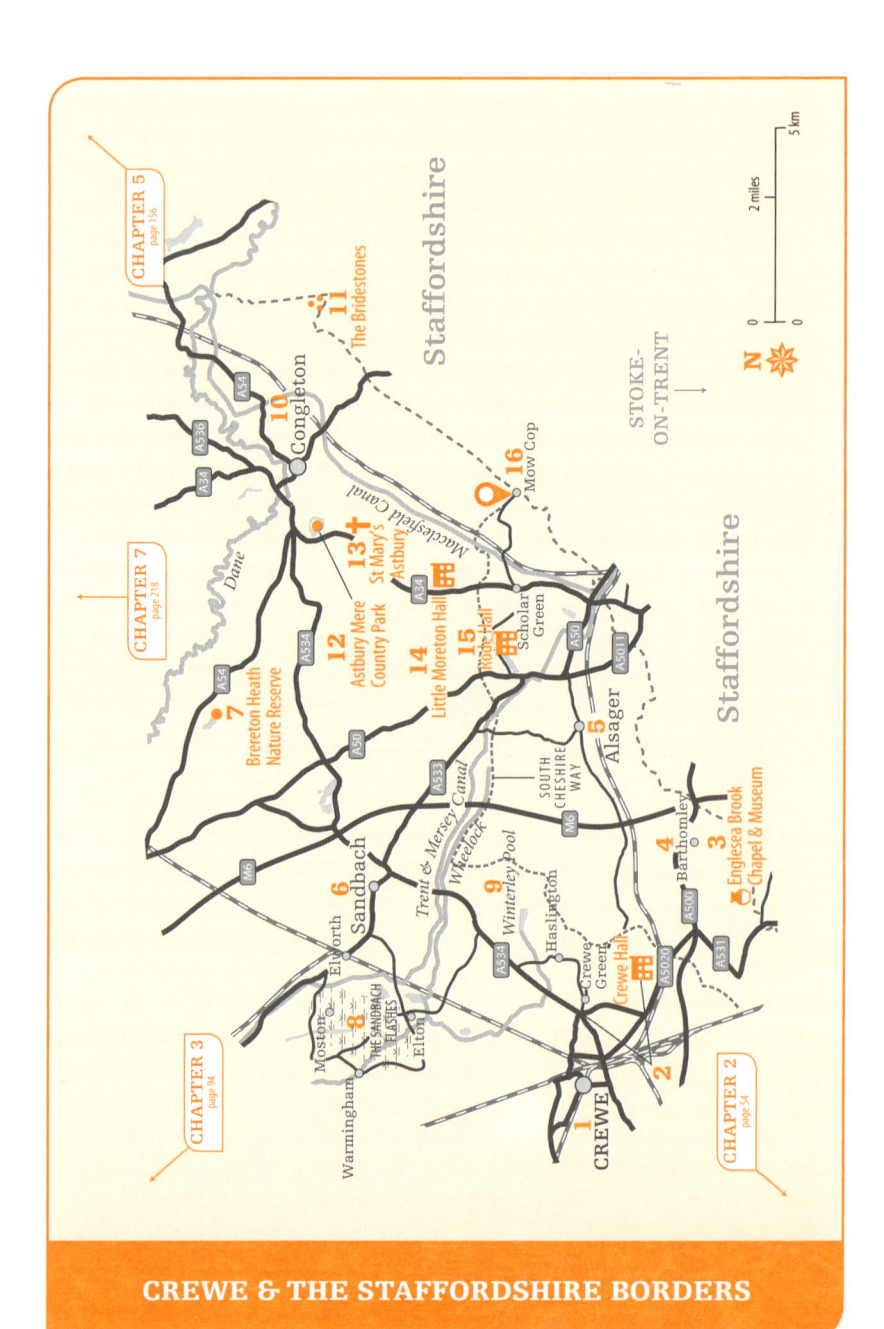

CREWE & THE STAFFORDSHIRE BORDERS

4
CREWE & THE STAFFORDSHIRE BORDERS

Cheshire's eastern edge is an industrious place, focusing on four busy towns: Crewe, Alsager, Sandbach and Congleton. Each was once a country backwater but all have transformed into populous centres, thanks to the roles they played in the agricultural and industrial revolutions and, most importantly, the arrival of the railway, which shaped the towns we see today. These are not conventional tourist destinations, but rather are the working towns they appear to be, though that has been used as a reason to overlook them for too long. If you take the approach of uncovering their history you'll reap rewards, because a closer look reveals medieval alleys and cobbled market squares, black-and-white half-timbered houses and grand Georgian and Victorian mansions, lofty churches and proud municipal buildings, with the hand of Sir George Gilbert Scott witnessed at many turns. The place is bursting with tales about the noble families and wealthy benefactors that ruled over these lands and the local communities that served them, with walk-on parts for Romans, Saxons, Shakespeare's players, Civil War soldiers, radical preachers and even Buffalo Bill.

Amid these towns are well-planned parks, flower-filled pathways where tracks once lay for salt and sand to be hauled across and flooded quarries turned to use as places to walk and get out on the water. At their edges the plain gently rolls out, rising to the dramatic moors on which dance the shadows of the Peaks, begging you to pull on your walking boots and tramp across hill and vale. One distinct theme unites this area – the proximity to Staffordshire, on which many locals naturally orientate rather than look inward to their own county, perhaps because Staffordshire's mines and pot banks have provided work for people here for so long. It touches everything: arguably the accent, certainly a predilection for oatcakes and definitely some of the words you will hear. Don't be surprised to be called 'duck' or 'shug' in these parts; these are local terms of endearment.

GETTING THERE & AROUND

PUBLIC TRANSPORT

Crewe is one of the country's main **railway** junctions, decanting Cheshire-bound travellers from all directions courtesy of the 23 trains per hour that arrive on the six lines that meet here. When HS2 is completed, Crewe will be a stop on the western line. The station is about a mile from the centre of town, a historical anomaly explained herein. Sandbach station, on the Crewe–Manchester Line, is also remotely located at Elworth, about 1½ miles from the town centre. Alsager is served by slow trains from London, connecting it to the Potteries and Crewe, while Congleton is on the Stafford–Manchester Line.

Useful **buses** include the number 3 from Crewe to Alsager and onwards to Stoke-on-Trent, the 37 from Crewe to Sandbach, the 38 which connects Congleton, Sandbach and Crewe, the 317 between Sandbach, Rode Heath and Alsager, and the 318 calling at Congleton, Astbury, Mow Cop, Scholar Green, Rode Heath and Alsager.

WALKING

The scenic walking is to the east of Congleton, where the Staffordshire Moorlands give way to the foothills of the Peak District. From Timbersbrook Picnic Area, off Weathercock Lane just east of Congleton, you can climb to the Bosley Cloud, a gritstone outcrop on the edge of the Cheshire Plain. Alternatively, the 34-mile **South Cheshire Way** can be picked up at Weston, heading northeast past the villages of Haslington and Malkins Bank, then turning sharp east across the top of Alsager up to Mow Cop. The 92-mile **Two Saints Way** (page 21) passes through this area at Englesea Brook, Barthomley and Weston. Otherwise, you're generally on the flat, for which there are good greenway walks detailed in this chapter, including the **Mere Lake Way** (pages 130–1), the **Salt Line** (page 130), the **Wheelock Rail Trail** (page 130) and the **Biddulph Valley Way** (see box, pages 150–2). Maps for this area are OS Explorer 268 Wilmslow, Macclesfield & Congleton and OS Explorer 257 Crewe & Nantwich.

CYCLING

Unfortunately, there is nowhere to hire a bike in this area, although there is some good cycling on the local greenways mentioned above, as

> **TOURIST INFORMATION**
> **Congleton Town Hall** High St, CW12 1BN ⌕ 01260 271095 ⊙ 09.00–17.00 Mon–Fri, 09.30–14.30 Sat

well as National Cycle Network routes 5, 71, 73, 55, 451, and 573. The **Cheshire Cycleway** skirts Congleton's western edge, heading southwest via Hassall Green to Weston.

CANAL-BOAT HIRE
Heritage Narrowboats Heritage Marina, Scholar Green ST7 3JZ ⌕ 01782 785700 ⌁ heritagenarrowboats.co.uk. Boat holidays and day-boat hire is available here, close to the junction of the Trent and Mersey and Macclesfield canals.

CREWE TO ALSAGER

Crewe and Alsager would not exist if it were not for the railway. In just a few years, these sleepy villages transformed into thriving communities at the cutting edge of the steam age. However, their fortunes contrasted. Crewe became a centre of engineering, while Alsager was identified as a desirable place to live for the Potters, who built fine villas on its streets, an escape to the fresh air from the sooty factories that filled their coffers. Today, both are lively towns, until recently receiving a sustained injection of youth from their campuses of the Manchester Metropolitan University, which are now in the process of closing. Although you may feel that post-war modernisation hasn't enhanced their looks, there are still pockets of the past to uncover amid their streets and the surrounding area.

1 CREWE

Crewe is the railway gateway to Cheshire (and, more importantly, northwest England), and is probably the main reason why you will visit this town, even if only to literally pass through, without getting off your train. While Crewe has a reputation for being a rather drab place (which isn't completely unfair), it is one of the country's most important railway junctions and has an interesting story to tell.

Before the railway arrived, this patch of Cheshire was a pastoral scene, the location of Crewe Hall and the hamlets of Church Coppenhall and

Monks Coppenhall, whose residents were mainly engaged in dairy farming. In 1831, the census recorded that Monks Coppenhall – now modern-day Crewe – was home to just 148 souls. Within a decade, the place had become unrecognisable, the site of a huge engineering works and a hub for four railway lines from Birmingham, Liverpool, Manchester and Chester.

The development of Crewe began when the Grand Junction Railway Company laid the line from Birmingham to Liverpool and Manchester and decided to build a station where the track crossed the turnpike road from Wheelock to Nantwich, with the first train arriving on 4 July 1837. This junction, called Crewe after the nearby hall, was swiftly identified as a convenient and spacious point at which locomotives could be built and repaired (the first of which, *Columbine*, was completed in 1843), taking the strain off the company's Edge Hill site at Liverpool, which had reached capacity. And so Crewe Works was born, in the hinterland, where the Crewe Heritage Centre (page 124) and Tesco now stand. The railway company, seeking somewhere to house the workforce it needed to move here from Liverpool, created a model town around the works, and by the early 20th century the population had swelled to more than 43,000, with other industries also present. Hence the distance between the town centre, which grew up around the works, and the remote station, about a mile to the southeast. Not so long ago, one of the main roads to the centre bore a sign declaring 'To The Town' to aid confused visitors.

The problem for today's visitor is that Crewe has not preserved its railway history and there is little left to see. The Crewe Historical Society (cheshirehistory.org.uk) has produced a Town Trail in association with Crewe Town Council (01270 756975 crewetowncouncil.gov.uk), but it largely relies on the user's imagination. Still, you can't miss the influence of the railway; it's impossible to get in or out of Crewe without crossing a railway bridge over one of the six routes that now converge here, with the addition of lines to Wales and London.

A tour of the town

It's likely you'll arrive in Crewe by train, but before you head off to the town centre there are a couple of things to see in this historic **railway station**. Today's station isn't the original that stood on the north side of the bridge, but a second version built in 1867, to which more work was done at the turn of the 20th century and (a new entrance) in 2014.

Check out the Victorian platform buildings with their pretty bow fronts, once offices, now cafés and shops; they are said to be among the best of their kind on Britain's railways. On platform 5, near the lift, there is a lovely little find: a Victorian drinking fountain with a dog bowl, bearing the words 'For Ye Dogs'. Across the road from the station entrance is The Crewe Arms, one of Britain's first railway hotels.

In Crewe town centre, only a handful of the 800-plus dwellings built by the railway company remain. By far the best preserved are the Railway Cottages on Tollitt, Betley and Dorfold streets, which run south off Chester Street close to the Town Square and are quite different from anything else in the town. Each would have contained four apartments, supplied with gas and water, and once had long yards and gardens, with outdoor toilets to the rear. Each row was separated by paved 'backs', or alleys, although these areas have since been re-landscaped.

Another fragment of Crewe's architectural past can be found on the north side of Memorial Square: London architect Henry T Hare's **Municipal Buildings** (Earle St, CW1 2BJ), which opened in 1905. The yellow sandstone ashlar structure seems a suitably ostentatious statement for a town that had just been given the status of a borough. Its two outer bays bear small balconies at the first floor, flanked by four columns with reliefs of six giant figures, which are meant to represent the different Cheshire industries. They recline in pairs on the top of the arches of the two ground-floor windows and central door – spot the *Charles Dickens* locomotive in the hand of the figure above the right side of the door. Lift your eyes to the weather vane on top of the cupola, the rather fun finial of which is in the shape of Stephenson's Rocket.

"The yellow sandstone ashlar structure seems a suitably ostentatious statement for a town that had just been given the status of a borough."

Next door is the **Market Hall**, originally meant to be a cheese market, though plans to win business from nearby Nantwich were foiled. Instead, the market hosted cattle auctions, until the locals got fed up with so many animals being driven through their town. Finally, it became a general market.

Around the corner is **Crewe Lyceum Theatre** (Heath St, CW1 2DA ✆ 01270 368242 ✍ crewelyceum.co.uk ⊙ box office 10.00–17.00 Mon–Sat & until show begins on performance days). Behind its modern façade is a charming Edwardian theatre, a rebuild from 1911 following a fire.

It's possible to call in when the theatre's open outside of performances for a look around. If they aren't busy, the friendly staff will happily show you the auditorium, which has a proscenium arch stage where Charlie Chaplin and Stan Laurel were among the famous names to have trodden the boards. The place is richly decorated in red, blue, cream and gold, and festooned in elaborate plasterwork, the most eye-catching being the romantic scenes of reclining musicians playing instruments that adorn the front of the circle, gallery and boxes.

I was unimpressed on my first visit to **Crewe Heritage Centre** (Vernon Way, CW1 2DB ⌇ 01270 212130 ⌇ creweheritagecentre.org ⌇ Apr–Sep 10.00–16.30 w/ends) more than a decade ago with my then six-year-old son. At that time it was called The Railway Age, but a change of management and a makeover in 2007 has improved it somewhat, The centre is dedicated to telling the town's story with an emphasis on its railway heritage, and the main engine shed is sparsely filled with information boards about the railway and the town's history, culture and landscape, with a small children's play area and model train displays. Even the large locomotive at the back, the *Robert Burns*, barely makes a dent in the vast space. In the yard outside, you can look around an InterCity APT parked on the sidings and there are other trains to explore, including the steam engine *Duchess of Sutherland*, as well as vintage buses. The highlight for me is the large viewing window in the North Signal Box, which puts you between two tracks so that you can watch trains speed by.

An enduring gift of this town's benefactors, the London North Western Railway Company, can be found west of the town centre at **Queen's Park** (Victoria Av, CW2 7SE ⌇ 01270 686708 ⌇ Mar & from 2nd w/end of Oct–Nov 08.00–17.30 daily, Apr & Sep 08.00–19.30 daily, May 08.00–20.00 daily, Jun–Aug 08.00–20.30 daily, Nov–Feb 08.00–16.30 daily). This is as enjoyable a place to visit today as it must have been in 1887, when it was opened to mark Queen Victoria's Jubilee and Crewe's 50th anniversary. Designed by F W Webb, the engineer who rose through the ranks to run Crewe Works, and the landscape architect Edward Kemp, this oval space has every necessary accoutrement of a fine Victorian park: lawns and ornamental gardens, walkways, a boating lake, bandstand and pavilion. There are lodges, war memorials and a clock tower to see, while more modern facilities include a café, children's play area, outdoor gym, bowling green, boules pitch and a BMX track named after local Olympic hopeful Shanaze Reade.

ADA NIELD CHEW: FACTORY GIRL TURNED AGITATOR

It's hardly surprising to discover that the workers in industrial Crewe quickly became politicised. One of these was Ada Nield Chew, a woman from just over the Staffordshire border who worked as a tailor in the town in her twenties. She began writing letters to the local paper, the *Crewe Chronicle*, about the poor treatment of the workforce. In this excerpt from a letter of 1894 she takes issue with the wages:

'I wish some of those, whoever they may be who mete it [the level of pay] out to us, would try to 'live' on it for a few weeks, as the factory girl has to do 52 weeks in a year. To pay board and lodging, to provide herself decent boots and clothes to stand all weathers, to pay an occasional doctor's bill, literature, and a holiday away from the scope of her daily drudging, for which even the factory girl has the audacity to long sometimes – but has quite as often to do without. Not to speak of provision for old age, when eyes have grown too dim to thread the everlasting needle, and to guide the worn fingers over the accustomed task.'

Ada lost her job for complaining to the press, but a different destiny awaited. She became active in the Independent Labour Party, working as an organiser for the Women's Trade Union League. Later she joined the National Union of Women's Suffrage Societies and, a class fighter, she engaged in heated debates with Christabel Pankhurst and the members of the Women's Social and Political Union, an organisation she viewed as only interested in gaining the vote for middle-class women.

Also west of the town centre is the **Bentley Car Works** (Pyms Ln, CW2 8WD ☏ 01270 505851 ⊙ bentleymotors.com ⊙ factory tours available to book), opened in 1938 by Rolls-Royce to build Merlin engines for Spitfire and Hurricane fighter aircraft. Post-war it produced luxury cars such as the Rolls-Royce Silver Shadow (from childhood, I remember a sign at the Alsager border with Crewe that proclaimed you were about to enter the town that made 'the best car in the world'). Today it makes Bentleys. Fans of 20th-century architecture can admire, from the outside, the original 1939 Art Deco buildings at the Pyms Lane plant, while fans of motor cars can visit CW1 House, at the Middlewich Road end of Pyms Lane, where Bentley sometimes offers factory tours (book ahead).

EVENTS CALENDAR
Find out more at ⌁ crewelife.net.

May Steampunk Carnival
Oct Crewe Cosmopolitan Food Festival

🍴 FOOD & DRINK
Beerdock 159 Nantwich Rd, CW2 6DF ✆ 01270 848628 ⌁ beerdock.co.uk. This bottle shop and bar (which has a branch in nearby Nantwich) sells more than 3,000 beers, lagers and ciders from Cheshire and beyond. Communal tables keep the atmosphere convivial.
Hops 8–10 Prince Albert St, CW1 2DF ✆ 01270 211100. A selection of 230 beers feature at this Belgian-themed watering hole. The historic former railway cottages make for a cosy place to sup and enjoy a sandwich, either at one of the scrubbed wooden tables set with church pew chairs or out in the front garden.

🛍 MARKETS
Food, drink and general goods are on sale at **The Market Hall** (Earle St, CW1 2BL ⊙ 09.00–16.00 Mon & Thu–Sat, 09.00–14.00 Tue & 09.00–13.00 Wed), to the rear of which is the **outdoor market** (⊙ 09.00–13.00 Mon, 09.00–16.00 Fri–Sat)

2 CREWE HALL & CREWE GREEN
Weston Rd, CW1 6UZ ✆ 01270 253333 ⌁ qhotels.co.uk

Just outside Crewe, this Jacobean country pile was built by Sir Randolph Crewe, a 20-year project completed in 1638, and was the family seat until the 1930s. Travelling along the tree-lined avenue to its front door, you can't help but be impressed by the majesty of the place. Built of red brick with diaper work and stone dressings, it has shaped gables and balustraded battlements with multiple finials among its many flourishes. The general appearance is a sequence of bays that advance and recede as though engaged in a polite dance. During the 200 years following its creation, a service wing was attached to the hall and further changes were made, most significantly by E M Barry, designer of the theatre at the Royal Opera House in London, following a fire in 1866. Yet the façade is thought to remain largely true to the 17th-century original, if not in size (the original part is at the eastern end). Inside, there is plenty of intricate wood carving and plasterwork to goggle at, especially the staircase. Both Capability Brown and the 18th-century landscape architect Humphry Repton are believed to have been involved in designing of the surrounding parkland. The hall is now a hotel, which offers tours on request.

Many attractive estate properties ring Crewe Hall, including St Michael's Church at **Crewe Green**, designed by Sir George Gilbert Scott. Thomas Bower built the vicarage opposite, on Narrow Lane, where it's said Reverend John Ellerton wrote the hymn *The Day Thou Gavest Lord Is Ended* during his 12 years in the town. The old road from Crewe Green to Alsager, the B5077, which runs across the top of the Crewe Hall estate, offers up more quaint cottages dating from various times; look out for the names Hilltop, Nursery, Keeper's, Lobelia and Bluebell.

3 ENGLESEA BROOK CHAPEL & MUSEUM

Englesea Brook Ln, Englesea Brook CW2 5QW ℰ 01270 820836 ⌁ engleseabrook.org.uk
☉ Apr–Jul & Sep–Oct 10.00–17.00 Thu–Sat, 14.00–17.00 Sun, Aug 10.00–17.00 Tue–Sat, 14.00–17.00 Sun

A fold in the Cheshire countryside is the unlikely location for one of the Methodist Church's most important national venues. A chapel dating from 1828 and a school built in 1914 in the hamlet of Englesea Brook, between Weston and Barthomley, is the place to find out all about the 'Prims' (Primitive Methodists), the breakaway movement from Wesleyanism led by Hugh Bourne, who is buried in the graveyard opposite. Bourne and his followers rejected the Wesleyan tradition for a more radical interpretation of their faith, holding evangelical camps on nearby Mow Cop from 1807 before moving into the more formal setting of chapels such as this one. There is lots of treasure here, including a Ranters pulpit (not to be confused with the Ranters of the English Civil War), a slideshow of the huge collection of religious banners held by the museum, and, of course, the historic chapel. But as well as hosting interesting objects, it also tells stories that capture the imagination, in particular about the advance of women preachers and the quest to educate working-class folk.

4 BARTHOMLEY

With its clutch of black-and-white timbered cottages, some dating from the 17th century, Barthomley is one of the most beautiful villages in Cheshire. If this pastoral scene is not enough to make you pause, there is another reason to stop for a while: **St Bertoline's Church**

(barthomleystbertolines.org.uk during services), named after a little-known Saxon saint from nearby Staffordshire. It was built in the 1500s, though a Norman doorway in the north wall, relocated there during the 19th century, reveals the existence of an earlier building. The red sandstone edifice defines the word imposing; sitting on an ancient burial mound above the lane, its crenellated west tower looms over onlookers. Highlights inside include an intricately carved oak ceiling and the Crewe family's chapel, containing an alabaster effigy of a knight from 1390. The church was the scene of a massacre during the English Civil War when on Christmas Eve in 1643, some 20 Parliamentarians seeking refuge in the church came under fire from Royalist forces, leaving 12 dead.

FOOD & DRINK

White Lion Inn Audley Rd, CW2 5PG 01270 882242. This cosy half-timbered pub huddling beneath a thatched roof has been serving ale since 1614 (while it was still the home of the parish clerk).

5 ALSAGER

Mere Cottage (page 293)

How do you pronounce Alsager? The 'sager' part is straightforward, that's said with a soft g as in sage. But on the slow train from London to Crewe, which reaches its penultimate northbound stop at this town, the automated announcement declares that you have arrived at Alsager, with 'Al' pronounced as in 'Alan'. It's enough to make a local wince: Alsager should really have a double l, for it is pronounced 'All-sager' (Sandbach suffers similarly, mispronounced as though it has a connection with the classical composers). Recorded as Eleacier in the Domesday Book, this community's name today owes more to the Alsager family, who are thought to have first settled here in the 1200s and presided over the local area for several centuries. By the 1800s, however, they had run out of male heirs, and their residence, Alsager Hall, exists today only as a cartographic footnote. Yet, despite the demise of its benefactors, Alsager prospered thanks to the arrival of the railway in 1848, which swiftly transformed it from a scattering of cottages and farms into a village, a leafy retreat for the wealthy owners of the pottery factories – 'pot banks', as they are locally known – in Stoke-on-Trent. In 1940, a munitions factory opened at Radway Green, the war effort serving to boost the

CHESTER

Walk the Roman walls, browse unique shopping arcades and admire art in the cathedral – just a few of the many reasons to visit the historic county town of Chester.

1 The medieval Rows are a unique feature of the Chester shopping experience. 2 When it comes to clocks, only Big Ben is more popular with snappers than the Eastgate Clock. 3 Chester's cathedral dates from medieval times but had a Victorian makeover. 4 Artefacts from the Deva Victrix fortress can be found in the Roman Gardens.

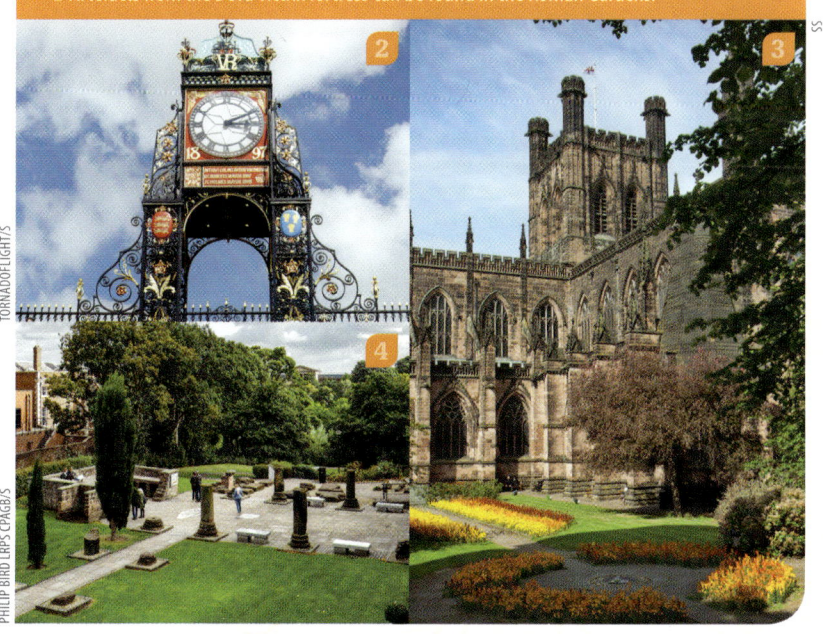

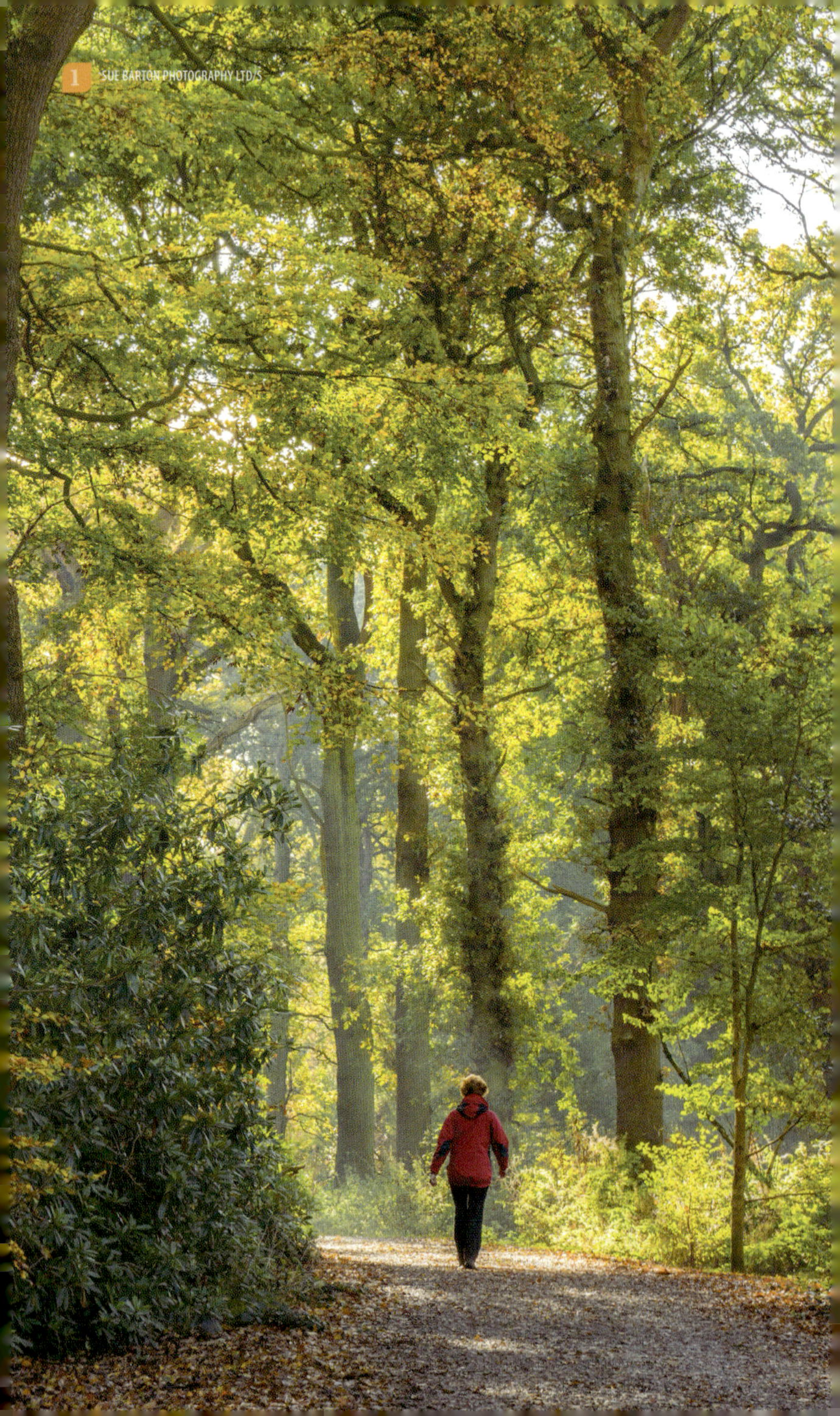
1
SUE BARTON PHOTOGRAPHY LTD/S

NATURAL ATTRACTIONS

Many perceive Cheshire to be all flat, farming country but there's far more variety to its landscapes than that, from the wild moorlands of the east to the sandy beaches, bird-rich marshes and little-known islands of the west.

1 The vast estate of Tatton Park offers plenty of scope for country walks. 2 A former sand quarry has been transformed into Brereton Heath Nature Reserve. 3 Cheshire's county flower is the cuckooflower, also known as Lady's Smock. 4 Head up Bickerton Hill for glorious views of the surrounding counties. 5 White Nancy is a distinctive landmark of the Bollington skyline.

6 The Dee Estuary offers an unexpected delight for walkers: at low tide you can stride across the sands from West Kirby to Hilbre Island. Elsewhere in the Cheshire countryside keep your eyes peeled for a variety of resident wildlife such as red deer (**7**), peregrine falcons (**8**) and redshanks (**9**).

population, while at the other end of town Twyfords manufactured bathroom products (by royal appointment) from 1958 until 2011.

Today's visitor might be surprised to read that Alsager has such a long history. On the face of it, this is a one-road town, connecting Crewe and the Potteries, with some rather unattractive late 20th-century architecture on its main road. Yet the village, as it is still known as by locals, offers a handful of attractions. Streets including Sandbach Road South, Chancery Lane, Ashmore's Lane, Station Road and Brookhouse Road are still graced by a smattering of 19th-century mansions; some in plain view, others peeping from behind hedges and high walls. One of the most impressive is **Milton House**, which takes pride of place in **Milton Park**, a pretty public space shrouded by tall trees and adorned with sunken and rose gardens. It's a good spot for a picnic, with the added benefit of a well-equipped playground if you're travelling with children. Milton House was once the home of Sir Ernest Craig, who, rather exotically, made his fortune in the silver mines of New Mexico before becoming the Member of Parliament for Crewe in the early 20th century. Fine Victorian homes can also be found along Church Road

WHEN BUFFALO BILL CAME TO TEA

Alsager may seem a one-horse sort of town for a larger-than-life character like Buffalo Bill to ride into. Yet in his book *Alsager: The Place and Its People* (Alsager History Research Group, 1999), local author James Sutton reveals that's just what he did.

'In 1890, William Burgess, the son of a potter who had moved to Baltimore in the 1850s, became the US Consul for Stoke-on-Trent ... During his time in Alsager (about four years), Colonel William Cody, known as Buffalo Bill, was at the height of his fame and came to Britain to present his exciting Wild West show. According to memoirs left by Burgess's son John, Buffalo Bill visited the family ... an event which naturally thrilled the children and formed a lasting memory in John's mind. William had Indian clothes made for the children and wanted them to spring out of the shrubbery in a mock attack as Buffalo Bill came up the drive, but when the time came they were too shy and overawed to act the part. The family visited the show and watched the shooting skills of Ann Oakley. Afterwards they were introduced to Chief Sitting Bull, who deeply impressed the children.'

and The Avenue, where gardens slope down to **The Mere** (see opposite). To look out over this large body of water, willows gently weeping on its shores, you'll need to go to one of the small public viewing points on Crewe Road and Sandbach Road North.

The town's most impressive church is **Christ Church** (01270 872291 christchurchalsager.uk in office hours and during services), built in 1789 thanks to the generous purses of the Misses Alsager. Created in ashlar sandstone, it has an imposing tower at its western end, with a doorway at its base bounded by Doric columns and topped by two pediments. Inside, further Classical decoration includes the huge pilasters separating the six arched bays on either side of the nave. Opposite the church entrance is a **school and schoolhouse** designed in 1848 by Sir George Gilbert Scott, two attractive red-brick buildings, with their multiple gables, quoins and lancet windows that reflect the religious connection. They stand closest to the road as part of Charles Tryon Court, a small upscale housing development inspired by Scott's design.

The Salt Line & Mere Lake Way

Alsager marks the start (or finish) of two gentle walks on well-maintained greenways. The **Salt Line** traces part of the Sandbach to Wheelock train track on the North Staffordshire Railway that once carried coal and limestone to the salt works at Malkins Bank. Now returned to nature, the 1½-mile route from Hassall Road in Alsager to the car park on Betchton Road in Hassall Green cuts through fields and is shaded by oaks, limes, silver birch and rowans. Depending on the season, primroses and harebells brighten the path, while bullfinches and yellow brimstone butterflies flitter by. When you reach Hassall Green, visit **St Philip's Church** on Smithy Grove (achurchnearyou. com/hassall-green-st-philip during services). It's hard to miss, being built of bright-pink corrugated iron. The church once stood in Alsager where you'll now find St Mary Magdalene Church and was moved here by horse and cart. The Salt Line connects to the **Wheelock Rail Trail**, a further 1½-mile stretch of reclaimed railway.

To the southeast of Alsager centre is **Mere Lake Way** (signifying neither a mere nor lake but, from the old English, a boundary stream). The mile-long path leads from Linley Road to Merelake Road on the outskirts of Talke, just across the Staffordshire border. Like the Salt Line, this shady avenue also follows a former railway track – keep an

CREWE TO ALSAGER

eye out for low-flying balls from the adjacent golf course. For self-guided route maps and further information about both walks, go to cheshireeast.gov.uk.

FOOD & DRINK

Kraftworks 58 Sandbach Rd South, ST7 2LP 01270 882871 nbkraftworks.co.uk. Take your pick from a wide choice of beers from around the world, including Offbeat from Crewe, at this bar and bottle shop with a sociable tap room.

Hall Farm Shop Alsager Hall Farm, ST7 2UB 01270 872478 hallfarmshopalsager.co.uk. This former milking parlour is the place to pick up local meat, fruit and veg, cheese, yoghurts, ice cream and more.

The Mere Crewe Rd, ST7 2HA 01270 879409 themereinn.co.uk. This cosy Victorian inn serves locally sourced solid pub grub and more adventurous dishes, such as mussel, chorizo and spinach linguine in a spicy tomato sauce.

The Real Food Company 48 & 50 Sandbach Rd South, ST7 2LP 01270 873322. Stock up on sustainably farmed and fished food at this trailblazing shop, which also sells herbal remedies and literature about environmental issues. Self-caterers can order boxes of fresh organic produce for collection on Wednesdays.

SHOPPING
Shops

Alsager Book Emporium Hassall Rd Methodist Church, Hassall Rd, ST7 2HH 01270 625444. Some 40,000 secondhand books on all subjects are sold here, with special sections on theology, local history and antiquarian books. All proceeds go to the Englesea Brook Chapel and Museum (page 127).

The Cottage Gallery 120 Crewe Rd, ST7 2JA 01270 878554. Resident artist Ged Mitchell is the creative force behind this independent gallery. Part studio, part shop, it's where you'll find Ged painting his signature watercolour landscapes, with work by others on sale, too.

Two Doors Studio 100 Crewe Rd, ST7 2JA 01270 877370. This gift shop keeps it local, selling handicrafts and art created by the owners Lorna Plant and Ruthie Williams and more than 50 other artists, most of whom live in the area. Contact the shop to check out upcoming artist events.

EVENTS CALENDAR

Find out more at @itsallaboutalsager.

Jun/Jul Art & Music Festival
Sep Italian Food Festival, Ceramics Festival

Markets

Pick up some fresh fish and fruit and veg at **Alsager Market**, held on Fairview car park on Wednesdays (⊙ 09.00–15.00). The **Olive and Stitch Market**, featuring food and artisan makers, takes place in the Civic Centre on the third Saturday of the month (⊙ 09.00–13.00).

SANDBACH, CONGLETON & AROUND

These two busy market towns remain as lively as ever, even if some of the industries that they made their fortunes from have now disappeared. There is plenty of history to unearth among their many half-timbered buildings and medieval streets and alleys: Congleton's last remaining hulking mills recall the town's heyday of silk and cotton manufacture, while Sandbach is a showcase for the architecture of Sir George Gilbert Scott. There are also pleasant green spaces to explore in the form of well-planned town parks and at wilder heaths and lakes in the surrounding countryside, where magnificent mansions still stand, including the Elizabethan treasure that is Little Moreton Hall. The distant past is present, too, in the Neolithic barrow at The Bridestones and the Anglo-Saxon crosses on the square at Sandbach.

6 SANDBACH

The Wheatsheaf (page 293)

Sandbach is arguably the most attractive of the four main towns in this chapter, with many centuries-old features still enduring today. The Saxons first settled here and the lands later passed through the noble hands of the Sandbach family, the Leghs of Booth, the Radcliffes of Ordsall, and the Crewes of Crewe Hall. Like many towns in the area, Sandbach's history was not untouched by the English Civil War. When a troop of weary Scottish soldiers on the retreat from the Battle of Worcester called by the town on 3 September 1651, during the September fair, they were attacked by the locals, a scrap that took place on what is now Scotch Common.

Sandbach was an important stop for coaches travelling from London and Birmingham to Liverpool and Manchester in the 19th century. Silk, shoes, ale and worsted yarns were among the town's industries and the Trent and Mersey Canal, which skirts the town, became the site of corn mills and salt works. By the 1900s, Foden and ERF had become major employers manufacturing heavy goods vehicles, and while those factories have shut, the annual Transport Festival they inspired continues to take place in April, and the musical legacy left by Foden, still the name of the Sandbach-based world-class brass band, lives on.

Market Square & Sandbach Crosses

Also known as the Cobbles for the stones that still carpet its floor, Market Square, a wide, open space, is the setting for one of Cheshire's jewels: the Sandbach Crosses, a pair of stone shafts believed to be the remains of two Anglo-Saxon high crosses, dating from the 9th century. We are lucky to be able to see them – they were broken up by Puritans in the 17th century and only returned to pride of place in the early 1800s. Apart from their very existence, the crosses are also remarkable for their intricate carvings (they were originally colourfully painted, too): the taller one, which is 16-feet in height, shows scenes from the Bible; the other,

"Market Square is a wide, open space clasping one of Cheshire's jewels: the Sandbach Crosses, dating from the 9th century."

about 10-feet tall, depicts animals and human figures. Now in the care of English Heritage, the crosses are enclosed by railings and surrounded by information posts offering insights into their history and the carvings.

The square is also bordered by three half-timbered inns. The thatched-roof **Olde Black Bear**, now known as DV8 (22 High St, CW11 1AX ⌀ 01270 368081), dates from 1634 and was named for the bear-baiting it hosted – Dick Turpin is said to have been a returning visitor. **The Market Tavern** (8 Market Sq, CW11 1AT ⌀ 01270 762099) was built in 1680, and **The Crown**, now The Saxon Grill at The Crown (10 Market Sq, CW11 1AT ⌀ 01270 762161), also dates from the 17th century, but is much altered. Peep behind The Crown to see what remains of substantial stables for the inns on the square.

The cobbles spill out of the square's northeast corner onto Crown Bank, where you'll find the town's oldest building, **The Lower Chequer** (Crown Bank, CW11 1DB ⌀ 01270 750214). This two-room pub, built in 1570, is thought to have been named for the chequer boards that were used to help illiterate customers count out their money. Of the original elements, you can still see the stone mounting block for horseriders. The inn is joined at the hip to the **Cake House**, a sweet little cottage that has more of its original timber-framed fabric intact.

St Mary's Church & the Scottification of Sandbach

High St, CW11 1HD ⌀ 01270 762379 ⌀ sandbachchurch.co.uk ⌀ during services, Thu mornings & often in daylight hours

Garlanded by high trees, this church dates from 1661 but it was the subject of a significant two-year restoration in 1847 led by Sir George Gilbert Scott. He encased the church in new stone and renewed the west tower (it is said to be a replica of the original), which has a high open porch and is unusual for having a public footpath run beneath it. To the right of the entrance, just outside the tower canopy, stand pieces of the Saxon Crosses. Inside, older features to spot include the original oak-carved ceiling and the font.

This was one of several projects Scott was commissioned to undertake in the area by the Rev John Armitstead, including Sandbach School on Crewe Road, the almshouses on The Hill, St John's Church at Sandbach Heath and its vicarage, now Tall Chimneys, at Betchton. In 1857, Scott designed the **Sandbach Literary Institution** (Hightown CW11 1AE ⌀ 01270 600800 ⌀ sandbach.gov.uk/literary-institute.htm ⌀ 09.00–14.00 Mon–Thu), which was originally a library, corn exchange, assembly room, ballroom and reading room, and is now the chamber of the town council. The main building of the institute was built of red brick with Scott's signature diaper work and an octagonal two-storey porch at the corner with Bradwall Street.

Old Hall & Front Street

Grade I-listed **Old Hall** (High St, CW11 1AL ⌀ 01270 758170) has been much added to over the years but was originally the half-timbered home of successive lords of the manor from 1656. The original section, made from wattle and daub and framed in oak felled in nearby woods, can be seen at its eastern end, encompassing an entrance and twin gables. In the mid 19th century, part of Old Hall became an inn, now its sole role. Internal gems include an ornate Jacobean fireplace on the ground floor, an unusual left-handed spiral staircase and a priest hole.

Across the road, drop down the stairs at the southeast edge of the churchyard to **Front Street**, a delightful terrace of red brick cottages with tall chimneys and a half-timbered dwelling at its far corner with Church Street. As its name suggests, this is the town's original main street, the route in from Stoke-on-Trent. It's also the site of the **town** spout, which was relocated here when a bridge was built over the River Wheelock that visitors still cross when arriving from the direction of The Hill and Old Mill Road.

Sandbach Town Hall
High St, CW11 1AX ⌀ 01270 600835 ⌀ sandbach.gov.uk/sandbach-town-hall.htm
⊙ by appointment

The Victorian Gothic town hall is at the centre of local life, especially on market day. The red-brick building, designed in 1889 by Thomas Bower, has an elegant arcade of four arches at ground level, echoed by four triple lancet windows with plate tracery on the first floor. At its eastern end is a clock tower with an entrance at its base, above which perch two statues – Bigod, the Norman lord of the manor, and Randolph Crewe, an ancestor of Hungerford Crewe, who granted the land on which the hall is built. Pass through the ground-floor arches of the main building

THE DIARY OF A GEORGIAN LADY

When Mrs G Linnaeus Banks wrote down her thoughts about the changing face of Sandbach between 1825 and 1832, she can hardly have realised she was creating such a precious historic document for the town, which runs to more than 4,000 words. Her reminiscences about the place she visited as a child, aged 4, 8 and 11 years old (she stayed in the house on the southeastern corner of Market Square) make for truly fascinating reading.

In the following excerpt, permission for its reproduction having been kindly granted by the Sandbach History Society, she reports the building of a bridge at the eastern edge of High Street, the parapets of which can still be seen today. Sandbach Library holds copies of her writings if you wish to read the whole piece.

'In Paterson's Roads, 1822, Sandbach is said to be 'pleasantly situated on an eminence near the little river Wheelock'. Evidently between that date and 1825, the main road had been considerably raised, and carried over a new bridge, thus levelling the town approach on the east, and reducing the steep ascent on either side; for I found not only a new bridge of two or three arches, but the debris of an old one, the thin shell of one low arch still upstanding, surrounded by water and detached portions of brickwork, offering a sad temptation to venturesome youngsters, who crossed to it on the scattered bricks in the water, regardless that the arch itself was unsafe, and falling brick by brick into the choked stream. It, however, had not wholly disappeared on my last visit in 1832.'

to find shops and the indoor market, which buzzes with business on Thursdays, Fridays and Saturdays. A table of tolls from 1890 is posted on the rear wall, shining a light on the scene that might have been witnessed by market-goers at the turn of the 20th century. It appears a fee of 4d was levied 'For any quantity of vegetables, fruit or agricultural produce brought into the market for sale or exposure for sale, in a cart drawn by one ass or mule'. But if your cart was pulled by two such beasts, the price rose to 6d. Bower also designed the Victorian drinking fountain, now marooned at the centre of the roundabout by the Literary Institute. It's awfully grand, with one central and four surrounding bowls, partially sheltered by a gabled dome held aloft by six Tuscan columns, and finished with a ball-shaped finial.

Sandbach Park
The Commons, CW11 1FJ 0300 123 5011 daylight hours

This lovely green space behind the library, which opened to mark the Diamond Jubilee of Queen Victoria in 1897, has ornamental lawns, play areas, outdoor gym equipment, a field for ball games, two bowling greens, a boules pitch, table tennis table, tennis and multi-sport courts, and a picnic area. At its furthest edge is a wetland habitat with a boardwalk and paths leading through woodland – a good spot for pond dipping – and a bug hotel has been installed recently.

FOOD & DRINK

The Beer Emporium 8 Welles St, CW11 1GT 01270 760113 thebeeremporium.com. This bottle shop and bar is continuing a fine tradition in the town, which was renowned for its ale in the 17th century. Take your pick from the beers, ales and porter that line the walls, or a drop from a keg.

Godfrey C Williams and Son 9–11 Market Sq, CW11 1AP 01270 762817 godfreycwilliams.co.uk. The Corner House, a Grade II-listed building with square-paned windows, is the charming setting for this award-winning delicatessen, which opened in 1875. Neatly stacked boxes, packets, jars and tins fill the shelves, while there are also extensive displays of cheese, charcuterie and pastries.

Jenny's Tea Shop 42 High St, CW11 1AN 01270 757702. Brick walls painted white and swagged with heart-shaped bunting, a teapot clock, floral china mugs hanging from hooks – the atmosphere here is dainty and cosy, just the place for a cuppa and slice of homemade cake.

The Wheatsheaf 1 High St, CW11 1AG 01270 762013 wheatsheafsandbach.co.uk. This coaching inn was recently spruced up gastro-pub style and serves British food with a

EVENTS CALENDAR

Find out more at 🌐 sandbachevents.co.uk.

Apr Transport Festival & National Town Criers' Competition
Jun Brass on the Grass
Sep Sandbach Day of Dance

modern twist. I can thoroughly recommend the inspired English Breakfast Salad: bacon, mushrooms, eggs, tomatoes, fried bread and haggis crumbs interlaced with dressed salad leaves.

SHOPPING
Shops

La Boutique Market High St, CW11 1AH 🌐 laboutiquesandbach.com. The latest use for the Town Mill, dating from 1825, is a one-stop shop for jewellery, handbags, vintage clothes, retro furniture and more by local artisans.

Markets

The **main market** day is Thursday (⏲ 09.00–16.00), when stalls spread out over High Street, Scotch Common, Little Common and around and inside the Market Hall. But there are smaller markets, too, centring on the Market Hall, at the same time on Friday and Saturday. There is a **Makers Market** (⏲ 09.00–15.00) every second Saturday of the month on Market Square.

7 BRREETON HEATH NATURE RESERVE

🏠 **Chequer Stable** (page 293)
Davenport Ln, CW12 4SU 📞 01477 534115 ⏲ 08.45–20.30 daily during British Summer Time, otherwise 08.45–17.00 daily

This local reserve northeast of Sandbach offers plenty of natural delights, including a rare lowland heath and a lake in a former sand quarry, as well as wildflower meadows and woods thick with birch, oak and rowan trees. It is a relaxing place to walk, with an accessible all-weather track around which are resting points with sublime views across the lake. Birdlife present includes nuthatches and green woodpeckers, redwing and fieldfare, as well as water birds (there is a hide) such as the great crested grebes that nest here. The heath was originally part of the **Brereton Hall** estate, at nearby Brereton Green, a prodigy house from the Elizabethan and Jacobean era that is now a private residence hidden behind high gates, although at the time of writing there were plans to turn it into a hotel.

FOOD & DRINK

Pear Tree Farm Shop Pear Tree Farm, Newcastle Rd North, CW11 1RR ⌀ 01477 533131 ⌀ peartreefarmshop.co.uk. Pedigree Dexter beef from the farm's own herd and what it claims is the best apple pie in Cheshire are among the local produce on sale at this small farm shop.

8 THE SANDBACH FLASHES

The Bear's Paw Warmingham (page 293)
⌀ sandbachflashes.co.uk

One for the birdwatchers, these fragile wetlands to the south and west of Sandbach (between Elworth and Crewe) are a chain of 14 saline pools created by the flooding of land that has subsided because of salt extraction. The flashes are a Site of Special Scientific Interest (SSSI), recognised as an important natural habitat for insects, plants and birds including pink-footed goose, sparrowhawk and oystercatcher. Although on private property, the flashes can be seen from surrounding public roads, such as the wide view of Watch Lane Flash on Watch Lane.

FOOD & DRINK

The Bear's Paw School Ln, Warmingham CW11 3QN ⌀ 01270 526317 ⌀ thebearspawinn.co.uk. In the idyllic village of Warmingham, a few miles west of Sandbach, this beautiful 19th-century inn is a relaxing place for a drink or a meal. You'll find buffed up oak panelling and huge fireplaces, walls hung with old prints and vintage photos, shelves stacked with books, and leather chairs and polished wooden tables. Run by Nelson Hotels, it also has rooms (page 293).

9 WINTERLEY POOL

Crewe Rd, CW1 5TR

Blink and you could miss this mill pool near Haslington. Unfortunately, its banks have been encroached upon by building development, but it's still possible to look out over the water from the main road to see house martins, pied wagtails, lapwings, black-headed gulls, tufted ducks and moorhens. Dragonflies and damselflies skip across the water,

SANDBACH, CONGLETON & AROUND

beneath which carp, pike and sticklebacks lurk, making this a popular haunt of anglers. Call by in the evening and you may catch sight of a Daubenton's bat.

FOOD & DRINK

Wheelock Hall Farm Shop Crewe Rd, CW11 4RE ⌀ 01270 764230 ⌀ wheelockhallfarm.co.uk. This family-run business isn't a place to just swing by for a few fresh eggs; it sells a huge array of produce from the farm and beyond, has a garden centre, and, if you're travelling with children, you'll appreciate the play area and the farmyard petting zoo. There's a café, too.

10 CONGLETON

⌂ **The Alexandra Court Hotel** (page 293), ⌂ **Dane Cottage Holidays** (page 293)

Set on a bend of the River Dane below the Staffordshire Moors, Congleton has the air of a busy modern town but its lanes are rich in history. Once, more than 50 mills congregated on the banks of the Dane, which snakes along the northern edge of the town, the free-flowing water tumbling from the moors to power the production of silk and cotton (and for copper beating). This natural asset put the town at the forefront of 18th-century technology and industry as part of the 'Silk Triangle' with Leek and Macclesfield. However, Congleton had long since made its mark on the local map. When the Vikings sacked nearby Davenport, Congleton is thought to have quickly positioned itself as the alternative trading centre, gaining a charter by 1272, and later found a niche in the market making Congleton Points, silver-tipped leather strips for fastening garments. Even in the mid 19th century, when the French were finally allowed to import silk to Britain duty-free, nimble Congleton – by now enjoying a strong transport network, with good roads, the Macclesfield Canal and the railway – found new work cutting fustian and became a leader in ribbon-making (later even making cigars at nearby Havannah, a cute marketing ploy). Today, Congleton's main attractions are divided into two areas bisected by Mountbatten Way, a dual carriageway that may have unclogged the town's old streets of traffic but has done little to enhance its looks. Most of the historic architecture is concentrated

"Once, more than 50 mills congregated on the banks of the Dane, the free-flowing water tumbling from the moors to power the production of silk and cotton."

on and around High Street, while the river, remaining mills, park and woods generally lie on the other side of the highway.

A tour of the town

Congleton's shopping thoroughfare, High Street, is a trove of historic buildings, built here on high ground after the settlement's centre was relocated following a devastating flood of the Dane in 1451. Start your tour at **The Olde King's Arms** (1 High St ⌁ 01260 408718), the town's oldest pub and surely its star attraction, a half-timbered Elizabethan beauty dating from 1585. Cast your eyes down to pavement level and you'll see the shape of the top of a door to an even older building – the pub's cellar was once the living room of an earlier house that stood here.

Next up is the town's most striking piece of architecture, E W Godwin's **Town Hall**, dating from 1864. This Victorian-Gothic creation owes a lot to Godwin's close associations with the theatre (his mistress was the actress Ellen Terry, with whom he had two children, including the theatre practitioner Edward Gordon Craig). Arcaded at ground level, the hall has eight lancet windows on the first floor, six gabled windows in its steep roof, and a central crenelated square tower, decorated with more lancet windows and surmounted by an inset clock tower. As if all this was not enough to divert the eye, the façade is adorned with four different shades of stone and bands of chevrons and blank shields (the latter were never completed with the crests of the local great and good because of a financial squabble that ended the project in acrimony). There were three statues at its centre: two on the first-floor level depicting Edward I and Henry de Lacy (now missing), and, in a suitably elevated position at the roofline, Queen Victoria. The building appears even more monumental due to the fact that it stands shoulder to shoulder with smaller neighbouring buildings and perches on the edge of a shallow pavement. It positively looms over pedestrians and you'll need to cross the road to get a better perspective of the whole edifice.

If you go inside, you'll find that Godwin's quest to impress continues. The big stone staircase, with beehive domes over the half landings, feels more akin to a castle than an administrative centre. The hall's centrepiece is a vast double-height Grand Hall with galleries on three sides and flourishes include exposed hammerbeams, a clerestory with huge round windows, and a minstrels gallery supported by (rather bashed about) statues of St Cecilia and King David that was for years masked by a stage and suspended ceiling.

Peep through the grille gate between numbers 18 and 20 High Street to glimpse **Black Lion Court**, a small courtyard of 16th-century timber-framed buildings, with a first-floor jetty just visible on the right-hand side. At the risk of encouraging you to gawp through their front windows, number 18, currently the hair salon Clarity's, has a couple of ancient wall paintings as well as fine beam work; other examples of the latter also exist at number 16, now Whittaker & Biggs estate agents. Clues to the past also exist across the road at the clothes boutique **Davenports** (7 High St), built in the 1500s. Its former use by an apothecary can be detected in the symbol of a serpent on the coving above the first-floor window.

The 16th-century inn **Ye Olde White Lion** (22 High St ⌀ 01260 272702) bears a plaque explaining that this was once the site of the offices where John Bradshaw practised, the judge who was the president of the court that ordered the death sentence for Charles I. (**Bradshaw House**, back at 21 Lawton Street, is a Georgian building on the site of the house where he lived.)

At **Moody Street**, turn left to see some Georgian beauties including Moody Hall, one of several solid mansions from that era in the town, which was once a school run by prominent suffragist, Elizabeth Wolstenholme-Elmy. Further along, the pastel-coloured Georgian terrace at numbers 15 to 29 might momentarily persuade you that you are, in fact, in Brighton.

Continue along Moody Street to Chapel Street to see **St Peter's Church** (⊙ during services). This plain brick building hides one of the best examples of a Georgian Neoclassical church in the north of England. Inside its 18th-century walls is an unusually near-complete church of its time, the highlight of which is its oak boxed pews, many still bearing the brass plaques and armorial crests that identify their former occupants (the church was originally owned by the borough corporation and was very much a status symbol of the commercial community). There are many interesting facets to uncover here, including murals of St Peter and St Paul by Edward Penney, a founder member of the Royal Academy.

Just behind the church is the **Cockshoots**, a path where the townsfolk would once lay out nets to catch wild birds. Meanwhile, the front gate marks the start of the pleasant 1½-mile **Priesty Trail** that connects St Peter's to St Mary's at nearby Astbury (page 148), once the area's parish church, and retraces the steps of the priests who would preach at both places of worship. For directions, get the free guide *Walks and Wildlife South of Congleton* from the Congleton Information Centre (page 121) or download it at cheshireeast.gov.uk.

Return to High Street and turn left onto the pedestrianised stretch of the road to find the turning for **Little Street.** Here, at numbers 6 to 10, you can see a row of black-and-white half-timbered cottages from the 17th century. These days they are occupied by shops and a pub, their longevity emphasised by the fact that you must step down into these dwellings because the original floors are lower than today's street level. At the end of Little Street, cross over the junction to the 19th-century coaching inn **The Lion & Swan** (1 Swan Bank 01260 273115), the latest incarnation of a hostelry where travellers have rested and refreshed themselves since 1496 (the central portion dates from the 16th century). It is said to be haunted by a brown-haired woman who sits by the fireside in the bar, but a more likely vision of the past is an exposed preserved section of wattle and daub from the 16th century, which can be seen in reception. An earlier tavern on this spot was a regular stop on the journey north for The King's Men, William Shakespeare's touring troupe, who performed here between 1614 and 1633, payments for which are recorded in the town's accounts.

Congleton Museum

Market Sq, CW12 1ET 01260 276360 congletonmuseum.co.uk 10.00–16.15 Tue–Sat, noon–16.15 Sun

THE STORY OF BEARTOWN

Congleton rare, Congleton rare,
Sold the Town Bible to buy a new bear

Wherever you turn in Congleton, you're sure to see the image of a bear, usually in chains. The story goes that Congleton was rather fond of the sport of bear-baiting, so when, in the 1600s, the resident bear died, rather inconveniently just before the Wakes Holiday, the town sold its Bible to pay for a replacement – some say to stave off the possibility of a riot by the locals. Ever since, it has been known as Beartown and the subject of the above teasing rhyme. The furry beast is remembered more fondly these days, not only in the names of the breweries and art projects, but also through the recent sponsorship of a real-life bear at a sanctuary in Vietnam.

SANDBACH, CONGLETON & AROUND

At the rear of the town hall you'll find the door to Congleton Museum, which occupies part of the same building, where a comprehensive understanding of the town's history awaits. It packs a lot into just one room, charting the settlement's origins and progress from prehistoric to modern times in chronological order, in the basic if well-presented format of information boards, tableaux and some interactive displays. Coins from two 17th-century hoards, found in Priesty Fields and Moody Street, are displayed. The bookshelves in reception positively groan under the weight of an extensive collection of books and pamphlets about the area for those in search of in-depth reading. Friendly staff are on hand to tell you more about Congleton, and themed guided walks of the town depart from the front door at 14.00 on the first Sunday of the month (March to November).

Electric Picture House
Cross St, CW12 1HQ ⌀ 01260 270908 ⌀ electricpicturehouse.com ⊙ 10.00–16.00 Mon–Sat

The town's first cinema (also at different times a fustian mill and an ambulance garage) is now home to 13 artists pursuing a variety of disciplines, from painting and ceramics to textile design. You can see them beavering away in their studios and browse some of their work on display, which is available to buy. The space also hosts a lively programme of events, from exhibitions to open mic nights, as well as regular art workshops for adults on Tuesday evenings and children on Saturday mornings (book ahead).

Congleton's mills
Only a few classic mills remain on the Congleton skyline. Dane Mill, on Broadhurst Lane off the Clayton Bypass, is now a business park, and Riverside, on Mountbatten Way next to Aldi, houses offices. Martin's Mill, now private residences, is an impressive sight, sitting at the edge of a mill pond on Wards Lane at the southeast edge of the town. However, you can take a closer look, inside and out, at **Victoria Mill** on Foundry Bank in the centre, which is now an antiques centre and café (page 146).

Congleton Park & Town Wood
Opened in 1871, this pleasant green space on the River Dane's northern bank is believed to have been planned by Edward Kemp, while

Victorian horticulturalist James Bateman, of nearby Biddulph Grange (see box, page 154), is thought to have influenced the planting. You'll find everything anyone wishing to enjoy a breath of fresh air could want, including a bandstand, playground, bowling green and floral gardens set with interesting pieces including the original 16th-century market cross. Refreshments are available in the pavilion built to celebrate Queen Victoria's Golden Jubilee (page 146). A riverside walkway, shaded by limes and horse chestnuts, begs a gentle promenade, while the paths in the Town Wood, along the park's northern boundary, offer a longer walk with views across the town. Take the Park View exit for the open-air **paddling pool** (Park Rd ⊙ May–Sep 10.00–18.00 daily, depending on weather), where youngsters have splashed about since the 1930s. During summer, the meadow **Dane-in-Shaw Pastures**, a Site of Special Scientific Interest (SSSI), is a lovely place for a walk (see box, pages 150–2), an untouched wild grassland of national importance. You can access it from the six-mile-long Biddulph Valley Way, a greenway that follows

POCKET PARKS

Congleton has excelled as a multiple regional award-winner of Britain in Bloom, but the latest green-fingered initiative here is the transformation of greyfield land into 'pocket parks'. **Moody Street Gardens** has turned a piece of rough ground into a sensory garden, with splashes of colour and tactile elements such as mosaics, boxes to encourage songbirds and plants chosen not just for fragrance but to stimulate other senses, too.

Margaret's Place, formerly The Antrobus Street Gardens, has also received a makeover on the theme of health (it sits next to a medical centre), with outdoor gym equipment, fruit trees and a giant wood-carved apple core by local sculptor Andy Burgess. Even a neglected flowerbed at the foot of the steps to the library has been put to interesting use, now sewn with herbs that everyone is welcome to pick. Take a look, too, at the **Physic Garden** off Colehill Bank, which focuses on plants with properties used for industrial and medicinal purposes, such as angelica and valerian, often found in remedies, and woad and common madder, which were used for dying fabric. At the top of this garden you'll find the **Bath House**, a small two-storey brick pavilion with just two rooms: a sitting area with a fireplace, and, below it, a windowless room with a large bath, once fed by a spring, into which descends a flight of stone steps – a plunge pool of yesteryear. The levels do not interconnect; instead each has its own entrance. To find out more about this building, including upcoming open days, contact the Congleton Building Preservation Trust (⌀ congletonbpt.wordpress.com).

CONGLETON APPLE JUICE

When the Congleton Sustainability Group was left with a glut of windfalls after a seed swap event in 2009, little did they know that this would be the start of the cottage industry Congleton Apple Juice. Now, up to 12 tons of apples are gathered every October from local gardens and orchards, including 250 fruit trees that have been planted in the town's schools, and a community orchard at Astbury Mere. For years, the pressing was done at a local fruit farm, but the centre of operations is now The Old Saw Mill, a community hub and event space that opened in autumn 2016 to challenge loneliness and social isolation. All profits go back into community projects, a worthwhile cause to which you can raise a glass of juice, or cider, in the café (see below).

the old coal freight railway line from Congleton to the Potteries. For more information, go to cheshireeast.gov.uk.

FOOD & DRINK

Barleyhops 2 Swan Hse, Swan Bank, CW12 1AH 01260 270164 barleyhops.co.uk. There's an impressive array of beers on sale here, including Congleton's own Cheshire Brewhouse, as well as gins. Stop to sup a brew or spirit in this small, convivial bar and select something to take home, too.

Beartown Tap 18 Willow St, CW12 1RL 01260 270775 @beartown.tap. One for the serious beer drinkers, this simple pub is all about what's in your glass, much of which originates from the Beartown Brewery just around the corner. Beartown Bear Ass and Beartown Bearskinful are among the cheekily named stalwarts.

Crema Deli 5 Bridge St, CW12 1AY 01260 270511 @CremaDeli. In search of a great coffee? Try this little corner of Italy on Congleton's main shopping drag, where paninis and pizzas are among a huge variety of fresh food available to take away or enjoy in the upstairs café, alongside shelves groaning with superior comestibles.

The Loft Café at Victoria Mill Foundry Bank, CW12 1EE 01260 400050. After browsing three floors of antiques and collectables (page 146), you'll be relieved to pull up a chair or flop on a Chesterfield in this comfy vintage-style café where chef Ian Woodhouse is gaining fans for his delicious cakes and scones, as well as savoury dishes such as tapas.

The Old Saw Mill Back River St 07971 805372 @OldSawMill. An inspired community project, this homely, affordable café is a great place to order a glass of the thirst-quenching apple juice or cider pressed on-site (see box, above) and relax in the spacious sitting area, furnished with books and table games, or in the garden on warm days.

Soul Food Café 5 Mill St, CW12 1AB 01260 408289. A solid choice of breakfast fare, soups and jacket potatoes, with vegetarian, vegan and gluten-free options, is served in this warren of rooms, shared with a tattoo parlour.

CREWE & THE STAFFORDSHIRE BORDERS

EVENTS CALENDAR
Find out more at congleton-tc.gov.uk/discover-congleton/whats-on.

Feb Congleton Unplugged
Jun Food & Drink Festival
Jul Big Beer Weekend
Aug Jazz & Blues Festival
Sep Open Space Arts Festival

Stock at the Pavilion Mill Green, Congleton Park, CW12 8JG 07855 010780 stockpavilion.co.uk. The 19th-century pavilion in Congleton Park is now a laid-back contemporary space with a modish mishmash of vintage furniture. Dishes range from a fanciful roasted tomato salad with halloumi and basil couscous to a good honest Sunday roast.
The Young Pretender Beer Parlour 30–34 Lawton St, CW12 1RS 01260 273277 thebeerparlours.co.uk/the-young-pretender. Three former shops provide the rambling premises for this award-winning beer hall, which has a stated aim of being women-friendly, as well as welcoming kids and dogs, and hosts regular film nights and meet-the-brewer events. Discover sister bars The Treacle Tap in Macclesfield (page 164) and The Old Dancer in Wilmslow.

SHOPPING
Shops
Victoria Mill Antique and Collectors Centre Foundry Bank, CW12 1EE 01260 297838 victoriamillantiques.co.uk. Three levels of this former mill are crammed with antiques and collectables. Revive yourself after with a snack in the café (page 145).

Markets
Congleton Market is held on Tuesday and Saturday (09.00–15.30) in the Bridestone Shopping Centre.

ARTS & CULTURE
Attitude Gallery 12a Swan Bank, CW12 1AH 01260 299143 attitudegallery.co.uk. Contemporary work by established and emerging artists is on display and for sale at this innovative gallery.
The Daneside Theatre Park Rd, CW12 1DP 01260 271095 danesidetheatre.co.uk. Check out the varied programme of plays and musicals performed by local companies, plus film nights.

SANDBACH, CONGLETON & AROUND

11 THE BRIDESTONES

Congleton's story began long before the weavers arrived. The first evidence of a settlement here dates from Neolithic times, as evidenced by The Bridestones, the remains of a long **cairn** thought to have been constructed between 3500bc and 2400bc. You'll find it a few miles to the east of town on Dial Lane, as it rises on to the Staffordshire moors. Though the site's importance is recognised in its status as a scheduled monument, the stones are tucked up the driveway to Bridestone and Brydges stone quarry (the yard is private, park elsewhere if you arrive by car), without so much as an information board. Experts say that this group of stones reveals that the tomb was divided into at least two burial chambers, marked by the broken cross slab, while the two tall portal stones flanked the entrance, and the remaining three stones are thought to have belonged to a circle or semi-circle that enclosed a forecourt to the east of the chamber. A plan of the tomb drawn in the late 1700s suggests there were two more portal stones and a third chamber, but it seems some of the stones were used for road-building in the 19th century.

12 ASTBURY MERE COUNTRY PARK

Sandy Ln, CW12 4PF ⌀ astburymerecountrypark.uk ⊙ visitor centre 09.00–17.00 daily

At the southern edge of Congleton, east of the A34 Newcastle Road, stands Astbury Mere, a flooded former sand quarry that was saved from housing development and transformed into a country park in the late 1980s. This vast body of water is fringed by shrubland and woods and presided over by Sandy the Bear, a sculpture of a bear that sits on a platform high in the air, decorated from head to toe in a picture of the very landscape that he surveys as it looked when it was sand quarry. Astbury Mere is an easy and attractive place for a gentle walk, bounded by an accessible all-weather path. Depending on the season you can expect to see a changing colourful carpet of bluebells, orchids and roses, alive with butterflies and bees, swallows and willow warblers on the wing, and Canada geese resting on the water. Find out more about the mere's history and wildlife in the visitor centre, where you can also pick up leaflets about regular activities at the mere and other local attractions. If you're a runner, this is the site of the **Congleton Parkrun** (⌀ parkrun.org.uk/congleton ⊙ 09.00 Sat), and there's also a **Water Sports Centre** (⌀ peakpursuits.co.uk/peak-pursuits-centres/

13 ST MARY'S, ASTBURY

The Green, Astbury CW12 4RG ⌀ astburychurch.org.uk ⊙ during services

At first sight, the most striking aspect of St Mary's is its size and location. In the context of the cluster of houses, dating from the 17th to 19th centuries, in which it now sits, it appears misplaced, something plucked from a large town or city and dropped at random in the Cheshire countryside. To understand why it is quite so massive and why it stands where it does requires an appreciation of its longevity and purpose: St Mary's was the parish church of Congleton from Saxon times until 1867. In other words, it is our modern perspective of this building and its location that is skewed.

The yellow sandstone ashlar church, with its detached millstone grit tower and spire, has been remodelled and added to over the centuries, yet many of these alterations remain intact and there's a clue to the distant past in a fragment of a teaching cross from AD950. It's best to consult the myriad service and opening times on the website or book an appointment because to arrive and find the door locked would be a great shame. Anyone interested in church architecture will find a feast and a puzzle here, according to Nikolaus Pevsner. He described St Mary's as 'one of the most exciting Cheshire churches', mentioning the high clerestory 'crowded with noble windows' and 'thrilling' ceilings 'low-pitched with camber-beams … with plenty of carved bosses and also dainty openwork pendants of a type without parallels in the county'. My highlights would include the gallery of intriguing carved faces on the Caen stone reredos, the Welsh dragons in the rood screen (revealing where it was made), and a recently restored 15th-century wall painting above the nave showing scenes from St George and the dragon. Outside, don't miss the huge gargoyles along the sides of the church.

FOOD & DRINK

Glebe Farm Astbury Astbury CW12 4RQ ✆ 01260 273916 ⌀ glebefarmastbury.co.uk. To the rear of the church, this former dairy farm is now the site of a popular shop selling home-grown local produce, with other local businesses, including a fishmonger, operating out of surrounding cabins. If you're travelling with kids, there is a collection of farmyard animals to see, plus tractor rides and a playground. There's a café here, too.

SANDBACH, CONGLETON & AROUND

14 LITTLE MORETON HALL
Congleton Rd, CW12 4SD 01260 272018 National Trust

Little Moreton Hall was the furthest point northwest that my childhood friends and I would venture on our bike rides from Alsager back in the 1970s. I have a vague memory of cycling up to its gatehouse, but on this recent visit I had to pass through a shop to reach even its lawn. Once on the garden path the view opens up of an extraordinary black-and-white half-timbered cluster of gables and jetties, encircled by a moat. The scene remains much as it did some 500 years ago, and your first reaction to this house is likely to be astonishment at how the three-storey manor is still standing. Little Moreton Hall buckles beneath the weight of its stone-slabbed roof and the Long Gallery has had to be reinforced twice since. It is in the Long Gallery that the manor's fragile state is perhaps felt most – the floor is akin to one you might find in a fairground fun house (a place to exercise during the Little Ice Age of the late 17th century, speculated the room guide when we chatted).

"The scene remains much as it did some 500 years ago, and your first reaction to this house is likely to be astonishment at how the three-storey manor is still standing."

The hall exists thanks almost as much to the misfortunes as the fortunes of its owners, the Moreton family, powerful landowners who climbed the social ranks. They spent almost 100 years building this proud statement of their wealth. Their extravagance is evident at every turn: the inner courtyard with its multiple bays; the 30,000 panes of glass encased in lead circles, rectangles, diamonds and squares; the exquisite carving of quatrefoils and other symbols, including the wolf from the Moreton's crest, which also appears in stained glass. But suddenly, in 1642, the Moretons found themselves on the wrong side of the English Civil War and over the following three centuries, while they managed to keep hold of their manor they had to rent it out. Finally, it passed into the hands of the National Trust in 1938.

The grounds, courtyard and 15 largely bare rooms are open to visitors – the Great Hall, colourful Little Parlour, wonky Long Gallery and, of course, the Garderobe are particular highlights. Quill writing is typical of the themed activities laid on, especially during school holidays, plus other special exhibition and events. There are regular

CREWE & THE STAFFORDSHIRE BORDERS

A walk from Dane-In-Shaw Pastures to Mow Cop
❋ OS Landranger 118; start: Congleton railway station ticket office, ♀ SJ 872 623; 4½ miles; easy with some steep ascents

The Gritstone Trail is a classic ridge walk offering fantastic views; on a clear day, it's possible to see Cheshire, Shropshire, the Welsh mountains, Lancashire, Manchester and Merseyside, Staffordshire and Derbyshire. This section of the 35-mile linear walk between the outskirts of Congleton and Mow Cop can connect to public transport at either end. I have started it in Congleton to make the Victorian folly at Mow Cop (pages 153–4) the reward for your endeavours. Time your walk to catch a number 77 bus from Mow Cop to Kidsgrove or Congleton, or the number 315 bus to Alsager or Congleton, which departs from the bottom of Mow Cop at Scholar Green, a couple of miles from where this walk ends. Buses are limited and infrequent, check the timetables at ⊘ dgbus.co.uk. Alternatively, Kidsgrove railway station is a further two-mile walk. You may prefer to arrange a taxi – mobile phones should get good reception around the telecommunications tower but it's advisable to book ahead. For walk extensions, see the free leaflets 'The Gritstone Trail' and 'The Biddulph Valley Way', available to download at ⊘ cheshireeast.gov.uk.

1 At Congleton railway station, dip down from Platform 2 to the Macclesfield Canal turning left onto the towpath. Continue straight, passing beneath two bridges before the towpath bears left and a view opens up across Dane-in-Shaw Pastures to the mighty viaduct that speeds trains across these rare grasslands.

2 Soon the parapets of an aqueduct come into view. Just before, descend the stairs on the left to the Biddulph Valley Way. Turn right onto this multi-user path, passing beneath the aqueduct and continuing forward through wooded cuttings where trains once carried coal between the Potteries and Congleton. Although popular and close to traffic in places, this is a pretty walk, its canopy of trees providing shelter from rain and sun, waysides blooming with bluebells and white wood anemone, depending on the season.

3 Shortly after Whitemoor Local Nature Reserve information board, go down a flight of steps on the left and pass under the Biddulph Valley Way to follow a lane to Upper Whitemoor Farm. From here you will see frequent yellow markers for the Gritstone Trail. Clear the farm buildings and look for a footpath on your left continuing through a field and into Whitemore Woods. Continue forward through the woods.

4 Eventually you will emerge on a track that climbs to Nick I'th' Hill, a dip in the ridge fashioned during the Ice Age. When you reach the road through the hamlet, look out for a footpath upwards on the left marked Gritstone Trail.

SANDBACH, CONGLETON & AROUND

5 This path continues south along the western edge of Willocks Woods. Occasionally, the trees and bushes part to reveal tantalising glimpses of the Cheshire plain and Welsh mountains to the right and the Staffordshire Moorlands to the left, before levelling out briefly. It's a well-worn track, with plenty of gritstone outcrops to examine as your feet pass over them.

6 At the road junction at Pot Bank, cross the road that drops immediately to your left and continue forward uphill – take extreme care at this point as vehicles turn left into this junction at speed. You have no choice but to follow this road for almost a mile. Keep your wits about you and restrain yourself from taking in the views until you reach the viewpoints at the top on Congleton Road. There you can revel in the superb panorama.

7 Continue on, passing on your left a detached house with a pond. On the right, at the mouth of a private road, Roe Park, is a fingerpost with a Gritstone waymarker that, at last, directs you off the road into woods and back onto the familiar gritstone-studded track woven with tree roots, finally emerging for more views across the plain. Pass through a metal kissing gate and climb up the steep steps to continue along the drystone wall, passing a stables and telecommunications tower, to reach a gate. ▶

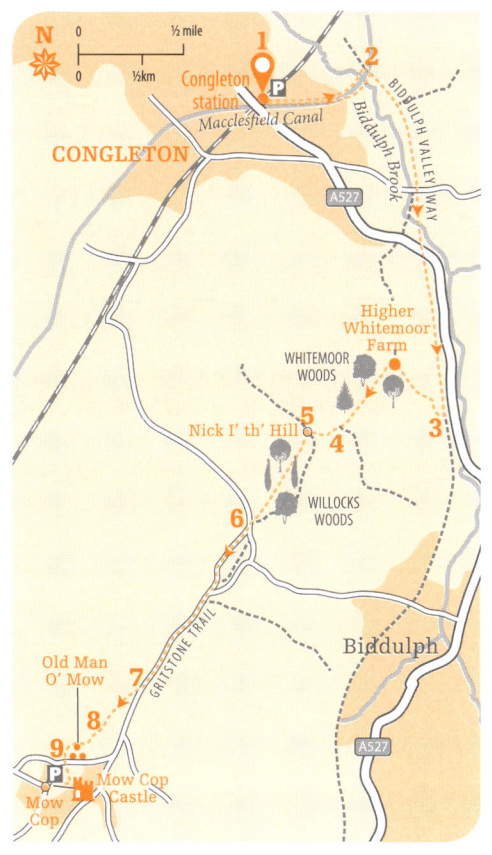

> ### A walk from Dane-In-Shaw Pastures to Mow Cop (continued)
>
> **8** Go through the gate, turning left then immediately right, before the road, to follow a track that passes a house on your left and loops the edge of a field, offering a fine view of the Old Man O Mow (page 154). Pass in front of this tower of stones and follow the track around until it doubles as a driveway to a house and leads you to Wood Street.
>
> **9** Turn right onto Wood Street and after a few yards turn left onto a track marked with a National Trust sign. Continue forward, then follow the track around to the right and along the base of the crag of rock on which sits Mow Cop. This is the end of the walk, leaving you free to explore these faux castle ruins and take in more views in your own time.

guided tours – or pick up a pocket guide at the shop on the way in and tap the knowledge of the room guides as you go around.

15 RODE HALL
Scholar Green ST7 3QP ⌀ 01270 873237 ⌀ rodehall.co.uk ⌀ Apr–Sep Wed & Bank hols, garden 11.00–17.00, house noon–16.00

This 18th-century country house, set in grounds designed by Humphry Repton, is one of Cheshire's true hidden gems. The handsome red-brick building with double bays has been played around with by successive generations of the Wilbraham family, as most obviously indicated by some bricked-up windows in the bows on its facade. In fact, the original house is the long low building to its side that sits in the shadow of a stable block (site of the tea room), which looks similar in style but was built later. On a guided tour of the elegant rooms, you can take an entertaining canter through history from 1669 to the present day, learning about the fortunes of the many Randle Wilbrahams who have inhabited this country pile (the name, too, of the present owner). Then wander at will in the lovely woodland and formal gardens, which lead to a lake. Don't miss the two-acre walled kitchen garden – produce from which is used in the tea room. If you visit in early spring, check out times for the popular snowdrop walks. Rode Hall is the location of a **regular farmers' market**, which takes place on the first Saturday of every month (⌀ 09.00–13.30). Top factoid: the gardener here holds the world record for the largest gooseberry. Nearby, on the corner of

LET THE KIDS GO WILD

Rode Hall is the home of the performance arts group Wild Rumpus (wildrumpus. org.uk), where the troupe creates the big family-friendly outdoor arts events for which it has become renowned. Wild Rumpus's theatrical experiences take place in wild spaces and Rode Hall itself is one such venue, hosting the annual Just So Festival each August. More outdoor adventure than arts festival, families gather to pitch camp for a weekend and immerse themselves in the magical world of music, comedy, art and literature that takes place in the woods, parkland and around the lake.

Church Lane and Holehouse Lane is **All Saints Church** (during services) designed for the Wilbrahams in late 13th-century style by Sir George Gilbert Scott.

16 MOW COP & AROUND

Castle Camping (page 293)

Mow Cop ST7 3PA 01625 584412 National Trust car park Apr–May 08.00–18.30 daily, Jun–Sep 08.00–20.00 daily, Oct–Mar 08.00–17.00 daily

Presiding over the eastern edge of these flatlands is Mow Cop, a 1,100ft-high hump of sandstone grit apparently crowned by the ruin of an ancient castle. Except, a castle never stood here; this is a folly, a summer house commissioned in 1754 by Randle Wilbraham of Rode Hall to look like a ruin. On a sunny summer's day, I climbed to the summit for a closer inspection, it being at least 40 years since my last visit. I rediscovered the familiar remnants of a round tower with arched and round windows, and an archway that frames a remarkable view of Cheshire, part of a panorama that also takes in the Staffordshire moorlands (in fact, on a clear day, you can see Lancashire, Derbyshire, Shropshire and the Welsh hills). In the silence, broken only by the sound of a bee busy at work and the breeze tousling the grass, it seemed as though the world below had, for a moment, stopped. Yet this contemplative spot has been the subject of bitter legal battles, first an ownership dispute between the Wilbrahams and the Sneyds of Keele Hall and later, in the early 20th century, a stand-off between the then owner, Joe Lovatt, and members of the surrounding communities who

"Presiding over the eastern edge of these flatlands is Mow Cop, a 1,100ft-high hump of sandstone grit apparently crowned by the ruin of an ancient castle."

> ## JUST OVER THE BORDER
> **Biddulph Grange** Biddulph ST8 7SD National Trust. A Victorian horticultural journey around the world at this National Trust-owned landscape garden.
> **Lud's Church** Leek ST13 8TA. A deep legend-filled crevice near Gradbach on the Staffordshire Moorlands.
> **Rudyard Lake** rudyardlake.com. The 18th-century reservoir turned pleasure park where Rudyard Kipling's parents first met.
> **Trentham Gardens** Stoke-on-Trent ST4 8JG trentham.co.uk/trentham-gardens. Parkland and gardens designed by Capability Brown.

protested his decision to quarry the land. Today, it is looked after by the National Trust.

There are other places of interest on the road up Mow Cop from the A34 at Scholar Green. Where Church Street meets Woodcock Lane stands **Saint Luke Mission Church** and **Woodcock's Well School**, a pretty terrace where local children have been educated for more than 150 years. A little further up, on the corner of Woodcock Lane and Primitive Street is the **Primitive Methodist Memorial Chapel**, an austere red-brick building with a wheel window over its door. This is the home of Primitive Methodism, standing on the spot where the first open-air gathering was held by this breakaway group from the Wesleyans (page 127). A carved stone close to the castle also remembers the occasion of the camp. Along a track off Wood Street is the **Old Man O' Mow**, looking out across the landscape. The unusual pile of stones is thought to mark either an ancient cairn or the Cheshire–Staffordshire boundary, which Mow Cop straddles.

> ## CHESHIRE ONLINE
> For additional online content, articles, photos and more on Cheshire, why not visit bradtguides.com/cheshire.

FOLLOW US

Use **#cheshire** to share your adventures using this guide with us – we'd love to hear from you.

- Bradt Travel Guides
- @bradtguides (#cheshire)
- youtube.com/bradtguides
- @BradtGuides & @Traveltappers (#cheshire)
- pinterest.com/bradtguides

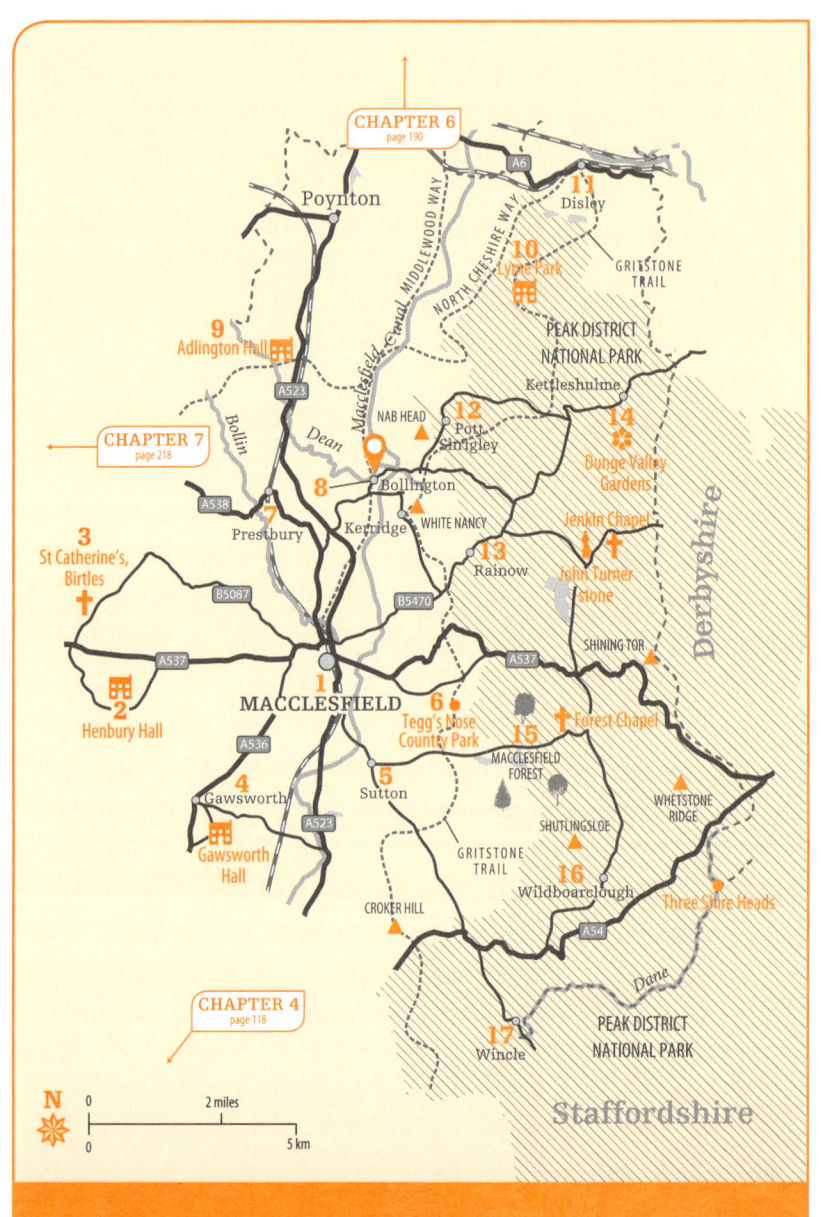

MACCLESFIELD & THE PEAK DISTRICT

5
MACCLESFIELD & THE PEAK DISTRICT

This corner of Cheshire, bumping up against the Pennines, gets gradually wilder the further inland you head. To the west of the Macclesfield Canal it's still gently rolling and pastoral, while to the east things get more extreme. Here, lush green fields and grazing cattle give way to dark wild moors and wind-whipped sheep; pretty villages of half-timbered cottages are replaced with isolated farmsteads of millstone grit; and instead of hedgerows, there are dry stone walls running across the hilltops.

Much of this wilder countryside is part of the Peak District National Park – a fact that may surprise the many who assume the park is contained within the Derbyshire borders. Cheshire's chunk may not be as well-known as the rest but it deserves recognition, including, as it does, one of the county's grandest stately homes (Lyme) in the north and one of its prettiest rivers (the Dane) in the south. In between, there are glorious views from the roads and footpaths that wind across the moors – including the dramatic A537 Cat and Fiddle road between Macclesfield and Buxton – so whether you're travelling by car, bike or on foot, take it slowly and factor in plenty of time to just stop, stare and soak up the peace of this sparsely populated region.

The commercial hub of the area is Macclesfield, where a handful of interesting museums tell tales of the silk trade that made the town's fortunes and left it with a stock of attractive Georgian buildings. In the valleys round about, former small mill or mining towns and villages are now considered desirable places to live, with spruced-up workers' cottages and glorious walking countryside on their doorsteps. Start exploring and you'll find some lovely stately homes and little-known ancient monuments, unusual churches and specialist museums, along with delicious ice cream, great micro-breweries, a large heronry and Cheshire's highest hills.

MACCLESFIELD & THE PEAK DISTRICT

GETTING THERE & AROUND

PUBLIC TRANSPORT

Macclesfield is the area's main transport hub, with a rail station on the West Coast Main Line. Virgin Trains from London and CrossCountry services from Birmingham stop here throughout the day *en route* to Stockport and Manchester. Local trains, operated by Northern, link Macclesfield and other smaller stations with Stoke-on-Trent to the south and Stockport to the north, both of which have connections to east–west lines. Disley is on the Buxton Line linking Manchester and Stockport to Buxton.

A short uphill walk from the train station is Macclesfield bus station, with routes radiating out in all directions – destinations served from here include Buxton, Manchester, Knutsford and Crewe, as well as towns and villages closer to home, such as Bollington, Prestbury, Sutton and Gawsworth. Some have a limited service and may not run on Sundays. For more detailed information and individual bus timetables, check out the Cheshire East council website (cheshireeast.gov.uk).

Realistically, if you want to explore the countryside round here and don't have the time or energy to do it all on foot, you'll need your own transport – and for most, that will mean a car. However, you should be aware that the more rural roads are often steep, narrow, poorly surfaced or muddy – or all four at once. Not great fun for nervous drivers, but passengers are generally too distracted by the fabulous views to care.

WALKING

As you'd expect, the walking here is some of the most challenging the county has to offer, and it pays to be prepared before you go striding off into the hills: come equipped with suitably sturdy footwear, appropriate clothing (the weather can change quickly) and maps (OS Explorer 268 or OL24). Best to take something to eat and drink, too – historic landmark pubs in the area continue to disappear so you never know when the next cosy country inn that you've earmarked for refreshment *en route* will be sold off and converted into private housing.

Clustered together either side of the Cat & Fiddle road (A537), you'll find Cheshire's three highest peaks: Shining Tor (1,1834 feet), Whetstone Ridge (1,795 feet) and Shutlingsloe (1,660 feet). They're all modest even by English standards, but they'll still give your legs a decent stretch, especially if you do a circle round all three on the same day.

Waymarked trails in the area include the 35-mile **Gritstone Trail**, which begins in Disley and winds its hilly way south, taking in many places covered in this chapter, including Lyme Park, Bollington and Tegg's Nose, before crossing over into territory covered in *Chapter 4*. The **North Cheshire Way**, too, starts in Disley and follows a different route through Lyme Park before heading west to Adlington and then into *Chapter 1*. Making the treble for Lyme Park is the ten-mile **Ladybrook Valley Trail**, which begins there and follows a river valley north and west until it meets the Mersey at Cheadle. Further south, the **Dane Valley Way** dips in and out of Cheshire for 41 miles as it runs from Buxton to Middlewich, largely following the river that marks this part of the county boundary. The 25-mile **Salter's Way** devised by marathon walker John Merrill (johnmerrillwalkguides.co.uk) follows old salt tracks through the region, on its way from the Northwich outskirts to Saltersford.

Despite the fact that much of the terrain round here appeals to hardy hillwalkers, the area has plenty to please those who prefer gentler strolls, too: there are scenic walks around lakes and reservoirs, plus round routes from pubs where you can warm up afterwards. Meanwhile, the ten-mile-long **Middlewood Way**, along the bed of an old railway line, offers a largely level route between Macclesfield and Marple. The 27-mile **Macclesfield Canal towpath** (part of the Cheshire Ring Canal Walk) runs roughly parallel, with plenty of opportunity to switch back and forth between the two.

CYCLING

Two main east–west cycle routes pass through this area. Part of the **Cheshire Cycleway** comes through Prestbury and Bollington and curves in a big loop through the hills and moors east of Macclesfield before returning to gentler terrain as it heads back west and south again via Gawsworth. **Regional Route 71** starts at Tegg's Nose Country Park (pages 170–1) and heads 62 miles through the heart of the county to Parkgate. You could ride it in the opposite direction, of course, but then you'd be leaving the toughest bit, the steep uphill climb from Fools Nook to Tegg's Nose, until the end. Running north to south is **National Route 55**, which follows the traffic-free Middlewood Way from Marple down through Bollington to Macclesfield, after which it continues on roads towards Gawsworth, Marton and Congleton.

> ### TOURIST INFORMATION
> **Macclesfield Visitor Information Centre** Town Hall, Market Pl, SK10 1DX ⌀ 01625 378123 ⊙ 09.00–17.00 Mon–Fri, 10.00–16.00 Sat (with slightly shorter hours, Oct–Mar)

BIKE & CANAL-BOAT HIRE
Bollington Boats & Bikes Grimshaw Ln, Bollington SK10 5JB ⌀ 01625 575811 ⌀ bollington-wharf.com. Here, on the banks of the Macclesfield Canal, you can rent sturdy vintage bikes, most of them ex-Post Office, with roomy wicker baskets up front (handy for stowing the picnic hampers the team can source from the local deli). They also have a couple of tandems and mountain bikes – and, as the name suggests, two narrowboats for day hire. The same team organises some interesting trips along the canal, including the odd meditation workshop or bat safari, and masterminds a folk boat festival in September.

MACCLESFIELD & AROUND

The hilly streets of Macclesfield (or Macc, as it's frequently referred to by locals) are filled with history, particularly relating to the boom years of the 18th and early 19th centuries, when it was famed for its silk manufacturing. Not that the town is stuck in the past – in recent years the monthly Treacle Market and revived Barnaby Festival have helped give the old town a welcome injection of new life and confidence. Beyond the suburbs lie attractive rural landscapes, where highlights include the pretty village of Gawsworth and the wonderful views from Tegg's Nose Country Park.

1 MACCLESFIELD
🏠 **Sleep, Eat, Repeat** (page 293)

Macclesfield's historic heart is high on a hill above the River Bollin: narrow cobbled streets converging on Market Place, where St Michael & All Angels, consecrated in 1278, sits next to the old market cross and the Georgian town hall. Central street names give clues to the town's past: a few – Chestergate, Jordangate, Back Wallgate – hark back to its importance in medieval times, while Castle Street is a reminder of the fortified manor house that once stood here, and King Edward Street honours Edward l, who granted Macclesfield its charter in 1261.

It was in the 18th century, though, that Macc really prospered, thanks to its flourishing silk trade. There had long been a cottage industry turning out buttons, made from moulds of holly wood twisted round with threads in intricate patterns. Then, in 1743, local button merchant Charles Roe opened the first silk-throwing mill, and it wasn't long before other mills and factories were popping up all over town, along with new houses and places of worship to cater for the burgeoning population employed in spinning, dyeing and weaving silk. Wandering round the streets today, you'll find a rich legacy of Georgian terraces and chapels, surviving mills and Victorian Gothic churches – and, in the gaps between them, sudden far-reaching views out to the hills.

A wander around town

Having climbed up the hill from the train or bus station, **Market Place** is the perfect spot to start exploring and is particularly lively on the last Sunday of the month, when it's the hub of the **Treacle Market** (page 165). On the east side of the square stands **St Michael's**, which, although clearly much altered since its 13th-century foundation, includes medieval elements, and is known for its fine alabaster effigies. It also has early 20th-century stained glass from the likes of Morris & Co and Christopher Whall. Follow the path along the left side of the church and you'll find the small **Sparrow Park**, with benches and a view. Head a bit further round, behind the church, and you come to the **108 Steps**, one of the town's most famous sights, leading down towards the station. Walk up them without taking a breath, they say, and you'll be granted a wish.

"Walk up the 108 steps without taking a breath, they say, and you'll be granted a wish."

Back in the square, pop in to the Visitor Information Centre (see opposite), next to the town hall, and pick up a copy of the **Macclesfield Heritage Trail**, a walking route around the town centre that explains some of the historical detail of the more interesting buildings. It directs you towards the odd point of interest you might otherwise miss, such as the late 17th-century chapel hidden away down a passageway off King Edward Street, or some lovely Georgian doorways on Sunderland Street. Not included in the trail leaflet, but an easy addition to the walking route, is **Paradise Street**, with a particularly well preserved terrace of weavers' houses: you can identify them by their distinctive third-storey garrets with long windows. Also worth a wander is the **High Street conservation area**, just south of the centre, where you'll find a cluster of handsome former chapels dotted among attractive early industrial housing.

The museums

Between them, Macclesfield's four central museums do a good job of filling you in on the town's history and leading characters (⌁ macclesfieldmuseums.co.uk). The best one to start off with is **The Old Sunday School** (Roe St, SK11 6UT ⊙ 10.00–16.00 Mon–Sat), built in 1814 to provide education for children working in the mills but now home to a heritage centre, complete with café, craft stalls and a good little shop. In the basement a series of display boards provides a potted guide to key events over the centuries, with topical eyewitness quotes adding extra colour here and there. I particularly like the cuttings from the *Macclesfield Courier*'s account of the 'Dreadful Fire' that destroyed Bollin Mill in 1845, relating the tale of a man whose barrowload of potatoes was accidentally roasted, and the news that on Park Green a fragment of hot stone 'burnt a young man's cotton handkerchief to a considerable extent'. The top floor of the building is now home to **Cinemac**, where you can watch the latest film releases in far more characterful surroundings than your average multiscreen. Just bear in mind that the vintage seats (rescued from the old Majestic cinema, when it was demolished) can be a bit hard – you might want to copy regular visitors and take a cushion with you.

"I particularly like the cuttings from the Macclesfield Courier's account of the 'Dreadful Fire', relating the tale of a man whose barrowload of potatoes was accidentally roasted."

A few minutes' walk down the road is **The Silk Museum** (Park Ln, SK11 6TJ ⊙ 10.00–15.00 (16.00 in summer) Mon–Sat), housed in the former School of Art, which numbered the celebrated artist Charles Tunnicliffe among its old pupils. It was originally founded to educate designers for the silk industry and is today dedicated to all things silk, with exhibits covering everything from 18th-century silk buttons to silk escape maps and parachutes used in the Second World War. It also houses an archive of pattern books, gathered together from local textile factories, which show how designs and colourways evolved between the mid 19th and mid 20th centuries.

Next door **Paradise Mill** can only be visited as part of an escorted tour from The Silk Museum so it's worth getting your timings right (⊙ tours noon Mon–Fri, noon & 13.00 Sat), as it's the best way to get a real insight into the life of a textile worker. This was a working mill until

1981 and up on the top floor they have the original (and still working) Jacquard silk hand looms.

Set apart from the other museums on the northwest edge of the town centre is **West Park Museum** (Prestbury Rd, SK10 3BJ ⊙ 13.00–16.00 Wed–Sun (Tue–Sun in summer)), brainchild of Marianne Brocklehurst, one of those indomitable Victorian women with a passion for travel and – thanks to her wealthy, mill-owning father – the funds to indulge it. Over the course of five trips to Egypt in the late 19th century, she amassed a collection of hundreds of ancient Egyptian artefacts and kept illustrated diaries of her adventures; samples of both are among the items on display in the museum today, along with Charles Tunnicliffe artworks and a rather sad but very popular giant panda, inexplicably shot by one of Marianne's descendants. No excuse. In the surrounding park you'll find three Anglo-Saxon cross shafts, brought here from outlying areas and incongruously sited in the children's playground.

FOOD & DRINK

The Button Warehouse Stanley Mill, Stanley St, SK11 6AU ⌀ 01625 433093 ⌀ thebuttonwarehouse.co.uk. This hidden-away wholefoods café serves organic and plant-based dishes in the attractive surroundings of an old mill. They're all about food that's healthy and, as far as possible, locally sourced, so the menu is ever changing but might include veggie burgers, spelt waffles and raw brownies or cheesecake.

The Cheshire Gap Deli 87 Mill St, SK11 6NN ⌀ 01625 425806 ⌀ cheshiregap.com. There's an appealingly old-school feel to this popular deli, just round the corner from the bus station. The shop window and counters are filled with a huge range of cakes, from retro faves such as Bath buns, snowballs and Viennese whirls to traybakes, cheesecakes and assorted cannoli. There's also a wide selection of cheeses plus savoury pies, pates, pasties and quiches, all homemade. You can take out or eat in at one of the dozen or so small tables squeezed into the space.

Lord of the Pies 19 Chestergate, SK11 6BX ⌀ 01625 615752 @lordofthepiesmacc. Like its siblings in Stockport and Chorlton, the Macc outpost of this northwest minichain serves high-quality pies featuring local ingredients such as Cheshire lamb and beef and Macclesfield-brewed beer, while its breakfast rolls are made with bread from local bakers Flour Water Salt. The menu here includes The Macc Pie (ground beef stew, Lyonnaise potatoes and Red Willow ale) and there are veggie or vegan options, too.

The Rustic Coffee Co 2 Church Mews, Churchill Way, SK11 6AY ⌀ 01625 423202 ⌀ rusticcoffee.co. They take their coffee seriously, use compostable packaging for take-outs and make their own cakes – a few of the reasons why this town-centre coffee house is so popular.

The Salt Bar 23b Church St, SK11 6LB 01625 432221 thesaltbarmacclesfield.com. Scandinavia meets Macclesfield in this little Nordic restaurant, where a menu of mostly meaty items includes a couple of veggie and gluten-free options, such as a Scandi Rarebit, made with Swedish Västerbotten cheese and Wincle beer.

The Treacle Tap 43 Sunderland St, SK11 6JL 01625 615938 thebeerparlours.co.uk/the-treacle-tap. Converted from a former saddlery shop, this friendly little micropub/café-bar belongs to the people behind The Young Pretender in Congleton (page 146) and The Old Dancer in Wilmslow (16 Grove St, SK9 1DR 01625 530775). Expect a good choice of local ales and plenty of social events – they host everything from quizzes and craft nights to German conversation or 'Stitch & Bitch' groups.

SHOPPING
Shops

Arighi Bianchi The Silk Rd, SK10 1LH 01625 613333 arighibianchi.co.uk. Passing through Macclesfield on the train you get a prime view of possibly its most famous building: the beautiful, Grade II-listed Arighi Bianchi furniture store, with its handsome façade of large arched windows set in ornamental cast-iron frames. The company itself was started by two Italian craftsmen, Antonio Arighi and Antonio Bianchi, who found their way here from Lake Como in the mid 19th century and built up a highly successful business supplying the northwest's well-to-do with fine furnishings for their homes. When the two Antonios moved premises into an old silk mill here they brought in local builder George Roylance to add this grand new showroom, inspired by London's Crystal Palace, which opened in 1892. Daringly democratic, it supplied 'goods for all classes', with the second floor stocking cheaper furniture for servants' rooms and artisans. In 1970, there were plans to demolish the building to make way for a new ring road. Hurrah then for Sir John Betjeman and the many others who came to the building's defence and saved it from the bulldozers.

Cheshire Fish 4 Roe St, SK11 6UT cheshirefish.co.uk closed Sun & Mon. It may be deep inland but this is a great little fish shop, its ice-packed counters well stocked with the pick of the day's catch, rushed in from ports around the UK – or, in the case of the trout, from the nearby village of Wincle.

The Conscious Bride 9 Church St, SK11 6LB 01625 439235 theconsciousbride.co.uk. The name may be slightly odd but the aim of this little bridal boutique is entirely admirable: it's all about helping people to have as eco-friendly and ethical a wedding as possible. The dresses they stock include fair trade, sustainable and vegan options and they have hair pieces made from upcycled jewellery.

Hadfield 89b Churchill Way (entrance on Stanley St), SK11 6AT 01625 423259 hadfield.since1755. As quirky and characterful as you like, this eclectic little store sells everything from bird seed to bath salts, wax tapers to wind chimes.

Markets
Treacle Market Market Pl, SK10 1EA ⊘ treaclemarket.co.uk ⊙ 10.00–15.30 last Sun of the month. Launched in 2010, this lively monthly market now spills out from the main square into the surrounding streets, with more than 160 stalls selling street food, crafts and vintage items.

FESTIVALS & EVENTS
Barnaby Festival ⊘ barnabyfestival.org.uk. This ten-day celebration of all things artsy and cultural takes place in June every other year, with plans for the 2018 event underway as we went to press. The programme includes a carnival parade, arts trail, live music and assorted installations and spoken-word events.

2 HENBURY HALL
School Ln, SK11 9PJ ℘ 01625 422101 ⊘ henburyhall.co.uk

Catching sight of Henbury Hall from a distance, you'd probably assume it was one of Cheshire's original old stately homes, its grand Neoclassical façade and central dome looking entirely at home in the rolling parkland that surrounds it. However, it's very much a newbie: the 18th-century house that once stood there, riddled with dry rot, was knocked down in 1958 and replaced by the current incarnation in the 1980s. That may not sound immediately promising but have faith: it's an elegant affair, built from creamy French limestone and modelled on Palladio's Villa Capra (or La Rotonda) in Vicenza.

The interior is closed to the public but the 12-acre gardens that surround the house (and predate it by a long way) open to visitors on a handful of dates throughout the year, offering a rare chance to enjoy the woodland walks, spot the dragonflies that hover round the lake and view the recently restored walled garden, complete with its original Georgian peach houses. Keep an eye on the website for forthcoming open days, and keep your fingers crossed that they continue – at the time of writing the whole 530-acre estate had just gone on the market. Yours for a cool £20 million or so . . .

3 ST CATHERINE'S, BIRTLES
Birtles Ln, SK10 4RX

Hidden away down a lane off the main road (A537) between Macclesfield and Knutsford, this parish church was originally built (in 1840) as a private chapel by Thomas Hibbert of nearby Birtles Hall, who set about

MACCLESFIELD & THE PEAK DISTRICT

filling it with the family collection of ecclesiastical antiques, including 16th- and 17th-century roundels from the Netherlands. Simon Jenkins included St Catherine's in *England's Thousand Best Churches*, describing it as 'a veritable treasure trove of fittings acquired from the churches and monasteries of Europe in the wake of the Napoleonic wars'.

4 GAWSWORTH

The Buildings of England give Gawsworth a grand build-up. 'There is,' it says, 'nothing in Cheshire to compare with the loveliness of Gawsworth: three great houses and a distinguished church set around a descending string of pools, all within an enigmatic large-scale formal landscape'. Pevsner wrote those words in 1971 but if he were alive today I doubt he'd see any reason to change his views. You might question it if you ever pass through on the busy Congleton Road, but turn off on to Church Lane, carry on past the little green with its old cross and water pump, and keep going until the road bends sharply to the right and suddenly there all the loveliness is: Gawsworth Hall peeping through the trees and the tower of St James church reflecting in a broad sheet of water.

"Suddenly there all the loveliness is: Gawsworth Hall peeping through the trees."

Two of Nikolaus Pevsner's 'three great houses' are not open to the public, but you can catch glimpses of them as you pass: the 18th-century New Hall, on your left just as the road bends right, and the timber-framed Old Rectory, across the pool from the church. The third, Gawsworth Hall (aka the Old Hall), is also a private home but allows visitors at certain times.

Gawsworth Hall

Church Ln, SK11 9RN ⌔ 01260 223456 ⌔ gawsworthhall.com ⊙ late Jun–late Aug 14.00–17.00 Wed–Sun, & for a few weeks either side of that period (from late May & up to mid-Sep) Sun only

The hall is chocolate-box pretty, a beautifully preserved black-and-white affair with pink and red roses rambling round the latticed windows in summer. It was built in the late 15th century by the Fitton family, lords of the manor from 1316 to 1662, whose monuments are a feature of the neighbouring church. Among their number was Mary Fitton, maid of honour to Queen Elizabeth l and said by some to be the mysterious Dark Lady of Shakespeare's sonnets. Her father, Sir Edward, spent a fortune beautifying the house and gardens in the hope that Mary's connections might prompt a royal visit, but it never came. Instead, his daughter was banished from court after falling pregnant by William Herbert, Earl of Pembroke.

Today, the hall is the lived-in home of the Richards family, responsible for introducing the popular **garden theatre**. It began modestly with a Shakespeare play in the old tilting ground in 1969; now there's a covered stage and seating stand in the sunken garden, and a six-week summer programme of events (⊙ Jun–Aug), including plays, concerts, opera and comedy. On a balmy summer evening it's a magical place to sit and watch a performance, with a backdrop of the Tudor courtyard and rose garden, and fairy lights twinkling in the bushes. Regulars get there early to enjoy a pre-show picnic on the lawn first, setting up their spots in varying degrees of grandeur – everything from a blanket on the grass to a full-on table, chairs and lanterns – before cracking open the hampers and bottles of fizz. A word to the wise: the seats may be protected from summer showers these days, but they're still very hard, so take your own cushions and put them on your chosen seats as soon as you get there. (Banish any embarrassed thoughts of sunbeds and beach towels – there are enough seats for everyone and the system works.) I recommend taking a couple of fleecy blankets as well, just in case the evening turns chilly.

St James the Great

Church Ln, SK11 9RJ gawsworthchurch.co.uk

The altar of this 15th-century church is flanked by some fascinating memorials to the Fytton (or Fitton) family. Oldest of them is the table tomb commemorating Francis Fitton, with a headless, shrouded cadaver beneath his effigy. Elsewhere, there's a mournful-looking Dame Alice Fitton, resting one elbow on her husband's tomb, with statues of her two sons in front of her and two daughters (including Mary) behind. Next to them lie the first baronet and his wife, with effigies of their ten surviving children lined up alongside the chest, accompanied by one other little figure, unpainted and frustratingly unidentified.

Maggotty's Wood

Some 500 yards north of Gawsworth Hall, on the corner of Church Lane and Maggoty Lane, is a little spinney, where a few minutes' walk through the beech trees brings you to a brick-built tomb, topped with an engraved stone slab. This is the burial place of Samuel 'Maggotty' Johnson, 18th-century actor, musician and playwright, possibly Britain's last professional jester, and certainly the former dancing master at Gawsworth Hall. Unusually, the grave comes with two inscriptions: on top of the tomb is the original 1773 inscription Johnson chose for himself, jesting as it rhymes; next to it is another, added in 1851 by a disapproving vicar, who clearly considered Johnson's levity ill-judged:

> 'A thoughtless jester even in his death,
> Uttering his jibes beyond his latest breath...
> Look on that stone and this, and ponder well,
> Then choose twixt Life and Death,
> Heaven and Hell.'

Perhaps Maggotty had the last laugh. It's said that on summer evenings his ghost can be seen dancing down the street. No, I haven't seen it.

5 SUTTON

The Ryles Arms (page 293)

Sutton parish, on the southeastern outskirts of Macclesfield, includes the attractive villages of Sutton Lane Ends and Langley and the neighbouring hamlet of Gurnett, where canal builder **James Brindley** was once a young apprentice. As you head into Sutton along Byrons Lane, shortly after passing under the Macclesfield Canal (one of Telford's rather than Brindley's), there's a cottage with a plaque above the garage recording the fact that this is where Brindley served his apprenticeship to Abraham Bennett, a millwright, between 1733 and 1740.

He isn't Sutton's only famous former resident: another stone plaque, at Lane Ends Farm on Walker Lane, marks the childhood home of artist **Charles Tunnicliffe**, and Sutton Hall (see opposite) is said to have been the birthplace of **Raphael Holinshed**, the 16th-century scholar whose *Chronicles of England, Scotland and Ireland* provided the source for many of Shakespeare's history plays.

The area was once known for its silk production, but these days it has more pubs than mills and you could do a good round walk stringing them all together and lunching *en route* at whichever takes your fancy. The 14 bus from Macclesfield stops near **Church House** (Church Ln, SK11 0DS 01260 252436 churchhouse.pub) with its beer garden, children's play area and local cask ales. From here, it's less than a mile's walk along Langley Road to the **St Dunstan Inn** (Main Rd, SK11 0BU 🕾 01260 252615 🔗 stdunstaninn.co.uk), in the middle of a row of terraced cottages at Langley. There's no kitchen here but licensees Will and Sarah are happy for people to bring in their own food or order in a take-away.

Next leg, again just under a mile, heads along Clarke Lane, passing beneath Tegg's Nose on the left, to **Leather's Smithy** (page 186) at Macclesfield Forest. Then it's onwards and upwards, surrounded by rolling countryside and following the Gritstone Trail for most of the way, to **The Ryles Arms** (Hollin Ln, SK11 0NN 🕾 01260 252244 🔗 rylesarms. com) at Higher Sutton, where the meaty menu is big on steaks and burgers but also includes fresh trout from nearby Danebridge Fisheries. From here, it's downhill back to Sutton, where, as you re-enter the village, you find **The Sutton Gamekeeper** (13 Hollin Ln, SK11 0HL 🕾 01260 252000 🔗 thesuttongamekeeper.co.uk), set back from the road on your right. Once the Lamb Inn, it's been given a new lease of life thanks to a recent makeover: expect rustic-chic shades of grey, a real fire, candles on the tables and Cheshire ales and gin behind the bar.

Heading north into the village, past the war memorial and along Hall Lane, you'll find a little path on the left by Rossendale Brook. Follow it, first along the brook then veering right across a field (noticing on your left the remains of a Bronze Age barrow), and you reach a drive, where a left turn brings you out on to Bullocks Lane. Turn right, and it's just a few yards to the entrance to **Sutton Hall** (Bullocks Ln, SK11 0HE 🕾 01260 253211 🔗 brunningandprice.co.uk/suttonhall), well on the way to celebrating its 500-year anniversary. In the past it's been a manor house and a convent; now it's one of the Brunning & Price group's characterful pubs, with plenty of little rooms and cosy corners where you can hide yourself away. From here, turn right out of the drive and right again when you get to Byrons Lane and in 10 minutes' time you'll be at **Ye Olde Kings Head** (30 Bradley Smithy, Byrons Ln, SK11 0HD 🕾 01625 611444 🔗 yeoldekingsheadgurnett1695.co.uk), built in 1695 and named after James ll, who features in one of the stained-glass windows. The pub is right next to the Macclesfield Canal, so you could join the towpath here and walk into central Macclesfield. Alternatively, a half-mile stroll along Byrons Lane and Jarman Lane will bring you back round to your starting point at the church, to catch the 14 bus back.

6 TEGG'S NOSE COUNTRY PARK

Buxton Old Rd, SK11 0AP teggsnose.co.uk

This popular country park, on the site of an old stone quarry, is one of the most accessible places to enjoy the hill country thanks to the fact it has a proper car park and a visitor centre, complete with tea room and a small gallery where local artists exhibit their works. It's a good place to walk at any time of year, but each season brings extra attractions to add to the ever-present stellar views. In spring there are lambs in the fields, in summer, colourful displays of delicate yellow mountain pansies; in autumn there are winberries to be picked and in winter, slopes to be sledged.

From the visitor centre there's an easy-to-follow two-mile **circular trail** around the hilltop with wonderful views along the way and the odd information board to help you identify major landmarks. Follow the sandy walled path across fields then take the left-hand fork; it brings you to the main quarry face, where you can clearly see layers of the millstone grit that was extracted here from Tudor times right up until 1955. Today nature has reclaimed its territory, with purple heather covering the old spoil heaps, but there are some pieces of old machinery left to remind you of more industrial times. When the Americans arrived during the Second World War, they brought pneumatic drills to help quarry rock for airfield runways – a move much welcomed by the locals, as the previous blasting method used to send rocks flying across the valley and landing in the nearby farms.

Continue along the trail beyond the machines for a few minutes and look out for a little path off to the left, which leads to a bench with a view across to Ridgegate Reservoir and Macc Forest, with Shutlingsloe popping up behind them. It's not the only bench with a view (you'll find several of them dotted around the park) but it *is* the only one that comes with a 'Library in the Landscape' – a mini bookcase on a pole, so if the view alone isn't enough, you can choose something to read while you're there.

At the southernmost point of the circular route, a path leads down to a viewing area with a fabulous outlook over the butterfly-shaped twin reservoirs at Langley to a patchwork of green fields and trees leading up to the telecoms tower on top of Sutton Common/Croker Hill and, to the right of the ridge, the Cheshire plain stretching away to the horizon.

Back on the main track, the path curves back around to return to the car park but detour *en route* to climb up to the summit of Tegg's Nose, where you'll find the gate/bench/toposcope created by sculptor, Reece Ingram. It's a drystone wall circle, with a wooden bench seat inside and aluminium rings set around the top stones, where you can look through little peepholes to focus on specific landmarks, such as Mow Cop, Alderley Edge and Kinder Scout.

The Gritstone Trail passes through the park and there are longer circular walks too, including one that goes across the valley to Macc Forest and round the reservoirs. Just bear in mind that they end with a steep slog back up Tegg's Nose on the way back …

NORTH OF MACCLESFIELD

To the north, Macclesfield's growing suburbs reach almost to the prosperous village of Prestbury (beloved of Premier League footballers) and the down-to-earth former mill town of Bollington. Between here and Poynton, the A523, West Coast main line and Macclesfield Canal wend their way up towards the Stockport borders, the River Dean careers in drunken squiggles across the fields and the narrow lanes criss-crossing the largely flat rural landscape are shared between flash cars from pricey private homes and tractors from working farms.

7 PRESTBURY

⌂ **Legh Arms** (page 293)

Long a byword for affluence, Prestbury is (along with Alderley Edge and Wilmslow) one point of the 'Golden Triangle' – estate agent speak for a millionaire belt that's a favourite place for footballers, pop stars and wealthy business folk to buy their mansions. Or, more likely, knock down the mansions already there and build new ones with the requisite home cinema, pool and games room. The leafy roads around the village are lined with their huge, and hugely expensive, homes, well hidden from prying eyes by high hedges and electric gates. All of which would be understandable reason to give it a wide berth, were it not for the fact that at the heart of it all is an attractive village centre that's worth a wander for those who aren't too worried about damaging their Louboutin heels on the old flagstones and cobbles.

To the south of the River Bollin, which flows through the centre, is the parish church of **St Peter**, sitting pretty in the middle of an attractive churchyard, where drifts of snowdrops and crocuses cover the graves in early spring. You get two for the price of one here – not just the main church, with its blend of 13th-, 14th- and 15th-century elements (and a 19th-century restoration planned by Sir George Gilbert Scott), but also its predecessor, a small Norman chapel. Set slightly back on the southeast side of the church, the chapel has been much repaired and remodelled over the years but retains its original, very weathered, 12th-century arched doorway. There's a relic of an even older church here too: fragments of a Saxon cross, discovered in the masonry of the chancel in the mid 19th century and now reassembled.

Stepping back on to the high street (called The Village) you're faced with a pretty prospect: handsome Georgian townhouses and, between them, the black-and-white Priest's House – a Jacobean building that until recently provided handsome premises for a branch of NatWest, but is now being converted to residential use. Along the churchyard wall there are wooden benches where you can sit and enjoy the village scene; the stocks are here too, along with that very English twosome: a red phone box and matching pillar box. At the southern end of the street is a row of weavers' cottages curving round the corner; the 18th-century Prestbury Hall, mostly hidden behind trees; and, to the right of it, the old school house, now a bank and Prestbury Library, with an impressive display of 'Best Kept Village' plaques on its wall.

Heading in the opposite direction takes you across the Bollin on to New Road, where an old tree trunk has been carved into a sculpture of two nesting herons and a picturesque row of stone-roofed, whitewashed cottages on the left faces the village green, Parrott's Field, on the right. If you turn left here on to Bollin Grove, past attractive old cottages, you can join the Bollin Valley Way and follow it along the river to Macclesfield in one direction or Wilmslow and beyond in the other.

FOOD & DRINK

There are several places to eat, including the Grade II-listed pubs that top and tail the main street: at the northern end, the 17th-century **Admiral Rodney** (⌂ robinsonsbrewery.com), all cosy little rooms and low ceilings; at the other, the older and larger **Legh Arms** (⌂ legharmsprestbury.pub), an Elizabethan building with plenty of old wooden beams, and seven guest bedrooms above the pub. Diagonally over the road from the Legh Arms is **The Chocolate Box Café** (✆ 01625 820268 TheChocolateBoxPrestbury), an independent family-run venture that's open seven days a week for breakfast fry-ups, light lunches, afternoon teas and homemade cakes, all served up on mismatched vintage china.

NORTH OF MACCLESFIELD

8 BOLLINGTON

Four miles north of Macclesfield and just outside the Peak District National Park boundary, the old mill town of Bollington stretches out along the valley floor and up the hill towards the pretty village of Kerridge. Don't be misled by the name: it's not the River Bollin winding its way through the centre but the River Dean, *en route* to join forces with the Bollin in Wilmslow. The **Macclesfield Canal** runs straight through town too, carried on top of a mighty stone embankment, as does the **Middlewood Way**, a former railway line that closed in 1970 and is now a popular track for walkers, cyclists and horseriders (see box, pages 176–7).

Today's Bollington was born during the Industrial Revolution, a collection of neighbouring hamlets gradually merging together to form a town when sheep farming gave way to cotton spinning, stone

BOLLINGTON'S PUB CULTURE

One of Bollington's big claims to fame has always been its abundance of pubs, and while some have closed down in recent years, the locals still have a respectable choice of places to pop into for a quick pint. Some are instantly visible as you wander along the main street, including the **Holly Bush** (75 Palmerston St, SK10 5PW ℰ 01625 574573), Grade II-listed as a fine example of interwar 'Brewer's Tudor' architecture. Two of the best, though – both freehouses, both big on community involvement, and both walker- and dog-friendly – are hidden away on side streets.

Head to the eastern edge of the village to find **The Poacher's Inn** (95 Ingersley Rd, SK10 5RE ℰ 01625 572086 ♂ thepoachers.org), which sits at the end of a row of terraced cottages at the foot of Blaze Hill. The Gritstone Trail passes within 350 yards of the front door and it's a popular place for walkers and cyclists to stop off to refuel. There's an open fire in winter and a beer garden for summer, the bar serves local real ales and interesting gins, and evening events range from quiz nights and live music to a monthly wild food supper club in collaboration with a local foraging group.

Also forming part of a terraced row, **The Vale Inn** (29–31 Adlington Rd, SK10 5JT ℰ 01625 575147 ♂ valeinn.co.uk) is just across the road from the steps leading up to the viaduct that carries the Middlewood Way across the valley (see box, pages 176–7). The pub serves real ales from its own microbrewery, The Bollington Brewing Co, as well as other guest ales and real ciders. It also sponsors the local cricket club, organises an annual fell race, and plays host to a variety of local organisations and events, including a Sip and Knit group and SciBar, with guest speakers and debates on scientific subjects.

quarrying and coal mining as the main sources of employment. There's no coal mining any more, of course, but the fawn-grey Kerridge stone is still quarried up on Kerridge Ridge and a few of the old cotton mills remain. Rather handsome beasts they are, too, now that they've been suitably spruced up and repurposed. Bookending the canal to the south and north of town are the **Adelphi Mill** (Grimshaw Ln), home to dozens of small businesses, and **Clarence Mill** (Clarence Rd), converted into apartments, offices and the local radio station. The latter also houses the **Discovery Centre** (@BollingtonDiscoveryCentre ⊖ 13.30–16.00 Wed, 11.00–16.00 w/ends), where you can learn all about the history of the town and the people who manned the mills.

Bollington's always been more down to earth than nearby Prestbury, Wilmslow and Alderley. While they spent the 20th century getting ever swankier, Bollington stayed closer to its industrial roots, perhaps because the majority of its housing stock was made up of small terraced cottages rather than big detached villas. Today, though, especially in the part of the conservation area around **Market Place**, those stone terraces are looking increasingly smart, with chic chalky colours painted on front doors framed by flourishing hanging baskets. Walking the triangle formed by Water Street, Palmerston Street and High Street makes for a pleasant stroll, taking in the small memorial gardens and coronation gardens *en route*.

White Nancy

High up on Kerridge Hill, visible for miles around, sits White Nancy, a conical stone monument built by the Gaskell family in 1817 to commemorate the British victory at the Battle of Waterloo a couple of years earlier. Originally it was possible to sit inside, with a seat running round the wall and a central round table, but the entrance has long been blocked up.

The landmark serves as a symbol of Bollington, its likeness featuring on everything from the town council website to keyrings, mugs and other items for sale at the Love Bollington Market (page 178). Usually pristine white, it occasionally gets a special makeover to commemorate a particular event or anniversary such as the London Olympics, the Queen's Diamond Jubilee or, in May 2017, the Manchester Arena attack when, in sympathy with the victims, it was painted with Manchester's symbol, a worker bee.

If you come up here following the most direct way from the town centre, try looping round west on your return, so you can take in the pretty conservation-area village of Kerridge on the way back down.

Walks around Bollington

Bollington became Cheshire's first 'Walkers Are Welcome' town in 2013 – entirely fitting for a town that's surrounded by good rambling country. One of its big attractions is the fact that it caters to different levels of walker, whether you prefer the challenge of the Peak District hills to the east or the flatter terrain of the Middlewood Way and Macclesfield Canal to the north and south. It's easy to find details of local routes, too: the town council website (⌀ bollington-tc.gov.uk) has a useful page of links to trails and walking groups, and down on the ground you can pick up leaflets and parish path maps at both the Discovery Centre (see opposite) and the **Bridgend Centre** (104 Palmerston St, SK10 5PW ⌀ 01625 576311). The latter also serves as the main information point for the annual **Bollington Walking Festival** (late September/early October), which features an ever-growing programme of special guided walks and social events.

Among the leaflets available is one that will guide you up to White Nancy (see opposite), the classic Bollington walk; it's a steep slog but one that rewards you with marvellous views from the top. You'll get even better views, though, if you climb **The Nab**, a slightly higher hill on the other side of the valley. Follow Shrigley Road east from Bollington, turn left in to Beeston Mount, then right into Cocksheadhey Road. Continue through the gate at the end and follow the drive to the end, then cross a stile and follow the path up to the barrow and trig point at the top, where there's a 360° panorama, including south to White Nancy.

FOOD & DRINK

Belfield's Village Bakery 80 Palmerston St, SK10 5PW ⌀ 01625 572397 ⊖ closed Sun. For the best part of three decades, this village stalwart has been baking its own pies, fresh bread and cakes, as well as selling a few other staples.

Café Waterside Clarence Mill, Clarence Rd, SK10 5JZ ⌀ 01625 575563 @cafewaterside. On the ground floor of Clarence Mill, this easy-going café has a menu of soups, sandwiches, salads and the odd more substantial dish, plus a decked outdoor seating area overlooking

MACCLESFIELD & THE PEAK DISTRICT

A walk along the Middlewood Way & Macclesfied Canal

OS Explorer map 268; start: Adlington Rd, SJ931780; 2½ miles; easy, along footpath, towpath & (briefly) minor roads

The beauty of combining the Middlewood Way and Macclesfield Canal in a circular walk is that it's endlessly flexible, and can be as long or as short as you want it to be. The route described here is a short one but if you want to walk further you can just extend it at either or both ends – the path and canal run close together for much of their length, making it easy to switch and swap from one to the other. Go to cheshireeast.gov.uk to download a copy of the Middlewood Way leaflet, which also includes details of the canal path. Apart from a few access steps, this route is largely flat, making it perfect if you're after a gentle stroll rather than a more taxing climb.

If you're driving, park in the cark park on Adlington Road (SK10 5HG). If arriving by bus, get off at the stop by the Arts Centre and walk along Wellington Road towards the Dog & Partridge, where a sign points left on to Adlington Road, with the car park on your left.

1 From the car park, take the flight of steps up on to the viaduct, which brings you out on to the Middlewood Way. Turn right and head north along the path until you come to bridge 8 (Holehouse Ln).

2 Come off the path here and up on to the road. If you turn left here, the Windmill Inn (Holehouse Ln, Whiteley Green SK10 5SJ 01625 574 222 thewindmill.info) is just a short distance down the road. It serves a selection of local ales and is a popular stop for a pub lunch, especially in summer, when you can take advantage of the large beer garden, and kids can have fun exploring the small windmill-shaped maze. Otherwise head right and it's only about a minute's walk to the canal.

3 Go down on to the towpath to the right and head back towards Bollington. Before too long, you'll come to Clarence Mill on your left, a large 19th-century cotton mill.

4 At this point you can cross over the bridge to the other side to visit the Discovery Centre (page

the canal, making it a good place to stop off for refreshments mid-stroll or after a visit to the Discovery Centre.

The Green 15 High St, SK10 5PH 01625 576691 @TheGreenBollington closed Tue. This small independent cafe is a very popular spot for brunch or lunch and also opens for the occasional pop-up night. The short but appealing menu of home-cooked food includes smashed hash browns, pancakes and toasted sourdough with assorted toppings.

174) or just have a coffee and cake at Café Waterside (page 175). Then, suitably refreshed, carry on, past houseboats moored up, and look left to catch a glimpse of White Nancy high on the hill (page 174).

5 Continue along the canal as it crosses over Palmerston Street, then past houses with gardens that come down to the water, and soon, on your right, you'll see another big mill, the Adelphi, and some metal railings.

6 Come off the towpath at the gate just before the mill and go down the steps on to Grimshaw Lane, then turn left and walk for a short distance, past Bailey Business Park on the right, until you reach a grassy area on your right, signposted Middlewood Way.

7 Turn right on the footpath here, with a finger post pointing to Higher Poynton. You'll soon pass the labyrinth on your right, a stone circle maze that was created for the Bollington Festival in 2009. Carry on, under a bridge then over a bridge (crossing the main road) and then you'll be back where you started, on the viaduct by the skate park, where going down the steps will return you to Adlington Road. The Vale Inn (see box, page 173) is a very short distance up the road on your right if you're ready for a post-walk drink.

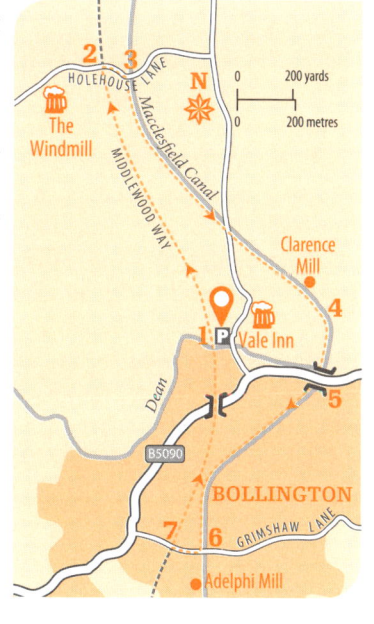

Lime Tree Bollington 18–20 High St, SK10 5PH ⌀ 01625 578182 ⌀ limetreebollington. co.uk ⊙ closed Mon. They don't just use locally sourced meats at this family-run restaurant – they go one better and rear their own livestock. The family farm, keeps the kitchen supplied with free-range eggs, lamb, beef and rare-breed pork. They also have an in-house baker producing the breads and pastas. Converted from two Victorian shops, the space is divided into different restaurant and wine bar areas, and there's a terrace garden for sunny days.

No 74 Delicatessen 74 Palmerston St, SK10 5PW ✆ 01625 573648 ⓕ @no74deli.co.uk ⊘ closed Sun & Mon. Locally produced goodies on the shelves at this deli/café include delicious bread from Macclesfield's Flour Water Salt bakery, Burt's cheeses from Ollerton and Bollington honey.

MARKETS

The monthly **Love Bollington Market** (ⓕ @LoveBollingtonMarket) takes place on the second Sunday of every month apart from January. The venue varies (keep an eye on their Facebook page to see where the next one is) but there's always a good mixture of craft and food stalls.

9 ADLINGTON HALL

Mill Ln, SK10 4LF ✆ 01625 827595 ⌖ adlingtonhall.com ⊘ Apr–Sep 14.00–17.00 Sun & bank hols. Private tours for groups of 20 or more can be arranged year round.

Adlington isn't as well-known as other Cheshire halls, possibly because it's still very much a family home (successive generations of Leghs have lived here for more than 700 years) and has very restricted opening hours, with public access on only 28 days a year. Time your Cheshire trip right, though, and you're in for a treat. The house itself is a beautiful blend of different architectural eras, from the handsome herringbone timber framing of the Elizabethan east wing to the classic Georgian lines of the red-brick south front, added in the mid 18th century. The Tudor part of the building underwent a substantial restoration a few years ago, taking the oak beams back to their more historically accurate brown colouring, rather than tarring them black as the Victorians did.

"The jewel in the Adlington crown is the medieval Great Hall."

The jewel in the Adlington crown is the medieval Great Hall, a neck-cricking space where you'll need to lean well back to appreciate the handsome hammerbeam roof, supported by doleful angels, and the elaborate oak canopy painted with the shields of leading Cheshire families. Built into the east wall, two carved oak trunks, still rooted in the ground, support a gallery housing the grand 17th-century organ, topped by trumpeting angels and a unicorn head and said to have been played by Handel, who was a friend of the family.

The hall is surrounded by a 2,000-acre estate, around 60 acres of which have been transformed into attractive landscaped gardens. On one side of the house, a laburnum arcade leads through to a formal rose garden and neatly clipped yew tree maze. Make it to the centre of the maze and you'll find another unicorn waiting for you – it's the family symbol so you see them popping up here and there as you wander round. On the other side of the hall, heading towards the back of the estate, along a lime tree walk, you'll come to The Wilderness, a woodland area on the banks of the Dean, with the odd folly dotted around and, in spring, a thick haze of bluebells beneath the trees.

Just over a mile east of the hall, on the other side of Adlington, there's a complete contrast on the architectural front: a tin tabernacle. A tiny corrugated iron church erected in Victorian times and only ever intended to be temporary, **St John's** is still going strong today and can be found at the junction of Brookledge Lane and Roundy Lane.

PEAK DISTRICT NATIONAL PARK

Most people are surprised to find that part of the Peak District National Park lies within Cheshire, generally believing the park to be a purely Derbyshire affair. Cheshire's is, admittedly, a fairly small chunk, amounting to just over 34 of the total 555 square-mile park area. That said, it manages to cram plenty of scenic variety into that space, from the stately surroundings of Lyme Park to the natural beauty of the Dane Valley.

10 LYME PARK

East Lodge (page 293)
Disley SK12 2NX National Trust year round but opening times for house & gardens vary; check website for details

On the northernmost tip of Cheshire's Peak District, just within the national park boundaries, sits one of Cheshire's grandest stately homes, surrounded by a glorious 1,400-acre estate. This is the place to come on days when you need to blow the cobwebs away; it's stirring stuff, striding across the parkland and soaking up the far-reaching views across hills and moors and down to the Cheshire Plain.

For many, that's the main attraction – wandering free in the wide open spaces, picnicking, flying kites and looking out for the resident red deer – but it's far from the only one. There's the hall itself, handsome formal gardens, an adventure play area in the woods, and an imaginative programme of events throughout the year, from historical re-enactments and themed afternoon teas to author talks and guided walks.

You can also go in search of locations seen on screen: Lyme is often used as a filming backdrop, most famously serving as Pemberley in the BBC's 1995 adaptation of *Pride and Prejudice*. This is where Colin Firth as Mr Darcy took his famous dip in the lake, and the self-guided Pemberley Walk (downloadable from the website) will lead you to that and other familiar spots.

"Lyme is often used as a filming backdrop: this is where Colin Firth as Mr Darcy took his famous dip in the lake."

Before being transferred to the National Trust in 1946, the estate was the property of the Legh family for nearly 550 years (having been granted to the first Piers Legh by Richard ll in 1398), and the **mansion** that stands here today has evolved gradually since the family first made Lyme its main home in the late 16th century. Entrance is via the classical north façade, which has at its heart an Elizabethan frontispiece, topped by a lead statue of Minerva. If it doesn't look quite as you expected that's because the image usually shown in photos of Lyme is the monumental south front on the other side of the hall, added in the 18th century, which stretches either side of a grand Ionic portico, overlooked by figures of Neptune, Venus and Pan.

There's much to see inside the house, and no space here to cover it in detail, but highlights include the richly ornamented **Drawing Room**, with its intricately patterned plaster ceiling, beautiful stained-glass windows and 17th-century oak panelling. In the **Stag Parlour**, look up to see a frieze running round the top of the room depicting the life of a stag; in the **Saloon**, where the walls are festooned with fine lime wood carvings by Grinling Gibbons, ask nicely and the staff will open up the French windows so you can step out onto the balcony and look over the gardens.

Treasures in the **Library** include the Sarum Missal, a pre-Reformation prayer book printed in Paris in 1487 by William Caxton and considered the most important book in the National Trust collection. Naturally enough, you won't get to handle the book itself, but there are a couple of facsimiles you can flick through and a virtual version you can view on one of the well-camouflaged PCs.

Last but not least, there's the **North Dressing Room** (◯ 11.00–15.00 Fri–Tue), filled with dozens of outfits and accessories created by a team of dedicated volunteers working from authentic period patterns. The exact clothing era changes every few years, to fit in with the displays and themes in the house, but at the time of writing you can dress the whole family up in Regency garb, complete with feathered bonnets, top hats and fans, and stay in costume as you wander round the house.

For a reduced admission fee, you can skip the house and just enter the **gardens**, part formal and part naturalised, which are laid out on three sides of the hall. My preferred route would be to turn right as you step through the south entrance and wander round in an anti-clockwise circle. That way, you start with views over the **Dutch Garden** (where box-edged beds filled with spring and summer bedding create intricate colourful patterns around a fountain pool), then head round the south side of the **lake**, which, on still clear days, frames a photogenic reflection of the house. Carry on round to find a rhododendron walk, a deep ravine filled with lush greenery, herbaceous borders and, as you come back towards the house, an Edwardian rose garden and formal terrace. Near here, beside the path, is a weeping silver linden, which you might pass unnoticed unless you happen to be there in summer, when its pale yellow flowers fill the air with the most beautiful fragrance.

11 DISLEY

Disley Hall (page 293)

One of two 'Walkers Are Welcome' towns in Cheshire (the other is Bollington, pages 173–8), Disley is just outside the national park but as the gateway to Lyme Park this feels like the right place to include it, alongside its most famous attraction. Its appeal as a village is undeniably spoiled by the fact that the busy A6 thunders right through the middle but it's still easy to see why people choose to live here, with its handsome buildings, beautiful countryside all around, and the Peak Forest Canal and River Goyt running through the valley below.

"It's easy to see why people choose to live here, with its handsome buildings, beautiful countryside all around, and the Peak Forest Canal and River Goyt running through the valley below."

At the central crossroads, there's a chunky 19th-century fountain, a war memorial and a large coaching inn, the Ram's Head, with a mounting block by the door and a carved ram's head (the crest of the Legh family) above the porch. The bicycle sculpture on the green in front of the pub is a tribute to cyclists Dame Sarah Storey and her husband Barney, Disley residents who've won 14 Paralympic gold medals between them. (The wall post box next to the post office is painted gold in their honour, too.)

Take the road to the left of the pub and it leads you up, past the castellated old schoolhouse, to the village church of **St Mary the Virgin**, hidden away behind a screen of mature trees. There's some good stained glass inside, including 16th-century windows from a Bavarian abbey, and if you walk through the churchyard to the other side you'll find a little memorial garden and a spring where the annual well dressing is held. Beyond that, walking half a mile along Red Lane brings you to a side entrance to Lyme Park.

Heading out of town on the Buxton Old Road, there are two points of interest that most visitors understandably miss. The first, directly opposite the end of Dane Hill Close, is a private house, which until recently was the **Ploughboy** pub, frequented by Dylan Thomas when he came to Higher Disley to stay with historian A J P Taylor in the 1930s. A lecturer at Manchester University at the time, Taylor and his wife Margaret had bought a house a little further up the hill and when Taylor became perturbed by the rapid rate at which his house guest was depleting his beer stocks, Thomas headed down the road to this, the nearest pub, instead. Author Christopher Isherwood used to drink here too – he was born nearby and namechecked 'the

MADE FOR WALKING

Growing up in this hilly region makes for strong legs, so it's maybe not so surprising that some locals have been happy to take on long-distance walking challenges.

In Disley, St Mary contains the grave of **Joseph Watson**, who spent 64 years of his life as park-keeper at Lyme and in 1710, as the parish website records, 'drove 12 brace of stags from Lyme to Windsor as a present for Queen Anne to win a 500 guinea wager for his master'. Nearly 300 years later, Lyme's then head warden **Emily Orford** followed in his footsteps (though without the 24 stags), raising £23,000 in sponsorship to help fund the restoration of two derelict landscape ponds on the estate.

Also not afraid of tackling the long road south was **Joseph Edge** of Macclesfield. In 1860, at the age of 62, he made a bet that he could walk the 172 miles from his home town to London in 50 successive hours – and proceeded to do just that, leaving the Market Place at noon and arriving in the City, not far from St Paul's, 49 hours and 20 minutes later. Another Macclesfield native, **John Alcock**, went for difficulty rather than distance: in 1875 he walked from Macc to Buxton in 2 hours 43 minutes – going backwards all the way. And once wasn't enough: 27 years later he did it again. It took him half an hour longer the second time around but given that he was 62 at the time, that seems fair enough.

little pub called The Ploughboy, which I used in *A Single Man*' in his 1960s diaries.

Carry on up the road for 1½ miles (with beautiful valley views opening up as you crest the hill), and you come to a sign marking the Derbyshire county border. A few yards behind it, set into the wall on your left, is one of the hill country's roadside curiosities: the '**Murder Stone**'. It marks the spot where William Wood, a weaver from Eyam, was robbed and killed on 16 July 1823 by three men who followed him from Disley as he was walking home after a successful day's trading at market in Manchester the day before. A memorial service held here shortly afterwards brought a crowd of at least 2,000 people to this remote spot; between them, they raised a collection of £4 10s 4d for the widow and three children William left behind. For a full account of the sorry tale, visit ⌂ stevelewis.me.uk.

FOOD & DRINK

Malt Disley 22 Market St, SK12 2AA ✆ 01663 308020 ⌂ maltdisley.co.uk. Disley's first micro-pub is converted from a former homewares shop, which still makes an appearance here now and again as a pop-up outlet, perhaps in the run-up to Christmas or Mother's Day. Beer is the big thing, with a good, ever-changing selection of ales from local brewers to drink in or take out, but they also stock traditional ciders, wines and spirits.

12 POTT SHRIGLEY

Just north of Bollington, three valleys meet at this pretty little hamlet, where a handful of attractive stone cottages cluster round a church, a school and a cricket pitch with a view. It's sleepy and scenic – but nearly 200 years ago it was in the limelight, as Georgian England was gripped by the unfolding drama of a scandal that made national headlines: the Shrigley Abduction.

In 1826, Ellen Turner, 15-year-old only child of wealthy William Turner of Shrigley Hall, was abducted from her Liverpool boarding school by 30-year-old Edward Gibbon Wakefield, who duped her into travelling to Gretna Green and marrying him – something he'd already done once before with another wealthy young heiress – before taking her over the channel to Calais. Her father pursued them; Ellen was rescued, the marriage annulled, and Wakefield and his accomplices imprisoned. After his release, he went on to become a major force in the colonisation of New Zealand, eventually dying there at the ripe old age of 66. Ellen didn't fare so well: at the age of 17 she was married again, to Thomas Legh of Lyme Hall, and died in childbirth two years later.

FOOD & DRINK

Coffee Tavern Shrigley Rd, SK10 5SE ⌀ 01625 576370 @TheCoffeeTavernPottShrigley ⊙ closed Tue. A little north of the village, on the road to Middlewood, this quaint tin shack was built to mark Queen Victoria's Golden Jubilee in 1887 and once housed a reading room and lending library. It's a popular stop-off for cycling groups, so don't be surprised to find yourself surrounded by a sea of sporty Lycra as you order from a menu that includes fry-ups, oatcakes, toasties and homemade cakes.

13 RAINOW & SALTERSFORD

Common Barn Farm (page 293), **Robin Hood Inn** (page 293), **Cheshire Hunt Holiday Cottages** (page 293), **Kerridge End Cottages** (page 293)

Like Pott Shrigley, **Rainow** sits right on the border of the national park, with one of the familiar millstone boundary markers just down the road from the Robin Hood pub. Within its far-reaching parish is the rather eerie **Saltersford**, home to a lonely chapel and a chilling roadside monument. **Jenkin Chapel** (officially St John the Baptist) is about as isolated as a church can be, standing all on its own at a meeting place of ancient trackways high up in the hills. Built in the early 18th century, it looks for the most part like one of the local farmhouses (complete with chimney and normal windows), with just a small tower and the graveyard marking it out as an ecclesiastical building.

About a mile southwest of the church, on Ewrin Lane, you'll find the **John Turner stone**, with its haunting inscription. On one side it reads, 'Here John Turner was cast away in a heavy snow storm in the night in or about the year 1755'; on the other, enigmatically, 'The print of a womans [sic] shoe was found by his side in the snow were [sic] he lay dead'. No wonder it fired the imagination of novelist Alan Garner, resulting in his 2003 novel, *Thursbitch* – a poetic tale of this landscape and its people, slipping between present day and pagan past.

FESTIVALS & EVENTS

If you pass through Rainow in July, don't be surprised to find it filled with curious straw figures, when the annual **scarecrow fortnight** sees the locals coming over all creative, transforming old clothes and assorted props into amusing and inventive tableaux on a

STONES & CROSSES

Cheshire isn't particularly known for ancient sites, but that's not to say it doesn't have any, particularly in this corner of the county. Keep your eyes peeled as you're out exploring the areas covered in this chapter, as you never know quite when you might stumble across a Saxon cross, boundary marker or prehistoric standing stone.

A little south of Macclesfield Forest on Nabbs Road, for example, is a medieval waymarker, the **Greenway Cross**, while further south again, just off the A54 in a grove of trees on private land, you can just about see the ancient monument of Clulow Cross. Nearby, on the edge of Cessbank Common, is the yet-to-be-fully-understood site of **The Bullstones** (♀SJ955676), with an upright gritstone slab at its centre. Lyme Park has the equally enigmatic **Bowstones**, thought to be the shafts of Saxon crosses, which stand beside the Gritstone Trail, and you'll find more Saxon crosses in **West Park** in Macclesfield.

There are standing stones in the fields around Rainow and Macclesfield Forest, and then there are less ancient but no less intriguing wayside monuments such as the **Murder Stone** near Disley (page 183) and the **John Turner stone** at Saltersford (see opposite).

---

different theme each year. The theme is carried through to the **Rainow Fete**, which takes place midway through the fortnight and starts off with a parade though the village. Samba drummers lead the way, and farm vehicles (given a lick and a polish for the occasion) pull trailers of fancy-dressed children and assorted rose queens sitting atop straw bales.

14 DUNGE VALLEY GARDENS

Dunge Rd, Kettleshulme SK23 7RF ⌀ 01663 733787 ⌀ dungevalley.weebly.com ⊙ May w/ends, by appointment only

At the head of a dead-end track in the hills south of Kettleshulme, David and Elizabeth Ketley have spent the past four decades creating a beautiful woodland garden. Threaded with streams and waterfalls, it's rather like a mini version of Bodnant Garden in north Wales and is at its best in May, when it's ablaze with colour from the hundreds of rhododendrons and azaleas that grow here.

15 MACCLESFIELD FOREST

🏠 **Stanley Arms** (page 293)

Less than five miles from central Macclesfield lies Macclesfield Forest, flanked by Tegg's Nose to the northwest and Shutlingsloe to the southeast, and criss-crossed with paths and trails for walkers, riders and cyclists. From the ranger centre at Trentabank car park there are colour-coded routes that wind, with varying degrees of difficulty, through forest and across moorland. Follow the easy green path (just over half a mile long) and it leads you through a small wooded area to the reservoir's edge, where, in early spring, you have a great view of the action in the **heronry** on the far side. Twenty-plus pairs of birds nest and rear their young here each year, and a noisy lot they are, too, with loud clacking calls carrying across the water – yet surprisingly graceful as they come in to land high in the trees or down by the water's edge. There are other birds to spot here too, including golden eyes, little grebes and mandarin ducks. Other wildlife tends to be on the shy side but if you're lucky you might see a red deer, and we once had a fleeting glimpse of a stoat, just registering the black tip of its tail as it bounced across the path and disappeared into a hole.

The longest of the waymarked trails is the red route, which takes you on an up-and-down circle around the forest, passing the tiny church of St Stephen along the way. Better known as **Forest Chapel**, it's famous both for its isolated hilltop setting, with just a couple of cottages to keep it company, and for the traditional rush-bearing ceremony still held here every August.

At the southern edge of the forest, a gate opens on to **Piggford Moor** where (doubtless buffeted by wind every step of the way) you can follow a slabbed path then a flight of steep steps cut into the rock, to reach the summit of **Shutlingsloe** with its glorious panoramic views. It's nicknamed Cheshire's Matterhorn – not that it's anything like as high, at a far more modest 1,660 feet, but seen from the right angle, its distinctive triangular top bears a resemblance to its Alpine counterpart.

FOOD & DRINK

Leather's Smithy Clarke Ln, SK11 0NE ⌕ 01260 252313 @Leathers-Smithy-Pub. This traditional stone-built pub has a great location overlooking Ridgegate Reservoir and serves hearty pub grub, including plenty of choice for vegetarians. Understandably, it's hugely popular with visiting walkers, vying for the prime seats by the fire in winter and the outdoor trestle tables in summer.

16 WILDBOARCLOUGH

Crag Hall (page 293), **Underbank Camping Barn** (page 293)

Crossing the top of the moors, it's easy to think all is bleak and wild for miles around. But turn off one of the side roads that lead to Wildboarclough (pronounced Wilbercluff) and it's not long before you're in a different world. Down in the valley, all is lush and lovely, Clough Brook rushing happily along on its way south to join the Dane and the road sticking close to its side, its verges sprinkled with tall stems of purple foxgloves and hedge parsley in summer. Here, tucked away in a fold of the hills, pretty little Wildboarclough is such a tranquil spot now it's hard to believe it was ever any other way, but the Industrial Revolution made its mark here too. In the 18th century the river waters powered a textile mill and the Gothic-windowed **Edinboro Cottages** were built to house the workers. Cross the bridge just south of the cottages and head up the hill and you'll see a surviving wing of the old works buildings, which later became a rather grand post and telegraph office (hence the old red phone box by the gate) while further up again is **Crag Hall**, the former mill-owners' mansion, now owned by the Earl of Derby and available for rent as a very swish holiday home (page 298). In between the two is the prettily situated **St Saviour's Church**, built in 1908–09 by the 16th Earl, in gratitude for the safe return of five sons who had served in the Boer War.

A little further along the road, you can turn off onto a footpath that leads you east to **Three Shire Heads**, where three counties (Cheshire, Staffordshire and Derbyshire) meet in a picturesque tumble of little waterfalls and rocky pools, complete with brackeny, heathery banks and an 18th-century packhorse bridge. Take a dip if you dare – it's popular with wild swimmers but the water is a tad chilly. The spot can also be approached via footpaths from Clough House car park just north of the village (SJ987698) or along the Dane Valley Way.

FOOD & DRINK

Blaze Farm SK11 0BL 01260 227229 blazefarm.com closed Mon except bank hols. Cheshire is building up a good stock of small-scale ice-cream farms and this family-run venture is one of them, using milk from its own dairy herd to produce its Hilly Billy ice cream. There's also a tea room, nature trails and, at weekends, a ceramic paint-a-pot studio.

Rose and Crown Inn Buxton Rd, Allgreave, Macclesfield SK11 0BJ 01260 227232 roseandcrownallgreave.co.uk closed Mon. There's a great view from the beer garden at this roadside country pub, just south of Blaze Farm in Allgreave. The bar serves a selection of real ales from several local breweries and the hearty food has earned it legions of fans.

MACCLESFIELD & THE PEAK DISTRICT

> ### JUST OVER THE BORDER
>
> For more on the Peak District, check out *Slow Travel: The Peak District*.
>
> **Buxton** visitbuxton.co.uk. The Derbyshire spa and market town known as the gateway to the Peak District has handsome Georgian architecture and a calendar full of festivals.
> **The Roaches** A dramatic rocky ridge that is popular with hikers and climbers.
> **Tittesworth Reservoir** visittittesworth.co.uk. Excellent birdwatching, pleasant waterside strolls, and a large, modern visitor centre and café..

17 WINCLE

Hill Top Farm (page 293), **The Apartment at Bartomley Farm** (page 293), **Clough Brook Cottage** (page 293), **Dane Cottage** (page 293), **Otter's Retreat** (page 293), **Swythamley Chapel** (page 293)

Turn off the A54 on to Barlow Hill and a road-with-a-view takes you gradually down to lovely Wincle, tucked away on the banks of the River Dane, which carves a pretty, wooded boundary between Cheshire to the north and Staffordshire to the south. As teenagers we used to come up here to have a drink in the pub, a picnic in the fields and a dip in the river – not quite wild swimming perhaps but certainly wild paddling. It was idyllic then and so it still is today, though now it has a couple of added attractions.

One is **Danebridge Fisheries** (SK11 0QE danebridgefisheries.com 01260 227293), where you can catch your own fish from a spring-fed lake stocked with brown, rainbow, blue and golden trout. Smaller ponds of varying sizes are perfect for kids of different ages. There's also a play area and a barbecue area. Next door is the **Wincle Beer Co** (SK11 0QE 01260 227777 winclebeer.co.uk), an award-winning brewery housed in a converted barn. Started in 2008, it's been a great success and you'll find its cask and bottled ales stocked in many local pubs, instantly recognisable by the sepia-tinted photos on their labels and their unusual names, all with local roots. Wibbly Wallaby, for instance, is a nod to the wild wallabies that used to live in the nearby hills after being released in the 1930s from a private menagerie. The animals are generally presumed to be extinct now but there's still the occasional

"As teenagers we used to come here to have a dip in the river – not quite wild swimming but certainly wild paddling."

report of a sighting. You can sample the beers (as well as ale flapjacks and stout brownies) in the cosy rustic tasting room, and buy bottles to take home. They also offer Brew for a Day experiences and recently introduced a summer beer festival (in June), with food, live music and camping in the field.

FOOD & DRINK

Ship Inn Barlow Hill, SK11 0QE ⌀ 01260 227217 ⌀ theshipwincle.co.uk. Cosy in winter and pretty in summer, when the hanging baskets and plant troughs are in bloom, the 18th-century Ship is popular with ramblers, dog walkers and country-pub-lunchers. Much of the food is locally sourced, with cheese, lamb, steaks and ice cream all from Cheshire, and there's a beer garden plus a few seats out at the front. One side of the pub sign shows a painting of *Nimrod*, the ship used by Shackleton on his 1907–09 expedition to Antarctica. It's not as famous as his subsequent vessel, *Endeavour*, but it's the one on which he was accompanied by local man Sir Phillip Brocklehurst, the youngest of the expedition team at a fresh-faced 20 years of age.

UPDATES WEBSITE

You can post your comments and recommendations, and read the latest feedback and updates from other readers online at ⌀ bradtupdates.com/cheshire.

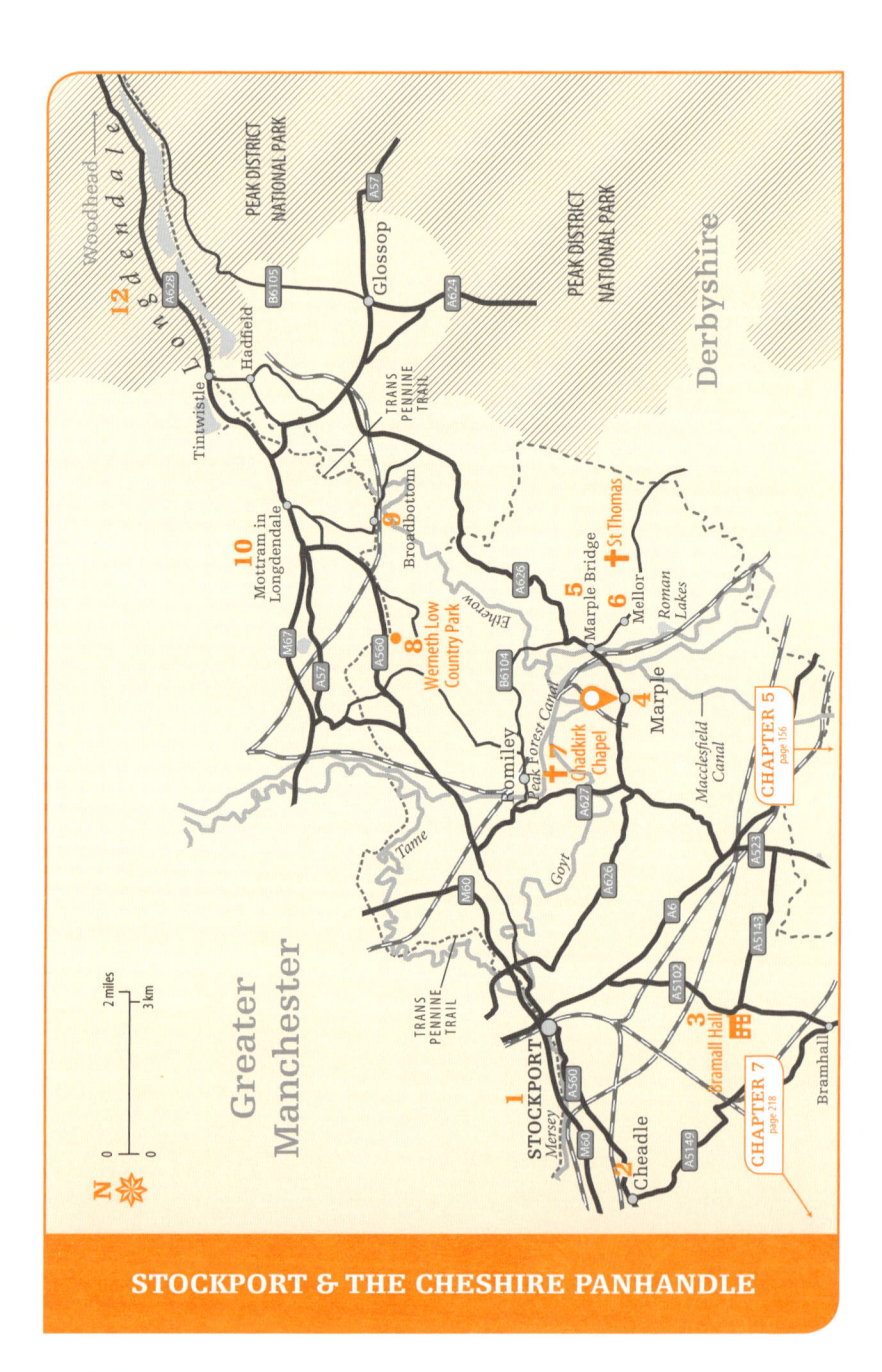

STOCKPORT & THE CHESHIRE PANHANDLE

6
STOCKPORT & THE CHESHIRE PANHANDLE

Some might feel that this chapter has no place in a 21st-century guide to Cheshire, the whole of the area within it having been parcelled up and hived off to neighbouring counties more than four decades ago now. But the Cheshire roots here stretch back centuries rather than mere decades, so we quickly dismissed the idea of leaving it out. To anyone who remembers Cheshire pre-1974, the shape of the new county looks all wrong without the 'panhandle', the distinctive little spur that used to reach up between Derbyshire, Lancashire and Yorkshire.

"Few realise that exploring this varied area leads you to some beautiful churches and glorious country views."

You can see the logic to the border reorganisation. The wild moorland region of the far northeast somehow feels better suited to its new addresses of Derbyshire and Yorkshire, and there's an obvious affinity between the old Cheshire mill towns on one side of the Tame and their once-Lancashire equivalents on the other, which came together to form the newly created Tameside. Yet even now many residents of the region retain Cheshire as their postal address and, especially in the south and west, still feel that Cheshire is where their allegiances lie.

But enough of arbitrary administrative borders. The important thing is that there's plenty for a Slow traveller to enjoy here. The impressive industrial heritage of towns such as Stockport might be expected, along with their big old mills and factories, towering over terraces of tiny workers' cottages. Few realise, however, that exploring this varied area also leads you to some beautiful churches and glorious country views; to one of England's finest black-and-white mansions and one of its steepest flights of canal locks. As you journey around, you'll also come across unlikely connections to such famous cultural figures as L S Lowry, Agatha Christie and Christopher Isherwood.

GETTING THERE & AROUND

PUBLIC TRANSPORT

Stockport is the transport hub of the region and a gateway to many other parts of Cheshire, including Chester, Crewe and Macclesfield. Several railway lines, including the West Coast Main Line, converge here before continuing up to Manchester, and from Stockport station there are frequent connections to and from London Euston. Northern trains link the town to its southern suburbs but frustratingly there's no direct rail connection from Stockport to the towns and villages to the east, so if you want to travel to places like Broadbottom and Marple by train, you'll need to go via Manchester.

There's a similar situation with the buses: there are good connections from Stockport to its immediate suburbs (including Marple this time) but places further afield to the east are a tad trickier to get to and usually require a couple of changes *en route*. Your best course of action is to consult the Transport for Greater Manchester website (⌀ tfgm.com), a central resource for all buses, trains and trams in the region.

WALKING

There's plenty here to keep keen walkers interested, with a range of routes that offer something for pretty much all fitness levels. Several long-distance trails pass through the area, including the granddaddy of them all, the 268-mile **Pennine Way**, which cuts across the Longdendale valley in the far east and climbs up to Black Hill, which was, once upon a time, the highest peak in Cheshire. You're exposed to the elements up here on the wild and windy moorland, so make sure you're suitably dressed and carrying all the appropriate equipment, including OS Explorer map OL1.

The 215-mile **Trans Pennine Trail** makes an appearance in the region, as does the 98-mile **Cheshire Ring Canal Walk**, following the Macclesfield and Peak Forest Canals, which meet at Marple. The mostly urban – and rather random – **Fred Perry Way** (named after the famous tennis player, who was born here), runs for 14 miles through Stockport borough from north to south, while the 15-mile **Etherow Goyt Valley Way** links central Stockport with Hadfield in Longdendale, passing through some lovely scenery as it follows the course of the rivers Goyt and Etherow. Other walking routes include the 225-mile **Midshires**

> **TOURIST INFORMATION**
>
> **Stockport Museum** 30–31 Market Pl, SK1 1ES ⌀ 0161 474 4444 ⊙ 10.00–17.00 Tue–Sat, 11.00–17.00 Sun & bank hols

Way, the 11-mile **Middlewood Way** and the 10-mile **Ladybrook Valley Interest Trail**. You can find more information on all at the Long Distance Walkers Association website (⌀ ldwa.org.uk).

CYCLING

Some parts of this area have fairly punishing gradients that are probably better suited to dedicated road cyclists in search of a full thigh-burning workout rather than those who are just looking for an easy-going weekend pootle. That said, there are also some less demanding routes such as the well-surfaced **Middlewood Way** (a former rail track that forms part of National Route 55), and the narrower, bumpier towpath along the **Macclesfield Canal**, both of which head south from Marple.

Local libraries carry copies of **Stockport Green A to Z** leaflets, each one providing information on cycling (and walking) routes in a different part of town. There's also a useful series of cycle network maps, produced by Transport for Greater Manchester, with details of cycling routes and conditions across the region – for this area, maps 7 (Stockport) and 6 (Tameside) will come in handy.

There are no cycle-hire places within this immediate area but it's not that far into Manchester, where you can hire all kinds of bikes from the helpful team at **Manchester Bike Hire** (198–200 Chapel St, Salford M3 6BY ⌀ 0161 769 5050 ⌀ manchesterbikehire.co.uk), whose range includes tandems, cargo bikes, mountain bikes and family bikes. There is also a Brompton bike hire dock (⌀ bromptonbikehire.com) just outside Manchester Piccadilly station.

STOCKPORT & AROUND

It may be officially part of Greater Manchester now, but until 1974 the hilly town of Stockport was one of the largest in Cheshire, and there are still many locals who identify more closely with the more rural county to the southwest rather than their mighty metropolitan neighbour to the north. There's a bit of both within the Stockport boundaries, with some interesting museums, industrial heritage and an emerging foodie scene in the town centre, while just a few miles away on the outskirts highlights include one of the county's most beautiful timber-framed mansions in Bramhall and, in Cheadle, a little-known wetlands area and a Victorian hall that inspired Agatha Christie.

1 STOCKPORT

The Red Bull (page 294)

Oh, to have seen Stockport through the eyes of 19th-century publisher Samuel Bagshaw, who waxed quite lyrical in his 1850 *History, Gazetteer and Directory of the County Palatine of Cheshire*. 'It is irregularly built upon ground in some parts precipitous,' he wrote. 'Around this precipitous acclivity, and along the south bank of the river the houses rise in successive amphitheatrical tiers from the base to the summit in a very romantic form, while the surrounding scenery is bold and picturesque.' Less impressed was Friedrich Engels, who also visited in the mid 19th century when the town was a major centre of cotton manufacturing and hat-making, and described Stockport as 'one of the duskiest, smokiest holes'. It looked, he said, 'excessively repellent', with 'repulsive' cottages and cellar dwellings.

What would they both make of it now, I wonder? The smoke may have gone, but so too has much semblance of romance. The past century has seen the town poorly served by its planners, its centre blighted by ugly post-war developments that seem to keep on coming. The River Mersey (born here, where the Tame and Goyt come together) is buried beneath a 1960s shopping precinct; the M60 carves its way through the sandstone outcrop on the northwest side of town.

At first glance, it might not seem a pretty prospect for visitors – but dig a little deeper and you'll find some interesting and attractive little pockets, particularly around the Market and Underbanks conservation area (now officially branded Stockport Old Town), where exciting independent ventures and initiatives are bringing welcome new life to the original heart of the town.

The most impressive way to arrive in Stockport is by train from Manchester, which takes you over the mighty railway viaduct that carries the tracks 111 feet above the valley floor. At the station, there's a free Metroshuttle bus that runs a circular route every 12 minutes, and stops near most central attractions.

Around the Market Place

The perfect place to start exploring historic Stockport is the hilltop Market Place – which, in the days before motorised transport, must have been roundly cursed by traders driving livestock and carrying heavy goods up the steep little paths and streets around its edges. At its eastern end, the parish church, **St Mary's in the Marketplace** (SKY 1YG ◯ Tue & Thu–Sun), is a handsome 19th-century affair that still includes architectural features of an earlier medieval church, such as the unusual scissor-braced timbers of the chancel roof, which date back to the 14th century. There's also a little heritage centre here, manned by members of Stockport Heritage Trust, where you can view old photos of the town, buy booklets about local sites and pick up tourist information leaflets, including a guide to the Stockport Town Centre Heritage Trail.

Dominating Market Place is the glass and iron Victorian **market hall**. It was built in 1861 but it's believed that markets have been held here for more than 900 years. In the late 19th century, one local farmer protested against a tax on saddle horses (imposed to raise money for wars against France and America) by riding to market on a saddled cow instead. Now, the area is the focus of much of the recent regeneration that's gone on in the town and the venue for hugely popular events such as **Foodie Friday** (pages 197–8) and **The Vintage Village** (page 198).

On the north side of the Market Place, you'll find **Staircase House** (30–31 Market Pl, SK1 1ES ◯ 13.00–17.00 Tue–Fri, 10.00–17.00 Sat, 11.00–17.00 Sun & bank hols). Don't be fooled by the nondescript façade, which has something rather Western saloon about it. Behind that simple brick front is Stockport's oldest town house, a 15th-century merchant's warehouse and home. It's famous for its rare Jacobean cage-newel staircase (one of only three surviving examples in the country) and is well worth a visit. Next door, **Stockport Museum** (◯ 10.00–17.00 Tue–Sat, 11.00–17.00 Sun & bank hols) provides a potted history of the town, and serves as the tourist information centre.

Leave Market Place via the southwest corner and suddenly you find yourself on an iron bridge crossing another street below, **Little Underbank**, which follows a natural ravine. Opened in 1868, the bridge finally provided traders and shippers with a level access to the market, sparing them the steep uphill climb. Pause for a moment to get to grips with the town's confusing topography and look east across the jumble of roofs to the towers of Robinson's brewery and St Mary's, then retrace your steps along the west side of Market Place, past **Seven Miles Out** (sevenmilesoutarts.co.uk), a creative social space that hosts quiz, comedy and folk nights, and the **Produce Hall**, which, at the time of going to press, was about to be transformed into a foodie hub. Turn left down the steep slope of Bridge Street, then left again on to Great Underbank and you'll find one of Stockport's jewels, the 16th-century **Underbank Hall**. This splendid black-and-white timbered town house once belonged to the wealthy Arderne (or Arden) family until they were forced to sell it in 1823 to pay off debts. It then became a bank and remains one today – possibly the most characterful branch of NatWest you're likely to find. And also, say NatWest, their most haunted: 'cash isn't the only thing that lives in our vaults' they once announced in a Halloween Facebook post.

"It then became a bank and remains one today – possibly the most characterful branch of NatWest you're likely to find."

A few doors down the road is **The White Lion** pub (now closed), where visitors could once fish in the River Mersey that ran past the bottom of the garden. Here, in 1831, the particularly charming William Clayton sold his wife for five shillings, handing her over to purchaser J Booth with a halter round her neck. Head a little further for a quick look at **Three Shires Hall**, another 16th-century house with decorative timber-framing, then turn back and up **Little Underbank**, which recently won a substantial regeneration grant – welcome news for a characterful street that doesn't deserve to have so many boarded-up shopfronts. Ahead you'll see the bridge you stood on earlier; pass under it and you reach **Winter's**, once a famous local jewellers and sadly now a bar, but at least it retains its landmark clock. Look up to see the figurines of Old Father Time, a soldier and a sailor, who used to strike the hours on the bells over their heads but have been silent in recent times. If you're really keen, nip in and go upstairs to the first floor where you can see the mechanics behind the clock – and maybe get it working while you're there.

Around Mersey Square

Mersey Square itself isn't the prettiest of places. It's not even really a square, and you won't see the Mersey without making an effort (it's hidden away, under the bridge by the bear ring). There are, however, a few good reasons for heading in that direction. First up, it gives you a good view of **Stockport Viaduct**, a mighty many-arched bridge that carries the railway high over the valley. Next, this is where you'll find **The Plaza** (Mersey Sq, SK1 1EP ⌀ 0161 477 7779 ⌂ stockportplaza. co.uk), a 1930s Super Cinema that has been painstakingly restored to mint condition so that you can now watch films, concerts and other theatrical events in the most glamorous of Art Deco surroundings. Even if there's nothing on, it's worth taking one of the volunteer-led tours just to admire the building itself and to hear about the painstaking work that's gone into restoring all those period features, including the original Compton organ, an absolute beauty to behold when it rises out of the ground in all its illuminated, etched-glass glory.

Come out of The Plaza and turn left up the steps, and you're just a couple of minutes' walk away from **Hat Works** (Wellington Rd South, SK3 0EU ⌀ 0161 474 2399 ⌂ stockport.gov.uk/topic/hat-works ⊙ 10.00–17.00 Tue–Sat, 11.00–17.00 Sun & bank hols). Housed in the 19th-century Wellington Mill, whose huge chimney is a very visible local landmark, this award-winning museum tells the story of the town's hatting industry – once so thriving that Stockport County FC is nicknamed the Hatters. There are recreated workshops and working machinery, plus a wonderful collection of all kinds of different headgear.

Turn right out of The Plaza instead and it's a short walk to another unusual museum, the Stockport **Air Raid Shelters** (61 Chestergate, SK1 1NF ⌀ 0161 474 1940 ⌂ stockport.gov.uk/topic/air-raid-shelters ⊙ closed Mon). You couldn't accuse the authorities of the time of being unprepared: in 1938, in readiness for the war they knew was coming, they started digging a huge network of tunnels out of the Stockport sandstone, with room to shelter thousands of people in what became nicknamed the Chestergate Hotel. It's a fascinating, informative and moving place to visit – and the communal toilets always get everyone talking.

🍴 FOOD & DRINK

The Allotment 6 Vernon St, SK1 TY ⌀ 0161 478 1331 ⌂ allotmentvegan.co.uk ⊙ 17.00–23.00 Thu–Sat, noon–16.00 Sun. One of the most exciting new arrivals near the market hall is this vegan restaurant, where chef Matthew Nutter promises to 'make aubergine taste better than steak'. Judge for yourself: an aubergine dish regularly features on both the à la carte and ten-course tasting menu. The restaurant isn't licensed so take your own wine.

Foodie Friday Market Sq ⌂ skfoodiefriday.co.uk ⊙ 18.00–21.00 last Fri of the month. The one thing above all that has put a spring back in Stockport's step is this hugely popular monthly event, with street-food stalls in and around the market hall, tables set out on the cobbles and live music in the surrounding bars. It's an all-ages, all-types, all-welcome affair that creates its own special party atmosphere, especially if you catch it on a sunny summer evening.

Lord of the Pies 42 St Petersgate, SK1 1HL ⌀ 0161 478 1920 @LordofthePiesGB. Launched in 2012, Lord of the Pies is now turning into a minichain, with branches in Macclesfield and Chorlton as well as Stockport, but this is the original, and the one that first garnered legions of fans for its traditional handmade pies, to eat in or take away. There are eight or so to choose from – I'll vouch for the cheese and onion and my other half is a big fan of the beef and ale.

Where the Light Gets In 7 Rostron Brow, SK1 1JY ⌀ 0161 477 5744 wtlgi.co dinner only Wed–Sat. Chef Samuel Buckley created a stir when he opened this edgy new restaurant in 2016, with a daily-changing set tasting menu based around seasonal and locally foraged ingredients. The restaurant itself is a light, airy loft space, converted from an old warehouse near the market. And the food? It won't be for everyone, with a no-choice series of small plates that sometimes feature challenging ingredients, but *The Guardian* gave it a rare 10/10 rating.

SHOPPING

20th Century Stores 26–27 Market Pl, SK1 1EZ ⌀ 07749 937994 20thcenturystores.com Thu–Sat plus 2nd Sun of the month & sometimes Tue. Following the success of the monthly Vintage Village markets, this shop opened in 2015 to provide a permanent hub for traders specialising in vintage clothing, furnishings and accessories. As the name suggests, they stock 20th-century items, mostly from the 1920s to 1980s, and though the shopfront may look small, the premises stretch back and down in a series of little rooms that run the length of Park Street.

Agapanthus 77 Wellington St, SK1 1FE ⌀ 0161 429 9710 agapanthusinteriors.com. This fabulous little interiors shop will appeal to lovers of distressed chic, with its dilapidated (in a cool way) interiors, and stock of vintage lighting, homewares and chalk paints. They create their own chandeliers, repair antique ones and run furniture-painting workshops, but my favourite bit is in the basement: stacked trays filled with glass and crystal droppers, little jewels just crying out to be used in some creative, crafty way.

The Vintage Village Market Hall www.thevintagevillage.co.uk 10.00–16.00 2nd Sun of the month. Once a month things take a retro turn in the market hall, with dozens of traders laying out stalls covered with all kinds of vintage finds, including clothing, jewellery, accessories and homewares.

2 CHEADLE

Oddfellows on the Park (page 293)

Despite the natural boundary of the Mersey floodplain to the north, separating it from Manchester, Cheadle has long been very much a commuter suburb – which is probably why many people, even locals, fail to appreciate that it's not without its treasures. You might not make a special visit, but if you happen to be passing through, it's worth a wander.

At its heart is the Grade l-listed **St Mary's Church**, at its prettiest in spring when the cherry trees blossom in the churchyard. Look up at the tower and you'll see that instead of numerals on the clock faces it has letters, which spell out 'Forget not God' (over the porch), 'Trust the Lord' (west side) and 'Time is flying' (on the east). Inside, look up again to admire the fine camber-beamed roof, with gilded bosses. The building itself is 16th century but some of its contents are older, including the well-preserved head of a Saxon cross found nearby and the 15th-century alabaster effigies of two knights.

At the other end of the High Street is **Cheadle Village Green**, where the Cheadle Civic Society has done grand work in recent years, re-landscaping, marking out the foundations of the hall that once stood here and reinstalling the Victorian drinking fountain that had been banished further down the road. The green is now home to a popular **Makers Market** on the first Saturday of the month, where you can wander round a few dozen stalls selling a mixture of crafts and food and listen to live music. And if you're wondering who the old man carved out of wood is standing by the bus stop, that's Scotch Bob (real name James Telford), who used to drive the horse-drawn bus that ran between Cheadle and Manchester in the late 19th century.

Another Cheadle character, though a fictional one, was the 1980s Victoria Wood creation: the sherry-sipping, lip-pursing Kitty, beautifully written and just as beautifully performed by Birkenhead-born Patricia Routledge. Kitty's monologues were a regular feature of *Victoria Wood As Seen on TV* and made frequent references to her supposed home town. 'I still can't polka without wincing,' went one, 'but we're spunky in Cheadle, we totter on.'

Abney Hall Park
Manchester Rd, SK8 2PD

A few yards north of Cheadle Village Green is Newland Road, which leads straight into Abney Hall Park. Built in 1847, the hall itself was once the private residence of the Watts family, wealthy Manchester business folk who entertained the great and the good of the Victorian era here, including Disraeli, Gladstone, King Edward VII and Prince

Albert. The last of several James Watts to live at Abney (they weren't over-imaginative when it came to naming the sons) was married to Agatha Christie's sister, Madge, and the novelist was a regular visitor as a child. She later used the house as a model for some of her fictional country homes, such as Styles and Chimneys, and it's the location for an Hercule Poirot case in *The Adventure of the Christmas Pudding*, a collection of short stories that she dedicated to 'the memory of Abney Hall – its kindness and its hospitality'. In the introduction she recalled fondly all the festive seasons she spent here. 'What superb Christmases they were for a child to remember! Abney Hall had everything! The garden boasted a waterfall, a stream, and a tunnel under the drive!'

Waterfall and stream are still there, though I can't speak for the tunnel. The house, after a few decades as Cheadle Town Hall, is now given over to offices and out-of-bounds to the general public, though you can walk round the outside to admire the ornate Norman doorway, and peer through the windows to catch a glimpse of the lavish Gothic interiors, designed by A W N Pugin and completed after his death. I worked in the kitchens here one summer, during Abney's brief incarnation as a language school, and it's a wonder and a joy that the interiors seem to have survived the carnage caused by gangs of out-of-control schoolchildren running riot through the corridors!

At just over 200 acres, the park surrounding the hall is a fraction of its former size, and there's no escaping the sound of the M60 running along its northern edge, but as a Local Nature Reserve it's still a pleasantly tranquil space. I once brought a friend who'd grown up just a few miles away but had never visited Abney, and she was astonished to find, just yards from the main road, this hidden world, with its field of grazing cattle, orchard, ponds, and a boardwalk through wetlands that in summer are buzzing with beautiful, brightly coloured dragonflies and damselflies.

FOOD & DRINK

There are cafés and restaurants dotted along and around the High Street, so there's no shortage of places to stop off for tea and cakes or something more substantial, like the excellent street food at **Indian Tiffin Room** (2 Chapel St, SK8 1BR ⌀ 0161 491 2020 ⌀ indiantiffinroom.com ⌀ evenings only). During the day, head into Abney Park and support **Abney Café** (@abneygarden.teas ⌀ closed Mon), run by husband-and-wife team Kate and Steven Peacock, who are such big fans of the park that they got married there and gave both their children Abney as a middle name. There's nothing flash about the venue (it's the old football changing rooms given a hippyish makeover with prettily flower-painted walls, chairs and tables) or the food (think bacon, egg and sausage barms or cheese toasties), but it's freshly cooked and good value. And, more importantly, Kate and Steven have created a great little community hub, hosting local groups, fundraising for the park, keeping a watchful eye on kids playing outside and generally being all-round good (and friendly) eggs.

SHOPPING

Much of the main street is taken up with the usual mix of chains and charity shops, but it hasn't completely lost its independents, including a proper fishmonger, butcher and greengrocer. **W Hulme** (36 High St, SK8 1AE), so old-fashioned-looking it's almost hipster, was selling farm produce long before farm shops came into vogue, and stocks good Cheshire and Lancashire cheeses.

A couple of those charity shops are worth popping in to, too. Just along from the church, **Barnardo's Vintage** (76 High St, SK8 1AE) won the Charity Retail Association's Specialist Shop of the Year award in 2017 and, as the name suggests, is dedicated to all things retro. You'll find a rich assortment of stuff in there – not just vintage clothes and accessories but also old ceramics displayed on granny-style dressers, and a box full of decades-old knitting and sewing patterns, plus lengths of retro fabrics, cotton reels and sewing machines to make them with.

At the other end of the road is **St Ann's Hospice** (3 High St, SK8 1AX), where it's not the stock so much as the building itself that's interesting. In the 1930s this opened as the rather swish Premier Café, where August Wienholt introduced the good folk of Cheadle to continental patisserie. Sadly, the gateaux have long gone – but you can at least still see the Art Deco interior, now Grade II-listed. At the back of the shop an intact chrome-railed staircase leads up to the first floor, where, among bridal gowns and hats, you can still see the glass dome, wall clocks, vintage tiles and other period fixtures, making you long for some enterprising soul to turn it back into a glamorous little tea room.

Another surprise, hidden away through an archway near the George & Dragon, is **Collector's Yard** (2b Stockport Rd, SK8 2AA), a bramble-bordered paved area with a few cabins, which turn out, on closer inspection, to be stuffed to the gills with interesting stuff. One is all vintage bric-a-brac, the other is piled from floor to ceiling with precarious piles of secondhand books and boxes filled with thousands of old postcards – a particular interest for owner Joao Da Silva.

3 BRAMALL HALL

Bramhall SK7 3NX stockport.gov.uk/topic/bramall-hall hall: 13.00–16.00 Tue–Fri, noon–17.00 w/ends, 11.00–17.00 bank hols; park: always open

We took Bramall Hall for granted as children. It was just one of the local places we used to cycle off to to play, picnic and fish for sticklebacks, or occasionally visit on school trips to learn about the Tudors. It never occurred to me until many years later how lucky we were to have such a treasure on our doorstep. Because it is a treasure. Pevsner declares it one of the four best timber-framed mansions of England (the others include Little Moreton Hall, pages 149–52) and devotes five pages to an in-depth description.

The Grade l-listed hall has been standing here for more than 700 years, a black-and-white Tudor beauty, raised above the surrounding parkland on a tier of grassy terraces. Whichever way you approach, it's impressive. Arrive from the east and you see the classic picture-postcard view, with the full width of the many gabled building and the terraces leading down to the park. Approach from the west and you arrive in the courtyard with wings on either side and a beautiful polygonal bay window straight ahead.

Thanks to a recent £2 million restoration, the hall is looking better than ever. Highlights such as the ornate plaster ceiling in the Withdrawing Room have been restored, and every single leaded pane of glass has been cleaned up to sparkle in the sunshine. New interpretation has been added throughout as well, bringing to life Charles and Mary Nevill, who owned the hall in the late 19th century and were largely responsible for the fact that it's in such fine shape today. It was the Nevills who uncovered the rare medieval paintings of the Solar Room and oversaw the creation of the surrounding park, transforming the grounds in the romantic fashion of the time, with ponds, specimen trees and rhododendrons. Take a walk through the woods and along the river and you stand a good chance of spotting a kingfisher.

FOOD & DRINK

Mounting Stone 8 Woodford Rd, SK7 2JJ ⌀ 0161 439 7563 ⌀ themountingstone.co.uk. This great little micropub in the centre of Bramhall specialises in real ales and craft beers, many of them from local brewers, but also carries some interesting spirits, including a couple of Cheshire gins. It has an equally popular older sibling a couple of miles down the road in Cheadle Hulme, The Chiverton Tap (8 Mellor Rd, SK8 5AU).

SHOPPING

The Bottle Stop 136 Acre Ln, SK8 7PD ⌀ 0161 439 4904. There can't be many off-licences prettier than this one, adorned as it is with dozens of hanging baskets. More important, though, is the superb range of drinks it carries, with all sorts of beers, wines, spirits and liqueurs you're unlikely to find in your average supermarket.

Simply Books 228 Moss Ln, SK7 1BD ℘ 0161 439 1436 ⊙ closed Sun–Mon. One of the best things about Bramhall is this excellent independent bookshop, run by a couple who are genuinely passionate about what they do. It's not huge but it carries a good range of titles, has a sweet little café area and hosts regular events, including author talks and craft workshops.

MARPLE & AROUND

This semi-rural area falls officially under Stockport's jurisdiction, but there's still enough green space between it and the town centre for it to feel slightly apart and much less urban. There's lovely countryside all round here, especially in the valleys of the rivers Etherow and Goyt, which come together near Marple Bridge. Thanks to Victorian mill-owner Samuel Oldknow, it's also a particularly rewarding area for fans of industrial heritage, while canal lovers are in for a real treat.

4 MARPLE

🏠 **Ring O'Bells** (page 294), 🏠 **Magpie Cottages** (page 294)

It's blessed with waterways is Marple. The River Goyt flows along its eastern and northern flanks, and in the centre the Peak Forest Canal and the Macclesfield Canal converge before heading off down one of the steepest flights of locks in the country. Sixteen locks later, the 100-foot-high **Marple Aqueduct**, designed by Benjamin Outram and built at the end of the 18th century, carries the canal over the river, with a dizzying view down to the Goyt Valley on one side and across to the slightly higher railway viaduct that runs alongside on the other. It's a superbly scenic combination of natural beauty and manmade ingenuity, making this an unsurprisingly popular destination for canal boaters and walkers (see box, pages 208–9).

The man responsible for much of that ingenuity was **Samuel Oldknow**, an entrepreneurial muslin manufacturer who, with the help of financial backing from Richard Arkwright, put in much of the early infrastructure that shaped modern Marple. In the 1790s, down on the Mellor side of the River Goyt, he built **Mellor Mill**, then the largest spinning mill in the world, employing hundreds of people. To access it he built a road and helped fund the construction of others. To house his workers he built homes and to help feed them, physically and spiritually, he invested in farms and funded the building of a church. He was a driving force behind the construction of the Peak Forest Canal, using it to transport limestone from the Peak Forest, which was then burned in the Gothic-inspired lime kilns he erected alongside the canal.

Oldknow died in 1828 and the mill burned down in 1892, nature gradually reclaiming the site. Until relatively recently you could have visited Marple and left again without being aware of the man and his achievements, but not any more. A few years ago the combined forces of Mellor Archaeological Trust and the Canal and River Trust, armed with Heritage Lottery funding, kicked off the Revealing Oldknow's Legacy project (oldknows.com) and all their hard work is finally coming to fruition, with the aqueduct restored, the mill excavated and the area round the lime kilns cleared.

Marple Memorial Park

SK6 6AX marplememorialpark.org.uk

One of the things I love about Marple is that there seems to be a real community spirit. Everywhere you look you can see the benign influence of the many local 'friends' groups, whether it's planters of help-yourself herbs and vegetables on the station platform and main shopping street or the Oldknow heritage sites being unearthed by amateur archaeologists. A shining example is the park at the heart of town, where the Friends of Marple Memorial Park have a hand in everything from maintaining the benches and looking after the flower beds to securing funding for new sculptures and campaigning to keep the public loos open. One of their latest achievements is a First World War timeline in front of Hollins House, where they've gathered together information about (and in most cases, a photo of) every soldier mentioned on the nearby war memorial, posting each one on the 100th anniversary of his death. It's a simple idea but very moving.

"One of the things I love about Marple is that there seems to be a real community spirit."

Running along the edge of the canal locks, the park makes a good picnic spot, with lovely views towards the Peak District, and contains a number of heritage features gathered together here from nearby sites, including the old sundial from Marple Hall and the decorative headstone once mounted on the front of Oldknow's mill. By the Stockport Road entrance to the park you'll also find the Regent, an independent cinema converted from a former coffee tavern, reading rooms and chapel.

St Martin's church
Brabyns Brow, SK6 5DT

When Ann Hudson inherited nearby Brabyns Hall and a fortune in 1866, she and her daughter Maria used some of their land and money to build this new church, which opened in 1870. It was designed by John Dando Sedding, one of the foremost church architects of the Victorian era and a leading light in the Arts and Crafts movement. The outside is simple but appealing, made from Pennine sandstone, with Gothic influences and a pretty half-timbered porch, and the inside is full of contributions from some of the most significant Victorian designers. There are stained-glass windows by William Morris, Edward Burne-Jones, Ford Madox Brown and Dante Gabriel Rossetti, another by Archibald Keightley Nicholson and a couple by Christopher Whall, who also contributed the altar piece, the gesso panelling on the ceiling of the Lady Chapel, and *Our Lady of the Goyt Valley* – a painting of the Annunciation with local scenery in the background. Elements designed by Henry Wilson, whose talents encompassed many branches of the arts, include a cast bronze war memorial, an Art Nouveau-style font cover and a large relief tablet of St Christopher. Sedding designed the painted alabaster reredos, the encaustic floor tiles and much more beside. There's a lot to see – go along on a Saturday morning in summer, when they're open to visitors, and let one of the volunteer guides talk you round the treasures.

FOOD & DRINK

All Things Nice 48–50 Marple St, SK6 7AD ⌀ 0161 427 2222 ⌀ allthingsnicedeli.co.uk. This popular deli/café has a good selection of cheeses, artisan breads and homemade dishes, with plenty of room for eating in and an al fresco seating area on the pedestrianised street.

Angkor Soul 12a Stockport Rd, SK6 6BJ ⌀ 0161 222 0707 ⌀ angkorsoul.co.uk ⊙ 11.30–15.00 Tue, 11.30–15.00 & 17.00–23.00 Wed–Sat, 17.00–21.30 Sun. It's not just locals who rave about Angkor Soul – people come from far around to sample the excellent Cambodian food prepared by chef-proprietor, Y Sok. It's fresh, delicious and all made from scratch, and there are lots of vegan options on the menu. There's also, unexpectedly, a record boutique in the basement, selling vintage vinyl and books.

Cloudberry Café 68 Stockport Rd, SK6 6AB ⌀ 0161 427 2435 @cloudberrycafe ⊙ closed Sun & Mon. Right next to The Bookshop is this relaxed café that sells craft items and homemade food, and runs craft and chat sessions. The owner puts in the effort to cater for different diets, tries to source ingredients locally and aims to keep waste to a minimum, for example by offering a discount on take-out drinks if you bring your own reusable mug or flask.

AGATHA CHRISTIE & MISS MARPLE

Devon seems to have staked its claim to being official 'Christie country', but the novelist found much of her early inspiration up north. Abney Hall in Cheadle (pages 199–200) appears, under different guises, in many of her books, and it was another Stockport suburb that gave her the name for one of crime fiction's most famous sleuths.

As reported on the Marple Local History Society website the 150th anniversary of Marple station in 2015 was attended by Christie's grandson, Mathew Prichard, who brought along a letter written by the novelist to a fan. In it, Christie recounts how, during one of her visits to Abney, her sister Madge took her to a house sale at Marple Hall (which, incidentally, was the former home of Judge John Bradshaw, who signed King Charles I's death warrant). Here, Agatha said, she not only picked up two Jacobean oak chairs but also found 'a name for my 'old maid' character' – and so, Miss Marple was born.

If you arrive in Marple by train today, you'll find a blue plaque on the station platform, along with some giant posters of Agatha Christie book covers.

The Samuel Oldknow 22 Market St, SK6 7AD ✆ 0161 425 9530 ⌖ samueloldknow.co.uk. In 2016 Billy Booth and co-owner Anthony Meynell set about transforming a former florist shop into a micropub – and a grand job they've made of it. It's tiny (just two rooms), friendly (dogs and muddy boots welcome) and serves a great choice of local cask ales, traditional ciders and craft beers. On a winter night you can cosy up by the wood burner with a mulled cider and one of the board games; on a sunny day you can take advantage of the bijou beer garden. There's live music on Thursdays and seasonal poetry evenings as well.

SHOPPING

The Bookshop 70 Stockport Rd, SK6 6AB ✆ 0161 427 4921 ⊙ closed Sun & Wed afternoons . Local bookshops always deserve support and this is no exception. It's traditional rather than trendy (if you want coffee, you can just go to the café next door) but if you can't see what you want, they'll order it in and it has a good little local history section where you can find booklets produced by local historians and walking guides of the area.

5 MARPLE BRIDGE

Marple Bridge is one of those places (admittedly there are a few) that has me doing online property searches as soon as I get back home. One of those pretty stone cottages in the central conservation area would do nicely, with roses rambling over the walls and a wrought-iron table and chairs set out on a little terrace overlooking the Goyt. The river runs along one side of Town Street, where the local shopkeepers club together to pretty things up even more with flourishing hanging baskets and planters.

FOOD & DRINK

Dutson's 22–24 Town St, SK6 5AA ⌀ 0161 484 5380 ⌀ dutsons.co.uk. This combined deli, café and wine shop, brainchild of brothers Paul and Matthew Dutson, stocks a very tasty range of products. On the shelves you'll find preserves from Pott Shrigley and honey from the Peak District, while local produce on the café menu includes Cheshire oats, used to make the breakfast porridge.

Libby's 1 Town St, SK6 5AA ⌀ 0161 427 2310 ⌀ libbysbreadandwine.com. The first thing you see as you walk into Libby's is racks of good-looking loaves, all made on the premises, followed by more temptation in the form of homemade cakes laid out on the bar. By day, this a place for sandwiches, salads and sharing boards; at night the lights go down and it's all about tapas and wine. Take a seat by the front windows and watch the world go by – or head out the back door, where there's a sweet little terrace overlooking the Goyt.

6 MELLOR

There's no obvious centre to Mellor – it's more of a strung-out affair, covering a wide area east of the River Goyt, which marks the boundary with Marple. Before being absorbed into Cheshire in 1936 and then into Greater Manchester nearly 40 years later, Mellor was traditionally part of Derbyshire, and that's what it feels like today – a hilly rural area of lush river valleys, scattered farmhouses and wonderful hilltop views.

From Mellor Mill (page 203) it's a 15-minute walk along a rutted road to **Roman Lakes** (Lakes Rd, SK6 7HB ⌀ 0161 427 2039 ⌀ romanlakes.co.uk), where there's a tea room (⊙ 10.00–16.00 Wed–Fri, 10.00–17.00 w/ends & bank hols) and a refreshment kiosk (⊙ 08.00–dusk Tue–Sun & bank hols). In the 19th century, the lakes formed part of a system of waterways created by Oldknow to harness the power of the river in the service of the mill, but after the mill burned down in 1892 the area was transformed into hugely popular pleasure grounds. On bank holiday weekends, nearby Marple station would be thronged by thousands of day trippers arriving on special excursion trains, ready to enjoy a day of picnicking, boating, dancing, watching the band and playing the penny slot machines. It's a quieter affair these days – more about walking (see box, pages 208–9), cycling and fishing – but in 2012 the tea dances were resurrected and are now held on the last Saturday of each month.

STOCKPORT & THE CHESHIRE PANHANDLE

A walk in the footsteps of Samuel Oldknow

Adapted from *Heritage Walks Around Mellor* with kind permission from Mellor Archaeological Trust (⌖ MATrust.org.uk)

❋ OS Explorer map 268; start: Marple station, ⚑ SJ962893; 4 miles; easy, along footpaths, towpaths & minor roads

This gentle circular walk leads you around sites associated with Samuel Oldknow, the 18th-century entrepreneur who made a real impact on this area (page 203). There are some lovely views along the way, plus a park where you can stop off for a lakeside drink.

1 Turn right out of Marple station on to Brabyns Brow and walk uphill until you reach the bridge over the Peak Forest Canal, with the number 9 lock gates on your left. Turn left after the lock and follow the towpath, passing Lockside Mill, which was Oldknow's warehouse for transferring raw and finished cotton between the canal and the road.

2 Shortly after lock 12, go up the steps on your right, before the bridge, then turn left over the bridge and immediately left into Oldknow Road, which runs along the edge of the recreation ground to Arkwright Road.

3 Cross over and continue straight ahead down Faywood Drive, passing Stone Row on the left and continuing into Lakes Road. At the bottom of the hill on the right is the site of Marple Lodge, home of the Mellor Mill manager.

4 Cross the bridge over the Goyt (footpath 78) and continue to the junction. Make a short detour some 50 yards left into Bottoms Mill Road. On the right is the site of the six-storey Mellor Mill, opened by Oldknow in 1792 and burnt down in 1892. On the left are the sites of a waterwheel, workshops, stable and a gas works. From here, walk back to Lakes Road and turn left on Bridleway 119. On the right is a gated bridge leading to the ruins of Oldknow's grand Mellor Lodge, with a narrow stone leat that fed water to power the spit in the kitchen. Pass the old millpond, now North Lake, on the left.

5 When the road forks, turn right, following Lakes Road (Bridleway 118). The road along the side of the lake runs on top of the dam made to create the millpond after Oldknow diverted the River Goyt. On your left is Roman Lakes leisure park, where refreshments and loos are available.

6 Continue under the railway viaduct and past Floodgates Cottage. One cottage was a home for the sluice man and one for a gate-keeper; the tollgate hinges are on the cottage wall.

7 Turn right opposite Strawberry Hill (signed 'Strines') and cross the packhorse bridge known as the Roman Bridge. The path (footpath 161) then swings left along the river bank; follow it uphill to Strines Road, cross over into Plucksbridge Road and walk up to the canal.

8 Turn right on to the towpath and walk along the canal, crossing over at Brick Bridge, the 'change bridge', where the towpath switches from the right to the left bank.

MARPLE & AROUND

9 Swing right over the next bridge at the junction with the Macclesfield Canal, noting the extensive vistas to the north, east and south, and the view of Top Lock House on the right. The left section was built by Oldknow for the canal engineer and the right section became Jinks' Boatyard. On your left is an information board on the Cheshire canal ring and a small information office, in the old toll house. Continue on the Peak Forest Canal down the side of the locks. The first ('top') lock is No 16 of the 16-strong flight that drops 200 feet to the aqueduct over the River Goyt.

10 At the side of lock 13, drop down through the horse tunnel to pass under the bridge you earlier crossed. This is Posset Bridge, where Oldknow is said to have encouraged his labourers to finish the building work faster by giving them ale posset for breakfast every day. Continue down the towpath to lock 9, before turning right to return to Marple station.

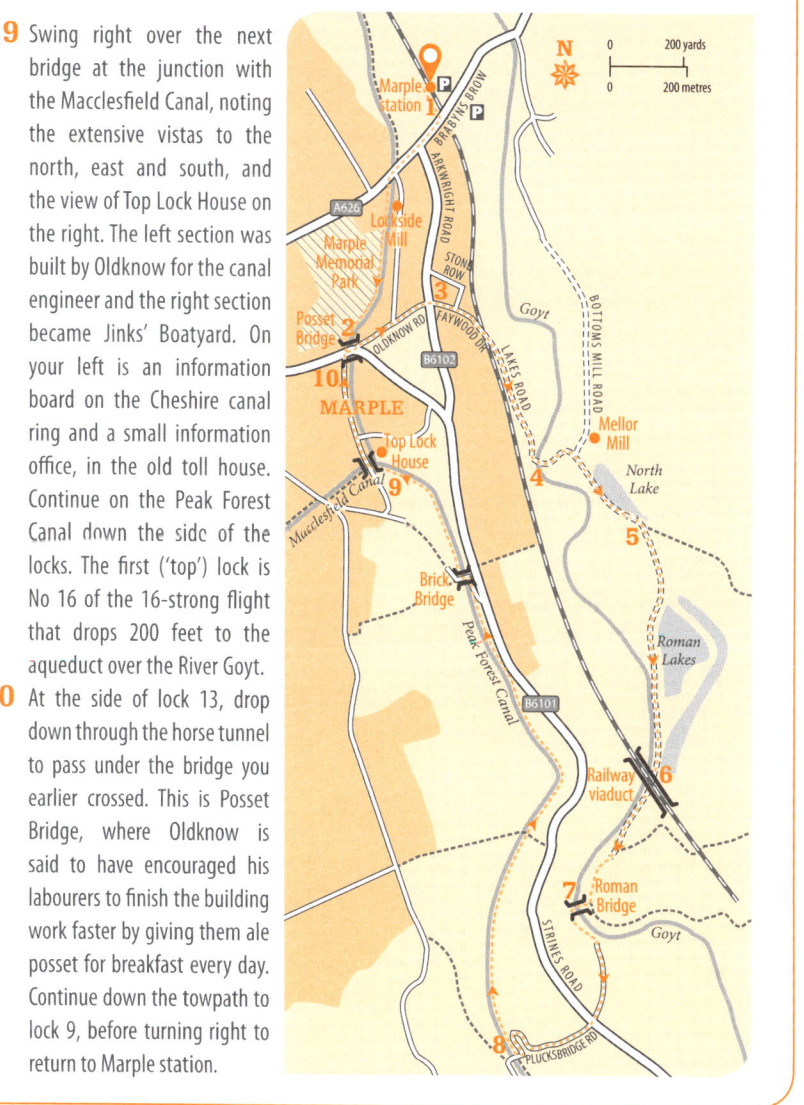

A couple of valleys away to the northeast is a Mellor must-visit: **St Thomas Church** (Church Rd, SK6 5LX), often just known as Mellor Church. Before you go in, look to the left of the church door where, tucked into a corner behind railings, you'll find the curious memorial stone for Thomas Brierley. If you're struggling to read it, it's not because there's anything wrong with your eyes – it's written in a cipher used by 18th-century Freemasons and covered in Masonic symbols. The church is only small inside so its two main treasures are easy to spot: to the right of the altar, a Derbyshire stone font, believed to date back to the 9th or 10th century; and to the left, a lovely oak pulpit, carved from a single tree trunk around 1340–50 and thought to be the oldest wooden pulpit in the country. It spent many years banished ignominiously to the tower, serving as storage for the gravedigger's tools, before it was returned to its rightful position in the 19th century.

"If you're struggling to read it, it's not because there's anything wrong with your eyes – it's written in a cipher used by 18th-century Freemasons."

The most striking thing about Mellor Church, however, is not the building itself but its location, set high on a hilltop (on the site of an Iron Age fort) with glorious views over the surrounding countryside – a lovely spot to sit and contemplate, with the sound of the breeze in the trees and the lowing of cattle drifting across the fields. Next to the church is a small garden, where archaeological excavations have unearthed Iron Age and Roman artefacts. Nearby, a stile beside a gate leads to a reconstructed roundhouse in a field. This is also where the annual well-dressing display takes place – the well is tucked away in a little glade at the far end of the field.

FOOD & DRINK

The Oddfellows Moor End Rd, SK6 5PT ⌀ 0161 449 7826 ⌀ oddfellowsmellor.com. From the outside, The Oddfellows ('Oddies' to its friends) looks every inch the traditional country pub, with its 17th-century stone walls, wisteria round the door and brightly coloured hanging baskets. Inside doesn't disappoint either, all flagstoned floors, low beamed ceilings and open fires. There's a leaflet of walks you can do from the pub, and when you've finished striding across the hills you can come back to fill up on their modern British grub, which includes pork from pigs reared in nearby Rowarth and, in season, fresh local game, and has earned the pub a listing in the Michelin Guide for the past five years.

WELL DRESSINGS

In June and July a number of villages along the Cheshire–Derbyshire border participate in the Peak District custom of well dressing, said to date back to pagan times when floral offerings were left for the gods of springs and wells in thanks for the gift of fresh water. Back then, they were probably simple bunches of flowers but since the Victorian era the displays have become far more elaborate, with beautiful, intricate pictures created from petals, berries, seeds and other natural ingredients.

Making them is a painstaking process. First, a large wooden frame is soaked in water for a few days then filled with clay, on to which the pattern is first pricked out and then outlined with something dark, such as wool, peppercorns or seeds. Next begins the patient business of filling it all in, layering individual petals and leaves in overlapping rows and working from bottom to top, rather like tiling a roof.

Wandering round Broadbottom in late July we arrived at the Church of the Immaculate Conception just as Sue Hickinson, Stella Quinn and fellow members of the well-dressing team were putting the finishing touches to their newest display. Fascinated, we looked on as they pointed out the different materials they'd used to create their picture of Catholic martyr Nicholas Garlick of Dinting, copied from a stained-glass window in a nearby church. Blue hydrangea petals formed the sky above his head, crushed coal and white gravel the tiled floor beneath his feet. There were panels of red begonias and purple statice; contrasting diamonds of ash and euonymus leaves; and a decorative trim of feverfew flower heads interspersed with St John's Wort berries. His face was made from crushed eggshell, with sheep's wool for his beard, peppercorns for hair and feathers for eyebrows. On the floor, representing his martyrdom, was a knife made from tree bark and a blade cut from a can of John Smith's bitter.

I wish I'd seen the previous year's display, when Joan of Arc memorably wore a suit of armour created from ring pulls saved from Boddingtons beer cans. Possibly even more, though, I'd love to have been here the year that St Margaret's face was outlined in lentils – which sprouted, leaving her with a curly white beard.

You'll also find well dressings at Disley, Tintwistle, Mellor, Bollington, Gee Cross and Chadkirk (as well as throughout the Peak District). For a comprehensive list of villages and dates, visit ⌀ welldressing.com.

7 CHADKIRK CHAPEL & COUNTRY ESTATE

Vale Rd, Romiley SK6 3LD

Stockport is full of the unexpected, like pretty little **Chadkirk Chapel** (⊙ 1 Apr–31 Oct 13.00–17.00 w/ends & bank hols, 1 Nov–31 Mar 13.00–16.00 w/ends), hidden away behind the suburban streets of Romiley.

Walk for 10–15 minutes from Romiley train station and the busy main road, crossing over the Peak Forest Canal, and you find yourself in the **Chadkirk Country Estate and Nature Reserve**, next to St Chad's Well. The well is adorned by a well dressing in July and for the days leading up to the official unveiling of each year's tableau, visitors are welcome to come along to see the work in progress and maybe push in a few petals of their own. From here you can follow the little rabbit signs that lead you on a trail round the fields and back again, or go straight to the chapel. It's tiny and unadorned and no-one seems quite sure how old it is – maybe 16th century, maybe earlier – but it's lovely in its simplicity, part stone-built and part timber-framed.

Next door is a **walled garden**, a peaceful spot, where you can sit and enjoy the tranquility and give quiet thanks to the Friends of Chadkirk (friendsofchadkirk.wordpress.com), who put in the hard work to look after it. Follow the footpath round the back of the garden into the ancient woodland of Kirk Wood and towards the tree trunk carved into the shape of a woodpecker (you can't miss it) for the prettiest view back over the church and garden. Take a photo of that, show it to other people, and they would never in a million years guess it was in Stockport.

From here, you could follow the Midshires Way through Kirk Wood to join the Peak Forest Canal or head south across Chadkirk Bridge and follow the footpath that leads to **Marple Hall**. Not that you'll find a hall there any more. There used to be: a substantial 17th-century affair once stood here, the family home of Judge John Bradshaw. Many years later, having passed down through successive generations of the Bradshaw-Isherwood family, it came into the hands of writer Christopher Isherwood, inherited from his uncle Henry, who had already auctioned off most of its valuable contents. By then living in the US, Isherwood passed it on to his brother, and the sad, sorry conclusion to the story is that, neglected by all, the hall was abandoned, looted, vandalised and eventually demolished in 1957. All you'll find there now, rather forlorn, is a plaque and the hall's old date stone.

WERNETH LOW TO LONGDENDALE

It was always a bit different, this part of Cheshire, far wilder than the softer plains to the southwest. Back in the early 1600s when cartographer John Speed likened the shape of Cheshire to an eagle's wing, this narrow

WERNETH LOW TO LONGDENDALE

strip of land, just a few miles wide in places, formed the 'first feather [that] toucheth Yorke-shire'. Or, as it was later, rather more prosaically, nicknamed, 'the panhandle', a small spur running northeast from Stockport up into the Pennines, flanked by the rivers Goyt, Etherow and Tame. Contained within its relatively compact area you'll find a varied range of landscapes, from unlovely, post-industrial urban sprawl at one end to wild, deserted moorland at the other, and, in between, some fabulous views and little unexpected pockets of loveliness

8 WERNETH LOW COUNTRY PARK
Higham Ln, Hyde SK14 5LR

Views – that's what you come here for. Great stonking views in just about every direction. Head up to the top of this Pennine spur on a clear day and you can look out towards Manchester in all its urban glory in one direction or turn and survey the Peak District hills in the other. The Domesday surveyors of the 11th century declared Werneth Low waste and of little value; almost a millennium later it's a much-loved recreational space, where people come to fly kites, feel the wind in their hair and walk, cycle or ride along the tracks that criss-cross the hillside. Up by the war memorial, gazing out at the views, is the perfect place to sit and contemplate all those who've been here before you, from the ancient Britons who buried their chiefs here and Bonnie Prince Charlie passing through on his journey south to the Victorians who built a racecourse on the hilltop and the soldiers who manned the anti-aircraft guns that were positioned up here during the Second World War.

9 BROADBOTTOM

Whichever way you approach Broadbottom, the initial impression is lush green valley – making it all the more difficult to believe that this lovely spot was once a place where huge textile mills, powered by the River Etherow, filled the air with smoke, dirt and noise as they churned out cotton and woollen fabrics.

Wander down Mottram Road from the station, almost to the valley bottom, and you find the turn off to **Broad Mills Heritage Site** (Lymefield SK14 6AG), where interpretation boards lead you round what remains of the textile works that once stood here, now all pretty little glades and picturesquely overgrown fragments of industrial archaeology. Flowing peacefully alongside all the while is the Etherow, subject of one of my favourite quotes from old Cheshire guidebooks, when Ralph Bernard Robinson, in an 1863 guide to Longdendale, spoke of it being 'full of trout and other of the finny race'.

You can carry on following the footpath up to the end of Well Row, then along the muddy track of Hodge Lane (passing the old dye vats on your left) and into **Great Wood Local Nature Reserve** (♀ SJ986935), one of Tameside's few remaining sites of ancient woodland, eventually coming back on to the main road, where a right turn will lead you back down to the station.

SHOPPING

Lymefield Arts & Crafts Centre SK14 6AG ⌀ 01457 764434 ⌀ lymefieldart.co.uk ⊙ 10.30–16.00 Wed–Sat. The former visitor centre is now a showcase for the creative talents of local artists and craftspeople. The range of work on offer includes patchwork, paintings, carvings, stained glass and lovely embroidered pictures from local textile artist Maxine Pigram, whose idea this was. They also host craft sessions and occasional literary evenings, and keep pond-dipping nets and magnifying glasses for children to explore with in the nearby play area.

Lymefield Garden Centre SK14 6AG ⌀ 01457 764686 ⌀ lymefield.com ⊙ 10.30–16.00 Wed–Sat. This small family-owned garden centre is home to Lymefield Farm Shop, where meats on the butcher's counter include home-reared lamb and locally sourced pork, while among the goodies on the shelves are homemade jams and pies, Peak District honey and northwest beers. At the back, there's a very popular tea room (which closes a little earlier), with good homemade food (using lots of local produce) and views over the fields of a working farm.

Mill Shop Lymefield Mill, SK14 6AG ⌀ 01457 764399 ⊙ 10.00–16.00 Thu–Fri, 10.00–15.30 Sat. I'm no fan of sewing but if anything could convince me to take up needle and thread it would be this wonderful little outlet for the mill next door. A tiny little square building on the edge of the river, it specialises in printed fabrics and is crammed full with a glorious selection of linens, poplins and assorted other textiles and accessories.

10 MOTTRAM IN LONGDENDALE

Most people know Mottram only as a traffic-snarled road, the A628, which crawls its way through *en route* to the Woodhead Pass. Turn south off the main road, though, and you discover an unexpectedly lovely little conservation area of stone-built cottages and a church with a view.

The triangle formed by Market Place, Ashworth Lane and Broadbottom Road bounds a little grassy area, at the centre of which is the **Crown Pole**, a lofty cast-iron mast topped with a weather vane and a golden

L S LOWRY

By the traffic lights in the centre of Mottram, where Market Street meets Stalybridge Road, you can take a seat next to a bronze statue of L S Lowry, besuited, behatted and bespectacled, and forever sketching the Crown Pole. The Stretford-born artist, best known for his paintings of northern industrial landscapes, retired up here, 'close to the wild hills', in 1948 and remained until his death in 1976. Just a short walk up Stalybridge Road, marked by a blue plaque, is The Elms, the detached stone villa where he lived surrounded by drawings from his favourite Victorian artist, Dante Gabriel Rossetti, and a houseful of clocks that he said kept him company.

cockerel. The village stocks stand nearby and in between the two is a rather sad looking little spruce. Meet **Twiggy**, planted with honourable intent by the council in 2014 as a sustainable, living Christmas tree but such a spindly specimen that it attracted immediate derision from the locals and spawned its own Facebook page, 'The Embarrassment of Mottram Christmas Tree'.

Overlooking the green is the 19th-century courthouse, where a handsome **drinking fountain** commemorates the introduction of piped water to the village, with instructions from the Members of the Local Board (including the splendidly named Adolphus Evill) that it's 'to be drunk on the premises'. Turn your back on the courthouse and walk up Church Brow then follow the broad stone steps ahead of you. They lead to a cobbled path that curves along the slope of the hill to emerge on top of the brow, where **St Michael and All Angels** (aka 'the cathedral of East Cheshire') stands proudly dominating the valley below, such a prominent landmark that it was used as a wayfinder by German aircraft heading towards Manchester during the Second World War. There's been a church on this site since at least the late 13th century but the one still standing here today is largely 15th century Perpendicular, at least on the outside. The interior was remodelled in the 1850s but retains reminders of earlier incarnations, including the Norman barrel font, carved from a single block, which for many years was banished outside to serve as a water butt. Other highlights include a finely carved alabaster pulpit and bread racks either side of the north door where they used to put loaves baked specially for distribution to the poor of the parish.

Keep your eyes down in the churchyard to find the grave of Lewis Brierley, a grim reminder that bodysnatchers haunted this area in the early 19th century, supplying surgeons with corpses for anatomical research. When the body of his 14-year-old son was stolen, Lewis's father James Brierley had the following inscription carved into his gravestone:

> 'Though once beneath the ground his corpse was laid
> For use of surgeons it was thence convey'd.
> Vain was the scheme to hide the impious theft
> The body taken - shroud and coffin left.
> Ye wretches who pursue this barb'rous trade
> Your corpses in turn may be convey'd
> Like his to some unfeeling surgeons room
> Nor can they justly meet a better doom.'

Head through the gate on the far side of the churchyard into the memorial garden, where you can soak up glorious views down the valley and pay your respects at the monument to one of Mottram's most remarkable sons, Lawrence Earnshaw. Born into a poor family at the start of the 18th century, he grew into a talented inventor and craftsman, with an extraordinary skill for all things mechanical and mathematical.

In *A Description of the Country from Thirty to Forty Miles Round Manchester* (1795), historian J Aikin hailed Earnshaw as 'one of the most universal mechanists and artists ever heard of' – a man who, among other talents, could make sheep's wool into cloth and cloth into clothes; who was a blacksmith, coppersmith, gunsmith and bell-founder; who could engrave, paint and gild; make sundials, mend fiddles and play assorted instruments. It's said that long before James Hargreaves and Richard Arkwright came up with their inventions that revolutionised the textile industry, Earnshaw had already created a machine that could spin and reel cotton but destroyed it because he feared it would put textile workers out of a job.

12 LONGDENDALE

From Mottram, Longdendale ('long wooded valley') leads up, via Tintwistle, to Woodhead and, a few miles further on, Salter's Brook, which marked the easternmost point of old Cheshire. The valley has always provided a corridor across the Pennines – this was the route followed centuries ago by the salters, carrying their valuable cargo from the Cheshire wyches into Yorkshire. Today, Longdendale falls

THE LONGDENDALE LIGHTS

Dr David Clarke is senior lecturer in journalism at Sheffield Hallam University, with a special interest in folklore, both ancient and contemporary. He has written many books on the subject, including *Supernatural Peak District* (drdavidclarke.co.uk).

It may be just 15 miles from Manchester city centre but Longdendale feels remote and eerie, especially at night. The top end of the valley has a long history of supernatural happenings, and everybody I've spoken to in that area, including mountain rescuers, park rangers and farmers, has had some sort of strange story to tell.

Many of them concern the 'Longdendale lights', which come in several different forms. Some people report seeing a large, pulsing ball of light hovering over the moors or a string of smaller coloured lights moving together; others have seen the whole valley illuminated by a cold blue light. Mountain rescue teams have been called out on many occasions, when people thought they were witnessing distress flares from walkers lost on the hills, but have found nothing.

Nobody knows yet what causes these lights. Some of the sightings are probably caused by aircraft approaching Manchester Airport, but stories of the lights go back long before there were regular flights coming in. Another theory is that they might be caused by geological faults – the area is riven with fault lines and perhaps mini earthquakes or rocks shifting underground are causing some kind of electrical current to build up and, on certain occasions, discharge into the sky. Personally, I think they're probably some kind of natural phenomenon, perhaps a mirage or optical illusion, rather like a rainbow.

Who knows? All these things could play a part in creating them. But people have seen these lights all through the ages and regarded them as supernatural. Over the years, they've been called devil's lanterns and devil's bonfires; while others have thought them to be the torches of ghostly Roman legionnaires marching across the moors or those of long-dead railway men haunting the Woodhead tunnel. Nowadays, of course, people see them and think UFOs and aliens. One thing's for sure: it's a very strange area ...

within the Dark Peak portion of the Peak District National Park and is a popular place for outdoors pursuits, with plenty of scope for walking, cycling and riding and sailing on the reservoirs. Among the paths that lead up into the high moorland is the **Pennine Way**, which crosses the valley at Crowden and heads north to Black Hill, once the county top of Cheshire. Less of a challenge is the **Longdendale Trail**, also open to cyclists and horseriders, which follows the old dismantled railway line to the south of the reservoirs, with plenty of access points where you can nip off and get down to the water.

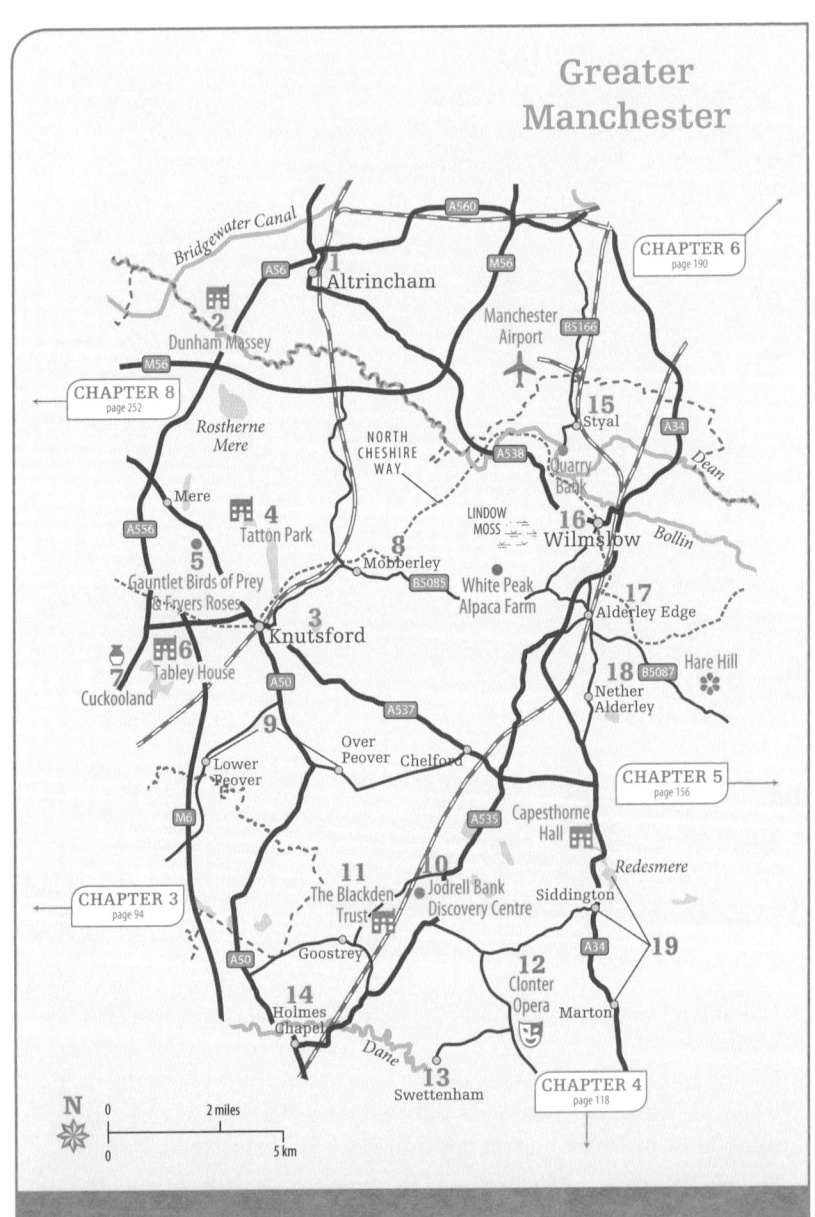

NORTHEAST CHESHIRE

7
NORTHEAST CHESHIRE

If northwest Cheshire is often dismissed by the unknowing as being all downtrodden industrial wasteland, the northeast is often sneered at for being all ostentatious wealth and bling. There's some truth in it, of course. The area does have a greater than average concentration of high-living high-earners. But then if you've made your millions, why *wouldn't* you choose to live here? It's an appealing, attractive part of the county.

The arrival of the railways in the mid 19th century transformed much of this region. It was largely rural until then, and indeed much of it still is today. The Royal Cheshire County Show (a celebration of all things agricultural) is held here and the lush farmland is dotted with blink-and-you'll-miss-them villages and prosperous market towns. But the new trains made it easy for those who'd made their fortunes in the dark, satanic mills of Manchester to live far from the smog and grime produced by the sources of their wealth. While the workers were crammed into tiny tenements in the inner city, the bosses moved out to build splendid, spacious villas in locations where the air was fresh and clean and the countryside rolled just enough to be prettily scenic without becoming too challengingly rugged. Some of those houses remain today, in the desirable avenues of places such as Bowdon, Hale and Alderley Edge.

The same railways made the same beauty spots popular destinations for workers to visit on their rare days off. In *Libbie Marsh's Three Eras*, Elizabeth Gaskell describes a Whitsuntide trip to Dunham Massey, recording the fact that at the time it was seen as a little old-fashioned next to the trendier delights of Alderley. The region is still popular with day trippers today, with some great country pubs, attractive rural walks, and a cluster of National Trust sites, including Tatton Park and Quarry Bank. It's home to the internationally significant Jodrell Bank Observatory, and it has unearthed the UK's oldest bog body (Lindow

Man) and produced famous adventurers such as George Mallory. It's also more than happy to embrace the eccentric, whether it's a museum devoted to cuckoo clocks or an opera house on a farm.

GETTING THERE & AROUND
PUBLIC TRANSPORT
Wilmslow has a **rail** station on the West Coast mainline, with direct Virgin Trains services between London and Manchester stopping off here once an hour. Arriva Trains Wales and CrossCountry Trains both link Wilmslow to Crewe and beyond in one direction and Stockport and beyond in the other. In addition, Northern trains between Manchester and Crewe stop at several stations in this area: Handforth, Wilmslow, Alderley Edge, Chelford, Goostrey and Holmes Chapel.

On the Mid-Cheshire Line, Northern Rail services between Stockport and Chester stop off at stations including Altrincham (connected to Manchester via Metrolink tram), Hale, Ashley, Mobberley, Knutsford and Plumley. The Mid Cheshire Community Rail Partnership (⌀ midcheshirerail.org.uk) is a mine of information about the line's services (including music trains), stations (they've produced attractive 1930s-style posters for each one), and nearby attractions. They also produce several Rail Walks booklets suggesting walks from stations along the line, and have teamed up with Chester Cycling Campaign to create three Rail and Ride Route leaflets. All routes (The Jodrell Jaunt, The Tatton Trail and The Ashley Amble) are 20–25 miles long, and start and end at stations on the Mid-Cheshire Line.

On the **bus** front Knutsford, Wilmslow and Altrincham are the best hubs, but it has to be said that this is not the best connected corner of the county. Services are infrequent and leave whole swathes of countryside untouched. In the land of flash cars, you're clearly not expected to travel by public transport.

WALKING
This is a region of gentle country rambles rather than challenging hilly hikes. That's not to say it's all flat – you'll find a few steeper slopes on the sandstone escarpment of Alderley Edge or on the banks of the Bollin in Styal. For the most part, though, it's a gently undulating landscape, where some of the best walks are along the river valleys or within the

> ### TOURIST INFORMATION
>
> **Altrincham Library** 20 Stamford New Rd, WA14 1EJ ⌀ 0161 912 3189 ⊙ 10.00–17.00 Mon–Tue & Thu–Fri, 10.00–19.00 Wed, 10.00–16.00 Sat
> **Cheshire East** ⌀ cheshireeast.gov.uk. This website has a page of links to information sources for different towns in the region, including Alderley Edge, Wilmslow, Knutsford and Prestbury. There's no obvious link on the home page so the easiest way to find it is to enter 'town information' in the search box at the top of the page.

grounds of the large stately homes – Dunham Massey, Tatton and Quarry Bank are all popular destinations for scenic strolls.

A few long-distance routes pass through the area. The 215-mile-long **Trans Pennine Trail** skirts across the northern edge of Altrincham and heads in a straight line to Lymm, following the route of the old railway line. Nearby, you can pick up the **Cheshire Ring Canal Walk** along the Bridgewater Canal, while the **North Cheshire Way** passes through or close to Alderley Edge, Wilmslow, Mobberley, Knutsford and Tabley on its 70-mile route from Disley to the Wirral. The **Salter's Way** (page 159) cuts across the southern part of the area covered in this chapter, around Goostrey, Jodrell Bank, Capesthorne and Siddington.

Cheshire East has published a couple of Walks for All leaflets containing details of more accessible walks for all abilities. You can pick the leaflets up at tourist attractions or download them from the Cheshire East website (⌀ cheshireeast.gov.uk). Most of the places included in this chapter are covered by OS Explorer 268.

CYCLING

The roads in this part of the county are very popular with cycling groups – some weekends it feels as if the Tour de France has come to town without telling anyone. The **Cheshire Cycleway** makes a couple of appearances in the region, cutting through the country lanes of Marton on its way to Gawsworth in the south, while to the north it skirts past Alderley, heads up through Mobberley to Ashley, then veers west to Rostherne before crossing the A556 into territory covered in Chapter 8. **CycleKnutsford** (⌀ cycleknutsford.org.uk) has produced a Knutsford Cycle Map, grading the town's roads according to the level of experience needed to ride them. You can pick up a copy at the library,

Knutsford Heritage Centre or Bikes n Gear (31 King St, WA16 6DW
⌁ bikes-n-gear.co.uk).

BIKE HIRE & REPAIRS
Bike & Go ⌁ bikeandgo.co.uk. Altrincham, Knutsford and Wilmslow stations have bikes available to hire through this scheme.
Tatton Park ⌁ 01625 374458 ⌁ tattonpark.org.uk. You can hire bikes at this National Trust property at weekends and during school holidays.

TRAFFORD

Between the River Bollin to the south and the Mersey and Manchester Ship Canal to the north is one of the chunks of 'lost' Cheshire. Although officially part of Trafford (one of the metropolitan boroughs that make up Greater Manchester) since the local government reshuffle of 1974, much of it still retains a very Cheshire feel, especially around the sylvan suburbs of Altrincham and the National Trust site of Dunham Massey.

1 ALTRINCHAM
🏠 **Birtles Farm B&B** Ashley (page 294)

Altrincham's swish southern and western outskirts have always been a desirable place to live. The attractive avenues of Bowdon and Hale – large swathes of which are covered by conservation zones – are broad, leafy and lined with handsome Victorian and Edwardian houses that have been highly sought after ever since wealthy Manchester merchants first built here, attracted by the area's scenic surroundings and famously salubrious climate. Wandering northwest from the hilltop **St Mary's** church along **Green Walk** will take you past some of the grandest, and lead to the pretty lych-gate entrance to **Denzell Gardens and the Devisdale** (157 Dunham Rd WA14 4QD ⌁ friendsofdenzellanddevisdale.com), where attractive formal gardens around the house lead through to a large area of grassland and woodland that's very popular with dog-walkers.

Central Altrincham, on the other hand, hasn't always fared so well. Once a busy market town, known for the quality of the local vegetables, it rather lost its way somewhere around the 1990s and by the noughties was looking decidedly down in the dumps, blighted by far too many boarded-up shop fronts. Now, though, it has a new spring in its step, due in no small part to the initiative of local couple Nick Johnson and

Jennifer Thompson, who came up with the bright idea of revitalising the dilapidated old market hall. Suitably renovated, it reopened in 2014 as Market House (see below) and proved an instant success, drawing people back into the centre and encouraging other new foodie and retail ventures to open up around it.

With no major cultural attractions and a still-fragile shopping scene, the market hall is the main reason for a visitor to come into town – but while you're there, you could pop round the corner to the **Old Market Place**, complete with cross, stocks and whipping post, and bring your imaginative powers to bear to see it as Thomas De Quincey did in the late 18th and early 19th century. Writing in *Confessions of an English Opium-Eater*, he recalled his first childhood visit to 'this cheerful little town of Altrincham' when, on a market day morning, the view from his window was 'the gayest scene I had ever beheld.'

FOOD & DRINK

Market House Greenwood St, WA14 1SA ⌀ altrinchammarket.co.uk ⊙ 09.00–22.00 Tue–Sat, 09.00–18.00 Sun. Inside the listed old market building are several independent food stalls, a wine shop and a bar selling craft beers. The food ranges from sourdough pizzas and artisan pies to handmade chocolates and cakes, with everyone eating at communal tables in the centre of the hall or at outside tables in summer. In addition, there are more street-food traders in the covered market area next door and a few 'Food Pods' round the corner on New Market Square.

The Garden 154 Ashley Rd, Hale WA15 9SA ⌀ 0161 941 6702 ⌀ thegardenhale.co.uk. From its 'Plant Power Breakfast' to its raw chocolate brownie, this trendy little café and wellbeing hub in Hale champions healthy eating and aims to source produce as locally, organically and sustainably as possible. There's a good range of healthy juices, shots and smoothies, but also vegan wines and gluten-free lager if you're feeling wicked.

Vegetarian Society ⌀ vegsoc.org Based in the northwest since the mid 19th century, the Vegetarian Society has its HQ in a large house in Bowdon. You can't just drop in for a veggie lunch, more's the pity, but you can book on to one of the regular classes held at the Cookery School here. They're enjoyable and instructive, and you get to eat all the results at the end.

SHOPPING

Shops

Abacus Books 24 Regent Rd, WA14 1RP ⌀ 0161 928 5108. At this independent bookshop, opened in 1979, Christopher and Elizabeth Lawton sell both new and secondhand books, with a particular emphasis on arts, crafts and local history.

NORTHEAST CHESHIRE

County Galleries 32–34 Railway St, WA14 2RE ⌁ 0161 928 9942 ⌁ countygalleries.co.uk. Housed in a large Edwardian building in the town centre, this long-standing gallery sells original paintings from both established and emerging artists, many of them from the northwest.
Edit & Oak 4 Greenwood St, WA14 1RZ ⌁ 07985 439630 🅵 @EditandOak. This attractive little lifestyle and interiors store was opened by owner Kate Harman in 2015. It carries an ever-evolving range of goods, including organic skincare, local ceramics and assorted reclaimed and vintage products, and many of the items are sourced from Fair Trade suppliers and responsible employers.
Idaho 56 Greenwood St, WA14 1RZ ⌁ 0161 941 1085 ⌁ idahoshop.co.uk. The homewares, stationery and jewellery at this independent boutique include organic toiletries and items from northwest craftspeople.

Markets
Altrincham Market Greenwood St, WA14 1SA ⌁ altrinchammarket.co.uk ⌁ 08.00–16.00 Tue, Fri & Sat, 08.00–15.00 Thu, 10.00–16.00 Sun. Next door to the food hub of Market House is the covered market, with a mix of fresh produce and crafts stalls. Different days bring different kinds of stalls (check the website for details), and the Sunday market changes theme on a weekly basis, rotating between design, food, vintage and crafts.

2 DUNHAM MASSEY
🏠 **Ash Farm** Little Bollington (page 294)
WA14 4SJ ⌁ 0161 941 1025 ⌁ National Trust ⌁ see website for details

Elizabeth Gaskell's portrayal of Knutsford in *Cranford* is familiar to most. Less well known, though, are her depictions of other parts of Cheshire. In *Libby Marsh's Three Eras*, it's Dunham Massey's turn to shine as 'the favourite resort of the Manchester workpeople'. The story describes a Whitsuntide outing to Dunham, where, after a 2-hour boat ride along the Bridgewater Canal from central Manchester, the characters land among 'soft, green meadows that [come] sloping down to the dancing water's brim'. For the city mill workers, the difference from their everyday surroundings couldn't have been greater:

> 'Its scenery presents such a complete contrast to the whirl and turmoil of Manchester; so thoroughly-woodland, with its ancestral trees (here and there lightning blanched); its 'verdurous walls'; its grassy walks, leading far away into some glade, where you start at the rabbit rustling among the last year's fern... Depend upon it, this complete sylvan repose, this accessible quiet, this lapping

the soul in green images of the country, forms the most, complete contrast to a towns-person, and consequently has over such the greatest power to charm.'

Dunham Massey still charms today, and continues to act as a natural oasis in an increasingly developed area. In Gaskell's day, the estate was the private property of the Earls of Stamford but in 1976 the 10th earl bequeathed it to the National Trust, in what the trust describes as one of the most generous gifts in its history.

Come here with kids in tow and there's no question what you do first – you go in search of the **fallow deer**. There's a 150-strong herd living in the park and on a good day you don't have to go far to find them. I've seen clusters of them on the lawns right up close to the house, though nothing has ever quite matched the thrill of one day coming across a solo stag, with a creamy coat and magnificent antlers, standing in one of the woodland glades at the far end of the park. If you're here in autumn, during the rutting season, you may get to hear the bucks bellowing at each other. In spring, when they shed their antlers, there's always the chance that you might find a cast-off lying on the ground – and if you do, you're allowed to keep it.

One of the other big highlights at Dunham is its **winter garden**, which comes into its own, inspirational best just as everyone else's garden is looking at its bleak and battered worst. On a crisp February day, the winter sun shows off the glossy coppery bark of the Tibetan cherries and the brilliant white trunks of the Himalayan birches, washed clean of moss by obliging volunteers. The Siberian dogwoods add extraordinarily vivid pops of red, while close to the ground there are snowdrops and golden aconites and carpets of blue and purple dwarf iris. Most unexpected of all is the fragrance, from winter-flowering honeysuckle, scented viburnum, *Sarcococca confusa* and *Daphne bholua*. My tip: join one of the guided walks with a gardener and take pen and paper to jot down all the plants you'll want to add to your garden wishlist.

"On a crisp February day, the winter sun shows off the glossy coppery bark of the Tibetan cherries."

Gratifyingly for Slow travellers, Dunham Massey is one of the easier attractions to reach by public transport: the number 5 bus between Warrington and Altrincham stops right by the entrance (see ⊘ tfgm. com for timetables).

NORTHEAST CHESHIRE

THE MERMAID IN THE MERE

It's not too often you get to encounter a mermaid inland – and to be honest, I can't promise you ever will. But this might be your best chance. Legend has it that Rostherne Mere, roughly midway between Dunham Massey and Tatton Park, is home to a mermaid who leaves the sea every Easter, swims up here via a network of secret underground waterways and rings a bell that tumbled into the water many years ago when the church tower was being repaired. Keep your eyes peeled ...

FOOD & DRINK

In the area round Dunham Massey there are a few places to eat, drink or pick up supplies. At **Little Heath Farm Shop** (Cow Ln, WA14 4SE ⌀ 0161 928 0520 ⌀ littleheathfarmshop.co.uk) the Jones family sell beef from their own Aberdeen Angus and Hereford cattle, plus a range of seasonal and local produce from other nearby farms and small businesses, including venison from Dunham Massey Park (Sep–Jan). A mile up the road, **Red House Farm** (Redhouse Ln, WA14 5RL ⌀ 0161 941 3480 ⌀ redhousefarm.co.uk) has a deli shop selling local produce, including their own preserves and organic free-range eggs, and a tea room where the menu is big on homemade and locally sourced food. In summer, they create a large maize maze, with paths big enough for wheelchairs and buggies.

You'll find traditional real ales at the small, family-run **Dunham Massey Brewing Company** (100 Oldfield Ln, WA14 4PE ⌀ 0161 929 0663 ⌀ dunhammasseybrewing.co.uk), while at **Dunham Massey Apple Juice** (⌀ 0161 928 3120 ⌀ dunhammasseyapplejuice.com) Alan Hewitt and family produce delicious organic juices and ciders from their orchards on the Dunham estate. You'll find them stocked at selected National Trust properties (including Dunham Massey of course) as well as some local delis and bars. In autumn, there's a pressing service, so if you have apples of your own you can take them along to be juiced, bottled and labelled, and in April/May, when the trees are covered in blossom, Alan occasionally opens up the orchard for blossom walks.

KNUTSFORD TO HOLMES CHAPEL

Centred around the genteel market town of Knutsford (Elizabeth Gaskell's *Cranford*) and the famous estate of Tatton, this part of the county is predominantly rural. So far, so normal, you might think. But it also throws up some surprises, including links with the Space Age, a cuckoo clock museum and a chance to see future opera stars in the making.

3 KNUTSFORD
⌂ **The Longview Hotel** (page 294), ⌂ **The Belle Epoque** (page 294)

This small town is regularly voted one of the best places to live in the northwest, and the appeal is easy to see. It has all the facilities of a proper town but retains a villagey feel; there's a pretty, historic centre framed by the open spaces of The Moor, The Heath and Tatton Park, and the whole happy parcel is wrapped up in attractive countryside sprinkled with good pubs and farm shops.

"It retains a villagey feel, and the whole happy parcel is wrapped up in attractive countryside sprinkled with good pubs and farm shops."

The town famously got its name (a contraction of 'Canute's ford') from the story of King Canute crossing the river here in 1016. You'll look in vain for a mighty waterway – so tiny is the Lily, the narrow culverted brook running through the centre, that it's easy enough to just hop across. Come after heavy rain, though, when the grassy area of The Moor on its eastern side is boggy with puddles, and you can imagine that getting from one side to the other may have been a trickier task all those centuries ago when this would probably have been much swampier land.

Arriving by train, turn right out of the station down on to **King Street** and you're straight into picture-postcard Knutsford. The narrow street (single file only on those teeny pavements) is lined with pretty little terraced houses and boutiques in an appealing mixture of architectural styles. There's multi-coloured Victorian brickwork, Georgian fanlights and bow windows, black-and-white timber framing and, mid-way along, an unexpectedly Italianate tower. Built in 1907 and designed by Richard Harding Watt (of whom more later), this is the **Gaskell Memorial Tower**, commemorating one of the town's most famous former residents.

Elizabeth Gaskell may not have been born here but she was sent to Knutsford as a baby to live with her aunt in a large house overlooking the Heath (Heathwaite, on Gaskell Avenue), and spent her childhood years in the town. She later married at nearby St John's and was eventually buried in the graveyard of **Brook Street Chapel** (Brook St, WA16 8DY ⌂ brookstreetchapel.org ⊙ 10.00–noon Tue, noon–13.00 Sun), where her grave can be visited today and there's an exhibition room dedicated to her. Mrs Gaskell famously immortalised the town as Cranford in the novel of the same name but it makes appearances in other works too, including *Wives and Daughters*, in which Knutsford serves as Hollingford and Tatton appears as Cumnor Towers.

Gaskell-themed guided tours can be booked further down the road at **Knutsford Heritage Centre** (90A King St, WA16 6ED ☉ 11.00–16.00 Tue–Sat, 14.00–17.00 bank hols, Apr–Sep also 14.00–17.00 Sun). Hidden away in a little courtyard, behind an ornamental gate depicting maypole dancers, this volunteer-run charity does sterling work in protecting and promoting the town's heritage. As well as running the Gaskell tours, it offers other themed walks and talks and has a well-stocked little gift shop. The big attraction here though is the **Knutsford Tapestry**, a needlework representation of the town at the end of the 20th century. The driving force behind this masterpiece, created to mark the millennium and completed in 2001, was local embroiderer Sue Newhouse, but it took the combined efforts of 3,000 locals to piece together, some filling in large areas, others adding just a single stitch. The result is absolutely captivating. Originally the idea was to do a two foot by ten foot depiction of the town's two main streets, but in the end the project grew and grew until almost every street was included and the canvas had grown to 40 foot long.

The delight is in the detail – individual houses, shops and civic buildings are clearly recognisable and it's all brought to life by the people and activities going on. There are swans swimming on the mere, firemen rescuing a cat from a pub roof and you can see the RHS flower show at Tatton and the dish of the Lovell telescope at Jodrell Bank. There are sheep in the fields, children playing croquet in a back garden, a car boot sale on The Little Heath, plus the white-suited figure of Martin Bell, former BBC foreign correspondent and one-time MP for Tatton. He's shown standing outside the Longview Hotel, his campaign HQ when he stood as an independent candidate against Neil Hamilton in the 1997 general election.

Legh Road & Richard Harding Watt

At the start of the 20th century, Richard Harding Watt left his very distinctive mark on Knutsford's skyline, despite the fact that he wasn't an architect but a glove merchant. Well-travelled and inspired by the sights he saw, particularly in northern Italy, he set about recreating some of his favourite looks at home, sometimes designing his own buildings, at other times calling in professional architects to bring

ANTI-CANOODLING PAVEMENTS

The narrowness of King Street's pavements is no accident – it's all down to Lady Jane Stanley, daughter of the 11th Earl of Derby. The inspiration for *Cranford's* Lady Ludlow, she remained single all her life and was no fan of public displays of affection between men and women. So when she died in the late 18th century and left money in her will to pay for paved footpaths, it was on the strict proviso that they be so narrow people could only pass along them in single file, hence preventing courting young couples from walking arm in arm.

Lady Jane herself usually travelled by sedan chair – hers is still used today as part of the May Day procession.

his visions to life. His mishmash of architectural influences and personal enthusiasms – here a Moorish dome, there a Mediterranean tower or balcony, everywhere ledges and niches for birds to perch on – didn't always win approval. Today, though, his eccentric creations are much loved and give an unexpectedly exotic air to corners of this quintessentially English town. You'll see his handiwork dotted about the centre including on King Street (the Gaskell Memorial Tower and King's Coffee House, which now houses the Belle Epoque restaurant) and on Drury Lane (the Ruskin Rooms and a row of cottages), but it's worth heading half a mile southeast of the station to Legh Road, home to what Pevsner describes as 'one of the most extraordinary sequences of villas in all England'. Among the grand houses lining the broad avenue are ten of Watt's creations, including The Old Croft, his own home for 18 years.

FOOD & DRINK

Barristers Restaurant Toft Rd, WA16 0PB ⌔ 01565 743333 ⌔ thecourthousecheshire.com/restaurant. Knutsford's former Sessions House – where, in 1952, the mathematician and code-breaker Alan Turing was so ill-served by the justice system of the time – has now been converted into The Courthouse Hotel, with Barristers Restaurant occupying the old Crown Court. The room itself is very impressive with its high coved ceiling and central dome, and the modern British food on offer includes a fine afternoon tea.

The Cheese Yard 69 King St, WA16 6DX ⌔ 01565 751697 ⌔ cheeseyard.co.uk. Owner Sarah Peak left the corporate world to open this specialist cheese shop and café in 2013. It stocks a good selection of well-kept artisan cheeses, including some award-winning products from Burt's Cheese in nearby Ollerton, all vegetarian and handmade in small batches from local milk. The small café serves brunch, lunch and drinks.

The Courtyard 92 King St, WA16 6ED ☎ 01565 653974 🌐 thecourtyardknutsford.co.uk. Yes, this little café gets good reviews for its homemade breakfasts and lunch, but to be honest it's the quirkiness of the place as well as the food that pulls people in. It doubles up as a Penny Farthing Museum, and you'll find around 30 examples of these extraordinary bikes suspended from the ceiling, including rare early wooden models and the Starley Giant, the largest ever made.

Dexter & Jones 20 Princess St, WA16 6DD ☎ 01565 650055 🌐 dexterandjones.co.uk. This friendly bottle shop and bar sells an impressive range of beers (more than 400) and gins (100 plus, including several from Cheshire distilleries). It also has a few wooden tables where you can sit in and have a drink – there's a changing selection of six beers on tap and six gins on the weekly gin board.

The Lambing Shed Moseley Hall Farm, Chelford Rd, WA16 8RB ☎ 01565 631027 🌐 thelambingshed.com. A couple of miles south of the centre on the road to Chelford, this farm shop showcases its own home-reared beef and lamb, with all burgers and sausages made in their own butchery. In addition, it stocks produce from more than 45 other local suppliers, including more meats, dairy products, preserves, veg and chocolates. The café menu is big on fresh, local produce with a specials board to take advantage of whatever's in season.

Seven Sisters Farm Holmes Chapel Rd, WA16 9ER ☎ 01565 723813 🌐 sevensistersfarm.co.uk. People come to this farm (two miles from central Knutsford) for the ice cream, made from their herd of pedigree Holstein Friesians, but there's also a tea room, serving a light lunch menu of homemade quiche, soup and oatcakes. Outside, you can sit at trestle tables with a country view, and there's a small covered play area for children.

SANDING THE STREETS

The custom of 'sanding the streets' – creating patterns of coloured sand on the pavements – is thought to be unique to Knutsford, and said to owe its origins to King Canute, who, after fording the Lily, sat down to shake the sand from his shoes. It landed in the path of a passing wedding party and he wished them luck. It then became tradition to sand the pavements outside the homes of bridal couples or on special occasions – when Queen Victoria visited in 1832 she recorded that 'we were most civilly received, the streets being sanded in shapes which is peculiar to this town.' Elizabeth Gaskell, too, remembered the streets being sanded for her wedding day.

These days, the practice is largely confined to the Royal May Day festivities (🌐 knutsford-royal-mayday.co.uk), which take place on the first Saturday in May. Held since 1864 (and 'Royal' since 1887), the event sees a costumed procession through town, the crowning of the Royal May Queen and a large funfair and firework display on the heath.

MARKETS

Knutsford Market Hall (6–8 Silk Mill St ⊙ 08.00–16.00 Tue & Thu–Sat) has traditional stalls. There's also a **Makers Market** held along Princess Street on the first Sun of the month (Feb–Nov), with food and craft stalls, plus a two-day **Christmas Market** in December, held when the festive lights are switched on.

4 TATTON PARK
Dairy Apartments (page 294)
Mereheath Dr, Knutsford WA16 6QN ⌔ 01625 374400 ⌔ National Trust ⊙ The park is open year round but times for the house & gardens vary; check the website for details. Although owned by the National Trust, Tatton is managed & financed by Cheshire East so NT members get free entry to the mansion & gardens, but charges apply for other things, including parking.

A giant of the stately home scene, Tatton Park is a vast and varied world that keeps the crowds coming with a wide array of attractions and a jam-packed calendar of events, including the RHS Flower Show in July. Whatever you expect from a country estate, you're pretty much guaranteed to find it here (including places to eat and drink during your visit). There's the **main house** itself, of course – a large Neoclassical mansion, its Regency interiors filled with the Egerton family's impressive collection of fine art and furnishings. Just for balance, you get to see the servants' quarters and kitchens below stairs as well. What many people don't realise is that Tatton also has another, older hall, called – appropriately enough – The Old Hall. Take a guided tour through its medieval rooms and see if you can spot one of the ghosts reputed to haunt it.

Then there are the justifiably famous **gardens**, all 50 acres of them, including the arboretum, rose gardens and 100-year-old Japanese garden, where the acers put on fabulous displays of autumn colour. There's an Italian Garden (designed by Joseph Paxton), a conservatory (designed by Lewis Wyatt), a fernery and a maze. They're all absolutely beautiful but I'm always particularly impressed by the walled kitchen gardens. Most places make do with one walled garden but Tatton has three, crammed with an abundance of fruit and vegetables that are sold in the garden shop in season.

Surrounding the house and gardens you get 1,000 acres of open **parkland** in which to wander, discovering ponds and woodlands and looking out for the resident red and fallow deer. Or, if you're with children, heading straight for the playground or the farm with its rare-breed animals. The farm's latest venture is a 'field to fork' project, bringing to life the story of how food is grown and reared – just one of the many entertaining and educational initiatives laid on within the grounds. You'll also find everything from the chance to experience life as a Viking or try your hand at longbow shooting to watching cinema under the stars or learning how to get the best from your digital camera.

5 GAUNTLET BIRDS OF PREY & FRYERS ROSES

Just north of Knutsford on the road to Mere is **Gauntlet Birds of Prey** (Manchester Rd, WA16 0SX ℰ 01565 754419 ⌀ gauntlet.info ⊝ Mar–Oct 11.00–17.00 daily, Nov–Feb 11.00–16.30 w/ends). Cheshire's largest bird of prey park, it's home to dozens of different species, from barn owls and buzzards to a golden eagle and griffon vulture. While there's no denying it would be preferable to see them all in their natural habitat, Gauntlet places great emphasis on educating people about birds of prey and the role they play in the wider ecosystem, and admission fees go towards supporting the work of the Gauntlet Conservation Trust. It's an interesting, informative and entertaining visit, the highlight of which is the twice-daily flying display. There wasn't a person there on my last visit who wasn't thrilled by the awe-inspiring finale, when the display area fills with an astonishing array of hawks, storks, vultures and more, swooping in over the trees and hopping along the path right next to you.

"It is home to dozens of different species, from barn owls and buzzards to a golden eagle and griffon vulture."

Right next door (and sharing the same car park) is **Fryers Garden Centre** (ℰ 01565 755455 ⌀ grosvenorgardencentre.co.uk/fryer). It sells all the usual garden centre stuff (clothing, candles and cakes as well as camellias, cosmos and chrysanths), but what it's particularly known for is its rose nursery. Arthur Fryer first started growing roses commercially in 1912 and the successful business he founded, although no longer owned by the Fryer family, is still producing award-winning new cultivars today. One of their latest, 'The Mayor', a pretty pink and gold floribunda, was launched at the 2017 RHS Flower Show Tatton Park, and some of the money from each sale goes to support charities nominated by the Mayor of Knutsford.

6 TABLEY HOUSE

Tabley Ln, Tabley WA16 0HB ⌀ 01565 750151 ⌀ tableyhouse.co.uk ⊙ Apr–Oct 13.00–17.00 Thu–Sun & bank hols

Nearby Tatton so effectively steals the stately home limelight round here that this fine Palladian mansion, surrounded by parkland, tends to be overlooked. Those who do discover it, though, are invariably delighted. You don't get to see all of the house (most of it is now a nursing home) but the one floor open to visitors contains the grandest areas, the State Rooms, which show off the finest 18th- and 19th-century art and craftsmanship, including original paintings and furnishings displayed in the rooms for which they were designed.

Next to the hall is a lovely little 17th-century chapel, which originally stood on an island in the mere before being moved and re-erected on its current site in the 1920s. The old hall that used to share the island wasn't so lucky, collapsing as a result of subsidence, but one of its grand fireplaces, a fabulously ornate affair, is preserved in the tea room, which opens on the same days as the house, serving teas, sandwiches and snacks.

7 CUCKOOLAND

The Old School, Chester Rd, Tabley WA16 0IIL ⌀ 01565 633039 ⌀ cuckooland.com ⊙ year-round, but contact them in advance to let them know when you'd like to visit

ROYAL CHESHIRE COUNTY SHOW

⌀ royalcheshireshow.org

For two days each June, all eyes are on Tabley when it plays host to the Royal Cheshire County Show, one of the area's flagship events. There can't be too many occasions that unite no-nonsense livestock farmers with giggling girls in designer wellies, gin-tasting foodies and kids firmly intent on whizzing down a giant bouncy castle slide all day – but this is certainly one of them.

This annual event brings together a wide range of tastes and talents. In one corner, young riders eagerly vie for show-jumping rosettes; in another, chainsaw-wielding artists compete to create the best carvings. You can have a ride on the big wheel or try your hand at country sports. There are marquees filled with flower displays and fluffy rabbits; arenas where sheep dogs show off and pipe bands parade; and a village green with entertainment in the form of folk singers, rock choirs and Morris men fully kitted out in ribbons, bells and flower-trimmed hats. And, of course, you get the chance to 'guess the number of blood tubes in the jar' (who needs sweets?), pick up a vintage tractor or win a year's supply of logs. Not to be sniffed at.

NORTHEAST CHESHIRE

Finding what's believed to be the world's largest cuckoo-clock museum hidden away somewhere in the depths of the Black Forest would feel entirely natural. But to come across it sitting on the A556 just outside Knutsford? That's a little more surprising. This gathering of chirruping, calling clocks is the labour of love of horologist brothers Roman and Maz Piekarski, who've dedicated several decades to acquiring and restoring the pieces now on display. There are more than 600 of them, their carved wooden cases and swinging pendulums covering every inch of available wall space, and the brothers know each one inside out.

8 MOBBERLEY

The Hinton Guest House (page 294), **The Roebuck** (page 294)
Owen House Farm (page 294)

Quite where Mobberley starts and ends is hard to pin down – it's a large, spread-out village with no obvious centre to it. What it does have, though, scattered round the parish, is a fine church, some appealing places to eat and drink, and an alpaca farm.

I can't look at the attractive country church of **St Wilfrid's** (Church Ln, WA16 7RA) without imagining a young George Mallory scaling its tower (see box, page 236) and wondering which route he took. It's

CHESHIRE CAT PUBS & BARS

cheshirecatpubsandbars.co.uk

This great little group is the baby of Mobberley residents Tim Bird and Mary McLaughlin, both dab hands at creating the perfect country pub. So far they've transformed seven closed or failing properties into just the kind of place you'd love to have as your local, all big on character, cosiness and cut-above pub grub, and all serving local craft ales and an interesting range of spirits. Lucky Mobberley is home to three of these.

Opposite St Wilfrid's is the **Church Inn** (Church Ln, WA16 7RD 01565 873178), a pretty brick building that now has loads of awards under its belt, including *Pub and Bar Magazine*'s 'Best Pub in the UK' title for 2016–17. Half a mile south, hidden away down a little dip, is **The Bull's Head** (Mill Ln, WA16 7HX 01565 873395), an early 19th-century pub with a large, family-friendly beer garden and a great choice of whiskies, and facing it over the road is **The Roebuck** (01565 873939), a romantic little slice of Provence adrift in the Cheshire countryside. Hard to choose between siblings, but I have a very soft spot for this one, with its weathered shutters and olive trees, lovely tiered garden and retro brasserie. It also has six quirkily decorated bedrooms, so you can stay over after dinner.

rather moving to think that one of Britain's most celebrated heroes found his climbing feet here in this unassuming village. Inside, as well as the Mallory memorial window (see box, page 236), there's more beautiful stained glass to admire, along with a splendid reredos and a richly carved rood screen, dating from 1500, with little faces peering out from the column tops. Looking up at the north wall of the nave you'll find the remains of a medieval mural depicting St George slaying the dragon, while high on the walls outside there are odd faces and figures carved in the stonework. For aviation anoraks, though, there's a more compelling reason to keep looking upwards – Mobberley is right beneath the flight path to Manchester Airport a short distance away and at this point the planes are flying low enough to alarm anyone who's not expecting them.

Just over two miles east of the church is **White Peak Alpaca Farm** (Paddock Hill, WA16 7DB ⌇ 01565 872012 ⌇ whitepeakalpacafarm.co.uk ⊙ 10.00–16.00 w/ends, appointment only in the week). There's something tremendously endearing about alpacas, especially when you catch them in happy mode, running round the field like spring lambs and pronking in the air. The herd here comes in all different shades, from pale cream to deep chocolate brown – one of the little nuggets of alpaca trivia you pick up on a visit here is that no-one ever knows what colour the new-borns (or crias) will turn out to be. The shop sells 'field to wardrobe' products including hand-knitted clothing, hand-spun yarn and raw fleece.

FOOD & DRINK

Barnshaw Smithy Pepper St, WA16 6JH ⌇ 01565 872286 ⌇ barnshaw-smithy.com ⊙ 08.30–16.30 Wed–Sun. Rustic shabby chic is the look at this revamped smithy, now part café, part reclamation shop. And very pretty it is too, with fairy lights and bare bulbs strung across the ceiling, mismatched wooden furniture and outdoor tables dotted between planters full of flowers. Service and food are a little more hit and miss but on a sunny day it's a pleasant place to sit out, and goods on sale include organic toiletries and locally made candles and honey.

The Mobberley Brewhouse Dairy Farm, Church Ln, WA16 7RA ⌇ mobberleybrewhouse.co.uk ⊙ noon–18.00 Thu–Fri, 11.00–17.00 Sat. Three minutes' walk from the church is this rural brewery producing cask and bottled beers, which you can buy in the on-site shop. On the first Tuesday of each month they hold an Open Taps Night where you can sample the beers and maybe have a tour of the brewery.

CHESHIRE MOUNTAINEERS

For a supposedly flat county, Cheshire has made a surprisingly prominent contribution to the world of mountaineering. Among the many famous climbers with a Cheshire connection is one of the most familiar names of all, **George Mallory**, who was born in 1886 in Mobberley, where his father was rector of the parish church, St Wilfrid's. From his first home in the grand Newton Hall (near the Bird in Hand pub), the family moved to Hobcroft Lane and a house that's now right at the end of Manchester Airport runway. Here, the young Mallory is said to have spent an adventurous childhood climbing anything and everything, including, on one occasion, the roof of St Wilfrid's, where there's now a memorial window to Archibald Keightley Nicholson, depicting the figures of King Arthur, St George and Sir Galahad. Below them, the inscription reads: 'All his life he sought after whatsoever things are Pure and High and Eternal. At last in the flower of his perfect manhood he was lost to human sight between Earth and Heaven on the topmost Peak of Mount Everest.'

Mallory's companion on that final expedition, **Andrew Irvine**, was another Cheshire man: born on Park Road South in Birkenhead in 1902 and still in his early twenties when the two disappeared in the ill-fated 1924 ascent of Everest. They were last spotted closing in on the summit but never returned, leaving the world not knowing for sure whether or not they actually made it to the top.

It was Mallory who gave us the famous and much repeated 'Because it's there' quote – his simple answer to a *New York Times* reporter who asked him, in 1923, why he wanted to climb Everest.

Waugh Brow Farm Shop Smith Ln, WA16 6JZ ⌀ 01565 872208 ⌀ waughbrowfarm. com ⏰ 09.00–17.30 Thu–Fri, 08.30–16.30 Sat, 10.00–16.00 Sun. When you see a parade of farmyard animals walking along the top of a wall, you know you've come to the right place. Run by the Jones family, this is a proper working farm and the shop sells meat from their own cattle, sheep and pigs, as well as lots of other local and deli produce. There's also a Snack Shack, selling homemade burgers, bacon butties and cakes, and in spring and summer, when the cows are back in the fields, the barn turns into a farmyard play area.

9 LOWER PEOVER & OVER PEOVER

These two neighbouring villages can be confusing to outsiders, who are never quite sure where one begins and the other ends. Best not to worry about it and just head straight to the heart of pretty **Lower Peover** (pronounced Peever), where school, pub and **St Oswald's** church sit snugly together at the end of The Cobbles (WA16 9PZ).

A very lovely church it is, too, all black-and-white-timbered apart from the 16th-century tower, made of pinky-gold stone from Alderley Edge.

Take the gate on the north side of the churchyard and follow the path straight ahead past the cottages, curving right up Barrow's Brow then right again and up to the T-junction, and you'll arrive at the rather wonderful **Tree of Imagination** (corner of Free Green Ln and Broom Ln, WA16 9PR). Faced with a dead tree on the green here, the villagers set about transforming the old trunk, carving a series of tiny rooms and putting in miniature front doors and windows (some open, some don't). They also added an owl box, a bat box, and, pointing out from under the roof, a small cannon. It's meant to delight and inspire children – but it works for adults, too.

A couple of miles east, in Over Peover, is **Peover Hall** (WA16 9HW ℘ 01565 757981 ℘ historichouses.org ⊙ guided tours only, May–Aug 14.30 & 15.30 Tue & Thu). A secret even to many locals, this Elizabethan house, still lived in today, has fine oak panelling, Grade l-listed stables and handsome formal gardens. Unlikely as it seems, during the Second World War it became HQ for General Patton and the US Third Army, stationed there to prepare for the D-Day Landings.

FOOD & DRINK

The Bells of Peover The Cobbles, WA16 9PZ ℘ 01565 722269 ℘ thebellsofpeover.com ⊙ noon–23.00 daily (22.00 on Sun). If you're wondering why there's a Stars and Stripes as well as a Union flag flying outside this beautiful old pub next to the church, it's to mark the fact that during his time in Peover General Patton was a regular and once lunched here with General Eisenhower when they were planning the D-Day Landings. It's one of the classics of the Cheshire country pub scene, with cosy rooms, good food, a gnarled old wisteria curling round the porch and a large beer garden by the stream.

Three Greyhounds Inn Holmes Chapel Rd, Allostock WA16 9JY ℘ 01565 723455 ℘ thethreegreyhoundsinn.co.uk ⊙ noon–22.30 or 23.30. Part of the Cheshire Cat group (see box, page 234) and every bit as appealing as its siblings elsewhere in Cheshire, this 300-year-old pub has scooped up multiple awards for its happy combination of warm relaxing atmosphere, local brews and cut-above pub grub, with many items locally sourced.

10 JODRELL BANK DISCOVERY CENTRE

Holly Tree Farm (page 294), **Cheshire Country Holidays** (page 294) SK11 9DL ℘ 01477 571766 ℘ jodrellbank.net ⊙ 10.00–17.00 daily

In this very rural landscape, you might think that a whopping great hulk of white steel, towering over the trees and visible from miles around, would be decidedly unwelcome. Far from it: there's immense local pride in the giant **Lovell Telescope**, the star attraction at Jodrell Bank – even more so, since Jodrell was confirmed as the UK's nomination for UNESCO World Heritage Site status in 2019.

The site has been a base for radio astronomy since 1945 but it was in 1957 that the Lovell first swung into action, just in time to track the progress of Sputnik 1, the first artificial satellite. It's still one of the largest and most powerful radio telescopes in the world and has played a globally significant role in increasing our understanding of the universe. Jodrell has become slightly trendy of late, as well – in 2016 the first **bluedot** festival (discoverthebluedot.com) was held here. An innovative combination of science and music, it proved such a huge success that it's now an annual event.

You don't have to be a total techy geek to enjoy a visit. Even if you wouldn't know a quasar from a Quaver, you can't fail but be impressed by the giant scale of the Lovell, which has its own special beauty and grace. If you're lucky, you'll be there on a day when it changes position so you can watch it moving – an impressive sight. If you do want to learn more about the science behind it, the visitor centre makes it as accessible as possible, with assorted interactive exhibits to add a bit of hands-on fun (the 'whispering dishes' are always good). If you don't, you could just enjoy the grounds instead. The observatory's founder, Sir Bernard Lovell, was a man with a passion for trees and initiated the transformation of 35 acres of farmland into a lovely **garden and arboretum**. It's now home to two national collections – Sorbus (whitebeam) and Malus (ornamental crab apple) – that put on beautiful displays of blossom in spring. Check out the shop, too; it has a fun line in science-themed items, from a periodic-table tea towel and solar-system coat hooks to rocket cufflinks and pulsar brooches.

11 THE BLACKDEN TRUST

CW4 8BY 01477 571445 theblackdentrust.org.uk

Virtually in the shadow of the Lovell Telescope, but a world away in time, is the Blackden Trust, which cares for two historic properties on an acre of Cheshire land. One is medieval **Toad Hall**, where author Alan Garner has lived since 1957. The other is **The Old Medicine House**, a 16th-century timber-frame apothecary's house that once stood 17 miles away in Staffordshire. To rescue it from threatened demolition in 1970, it was

GOOSEBERRY RULES

In the late 19th century, gooseberry shows were hugely popular around the country. Now there are under a dozen left, all but one of them here in Cheshire. They may be a dying breed but they're still serious business, as I found out at the Goostrey Gooseberry Show, held on the last Saturday of July in a back room of the Crown Inn at the heart of the village.

The day before the show, the berries are picked in the presence of a witness, placed in special boxes and tied with string that is then sealed with wax and stamped. At the start of proceedings on the Saturday, the boxes are placed on the table, seals are inspected and, with no tampering discovered, strings are cut and the cases opened to reveal the contenders, each little gooseberry jewel carefully cocooned in cotton wool.

And so the judging begins, each berry placed solemnly on a little set of scales, weighed out precisely in grains and pennyweights, and measured up against the others in its class. They come not just in green but in red, yellow and white, with different varieties of each.

The big prize is for the heaviest berry overall, the Premier Berry, whose owner's name will be added to the list of previous years' winners displayed on a plaque in the snug. There are other prizes up for grabs too including the heaviest of its colour, the heaviest twin (two berries on a single stem), the heaviest triplet (so rare there were no entrants in 2017), and the heaviest group of 12 on a single plate. As the winner of each category is decided, the berry takes its place in a special display cabinet, which goes on show in the snug before the contents are auctioned off for seeds, and preparation begins for next year's battle of the berries.

---

dismantled and re-erected here alongside Toad Hall. The trust's work is all about connecting people with different aspects of the past, and the activities organised here range from talks and tours to archaeological surveys and digs. They also have a gooseberry project, growing 17 prize-winning cultivars, and are developing a herb garden around the house, growing plants that a medieval apothecary would have known and used.

12 CLONTER OPERA

Swettenham Heath CW12 2LR ✆ 01260 224514 🜲 clonter.org

There are many things you'd expect to find in the middle of the Cheshire farmlands, but an opera house probably isn't one of them. Clonter began in 1974 when Jeffery Lockett and wife Anita put on a one-off charity concert in their barn, with the audience sitting on bales of hay. Now the barn has become a theatre, with a 400-seat auditorium, orchestra pit, stage, bar and dining area, and an annual programme that takes in all kinds of musical performances as well as opera. You may not get the lavish gilt-and-velvet surroundings of a traditional opera house, but you'll enjoy a far more intimate setting and the chance to see tomorrow's stars before they make it big – encouraging emerging talent is all part and parcel of the Clonter ethos. A big plus for anyone who hates getting poshed-up is that there's no pressure on the dress-code front: if you like doing black-tie-and-ballgowns, go for it; if not, that's fine, too. The name, in case you're wondering, comes from the nearby stream, the Clonterbrook, which runs through the woodland on its way to join the Dane.

13 SWETTENHAM

A word to the wise: don't, as I once did, take a friend to Swettenham for a summer pub lunch without first checking if she has a bee-sting allergy. In July and August the two-acre lavender meadow beside the **Swettenham Arms** (Swettenham Ln, CW12 2LF ✆ 01477 571284 ◊ swettenhamarms.co.uk) is in full, fragrant bloom, and a lovely place to sit out, looking across to a sea of flowers and listening to the buzzing of thousands of bees. Unless, that is, you've brought someone who's rooting through her handbag and realising she's left her EpiPen at home.

Fortunately, this little village has an even lovelier natural diversion on the other side of the pub as well: the **Lovell Quinta Arboretum** (Swettenham Ln, CW12 2LF ◊ lovellquintaarboretum.co.uk ⊙ 09.00–sunset daily). Home to around 2,500 trees and more than 800 different species (including the national collections of pine and ash), it was created by Sir Bernard Lovell (of Jodrell Bank fame) and is a blissfully peaceful place to wander. Indeed, at the risk of jinxing it, I'd say I've never shared the 28-acre site with more than one or two other people at the same time. Favourite things? For me, the wonderful variety of unusual pine cones, the carpets of snowdrops in February and the view over the Dane Valley from the far end, but everyone finds their own highlights. There are maps at the entrance gate to guide you around, along with an honesty box, inviting a £2.50 contribution per person. Worth every penny.

Completing a trio of natural beauties, Cheshire Wildlife Trust (◊ cheshirewildlifetrust.org.uk) also has a reserve here, **Swettenham Meadows**, with a rich range of wildflowers, including devil's-bit scabious, heath spotted orchids and Cheshire's county flower, the cuckooflower, also known as Lady's Smock. Download a self-guided trail on the CWT website.

TOWNS & VILLAGES

Exploring Cheshire's remote villages, rural hamlets and handsome market towns reveals a wealth of tea rooms, roadside honesty stalls and great little pubs.

1 Rainow has a scenic setting on the edge of the Peak District National Park. **2** Sandbach is home to two rare Saxon crosses, which can be seen in the town square. **3** Great Budworth is one of Cheshire's prettiest villages. **4** Canals are a key feature of the Marple landscape.

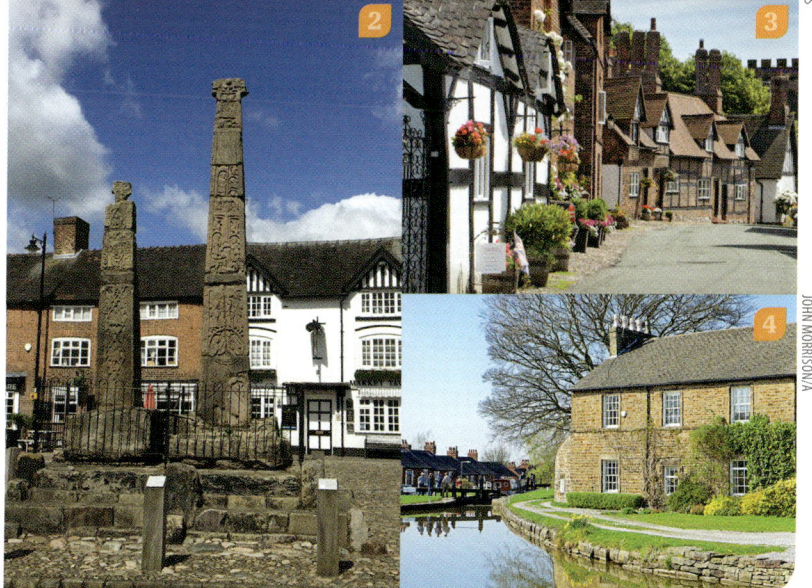

EVENTS & ECCENTRICITIES

Cheshire's calendar takes in everything from traditional well dressings and scarecrow festivals to Christmas markets and major agricultural fairs. There are regular farmers' and makers' markets year-round; summer brings a wide range of outdoor events and activities; and as you explore the countryside, you never know quite what eccentric sight might be waiting round the next corner ...

1 A well dressing in Broadbottom. **2** Peter Rabbit is the latest straw sculpture at Snugbury's ice-cream farm. **3** You need a sturdy pastry case to win the day at Wybunbury's annual Fig Pie Roll. **4** Children can immerse themselves in the theatrical experience that is the Just So Festival. **5** The Tree of Imagination at Lower Peover. **6** Shop for food and crafts at Macclesfield's Treacle Market. **7** Competitors race to unearth the most critters at the Willaston World Worm Charming Championships.

CHURCHES

Cheshire's many beautiful churches run the gamut of architectural styles, from simple tin tabernacles to a grand Gothic cathedral.

1 St Mary's Astbury has gigantic proportions for a village church. 2 Chadkirk Chapel reveals a surprising side to Stockport. 3 Detail of the Lewis Carroll memorial window at All Saints Church in Daresbury. 4 Corn dollies decorate All Saints in Siddington for harvest festival.

14 HOLMES CHAPEL

The Vicarage Freehouse & Rooms (page 294)

Holmes Chapel has an attractive setting in the Dane Valley, with the river itself meandering picturesquely along on the northern edge of the village, and an attractive little conservation area at its heart. Still, it's never been much of a tourist destination. Until, that is, One Direction shot to fame, and, as the home town of Harry Styles, Holmes Chapel found itself suddenly a place of pilgrimage for pop fans hoping to catching a glimpse of their idol. The closest most come is if they pop into the traditional village bakery where he used to work – step inside **W Mandeville** (2 Macclesfield Rd, CW4 7NE ☎ 01477 533148) and you'll find a giant photo of him, holding up a loaf above the slogan 'People come from miles and miles for craft baking and Harry Styles'!

"As the home town of Harry Styles, Holmes Chapel found itself suddenly a place of pilgrimage for pop fans."

Round the corner is the Grade l-listed **St Luke's** church, an attractive patchwork of architectural styles, with the original 15th-century half-timbered building encased within early 17th-century brickwork. It makes a pretty picture, sitting in the centre of a lawned churchyard against a backdrop of cobbled square and well-kept cottages.

STYAL TO MARTON

This part of the chapter takes you in a more or less straight line though a particularly prosperous part of Cheshire, from the outskirts of Greater Manchester (there be dragons) in the north to the outskirts of Congleton (there be timber-framed churches) in the south. Highlights include the industrial heritage site of Quarry Bank in Styal, the beautiful sandstone ridge of Alderley Edge and assorted mosses and meres *en route*.

15 STYAL

Tiny Styal is home to one of the country's greatest industrial heritage sites: **Quarry Bank** (Styal Rd, SK9 4LA ☎ 01625 527468 ◊ National Trust ⊙ see website for details), where, in 1784, Samuel Greg built a vast cotton mill on a picturesque stretch of the River Bollin. Greg was one of those at the forefront of change in the 18th century, taking full advantage of the new technology that turned cotton production from a small-scale home-working affair to a mighty manufacturing industry. As the mill grew, so did the number of employees, all needing somewhere to live. Former farms were turned into workers' accommodation, and Greg built first the **Apprentice House** (home to the many child labourers who put in hard 12-hour days alongside the adults) and later a whole little village of cottages, complete with church, chapel, school and shop.

The mill itself closed temporarily in November 2017 and is due to reopen in summer 2018, with redesigned galleries and a new passenger lift making them more accessible to all. Even without the star attraction, though, this is still a great place to visit. The site is beautiful, the mill so well hidden by the surrounding woodland that even from the car park it's hard to spot where it is.

From the new reception area a wide drive leads down to the mill but at the top of the drive a footpath leads off to the left and gives a better view on approach, at least in winter, when the trees are bare. Follow it along the edge of the car park, then right by the square pond (signposted Mill Yard) and as you round the next bend the mill appears in the valley below you, its huge chimney silhouetted against the sky. To get a better impression of just how large it is, cross over the river to the lawn on the far side and look back – there are a few benches there where you can kick back, relax and listen to the sound of the water rushing over the weir just upstream. On the left-hand side of the mill you'll see **Quarry Bank House**, Greg's own home, which recently opened to visitors for the first time. You can nip in there to get an idea of the owners' lifestyle then head up the hill to the Apprentice House to see how the other half lived. Both the Apprentice House and a newly opened **worker's cottage** in the village are guided tours only, so it's a good idea to ask about timed tickets at reception when you first arrive.

"The site is beautiful, the mill so well hidden by the surrounding woodland that even from the car park it's hard to spot where it is."

One of the biggest changes in recent years has been the renovation of the **walled garden**, now looking very fine. The rare curvilinear glasshouses, once derelict, have been magnificently restored and planted with vines and soft fruits, and in the back sheds you can learn about the work of the estate gardeners and visit the new shop. Vegetables from the new beds go to supply the café, with any surplus laid out on a produce stall for visitors to pick up.

To the north of the gardens lie **landscaped woods**, where you can take a walk along the lovely Bollin Valley. Go far enough and you come to the perimeter fence of Manchester Airport – bad news for the poor old Bollin, ignominiously culverted under the runway; good news for plane spotters who get a prime spot to watch aircraft landing and taking off.

FOOD & DRINK

Big pat on the back for the proactive locals who banded together to save the village shop. It had been closed for years before reopening in 2014 as **Earlams** (Altrincham Rd, SK9 4JE), a community venture mostly staffed by volunteers. It has three strings to its bow: the store, which sells a mix of everyday and deli foods, including some locally sourced produce; a café at the back, serving cooked breakfast, lunches, snacks and cakes; and an upstairs gallery where you can buy arts and crafts from local artists. Over the road, you have the choice between very good modern British fine dining at **The 39 Steps Restaurant** (🕿 01625 548144) or posh pub grub at the next door **Ship Inn** (🕿 01625 444888), where you'll need to be quick to grab one of the popular tables on the cobbles by the front door.

Near the main entrance to Quarry Bank is another, more unusual, restaurant option: **The Clink** (HMP Styal, SK9 4HR ⌀ theclinkcharity.org). It provides hands-on training for prisoners, with the goal of helping them find employment in the hospitality industry when they leave.

16 WILMSLOW

With its suntans-and-supercars reputation, Wilmslow might not seem an obvious Slow travel destination. But you don't have to venture too far from the Aston Martin showroom and Patek Philippe watch store to find yourself in a completely different world. Ten minutes' walk north from the centre brings you to **The Carrs**, a riverside park, where you can head off along the Bollin Valley to Quarry Bank in Styal. Ten minutes west, and you find yourself on **Lindow Common**, an area of ancient lowland heath that's a Local Nature Reserve with SSSI status. As well as the obvious heather and gorse, there are rarer plants here such as bog asphodel and the carnivorous round-leaved sundew, while butterflies include small heath and green hairstreak. Frogs and toads breed in Black Lake and there's said to be a small colony of water voles there, though stand and stare as I might I've never managed to see one.

Carry on heading west from the common, and things get even more unexpected as you reach the peaty, boggy wildness of **Lindow Moss**. Here, in 1984, peat cutters unearthed the UK's best-preserved bog body: the

2,000-year-old Lindow Man, who seems to have met an unnatural death some time between 2BC and AD119. Officially known as Lindow ll, and punningly nicknamed Pete Marsh, he now lives in the British Museum. Near the moss is **Rossmere**, a manmade lake used by anglers and a pleasant place to follow the footpath round before heading back into central Wilmslow.

FOOD & DRINK

Cheshire Smokehouse Vost Farm, Morley Green SK9 5NU ⌀ 01625 548499 ⌀ cheshiresmokehouse.co.uk ⊘ closed Sun. You could spend a lot of money at this very smart shop, and not just because it's fairly pricey. The shelves are stocked with serious temptation, from the in-house bakery's artisan breads to a range of smoked produce including home-cured bacon and smoked Wincle trout.

The Market Co Alderley Rd, SK9 1PB ⌀ themarketco.co.uk ⊘ 10.00–16.00 3rd Sat of the month. Wilmslow's monthly artisan market is a good one. Dozens of stalls line the main street, selling a range of foods and crafts, with a serving of live entertainment on the side.

17 ALDERLEY EDGE

🏠 **Goose Green Farm** Mottram St Andrew (page 294), 🏠 **Wizards Thatch** (page 294)

Alderley is one of those places where I'd love to turn back time. Not too far; just a few decades would do it, long enough to restock the high street with a few more normal shops in place of beauty salons and cocktail bars and to revert to the days before footballers started getting paid silly money and competing to see who could build the flashiest houses. The village always had plenty of wealthy residents and more than your average headcount of sports and TV stars, but things really ramped up a notch when the Beckhams moved in in the late 1990s. Suddenly Alderley found itself in the media spotlight and never quite returned to normal. Still, we are where we are and there are many who love the blingy new vibe, safe in the knowledge that they'll never be too far from their next injection of botox or Bolly.

And it has to be said there were the same grumbles about new money spoiling old Alderley back in the mid 19th century, when the arrival of the railway brought major changes to what, until then, had been a sparsely populated rural community. The land-owning Stanley family were far from enamoured of 'the Cottentots' – their nickname for the wealthy Manchester industrialists who started setting up home here, building grand Victorian houses surrounded by large, leafy gardens.

Nor did those homes impress contemporary James Croston, author of several northwest histories and guides. Writing in 1883, in *Historic Sites of Lancashire & Cheshire*, he was decidedly sniffy about what he called 'the aggregation of modern Swiss chalets, Italian villas, and imitation castles which Manchester's merchant princes have built for themselves on the wooded hill yclept Alderley Edge.' Yclept, mind you.

The railway also brought with it day-tripping factory workers from Manchester, who came on high days and holidays to escape the city smog, breathe in lungfuls of country air and soak up the glorious views from the Edge itself, the dramatic sandstone escarpment on the southeastern side of the village.

Now owned by the National Trust, the Edge was once the private property of the Stanley family, whose old hall stood where Alderley Park, a large life sciences campus and soon-to-be housing estate, stands today, on the shores of Radnormere. It was the Stanleys who planted trees on the escarpment, which until then had been bare, so we have them to thank for the fact it's now covered in mature woodlands of Scots pine and beech, which suddenly open up to reveal far-reaching views over the Cheshire Plain. Admittedly I'm biased, as the Edge plays a prominent part in happy memories of my teens and twenties, but it's always felt a special, atmospheric place – though it helps to catch it on a quiet, crowd-free day. There's not just natural beauty here but history and legend, too. According to the National Trust, it's the oldest known metal mining site in England, with activity dating back as far as 1900BC. Copper, lead and cobalt are among the minerals to have been extracted from the rocks and the many centuries of mining (which continued even into the 20th century) have left dramatic gashes in the hillside and a warren of tunnels beneath the ground. Much loved by potholers, they're now controlled by Derbyshire Caving Club (🌐 derbyscc.org.uk), who hold open days in April and September and run guided trips for groups at other times of year.

"It's always felt a special, atmospheric place – there's not just natural beauty here but history and legend, too."

As for legend, there all sorts of tales and superstitions attached to various landmarks on the Edge but the main tale told is that of the wizard and the sleeping knights lying underground (see box, page 246). It provided the inspiration for Alan Garner's classic 1960 novel

The Weirdstone of Brisingamen, a tale of good battling evil on and around the Edge. It was Garner's great-great-grandfather, Robert, a stonemason, who's said to have been responsible for the carving of a head above the Wizard's Well, where water trickles from the rock face into a stone trough and an inscription reads: 'Drink of this and take thy fill for the water falls by the wizard's will'.

Less than two miles southeast of Alderley Edge (from May to November a permissive footpath links the two) is a lesser-known (and hence less crowded) National Trust site in Over Alderley: **Hare Hill** (SK10 4PY ✆ 01625 827534 ◯ Feb–Nov 10.30–17.00 daily). A pretty little package it is, too. Around the edges you can follow woodland paths, looking out for the carved statues of hares dotted here and there,

THE LEGEND OF THE EDGE

Once upon a time, so they say, there was a farmer from Mobberley who had a fine milk-white mare and took it to Macclesfield fair to sell. On his way there, as he was crossing the Edge, he was stopped by an old man, with long robes and flowing beard, who offered to buy it from him. The farmer, confident of getting top price for his animal at the market, refused and took no heed when the old man predicted that he would have no joy in selling his mare that day.

The prediction, however, came true. Despite the fact that many admired the horse and remarked on what a fine beast it was, no-one wanted to buy. At the end of the day, disheartened, the farmer was leading the mare back home when the old man once more appeared in his path as he reached the Edge. This time, the farmer agreed to sell and followed along woodland paths until they came to a large rock, which the man struck with his staff. To the farmer's amazement, the rock split open, revealing large iron gates.

Clearly this was no ordinary old man he was dealing with but a wizard, who beckoned him through the gates and down, down, down through the hillside to a vast cavern, where 140 armoured knights lay sleeping. By the side of all but one lay a slumbering milk-white steed, the final missing place now filled by the farmer's mare.

This army, explained the wizard, would one day rise to save England when the country was in her hour of direst need. Until then, his job was to safeguard them as they lay deep in their enchanted sleep beneath the hillside. As payment for the mare, he pointed the farmer towards another cave filled with treasure and invited him to take his fill. The farmer stuffed his pockets with all the jewels and gold he could carry, before the wizard ushered him back through the tunnels and through the iron gates. Turning round to say farewell, he found both wizard and gates had disappeared, leaving just a solid rock – and try as he might, he never saw either again.

but the real star is the walled garden at its heart. In spring, one end is awash with colour from rhododendrons and azaleas, while the other has wisteria blossoms draping prettily over a white pergola; in summer, the borders of predominantly white perennials come in to their own. If you haven't visited for a while, it might be time for another look: they've done a lot of restoration work in the past couple of years. Plus, the hares have moved, so you'll have the challenge of finding them all over again.

FOOD & DRINK

G Wienholt Bakery 25 London Rd, SK9 7JT ⌀ 01625 583275 ⌀ gwienholt.co.uk ⊙ 09.00–17.00 Wed–Sat. Other shops have come and gone but Wienholt (pronounced Weenholt) is an Alderley institution, with a busy team of pastry chefs slaving away behind the scenes to produce all the homemade goodies that have people queuing out the door. The gateaux are gorgeous but they also do fine pies and lunchtime sandwiches. Just remember that they only open four days a week – it's too disappointing to come in search of one of their famous vanilla slices only to find the door closed against you.

Grantham's Fine Food 68 Heyes Ln, SK9 7HY ⌀ 01625 583286 ⌀ granthamsfinefood.com. This family-run deli isn't on the main road through Alderley, so in the normal run of things you wouldn't discover it unless you lived locally. Less than a 10-minute walk from the station, it's worth seeking out for its excellent range, which includes cheeses, home-cooked hams and Cheshire bacon. The owners make a point of supporting other family-run small specialist producers.

18 NETHER ALDERLEY

🏠 **Millbrook Cottage Guesthouse** (page 294)

On its southern side, Alderley Edge gradually turns into Nether Alderley, where **Nether Alderley Mill** (SK10 4TW ⌀ 01625 527468 ⌀ National Trust ⊙ Mar–Sep 13.00–16.30 Tue & w/ends, by guided tour only), a working medieval corn mill, sits right by the roadside, its heavy Kerridge-stone roof sloping down almost to the grass. Access to the small, wonky-floored interior is by guided tour only but that's no bad thing – the guides explain things that would otherwise be a complete mystery and give you a far better feel for the hard, dusty, back-breaking life of a miller.

Hidden away down a lane on the opposite side of the road is the lovely **St Mary's** church. At the entrance to the graveyard (where you'll need to give the very stiff gate a hefty push to make it budge) stands the old schoolhouse, now the parish hall. A stone over the door dates it to 1628 and the intervening centuries have weathered its sandstone blocks to prettily pale shades of pink. Round the corner is the unexpected sight of the **Stanley mausoleum**, neo-Jacobean in style and dismissed by Pevsner as a 'soulless rectangular block', though catch it at the right time of day, with the setting sun sparkling on its latticed windows, and it looks rather pretty against its rural backdrop. Obscure trivia time: the architect who designed the mausoleum was Paul Phipps, father of Joyce Grenfell. Take a walk round the outside of the church to admire the gargoyles on the tower (but take care – the slabs are mossy and slippery), then head inside, where highlights include some lovely stained glass (including a Morris & Co depiction of Raphael and Gabriel and a moving memorial window by Irene Shakerley) and the very grand Stanley pew. Often compared to an opera box, it's set high on the south wall, adorned with plush red fabrics and Jacobean panelling, and accessed via its own private staircase from the churchyard.

19 MARTON, SIDDINGTON & REDESMERE

Passing along the A34, you'll spot two interesting-looking churches on the east side of the road. To the south, in **Marton**, is the black-and-white **St James & St Paul**, founded in 1343 on top of what's thought to be a prehistoric mound. It has a very specific claim to fame: it's the oldest longitudinal-aisled timber-framed church in the world. When it was restored at the start of the 1930s, early medieval frescos were discovered hidden under the plaster of the west wall, and you can see above the door the faint faces of souls awaiting judgement. On the same wall are two large oil paintings by Edward Penney (one of the founders of the Royal Academy), in which Moses and Aaron hold tablets displaying the Ten Commandments.

"St James & St Paul has a very specific claim to fame: it's the oldest longitudinal-aisled timber-framed church in the world."

The church features in *Strandloper*, Alan Garner's fictionalised account of real-life William Buckley, a Marton man who was transported to Australia in 1803, escaped from his prison camp and ended up spending more than 30 years living with an Aboriginal tribe who believed him to be a reincarnation of their dead chief. Elsewhere in the village is the **Marton oak**, one of the oldest oak trees in the country, thought to have started growing back in the 8th century when King Offa ruled over this region, which was then part of Mercia. These days it looks more like a little grove of trees, its mighty trunk having fractured into three or four fragments. It's hidden away in a private garden on – what else? – Oak Lane.

A couple of miles up the road in **Siddington** is **All Saints**, also black and white but this time deceptively so, because, although some of the timber-framing is real, a large part of the church is painted brickwork. In the 18th century the old thatched roof was replaced with Kerridge flagstone slabs, the weight of which caused the nave walls to buckle, so they were encased in brick, which was then painted to resemble the original timbers. If you can visit All Saints in autumn, so much the better. Every year for Harvest Festival, the church is decorated with hundreds of beautiful corn dollies, made by retired farmer Raymond Rush, master of a disappearing art, who lives in the house next door. At other times of the year, you'll have to content yourself with admiring the corn dolly cross and three attendant angels over the rood screen and checking out the notelets and postcards for sale at the back of the church, which show the building in all its harvest glory.

Half a mile from All Saints is **Redesmere**, a large manmade lake, with plenty of benches along the water's edge where you can sit with an ice cream (if it's a nice day, there's usually a van parked in the layby), enjoy the view and feed the mallards, coots, tufted ducks, geese and swans, all so tame they'll be practically tripping you up. In July, when the Redesmere Fete takes place, the Water Lily Queen is rowed across the lake in a swan-shaped boat, before being crowned on the lake shore.

Capesthorne Hall

▲ **Capesthorne Hall Caravan Park** (page 294)
Congleton Rd, Siddington SK11 9JY ⊘ capesthorne.com ⊙ Mar–Oct noon–17.00 Sun, Mon & bank hols (gardens & chapel), 13.30–16.00 (hall)

Driving past Capesthorne a few years ago, we were puzzled to hear, drifting across the fields, the faint strains of Chesney Hawkes singing *The One and Only*, and to pass, a few yards later, a crowd of crimped-haired girls in pink rara skirts waiting to cross the road. That's not normal on this stretch of the A34. It was, we later discovered, the weekend of Rewind North, a very popular retro-themed music festival that takes over the estate for a weekend each August. It's one of a number of large events held in the grounds throughout the year, including antiques and collectors fairs and a classic car show.

> **CHESHIRE ONLINE**
> For additional online content, articles, photos and more on Cheshire, why not visit
> bradtguides.com/cheshire.

A very pleasant setting it is too, with 100 acres of parkland that takes in rolling pastures, lakes, woodland and flower gardens. In summer, roses ramble prettily over red brick walls and balustrades, and in the lakeside garden there's a lovely path lined with white-trunked Himalayan birches and off-white hydrangeas. If you take a fancy to the wrought-iron gazebo at the end (a favourite spot for wedding photos), you could commission one for yourself – it was made just down the road at **Siddington Smithy** (Salters Ln, SK11 9LH ⌁ 01260 224362 ⌁ smithyironworks.com).

Capesthorne is the seat of the Bromley-Davenports, whose Elizabethan-style hall, all turrets and gables, dates back to 1719, though the building you see today is largely the work of two Victorian architects, first Edward Blore and then, when part of the building needed rebuilding after a fire in 1861, Anthony Salvin. Access to the hall is limited, and things are geared much more towards weddings and corporate events rather than individual visitors with an interest in stately homes. However, you can poke your nose round some of the interiors, including the American Room, which a previous, US-born Lady Bromley-Davenport furnished with items shipped to the UK from her Philadelphia home.

FOOD & DRINK

Chapeau! Church Farm, SK11 9HF ⌁ 01260 224344 ⌁ closed Mon. This smart little café is owned by six friends, all keen cyclists, who also have a company organising charity bike rides. The name comes from a cycling term of approval – saying 'chapeau!' is the equivalent of doffing your hat – and the café is very popular with cycling groups, who have a tendency to hoover up the cakes. You'll also find homemade burgers, quiches, pies and lighter meals. Cheshire produce for sale in their small shop next door includes local eggs and ice cream as well as rapeseed oil and rapeseed honey from Calvia, a nearby family-run farm.

SEND US YOUR SNAPS!

We'd love to follow your adventures using our *Slow Travel Cheshire* guide — why not send us your photos and stories via Twitter (@BradtGuides) and Instagram (@bradtguides) using the hashtag #cheshire. Alternatively, you can upload your photos directly to the gallery on the Cheshire destination page via our website (bradtguides.com/cheshire).

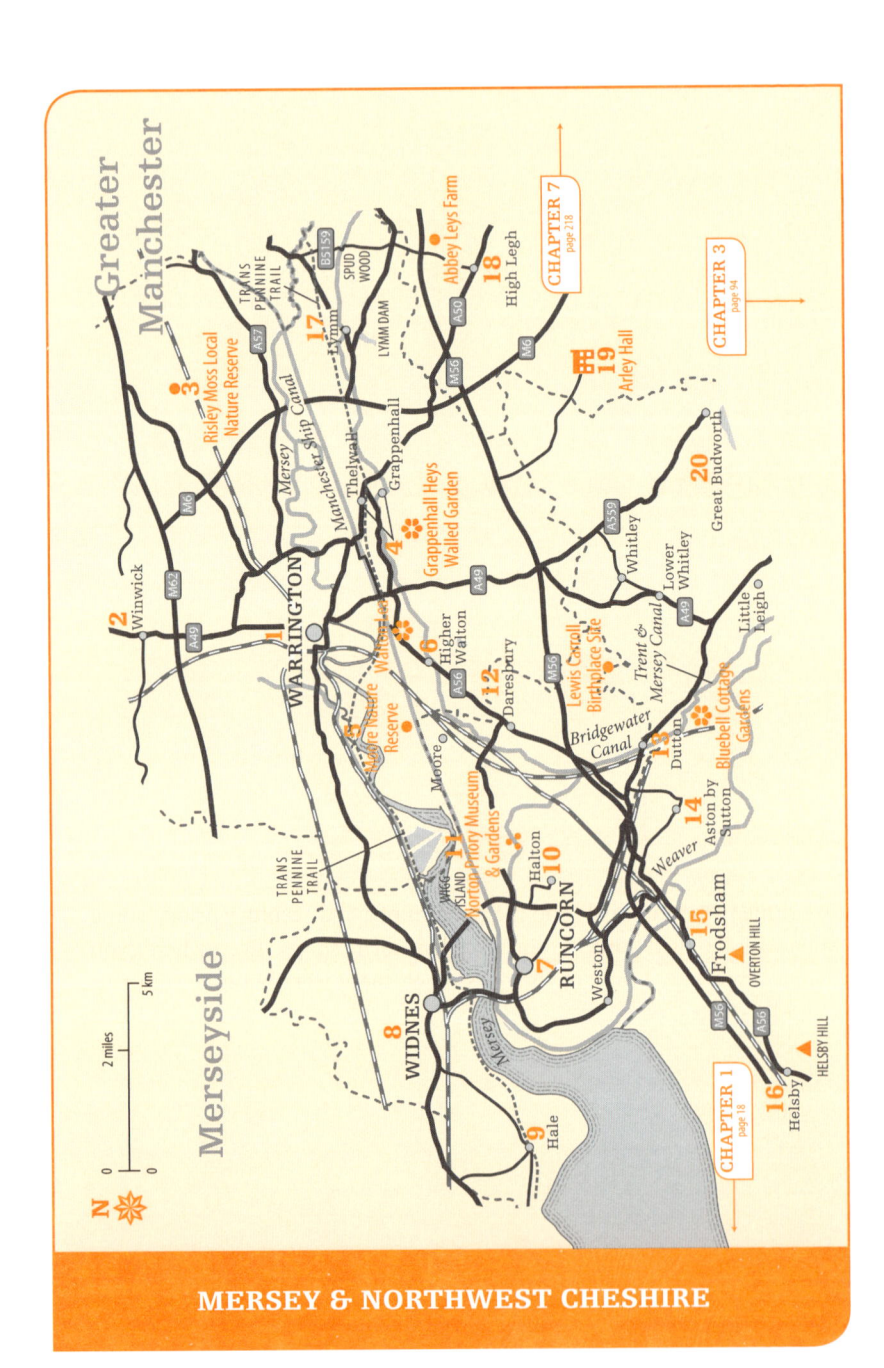

MERSEY & NORTHWEST CHESHIRE

8
MERSEY &
NORTHWEST CHESHIRE

Much of the northwest corner of the county belies the typically rural image of Cheshire, dominated as it is by the large towns of Warrington, Widnes and Runcorn that flank the Mersey and Manchester Ship Canal. When the Industrial Revolution came along, this area transformed rapidly: meadows were covered in mines and mills; farms gave way to factories; quarries and chimneys supplanted cattle and cheese. Today, of course, it has many of the problems typical of areas that have been industrial then gone into decline as the industry disappears.

It would be a mistake, though, to write it off as unworthy of a visit. The boom years have left the towns with some interesting buildings and tales to tell – rich pickings for lovers of industrial archaeology and social history – and the canals that once carried industrial freight are now the peaceful preserve of narrowboaters and towpath-strollers. For every chemical works or power station that blights the landscape, there's a quarry turned nature reserve or postcard-pretty village. There's a ruined Norman castle and the remains of a 12th-century priory, some beautiful walled gardens and excellent farm shops. Everywhere, you find tantalising traces of the days when there were big estates in this area – here an old family chapel, there a lodge house that once guarded the sweeping drive to a grand country manor. There are encounters with famous local characters, both fictional (including the Cheshire Cat and Alice – author Lewis Carroll was born here) and factual (including the vicar who earned 18th-century infamy by chopping down Shakespeare's mulberry tree). And there's plenty here to keep birdwatchers happy, with a variety of habitats (from the mudflats of the Mersey Estuary to the mossland and woodland of Risley Moss) encouraging a huge range of resident and migrant species.

In some of the areas covered in this chapter, such as the stretch from Lymm to Great Budworth and the area round Frodsham and Helsby, the appeal is easy to see and the attractions more obvious. In other areas you may have to dig a little deeper to find your rewards. But discovering the hidden beauties of a part of Cheshire I didn't know very well before was one of the joys of researching and writing this book – and a salutary lesson in not judging a place before you've been.

GETTING THERE & AROUND

PUBLIC TRANSPORT

The main rail hubs in the area are Warrington and Runcorn, each of which has, confusingly, two stations: Warrington Central and Warrington Bank Quay, Runcorn and Runcorn East. **Warrington Central** has connections east (Manchester and beyond) and west (Liverpool via Widnes) with East Midlands Trains, TransPennine Express and Northern. **Warrington Bank Quay** and **Runcorn East** both sit on Northern's line to Ellesmere Port and on the Arriva Trains Wales route from Manchester to Chester, in both cases calling at Frodsham and Helsby on the way. Virgin Trains from London call at either Warrington Bank Quay (on the Glasgow line) or **Runcorn** station (on the Liverpool line), which is also served by West Midlands Trains on their Liverpool to London line.

When it comes to buses, there are plenty around but, with services falling between different councils, no single information source. For Warrington and the surrounding area (including Lymm), you'll find a map of routes on the Network Warrington website (⌁ networkwarrington. co.uk), while for details of buses in and around Runcorn and Widnes, you'll need to visit the Halton Borough Council site (⌁ www3.halton. gov.uk). Cheshire West & Chester (⌁ cheshirewestandchester.gov. uk) has a bus map that includes services from Chester to Frodsham, Runcorn and Warrington – the X30, linking all of them, is particularly useful. Outside the main urban areas, bus services tend to be infrequent and usually stop early in the evening.

WALKING

There's some surprisingly varied walking to be had in this area, from flat towpaths to more challenging hill trails, sometimes passing through rural landscapes, at other times decidedly more urban. Several long-distance footpaths run east–west through the district. The 215-mile-long **Trans Pennine Trail** passes through, ploughing a resolutely direct route along an old railway line north of Lymm then crossing over the Manchester Ship Canal at Warrington and continuing westward to Widnes, Hale and beyond. Joining it for some of its 22-mile route is the **Mersey Way**, which begins inconspicuously in Rixton, east of Warrington, and ends just beyond Speke Hall in Liverpool.

The route of the **Mersey Valley Timberland Trail** (also 22 miles) is entirely confined within this chapter, starting at Spud Wood near Lymm and wiggling its way along to end at Runcorn Hill Nature Park. For some of its length it coincides with the 98-mile-long **Cheshire Ring Canal Walk**, which runs alongside the Bridgewater Canal.

On the more challenging side, there's the **Sandstone Trail**, which begins in Frodsham and heads instantly uphill to Overton Hill as it sets out on its 34-mile journey south to Shropshire. Other trails either passing through or starting in the area include the North Cheshire Way, Eddisbury Way, Delamere Way and Longster Trail. In addition, of course, there are lots of local walks, even in urban areas – when the new town districts of Runcorn and Warrington were built, they factored in plenty of green areas linked by foot and cycle paths.

The area finds itself, expensively, right at the edge of four different OS maps – to get full coverage, you'd need OS Explorers 266, 267, 275 and 276.

CYCLING

Some of the walking trails listed above, including the Trans Pennine Trail, are open to cyclists too, while **National Cycle Route 5** links Frodsham with Chester (including a traffic-free stretch through the marshes by the Mersey Estuary), and **Regional Route 82** runs a car-free ring around Runcorn. Warrington council produces a useful cycle map, which can be downloaded from ⌀ warrington.gov.uk. As well as showing where to find bike shops, parking and cycle paths across the borough, it also colour codes the roads to show how easy or tricky they are to negotiate, from yellow for the quieter streets to dark pink for those with heavier traffic and higher speeds.

BIKE HIRE & REPAIRS

Frodsham Bike Hire Lady Heyes Park (page 294) ⌀ 07541 347259 ⌀ frodshambikehire. co.uk. Offers a variety of bikes for hire, including children's models.

MERSEY & NORTHWEST CHESHIRE

> **TOURIST INFORMATION**
>
> Sadly there are no central sources of tourist information in the area, so the best way to find out about places to visit is at other visitor attractions such as Norton Priory (pages 275–6) or Warrington Museum & Art Gallery (page 257), where there's usually a display of assorted information leaflets.

Twelve50 Bikes 102 Main St, Frodsham ⌁ 01928 898011 ⌁ twelve50bikes.com. Although this shop doesn't hire bikes, it does repairs and has copies of the Cycle Frodsham map with suggested riding routes nearby.

CANAL-BOAT HIRE

Claymoore Canal Holidays The Wharf, Preston Brook WA4 4BA ⌁ 01928 717273 ⌁ claymoore.co.uk. This family-run company offers a range of different-sized narrowboats for canal holidays, along with a couple that can be hired by the day.

WARRINGTON & AROUND

Warrington straddles the Mersey, the river zigzagging ever more dramatically as it nears the estuary. To the north, the borough takes in Burtonwood, once home to the largest US airbase in Europe, and Winwick, site of a bloody Civil War battle and home to a legendary pig with a plan. To the south it reaches out across the Mersey, Manchester Ship Canal and Bridgewater Canal to gather in once outlying settlements such as Thelwall, Grappenhall and Higher Walton. Yes, this is a largely urban area, its countryside being steadily swallowed up by the large town at its heart, but it still has attractive old villages, farm shops, walled gardens and excellent birdwatching in nature reserves reclaimed from land where industry once ruled the roost.

1 WARRINGTON

It can be hard for outsiders to get a handle on Warrington. It's midway between Manchester to the east and Liverpool to the west yet bows to neither, keen to be recognised as a city in its own right. One minute it's being named the country's worst town for culture (the Royal Society of Arts placed it 325th on a list in 2015); the next it's been declared the second-best place in the UK to live (according to a 2017 Channel 4 TV programme, *UK's Best Places to Live*). For most of its life it was one of the oldest towns in Lancashire; then suddenly, in 1974, it found itself the biggest town in Cheshire instead. When the *Warrington Guardian* recently ran a poll asking its readers where they considered Warrington to be, the 47% who said Cheshire were narrowly outnumbered by the 50% who still felt themselves to be in Lancashire. Clearly, old loyalties run deep.

'Deus dat incrementum' says the Warrington motto on the coat of arms: 'God giveth the increase'. It feels particularly appropriate at a time when the town seems to be growing at a rate of knots, with big new housing developments planned on the outskirts, while in the centre, a £107 million regeneration scheme is underway to transform the area around Bridge Street and Time Square. It's not the prettiest of Cheshire towns, but it definitely has its eye on the future.

Whatever else you expect to find in Warrington town centre, it's probably not the extraordinary sight that greets you as you stand on Sankey Street and look across towards the Town Hall. There ahead of you, in all their ornate, cast iron, gilded glory, are the Golden Gates of **Town Hall Park**, topped with Prince of Wales feathers and statues of Nike, goddess of victory. They were made by the Coalbrookdale Company in Ironbridge, shown at the International Exhibition of 1862 and erected here in 1895 (after, it's said, having been rejected by Queen Victoria). They definitely steal the limelight from the Town Hall behind them, despite the fact that it's a Grade I-listed Palladian mansion, designed by James Gibbs, who was also responsible for the Radcliffe Camera in Oxford, King's College in Cambridge and St Martin-in-the-Fields in London.

> *"There ahead of you, in all their ornate, cast iron, gilded glory, are the Golden Gates of Town Hall Park."*

A few minutes' walk southeast of the Town Hall is the newly branded **Cultural Quarter**, in the conservation area around Palmyra Square. Here you'll find a little cluster of attractions giving the lie to the claim that Warrington doesn't do culture. **Warrington Museum & Art Gallery** (Museum St, WA1 1JB ⌀ 01925 442399 ⌀ warringtonmuseum.co.uk ⊙ 10.00–16.30 Mon–Fri, 10.00–16.00 Sat) is a little jewel, with an extensive collection of exhibits including Roman remains from the early days of the town, excellent natural history galleries and a large archive of local photos. Nearby **Pyramid & Parr Hall** (Palmyra Sq South, WA1 1BL ⌀ 01925 442345 ⌀ pyramidparrhall.com) hosts a variety of

RAF BURTONWOOD

Most Americans visiting the UK today probably fly into London. Rewind to the 1940s, though, and there's every chance their first sight of Britain would have been the outskirts of Warrington. In 1942, the RAF base at Burtonwood, just a few miles northwest of Warrington centre, was transferred to the United States Army Air Forces (USAAF) who stayed there, on and off, until the base was officially closed in 1993. During the Second World War, it was the largest airfield in Europe and at its peak more than 18,000 USAAF personnel were stationed there, thousands of whom ended up marrying Warrington brides.

It wasn't just GIs jetting in either. In their wake came Hollywood stars to keep them entertained – Bob Hope, Bing Crosby, Nat King Cole and Glenn Miller, to name but a few.

There's nothing left to see of the airfield – the M62 ploughs its way across the former runway, celebrity steeplejack Fred Dibnah demolished the control tower in 1988 and the base officially closed in 1993. The legacy lives on though – at one of the many new housing developments that have sprung up on the site all the roads have US-influenced names, such as Dallas Drive, Phoenix Place and Santa Rosa Boulevard. There is also a museum in Warrington where you can find out more about the history of the base – the RAF Burtonwood Heritage Centre (WA5 9YZ 07585 609781 rafburtonwood.com), which, bizarrely, can be found in the car park of theme park Gulliver's World, next to the Nerf Zone.

comedy, musical and theatrical events. Check out the programme of The Warrington Contemporary Arts Festival (warringtonartsfestival.co.uk), a rather cutting-edge celebration of the arts at venues across the town.

2 WINWICK

This small village just north of Warrington is dominated by the Grade I-listed **St Oswald's**, parts of which date back to the early 13th century. Look above the door on the exterior wall of the west tower and as well as niches housing statues of St Oswald (left) and St Anthony (right), you'll see a roughly carved animal with a bell round its neck. Meet the Winwick Pig. It's probably there because the pig is a traditional symbol of St Anthony, but local legend has a more colourful explanation. The church, it's said, was originally being built elsewhere but a pig appeared at night and carried the stones over here, near the spot where King Oswald, Christian ruler of Northumbria, was slain in battle against the heathen King Penda of Mercia in 642. (Residents of Oswestry in Shropshire might dispute that part of the story, as they make a similar claim for their own town.) The pig's actions were taken as a divine sign, and the church, consecrated to St Oswald, was duly built on the new site. During the English Civil War, the village was the site of another bloody conflict: the Battle of Red Bank (or Battle of Winwick), which took place less than a mile north of the church on 19 August 1648. It ended in terrible loss of life, with Cromwell and his victorious parliamentarian troops killing around a thousand of the mostly Scottish royalist forces.

"The church was originally being built elsewhere but a pig appeared at night and carried the stones over here."

While you're here, wander down to the little green below the churchyard and you'll find a **Travellers' Rest** stone (see box, page 260), where you can sit and ponder one final piece of Winwick trivia: on 13 January 1887 local girl Sarah Eleanor Pennington married Edward Smith in St Oswald's, 25 years before he went on to captain the RMS *Titanic* on its ill-fated maiden voyage.

FOOD & DRINK

Fiddle I'th Bag Inn Alder Ln, Burtonwood WA5 4BJ ⌀ 01925 225442. This eccentric one-off (and minimalist's nightmare) is crammed from floor to ceiling with antiques, bric-a-brac and memorabilia. Or, as landlady Emma refers to it, 'just stuff'. But what fascinating 'stuff' it is. There are vintage toys, money boxes and commemorative mugs, higgledy-piggledy stacks of books and comics, a ventriloquist's dummy next to a shop mannequin in beaded dress and life jacket, musical instruments and fishing rods strung on the beams, helmets, hats and dressing up clothes flung in a corner ... And if you can make out the bar behind the piles of old tins and glove puppets, you'll find they also serve local cask ales.

Kenyon Hall Farm Winwick Ln, Croft WA3 7ED ⌀ 01925 763646 ⌀ kenyonhall.co.uk. A couple of miles northeast of St Oswald, Kenyon Hall Farm carries a good selection of fresh seasonal produce plus preserves, breads, cakes and oils made on-site, along with organic meat, free-range eggs and speciality cheeses from local suppliers. They also have pick-your-own fields – the season starts in June when the first strawberries ripen and runs on, through other soft fruits and summer vegetables, to the final autumn crops of pumpkins and corn.

Winwick Farm Shop 47 Southworth Ln, WA2 0RA ⌀ 01925 651719 ⌀ winwickfarmshop. com. Easily missed (the entrance looks like a private driveway), this small farm shop is worth popping into if you're passing, to pick up eggs from their own hens, ducks and geese, honey from their own hives and fruit from their own pesticide-free trees. Other produce stocked on the shelves includes local rapeseed oil, bunched rainbow carrots and Cheshire potatoes grown in the field across the road.

TRAVELLERS' RESTS

Occasionally in this corner of the county you may come across a curious sandstone block by the roadside, looking a little like a stunted mounting block or diminutive medal winners' podium.

These are 'Travellers' Rests', brainchild of Dr James Kendrick, a Warrington doctor who, in 1859, first proposed that they be erected at two-mile intervals all along the route from Liverpool through Warrington and on to Manchester. The idea was to provide a resting place for weary pedestrians, in particular the Irish labourers who routinely traipsed miles from the docks at Liverpool in search of work in the fields inland.

A medical man, Kendrick thought long and hard about the design before settling on what he considered the optimum dimensions for a weary traveller's anatomy. Each block was to be 5 foot 3 inches long, with a central section of 3 foot 3 inches in length and 16 inches in height 'to allow of the body bending forwards, the elbows resting on the knees'. Either side of that was a lower seat, 10 inches high and 12 inches long, to be used either for children or as 'a convenient footstool for a mother with an infant at the breast'. The upper surface had to be rounded 'so as to throw off the rain', and was to be 22 inches from front to back, 'thus affording space to deposit a large bundle or to accommodate, if necessary, two other travellers'.

Kendrick paid for many of the rests himself and invited well-to-do citizens to fund others, at a cost of two guineas each, including an inscription. Many have been lost over the years but among the easiest-to-spot survivors are one in Winwick (at the junction of Newton Road and Golborne Road), one at Walton Hall (moved from elsewhere and now standing in the reclamation garden by the entrance), another in Lymm (dedicated to Mary Ridgeway, 'a nephew's affectionate remembrance'; in front of the Shell petrol station on Higher Lane) and two on Chester Road (A56): one at the junction with Walton New Road in Walton, the other opposite the end of Barrymore Road in Grappenhall.

3 RISLEY MOSS LOCAL NATURE RESERVE

Ordnance Av, Birchwood WA3 6QX ⊙ closed Fri, Christmas Day, Boxing Day & New Year's Day

Walk into the visitor centre at Risley Moss and you're greeted by a wall plaque bearing a quote from Daniel Defoe, who passed nearby in 1724 and recorded his reactions in his *Tour Through the Whole Island of Great Britain*. It's fair to say he wasn't impressed by the local landscape: 'The nature of these mosses,' he said, 'for we found there are many of them in this country, is this … the surface looks black and dirty, and is indeed frightful to think of, for it will bear neither horse nor man … what Nature meant by such a useless production 'tis hard to imagine but the land is entirely waste.'

Today we're more aware of the ecological importance of this lowland raised peat bog, which supports many species of plants, animals and birds, even more so as this is one of just a few remaining fragments of a system that once covered large areas of the Mersey Basin. Vast swathes of surrounding mossland were drained and turned into highly productive arable farmland, and in the late 19th century commercial peat cutting and processing began here. Then, in the Second World War, the Government acquired the land and built ROF Risley, a huge factory for filling bombs.

These days it's an altogether more peaceful, welcoming place, a Local Nature Reserve opened by Sir David Bellamy in 1980. Much of it is a protected mossland area that shelters elusive creatures such as great crested newt, adder, slow worm and water vole. This part can only be visited on guided walks but you can view it from the Mossland Hide or the spot where the observation tower once stood (the tower itself was destroyed in an arson attack in July 2017). The rest of the site is woodland, threaded with paths, dotted with grassy glades (complete with the odd picnic table or bench) and full of little ponds where dragonflies and damselflies dart across the water in summer.

It's a great place for bird-spotting, particularly in the Woodland Hide, where we've seen clouds of chaffinches and long-tailed tits; greenfinches, willow tits and reed buntings; great spotted woodpecker and many more, all happily flocking to eat the food the rangers leave out for them over the colder months. Commonly seen birds of prey include buzzards, kestrels and sparrowhawks and you might spot a short-eared owl cruising over the mossland on the hunt for voles.

4 GRAPPENHALL & THELWALL

For most of their existence, these two villages were small rural settlements. Then the 20th century brought the Warrington suburbs right up to their doorsteps – and now, with plans to cover swathes of greenbelt in thousands of new homes, they seem sadly destined to be engulfed completely. For the moment, though, the attractive conservation areas at the heart of each are still clinging on to their villagey, semi-rural feel.

Grappenhall's Church Lane is all cobbled and quaint, with the Bridgewater Canal at one end, some rather desirable houses and a couple of popular pubs. The **Parr Arms** (Church Ln, WA4 3EP ⌀ 01925 212120 ⌀ theparrarms.co.uk), right next to the church and the village stocks, gets my vote as the cosier of the two, though the **Ram's Head** (🕿 01925 269320 ⌘ ramsheadinn.co.uk), 70 yards down the road, houses the old village well, visible through a glass pane in the floor. The Grade I-listed **St Wilfrid's Parish Church** is well worth a visit, particularly for its beautiful stained glass, including the subtly coloured Revelation window and a 'jigsaw' window made up of many fragments of medieval glass. Another fragment is easily missed, hidden away as it is in a case on the wall to the right of the font: open the door and press the light to illuminate a slightly quizzical looking figure of St Mary Magdalene. There are information sheets and booklets inside the church and (nice touch) a basket of reading glasses to borrow in case you've forgotten your own. Remember to look up at the west wall of the church tower before you leave – the carving above the window there is said to be the inspiration for the Cheshire Cat in *Alice's Adventures in Wonderland*, whose author, Lewis Carroll, grew up five miles away in Daresbury (pages 276–7).

"The carving above the window is said to be the inspiration for the Cheshire Cat in Alice's Adventures in Wonderland."

Thelwall also has a couple of attractive old pubs, both on Bell Lane, two minutes' walk apart, and both featuring archive photos of the village on their walls. **Little Manor** (WA4 2SX 🕿 01925 212070 ⌘ brunningandprice.co.uk/littlemanor), originally built in 1660 but now much extended, was once home to the Percival family (whose crest features on the pub sign) and has a large beer garden that backs on to Elizabeth Park. The timber-framed **Pickering Arms** (WA4 2SU 🕿 01925 861262 ⌘ pickeringarmsthelwall.co.uk), sitting prettily across from the old post office and flower-decked cottages, bears an inscription on its gable end: 'In the year 923 King Edward the Elder [brother of Aethelflaed] founded a cyty here and called it Thelwall'. It doesn't mean Thelwall was once much larger than it is today, just that some early translator misinterpreted the word 'burh', which means fort rather than 'cyty'.

Stroll down Ferry Lane, past the 17th-century Thelwall Old Hall, and you come to the **Manchester Ship Canal**, where gliding mute swans carve V-shaped trails in the still water. The little silver skiff moored up at the jetty here is the 'penny ferry', established in 1894 to protect the right of way northwards when the canal cut off the previous route across the Mersey, and still running today.

Across the canal is **Woolston Eyes Nature Reserve**, a SSSI site where an astonishing 232 species of bird have been recorded. A public footpath runs alongside the canal but access to other areas is restricted; check the website (⌁ woolstoneyes.com) for details.

Grappenhall Heys Walled Garden
Witherwin Av, Grappenhall WA4 3DS ⌁ ghwalledgarden.org.uk ⊙ 13.00–16.00 Tue–Thu, 09.00–16.00 Fri, 10.00–17.00 w/ends

Just south of Grappenhall village, the walled garden at Grappenhall Heys is all that remains of a 150-acre estate created in the 18th century by wealthy local banker Thomas Parr. By the 1970s it was in a dilapidated state and only narrowly escaped being demolished and built over, so kudos to the local campaigners and volunteers who successfully saved it and helped transform it into the lovely, tranquil space it has become. The huge Victorian glasshouses have been restored, the beds are filled with vegetables and flowers, and more than 20 different varieties of apple tree are thriving. Look out for the fresh produce cart selling off surplus fruit and veg,

"Look out for the fresh produce cart selling off surplus fruit and veg, with profits ploughed back into the garden."

with profits ploughed back into the garden. There's also a café in one of the greenhouses (⊙ Fri–Sun for breakfast, lunch and afternoon teas). Adjoining the formal kitchen garden is a lovely pleasure garden, with lawns and three deep ponds, topped with water lilies and some very contented-looking mallards.

5 MOORE NATURE RESERVE
Lapwing Ln, WA4 6XE

There's a certain melancholy that sets in with any visit to Moore. The company that owns the 186-acre site has applied for permission to develop most of it once the reserve's lease on the land expires in 2021. Fingers crossed the protests of concerned locals and conservation groups win the day and save it, because this former sand quarry turned nature reserve is an unexpected beauty, its meadows, woodlands and lakes providing a haven for all kinds of wildlife, including protected species such as great crested newts. The birdwatching is particularly good; all five species of British owl live here, along with all three species of woodpecker; rare bitterns hide out in the reed beds and even rarer black-necked grebe breed here most years. Within minutes of a recent visit we'd lost count of the different birds we'd seen, including great spotted woodpecker, buzzard, tufted duck, grey heron, mistle thrush, little grebe and an obligingly stationery kingfisher.

There are paths all round the reserve, linking a dozen hides with views over lakes and ponds. The main area stretches east of the car park – but there's a lovely, varied walk on the other side of the track, skirting along the southern edge of Lapwing Lake, heading up to a raptor viewpoint, then curving back to walk along an old canal bed on the northern side of the lake. Turn left to the feeding station hide (usually abuzz with woodland birds) and it takes you through a moody little swampy area, where the combination of young saplings and still water creates beautiful photogenic reflections.

6 HIGHER WALTON

Higher Walton's origins date back to the 12th century but the heart of it today is a 19th-century estate village, with cottages, St John the Evangelist church and an old schoolhouse, all built for his tenants by Sir Gilbert Greenall of brewing family fame. The former Greenall family home was the mock-Elizabethan **Walton Hall** (Walton Lea Rd, WA4 6SN) of which only the east wing remains today. It's now council-owned, along with the large gardens that surround it, and is out of bounds unless you book it for a private function or attend one of the occasional musical events laid on by Friends of Walton Hall Music. The gardens, though, are open, free of charge, to all (and on a sunny summer weekend it can feel as if all Warrington is there), and offer enough variety to appeal to different tastes. As well as formal beds and borders, woodland areas and an ornamental pond full of koi carp, there's a bowling green, pitch and putt, adventure golf, excellent play area and small zoo (we're talking rabbits and goats rather than rhinos and gorillas). They also run a programme of events throughout the year, from guided tree walks to an annual Chilli Fest in August.

Just off the A56 is the walled kitchen garden of **Walton Lea** (off Chester Rd, WA4 6TB ⊙ 09.00–16.00 Mon–Fri & 10.00–16.00 summer w/ends) that once belonged to Walton Lea Mansion, built in 1864 for local soap manufacturer George Crosfield. The hall is long gone, demolished in the 1920s, and the garden has been through a few incarnations since then. For the past 20 years, though, it's been home to the Walton

Lea Partnership, a charity that provides horticultural training and employment for adults with learning difficulties, mobility issues and mental health issues. Inside there's a rather cool little tea room and a farm shop selling home-grown produce as well as other local foodstuffs including Higher Walton Honey. Outside, you can wander around the garden, shop for plants and pick up a chest of drawers or bargain set of wheels – there's a polytunnel filled with recycled bikes and upcycled furniture. Also available are hand-crafted wooden goods, including bird-feeders, bug houses and, at Christmas, quirky reindeer heads made out of logs and branches.

HALTON & AROUND

Created in 1974, the borough of Halton (not to be confused with the village of Halton) straddles the Mersey, taking in Widnes and Hale on the north shore and Runcorn on the south. Runcorn has plenty to fascinate lovers of industrial heritage, with its landmark bridges, famous canals and former quarries or manufacturing sites turned nature reserves. In among its modern housing estates you'll find little islands of the past, including the ruins of a Norman castle and 12th-century priory, while attractions on its eastern outskirts include Daresbury village (birthplace of Lewis Carroll) and Bluebell Cottage Gardens. Crossing over the new Mersey Gateway Bridge to Widnes, you can enjoy interactive science exhibits at Catalyst, take walks along the estuary shore and learn about the Childe of Hale, said to have been Britain's tallest man. Heading south across the River Weaver instead brings you to nearby Frodsham and Helsby, where high sandstone bluffs offer glorious views over the Mersey estuary.

7 RUNCORN

There were raised eyebrows the day I popped in to Runcorn Town Hall and asked if they had any tourism information leaflets. 'Not much call for those,' was the answer. 'We don't really get tourists in Runcorn.' It's probably not so surprising. The combination of a rundown old town and sprawling new town, fringed by chemical plants and encircled by an expressway network seemingly designed to whizz you off in all kinds of directions you never intended to go, isn't an obvious lure. One of the joys of Slow travel, though, is unearthing the diamonds in the dust – and Runcorn turns out to have a few sparklers.

It may be best known for the second-generation new town that more than doubled the population size between the mid 1960s and late 70s, but Runcorn's roots stretch back far further than such recent history suggests. Aethelflaed, eldest daughter of Alfred the Great, built a fort here in 915 to help guard her kingdom of Mercia against Viking invaders. For most of its history, though, Runcorn remained a fairly small backwater until, in 1776, everything changed with the arrival of the Bridgewater Canal (see box, pages 270–1) and the consequent industrial boom. More canals followed in the early 1800s, and Runcorn became a waterways hub, abuzz with a constant traffic of barges bearing raw and manufactured goods for export or import via the town's docks. It rapidly industrialised as a result: there were shipyards, timberyards and quarries, cargoes of coal from Lancashire, salt from Cheshire and clay bound for the Potteries. The town became a major centre for soap manufacture, leather – Runcorn tanneries are said to have supplied the leather for the boots worn by Wellington and his troops at the Battle of Waterloo – and, later, chemicals, before the late 20th century brought the familiar story of post-industrial decline.

Town centre

Runcorn Promenade, a little stretch of landscaped waterfront on Mersey Road, is a good place to begin an exploration. Start out at the blue '**Queen of Mercia**' metal sculpture (that's Aethelflaed's head on top, gazing towards the former site of her fort) and you can see how the Mersey narrows at this point, making it a natural crossing point. For centuries it was a ferry that carried people over to the other side – and inspired a comic monologue popularised by Stanley Holloway in the 1930s. *The Runcorn Ferry* can still raise a smile with its tale of the Ramsbottom family's determination to outwit Old Ted the boatman, who rowed people across for 'Per tuppence per person per trip … and them as can't pay 'as to walk.' After the ferry came the rail and foot bridge in 1868, followed in 1905 by the Transporter Bridge, Britain's first, which shuttled people and vehicles across the water in a kind of giant cable car, designed to hold four horse-drawn wagons and 300 passengers. Astonishingly for something that looked so Heath Robinson-esque, the bridge stayed open and working until 21 July 1961 when, superseded by the new road bridge (now known as the Silver Jubilee Bridge), it was closed down and demolished.

Walk towards All Saints church and on your left you'll pass a small Georgian terrace, **Belvedere** – a reminder of the fact, unlikely as it might seem, that Runcorn briefly enjoyed an incarnation as a spa town. In his early 19th-century *History of Cheshire*, George Ormerod recorded how 'Very considerable numbers of invalids from Manchester and Liverpool resort to the place in the summer months for the sake of sea-bathing and the enjoyment of an air which is reckoned particularly salubrious.'

Saltwater baths stood at the water's edge below the church, and the terrace was built as lodgings for the visiting bathers. It didn't last long – once the chemical industry took off, the air wasn't quite so salubrious any more.

"You'll pass a small Georgian terrace, Belvedere – a reminder of the fact that Runcorn briefly enjoyed an incarnation as a spa town."

You can do a circular stroll along the water and back into town, via **Bridgewater House** (a handsome Georgian residence, built so the Duke had somewhere to stay when he came to oversee construction on his canal), then along the route of the old flight of locks that used to bring boats down from the canal above to the Mersey and Manchester Ship Canal below. In the centre of town, at **Top Locks**, the handsomely balustraded Waterloo Bridge marks the modern-day terminus of the Bridgewater Canal, once a busy port, now just home to a few houseboats and swans. From here, you can stroll along the towpath to The Brindley (page 271) or take a walk along the **High Street**. For the most part it's a sorry, dilapidated affair, but it has two bright lights: the **Curiosity Bookshop** (page 270) and **Old Town Bloom**, a small but sweet community garden full of endearingly quirky touches, including a fireplace in the wall and a 'Little Free Library' housed in a carved out piece of fallen oak.

Runcorn Hill Nature Park

In the 19th century there was high demand for Runcorn sandstone and the town quarries provided the building blocks for many local houses and stately homes, as well as grander edifices such as the Anglican cathedrals of Liverpool and Chester. Those glittery red blocks, shot through with sparkly mica crystals, made their way further afield too – there's Runcorn sandstone in the docks of New York City, Galveston and San Francisco. Quarrying at Runcorn Hill tailed off in the late 1800s and eventually stopped altogether at the turn of the century, to be followed by major landscaping works in the 1920s. Today, the once noisy, dusty site is now a peaceful, picturesque landscape, where areas of rare lowland heath blend into shady woodlands or open up to reveal sudden, unexpected vistas. The park has bowling greens, tennis courts and a bandstand, there's a new café, Espositos (page 270), for refreshments, and over the road on the heath there are children's play areas and a model boating pond.

If you have the time, you could walk south from here to **Weston** (with its small conservation area clustered round the green and restored cross), then turn right along the fairly busy Weston Road, with far-reaching views over the estuary on the western side. It's an industrial landscape, with its chimneys and wind turbines, but bleakly impressive in its own way. When the tide comes in, a broad sheet of grey water stretches across the estuary to Wirral; when the tide's out, thin silver ribbons of water squiggle between huge sandbanks. Looking down to Weston Point, you may spot a rather forlorn church spire in among the industrial desolation – that's **Christ Church**, built in 1841 for the employees of the Weaver Navigation, but now deconsecrated, abandoned and off-limits to the public.

Eventually the road curves round to the right, bringing you to a little cluster of attractive listed buildings, then on to the **cenotaph** and a **memorial garden**. Over the road is a 17th-century farmhouse now known as **Brookfield Garden Centre** (2 Weston Rd, WA7 4JT); there's no sign on the gate but pass into the cobbled courtyard and you'll find trays of plants for sale and a shop in the barn selling their own chicken and duck eggs. From here, head up Highlands Road and follow the signs right then left into a car park, where an information board in the corner explains the background behind the creation of the Local Nature Reserve. Follow the path behind the board and less than 100 yards' walk brings you to an open plateau. Admire the views over the Mersey and the neatness of some of the graffiti carved into the rocky ground (Mary, whoever she is, is clearly a dab hand with a chisel) but heed the warnings – one side of the plateau is yellow flowering broom; the other sheer drops and crevices.

Town Hall Park
Heath Rd, WA7 5TD

There were mutterings back in 1932 when Runcorn Urban District Council forked out £2,250 to buy Halton Grange and almost 12 acres of grounds – it was felt to be far too extravagant a purchase at a time of economic depression. Fast forward to 2018 and presumably all is forgiven and forgotten, as that 1930s profligacy has left Runcorn with an unexpectedly attractive town hall. Once a private home, built in the 1850s for Thomas Johnson, a local industrialist, the building itself is a Grade II-listed Italianate villa complete with four-storey belvedere tower. The gardens around it, originally laid out by Edward Kemp, the leading Victorian landscape architect, are now a public park, with broad lawns, woodland, a pond and a play area for children.

Wigg Island
WA7 1SQ SJ523833

You have to cross a swing bridge over the Manchester Ship Canal to get to this Local Nature Reserve, a 15-minute walk north of the town centre. Opened in 2002 by Bill Oddie, it's another of the area's many reclaimed industrial sites – in this case a former alkali works and mustard gas production centre. Inevitably, it has been affected by construction work on the new Mersey Gateway Bridge that now crosses overhead (large sections of the park were still closed off at the time of writing), and it feels a little unloved, with overgrown plants in front of the bird hides and a visitor centre that looks permanently closed. However, there are well-laid footpaths and useful information boards and children will enjoy the Troll Trail of wooden and ceramic sculptures hidden away in a piece of woodland towards the western end of the island. Don't bother looking for the Saxon stone heads marked on the map, though – when construction work began on the bridge, they were moved and now stand outside the Brindley Theatre. Even with the new bridge in situ, the island is still a prime spot for birdwatchers, with great views over the sandbanks, salt marshes and mud flats of the Mersey Estuary, popular feeding grounds for large numbers of waders and wildfowl, particularly during the winter migration season. On a moody November afternoon, it

"The island is a prime spot for birdwatchers, with great views over the sandbanks, salt marshes and mud flats of the Mersey Estuary."

was a surprisingly peaceful place to stand, watching cloud shadows shifting across the water and listening to the incoming tide swirling in treacherous-looking eddies as a lone curlew called from a fast-disappearing sandbank.

MERSEY & NORTHWEST CHESHIRE

BRIDGEWATER & BRINDLEY

Look at the Bridgewater Canal on a map and you could be forgiven for failing to recognise it as a canal at all. Unlike the Manchester Ship Canal slightly to the north, which ploughs, business-like and direct, straight through the north Cheshire countryside, the Bridgewater takes its time, meandering its way westward through fields and villages *en route* from Manchester to Runcorn. That's because engineer James Brindley, a pioneer of British canal-building, designed it as a contour canal, closely following the lie of the land to avoid, as far as possible, the extra expense incurred in constructing embankments, tunnels and locks.

Brindley was recruited in 1759 by Francis Egerton, the third Duke of Bridgewater, who had decided on a canal as a more efficient means of transporting coal from his mines at Worsley to the factories of Manchester, where they fuelled the steam engines that powered the Industrial Revolution. It proved to be a good choice: Brindley was not only skilled and hard-working but also good at conveying complicated concepts to non-engineers. Making a presentation to a Parliamentary Commission, he famously carved a miniature aqueduct out of a piece of cheese to convince them that his plans to carry the canal over the River Irwell would work.

FOOD & DRINK

The Bake House 2 Highlands Rd, WA7 4PR @thebakehouseruncorn. Salads, sandwiches and jacket potatoes, plus homemade soup and cakes, form the basis of the menu at this popular tea room. They do a mean chunky chip, and if you can't finish your cake they'll give you a doggy bag to take home. Try to avoid the lunchtime rush, when service can be painfully slow.

Devonshire Bakery 43a Church St, WA7 1LX 01928 568210 devonshire-bakery.co.uk. A cut above most of the surrounding shops, this outpost of the original Devonshire Bakery in Frodsham (page 282) sells speciality breads, a wide range of cakes and tasty pies.

Esposito's Highlands Rd, Runcorn Hill Nature Park WA7 4PT espositosicecream.co.uk. It's the ice cream that's the big draw at Esposito's, a family-run business that started with ice-cream vans but recently opened this café and another in Victoria Park, Widnes. However, you can also get sandwiches, cakes and homemade pizzas – and can gen up on a bit of Runcorn Hill history, courtesy of the large information board that takes up much of one wall.

SHOPPING

Curiosity Bookshop 52 High St, WA7 1AW 01928 575956 09.15–17.15 Mon–Tue & Thu–Fri, 09.15–14.00 Wed, 09.15–16.00 Sat. This fine independent bookshop was opened by local author Liz Howard in 1990 and is now owned by son Chris. As well as all the usual fiction and non-fiction shelves and a bargain room upstairs, there's a good local history section, and they host regular evenings with visiting authors.

Opened in 1761, the first leg of the canal proved hugely successful, halving the price of coal in Manchester and sparking a new wave of waterways building: the 'canal mania' of the late 18th century. Brindley found himself in demand, with canal commissions pouring in: as well as designing the next leg of the Bridgewater, from Manchester to Runcorn, he went on to design the Trent and Mersey (page 15), Staffordshire and Worcestershire, and Coventry and Oxford canals, among others.

After many delays and huge costs for the Duke (who footed the bills), the section of the Bridgewater Canal that passes through Cheshire was completed in 1776, connected to the Mersey by a flight of Brindley-designed locks. Brindley himself died in 1772, so never saw the job completed.

The canal, though, prospered, even after the arrival of the Manchester Ship Canal and railways; indeed, it continued to carry significant amounts of goods traffic until well into the 20th century, when growing competition from road transport started its irreversible decline as a commercial waterway. The Bridgewater carried its last freight in the mid 1970s but these days is well used by pleasure craft and forms part of the popular Cheshire Ring canal route.

Frailers Guitar & Banjo Shop 89 Church St, WA7 1LG ⊘ frailers.com ⊖ 09.00–18.00 Mon–Sat. What do Joe Bonnamasse, Glenn Tilbrook and Billy Connolly have in common? They are among the many unlikely names who've made a beeline to Runcorn just to visit Frailers, which specialises in used and vintage American guitars and banjos.

ARTS & CULTURE
The Brindley High St, WA7 1BG ⊘ 0151 907 8360 ⊘ thebrindley.org.uk. Sitting in a prime spot right on the banks of the Bridgewater Canal, the Brindley opened in 2004 and promptly won an architectural award from RIBA. It's a bright, light space, with a busy programme of events that's heavy on the tribute acts but also takes in original music, comedy, drama, dance and author talks. The gallery space hosts free exhibitions featuring local artists and the Terrace Café serves light meals, cakes and coffees with a canal view.

8 WIDNES

Flanked by the much larger Liverpool to the west and ever-spreading Warrington to the east, the historically Lancastrian town of Widnes now shares its civic identity with the Cheshire town of Runcorn to the south, the two having come together to form Halton Borough Council in 1974. Like its twin, it's not an obvious tourist destination. In the 1800s, with the arrival of chemical factories, Widnes morphed rapidly from sparsely populated marshland to a densely populated and polluted industrial area. At the end of the 19th century it was described by the *Daily News* as the 'dirtiest, ugliest and most depressing town in England,' while another writer, comparing it to Sodom and Gomorrah, spoke of an area 'devoid ... of one single green leaf or sign of vegetation.' Happily, it's moved on a lot since then. It's still not the prettiest, but at least the grass grows again now that the air's been cleared up, and some former industrial sites are gradually being reclaimed and reinvented as more attractive green spaces.

In terms of visitor attractions, the town's big draw is **Catalyst** (Mersey Rd, WA8 0DF ✆ 0151 420 1121 ⌕ catalyst.org.uk ⊙ 10.00–16.00 Tue–Sun, closed Mon except for bank hols & school hols). Housed in a converted 19th-century tower on the banks of the Mersey, this science discovery centre is dedicated to illuminating the history and processes of the chemical industry. If you manage to find it first time round, congratulations – the gargantuan road works going on in the surrounding area make navigation decidedly tricky. It's worth persevering, though. 'We put the fun in science,' says the Catalyst website, and that's exactly what it did when we visited with three under-tens in tow. I wouldn't claim we came out a whole lot wiser about the construction of polymers but we had great fun trying out the many interactive exhibits in the Scientrific Gallery, solving the challenges in the Puzzle Room and clambering round the chemical-themed apparatus in the playground. There are good views from the top floor observation deck, too.

"There's good birdwatching on the estuary, especially in winter, and this is also a pleasant place to watch the incoming tide."

Outside, you can take a stroll along the **Sankey Canal** and around **Spike Island**, once the site of a huge chemical factory but now an open green space with clear views over the river estuary and the new Mersey Gateway Bridge. The Trans Pennine Trail passes through here, and if you follow it south it will take you round, along the Mersey shore, to **Pickerings Pasture**. This former waste-disposal centre was cleaned up in the 1980s and is now a Local Nature Reserve, with wildflower meadows and an occasionally open café. There's good birdwatching on the estuary, especially in winter, and this is also a pleasant place to watch the incoming tide; the Mersey has the second-largest tidal bore in Britain and while it's rare to catch a particularly big wave, you never

know – you might get lucky. The Friends of Pickering Pasture website
(⌀ thefriendsofpickeringspasture.org.uk) has details of how best to
time your visit.

9 HALE
🏠 Childe of Hale Cottage (page 294)

Hale is the westernmost outpost of Cheshire on this side of the estuary, with the end of the runway at Liverpool John Lennon Airport less than two miles from the village centre. Amazingly, given its location, it still feels quite rural, with green fields all around and footpaths leading down to the Hale lighthouse on the Mersey shores. The village's main claim to fame is John Middleton, aka the **Childe of Hale**, who was born here in 1578 and lived in a thatched cottage on Church End. It's said he grew to the lofty height of nine foot three inches, and though there may have been some exaggeration over the years, no-one knows for sure, so let's give the legend the benefit of the doubt. In 1617 the Childe was summoned to London by King James I, where he was pitted against the king's wrestler, won the match and was sent back home with £20. His old home is still here (and available as a holiday rental, page 294) and in the churchyard of St Mary's, just down the road, you can see his grave – it's the big one near the south porch. In between the two, you'll find a life-size bronze statue of the man, deliberately designed so you can have your photo taken standing next to him, holding his hand and seeing how you measure up.

To the east of the village, surrounded by salt marsh, is another curiosity (and a Scheduled Ancient Monument): the **Hale Duck Decoy**. Clearly visible on satellite maps, it's pentagonal in shape, with a central pond off which run five curving channels, all surrounded by woodland. One of the best preserved duck decoys in the country, it was once used to trap birds; now it's a sanctuary for them. Although usually off-limits to the public, outside breeding season it is sometimes possible to visit on a guided walk. Visit the Friends of Pickerings Pasture website for details (⌀ thefriendsofpickeringspasture.org.uk).

10 HALTON

It's an odd one, Halton. A little island of old Cheshire stranded amid a sea of new housing estates, it sits high on a hill crowned by the ruins of **Halton Castle**, a Grade I-listed Scheduled Monument. There's not much left of the Norman castle originally founded in 1071 by Nigel, first Baron of Halton, but it's instantly obvious why he'd want to put it here. From this high rocky spur, there are clear views in almost every direction, none the less impressive for taking in industrial sites such as Fiddler's Ferry power station and the distant chimneys of Stanlow Refinery.

Exact details of the castle's history remain vague, but it's said that King John visited in 1207 and it's certain that in the 14th century it passed into the hands of the Duchy of Lancaster, serving as a hunting lodge for John of Gaunt for the best part of four decades. Its downfall seems to have come with the Civil War when it was twice besieged by Parliamentary forces and subsequently largely dismantled on Cromwell's orders. Today it looks more romantic hilltop folly than forbidding fortress – indeed a section of wall in the southeastern corner is known as the Folly Walls, having been added in the early 19th century to make the castle a more appealingly picturesque view for the residents of nearby Norton Priory. (Connections between the castle and priory go back a long way, and it's the Norton Priory Museum Trust that manages the site today.)

"It looks more romantic hilltop folly than forbidding fortress – indeed a section of wall in the southeastern corner is known as the Folly Walls."

There's a path running right round the outside of the walls but you can also go inside when the **Castle Hotel** is open. This 18th-century building, on the site of the former gatehouse, served as a courthouse for many years but is now a no-frills pub with the castle grounds as its beer garden – go through the pool room, out the back door and there you are. There are some signboards round the edges, but the landlord also keeps an information folder behind the bar that provides more detailed information about the site, illustrated with old photos and engravings.

Next door to the castle is the slender-spired **St Mary's Church**, designed in Gothic Revival style by Sir George Gilbert Scott and built from local sandstone. Nearby stands the 18th-century **Chesshyre Library**, built (and once stocked with hundreds of books) by the wealthy, Runcorn-born Sir John Chesshyre, who also funded the neighbouring vicarage. It's worth a wander down Castle Road and north along Main Street to view these and other historic buildings, culminating in the brooding-looking Seneschal's House (near the junction with Halton Brow), which dates back to 1598. If you stop for a quick drink in the 18th-century

Norton Arms (Main St, WA7 2AD ✆ 01928 567642 ⌂ thenortonarms.co.uk) on your way back, pop round the corner for a quick look at the **Millennium Green** too: it has several chainsaw carvings, thousands of spring bulbs, a wildflower meadow and a community orchard planted with heritage fruit varieties.

11 NORTON PRIORY MUSEUM & GARDENS

Tudor Rd, Windmill Hill WA7 1SX ✆ 01928 569895 ⌂ nortonpriory.org ⊙ Apr–Oct 10.00–17.00 daily, Nov–March 11.00–16.00 daily (walled garden closed)

You'll need some imagination to picture this medieval priory as it was in the days when black-cloaked Augustinian canons lived here. Founded in the 12th century and flourishing in the 14th, when it was promoted to abbey status, Norton then became an early victim of Henry Vlll's Dissolution of the Monasteries and was disbanded in 1536. A few years later, the lands were bought by Sir Richard Brooke and became the family estate for the best part of four centuries until, in 1921, the contents of the 30-bedroom mansion that then stood on the site were auctioned off and, in 1928, most of the building pulled down.

Norton's new life as a visitor attraction began in 1970, when they broke ground on an archaeological dig that lasted 17 years and turned up everything from 130 skeletons and one of the world's largest medieval tile collections to an unexploded Second World War bomb. The pick of the finds are now displayed in the new visitor centre, opened in 2016, where you'll also find two surviving fragments of the original priory building: a Romanesque archway and the 12th-century undercroft. Norton's pride and joy is here too: a medieval statue of St Christopher, twice life-sized and carved from local sandstone. A sound and light show brings to life the bright colours the statue was once painted in – though the booming tones of Brian Blessed as its voice, and an accompanying light projection making the lips appear to move, is probably a step too far for me.

Outside, the unearthed foundations mark out the old priory buildings, including the church, cloister and kitchens, and beyond them there are lovely walks through the woodlands, dotted with sculptures, that stretch down to the Bridgewater Canal. There's a little orchard here, too, with a few picnic tables and, on a recent autumn visit, lots of tasty windfall apples. Cross the bridge over the busy A558 that divides the site, and you'll find more woodland (it's a great conker-hunting spot in autumn) and a 2½-acre walled garden. Built for the Brooke family in the late 18th century, it houses fruit trees, ornamental borders, vegetable beds and a rose garden, and is home to the national collection of tree quince, with 25 different varieties growing there.

FESTIVALS & EVENTS
Quince and Apple Day ⊙ Oct. At this popular event (one of many laid on throughout the year) you'll find craft demonstrations, music and stalls selling produce from the garden. If you're quick you might be able to snap up some of the fresh quinces; if not, you can console yourself with a jar of Norton Priory chutney or jelly instead.

12 DARESBURY
🏠 **The Partridge** Stretton (page 294)

Daresbury would probably fly under most visitors' radar were it not for two things. One, this well-heeled little village is familiar to fans of electronic dance music as the unlikely home of Creamfields, a massive festival that takes place there every August bank holiday. Don't even think about trying to visit then. Two, and far more famously, it's known for its connection to Charles Lutwidge Dodgson, aka Lewis Carroll, who was born here on 27 January 1832 and spent the first 11 years of his life in the village.

His father was vicar of **All Saints Church** at the time; and as you walk through the churchyard gate on Daresbury Lane you'll see on your right the old font (once indoors) where Carroll was baptised. Inside, in the Daniell Chapel, is Daresbury's most famous sight: the **Lewis Carroll Memorial Window**, installed to mark the centenary of the author's birth. Above a biblical nativity scene (in which Carroll is shown kneeling in the left-hand window, with the figure of Alice behind him) are panels that represent different aspects of his life, including a Cheshire wheatsheaf, mathematical dividers and the arms of Rugby School and Christ Church, Oxford. Below, based on artist John Tenniel's illustrations for the *Alice* books, are panels showing familiar characters such as the White Rabbit, Mock Turtle and Caterpillar. The window was designed by Geoffrey Webb, whose trademark signature was a tiny spider's web hidden somewhere in his designs – here, you'll spot it in the bottom right-hand corner, above the Queen of Hearts' head, together with the date, 1935, when the window was dedicated. Elsewhere in the largely Victorian church (all that remains of an earlier 16th-century incarnation is the tower), there's more fine stained glass and some interesting wood carvings, including those on the pulpit and on the Jacobean panelling behind the altar. And if you feel the need for a White Rabbit wall clock, Alice fridge magnet or Fish Footman key ring, you'll find a range of Wonderland-related souvenirs on sale by the entrance.

Tacked on to the north side of the church is a modern extension housing the **Lewis Carroll Centre**, which opened in 2012. Don't expect too much – it's basically a collection of large information boards – but it does fill you in on the details of the author's life and explains how to reach the **Lewis Carroll Birthplace Site**, a couple of miles away on Morphany Lane. Best to manage expectations here, too, as there's little to see, the parsonage having burned down in 1883. The National Trust has done what it can, though, with a couple of White Rabbits pointing the way along a path towards the site, where a brick outline marks the shape of the building and a wrought-iron sculpture, complete with dormouse design, covers the well. Take a seat and enjoy a moment's peace in what Carroll described as 'An island farm mid seas of corn, Swayed by the wandering breath of morn, The happy spot where I was born'.

There's even less to see at the **Lewis Carroll Centenary Wood**, a few minutes' walk away along a grassy verge, but for the sake of completeness you might want to visit this tiny patch of broadleaf woodland while you're there. Back in Daresbury village there are a few more Wonderland-related sights to spot before you leave – look out for the village sign (which includes a grinning Cheshire Cat), the Alice weather vane on top of the school, and a painting of Alice and cat on an old gate hanging on the side wall of the Village Hall.

FOOD & DRINK

It's a shame the village pub, the **Ring O'Bells** (7 Chester Rd, WA4 4AJ ⌁ 01925 740256), is part of a chain rather than an independent, but it does have open fires and plenty of outdoor tables, in the large beer garden at the back or on the cobbles at the front. There's more al-fresco seating, and Wonderland-themed décor, up the road at the **Dormouse Tea Rooms** (Chester Rd, WA4 4AJ ⌁ 01925 740289), where the menu (appropriately divided into 'Drink Me' and 'Eat Me' sections), includes good homemade cakes as well as sandwiches, soups and salads. If you head down to the Lewis Carroll Birthplace be sure to stop off at **Daresbury Dairy** (Penkridge Lake Farm, Newton Ln, WA4 4HZ ⌁ 07856 091601) for some yummy ice cream, made on the farm with milk from their own cows, which you can hear mooing in the background.

MERSEY & NORTHWEST CHESHIRE

13 DUTTON & AROUND

Dutton today is a scattering of farmhouses and cottages, with no centre, church or pub. You'd never guess it was once the seat of the powerful Dutton family, who held sway here at Dutton Hall for more than 500 years and could date their lineage back to Odard, the Norman knight who took possession of the lands in 1086. In the early 16th century, Sir Piers Dutton rebuilt the hall in grand Tudor style, a quadrangular, moated, black-and-white affair. Sadly, it's no longer standing, at least not in Cheshire. By the 20th century, the east wing, the only bit remaining, caught the eye of John Arthur Dewar, racehorse owner and whisky magnate, who decided it would go nicely with his family home in Sussex. He duly bought it, dismantled it and shifted it, piece by precious piece, down to East Grinstead.

Dutton does still have a star attraction, though, in the form of the **Bluebell Cottage Gardens and Nursery** (Lodge Ln ⌾ 01928 713718 ⌾ bluebellcottage.co.uk ⌾ Apr–Oct 10.00–17.00 Wed–Sun & bank hols). Tucked well away down a narrow lane off the A533, they're owned and run by Sue Beesley, former BBC Gardener of the Year, who's surrounded her home with cottage borders, an orchard, wildflower meadow, bluebell woods, grasses garden and vegetable plot. You can stock your own borders with plants from the on-site nursery, which specialises in flowering perennials, and enjoy locally made cakes in the tea room. From here you can also do a pleasant four-mile (ish) round walk, taking a halfway break at **Davenports Tea Room** (Bridge Farm, Warrington Rd, Bartington CW8 4QU ⌾ 01606 853241 ⌾ davenportsfarmshop.co.uk/tea-rooms), with its *Alice in Wonderland*-themed décor and popular afternoon teas. Opposite Davenports, you can buy Cheshire-grown roses at **Harefield Nursery** (⌾ 07884472883 ⌾ harefieldnursery.co.uk ⌾ closed Mon & Tue).

"You can stock your own borders with plants from the on-site nursery, and enjoy locally made cakes in the tea room."

🍴 FOOD & DRINK

If you fancy a pub lunch, nearby options include **The Chetwode Arms** (Street Ln, Lower Whitley WA4 4EN ⌾ 01925 640044 ⌾ chetwode-arms.co.uk), an old wayside inn that's now renowned for serving exotic meats cooked on hot stones, African-style. Or, further south, there's **The Hollybush** (Warrington Rd, Little Leigh CW8 4QY ⌾ 01606 853196 ⌾ thehollybush.net), one of the oldest pubs in the UK, which sources food from nearby Barnton and Whitley.

HALTON & AROUND

14 ASTON BY SUTTON

Around three miles east of Frodsham, the hamlet of Aston by Sutton is dotted with reminders that this was once part of a great country estate, where the late 17th-century Aston Hall, a 'spacious and lofty edifice', according to Ormerod, was surrounded by grounds landscaped by Humphry Repton. The house was demolished in the 1930s and some of the listed structures associated with it, such as the coach house and dovecote, are now on private land, but **St Peter**, the family chapel, is easy to find next to the school on Aston Lane. On summer Saturdays the church is usually open for visitors to go inside, where you'll find a late 17th-century chancel and early 18th-century nave plus family monuments, including one with a fulsome tribute to the virtues of Lady Magdalen Aston, a 'wife so perfect and refynd To be but body to her husband's mynd'.

If you turn up when the church is closed, all is not lost: a handy information sheet pinned to the noticeboard in the porch explains where to find points of interest in the churchyard, including the old font, a plague stone and the grave of the unfortunate Mary Illidge, who had a miserable time of it before dying in 1842. 'She was afflicted with the Dropsy,' says the inscription, 'and underwent 9 operations in 23 months. She had 178 quarts of water taken from her during that time.' Mind you, that's nothing compared with the even more unfortunate Peter Banner of Frodsham (page 281).

Elsewhere, as you head east along Aston Lane, you pass the sandstone war memorial, the walls of the old kitchen garden, the stumpy remains of the village cross and, just after the road bends left towards Preston Brook, the 18th-century Top Lodge, marking the point where the old driveway once began its long sweep down to the hall.

15 FRODSHAM

🏠 **Beechlands Cottage** (page 294), ⛺ **Lady Heyes Holiday Park** (page 294)

The attractive market town of Frodsham sits between a dramatic rocky outcrop on one side and the broad mashes of the Mersey Estuary on the other. Running through its centre, broad **Main Street**, lined with trees planted in 1897 for Queen Victoria's Diamond Jubilee and generously sprinkled with wooden benches, is like a living sampler of architectural styles over the past few centuries. There's a Stuart coaching inn (The Bear's Paw), 17th-century thatched cottages, Georgian houses,

19th-century barrack gates, a tin tabernacle and, just past the lights on High Street, a 20th-century supermarket – though the latter is the exception in a charmingly traditional country-town scene. Historic Frodsham information boards, helpfully dotted along the pavement, point out some of the more interesting buildings (identified by blue plaques on their walls), with little snippets of info about each and the odd black-and-white photo from the 1890s and 1900s.

You could do a very happy wander up one side and down the other, starting from the **Brook Stone** (a glacial erratic boulder at the corner of Main Street and Marsh Street) and heading northeast, past the clock in the centre of the road (erected in 1925 to commemorate a visit from George V), crossing into High Street and continuing up to **Trinity Gardens**, where a fine steeple and fragment of wall are all that remain of an 1873 Methodist church. Crossing the road and returning down the other side will bring you to a sandstone obelisk framed in wrought iron – starting point for the Sandstone Trail, which runs for 34 miles between Frodsham and the Shropshire town of Whitchurch.

Carry on along Main Street to the **Old Hall Hotel** (WA6 7AB ✆ 01928 732052 ⌂ oldhallhotelfrodsham.co.uk) for afternoon tea in the cosy bar, and nip into the garden to see the two stones marking the spots where the Mersey reached exceptionally high tide levels in 1802 and 1862. Take a peek into the dining room, too, to see some exposed sections of wattle and daub. Leading off Main Street is Church Street, where the eagle-eyed wandering past the Cholmondeley Arms will spot a rare **K4 phone box** opposite the approach to the station. A 1927 adaptation of Sir George Gilbert Scott's classic red design, it was one of only 50 ever made and incorporated a post box and stamp machine. These days, it's one of just a few K4s still in public use, with one of the other survivors just a little further north in Warrington.

Castle Park
WA6 6SB

This attractive park was originally laid out by leading garden designer Edward Kemp in the 1850s, when these were still the private grounds of Park Place, the Georgian house now turned into offices. It's larger than you might expect at first, stretching back and up from the main road and encompassing woodland, lawns, ponds, a bowling green, an imaginative play area and sports facilities. There are attractive formal beds; pretty pale lilac cyclamen growing by a channelled stream; bluebells and wild garlic popping up in spring. Throughout the grounds you'll find handsome specimen trees, including a veteran copper beech (fenced off for safety because it's started shedding branches in its old age) and a lovely weeping birch bowing over an old fountain basin.

St Laurence Parish Church
Church Rd, WA6 6AD

Frodsham's oldest building, and the only one with a Grade 1 listing, is a soothing place to visit, gentle music playing in the background as you wander round. It's Saxon in origin and fundamentally Norman in design but what you see today is largely the result of later extensions and a substantial restoration in the late 19th century.

Information leaflets in the church provide more historical detail and direct you towards points of interest such as the memorial tablet to former vicar Francis Gastrell (see box, page 283) and another that describes the ill health woes of local carpenter, Peter Banner. Before he died of dropsy in 1749, it records, poor old Peter had been 'tapped' 58 times and had 1,032 quarts of water taken from him. In the Kingsley Chapel (or Lady Chapel), the stained-glass window, installed in 1933, was designed by Archibald Keightley Nicholson, whose work appears in several UK cathedrals, and includes the figures of prominent scientists and artists among the martyrs – look out for Newton, Handel and Lister among others.

"Before he died of dropsy in 1749, it records, poor old Peter had been 'tapped' 58 times and had 1,032 quarts of water taken from him."

Overton Hill
WA6 6HH

Some call it Overton Hill; some call it Frodsham Hill. Some get there the hard way, walking up, up, up from the centre of Frodsham; others take the easy route and drive up to the little car park on Bellemonte Road, then follow the level footpath beyond the memorial gates. Either way, the result is the same: you come out onto a wide open rocky plateau where the striking sandstone war memorial (visible from miles around) stands sentinel over the town below and the marshes and Mersey Estuary beyond. The views are glorious, the landscape littered with easy-to-pick-out landmarks – the cathedrals of Liverpool and the mountains of Wales; the Manchester Ship Canal snaking its way along the coast; and a toy train trundling over the Frodsham Viaduct. Fabulous.

FOOD & DRINK

Devonshire Bakery 1 High St, WA6 7AH ⌇ 01928 731234 ⌇ devonshire-bakery.co.uk. Five generations of Crowther family are behind this smart little bakery/café, where the shelves are stocked with speciality breads and a wide range of cakes, all handmade on the premises. Their pies are small but delicious and they make a point of buying in produce from local suppliers to help create them.

Next Door 68 Main St, WA6 7AU ⌇ 01928 371053 ⌇ restaurantnextdoor.co.uk ⌇ closed Sun & Mon. Husband-and-wife team Richard and Vicki opened this restaurant in 2017, in the 17th-century cottage where several generations of Vicki's family ran a butcher's shop, H E Coward (still going, a few doors down the road). He's a chef, she's a sommelier, both have a background in big-name restaurants, and the modern European-style food they're serving not only showcases seasonal local produce but is earning rave reviews.

The Ring O'Bells 2 Bellemonte Rd, WA6 6BS ⌇ 01928 732068 ⌇ ringobells-frodsham.co.uk. Opposite St Laurence (and, for early flaggers, about half a mile from the start of the Sandstone Trail), this 400-year-old pub has cosy little rooms and friendly young staff. Its small courtyard garden is a pleasant spot for a summer G&T, with tables set round an ornamental pool, red admirals flitting around, and (depending on which way you're facing) a view of either the top of the church tower or the tip of the war memorial on Overton Hill. Trivia time: Daniel Craig lived here as a young child, when his father was the landlord.

Whitmore & White 72 Main St, WA6 7AU ⌇ 01928 734427 ⌇ whitmoreandwhite.co.uk. This fab little deli – part of a minichain with sister branches in Heswall and West Kirby – has only been open a couple of years but has already snaffled the 'Best Deli in Cheshire' award for 2016 and 2017. It's only small, but it's full of delectable foods, wines and spirits, including a good selection of gins. ('You can never have too much gin,' said manager Tom Scargill, 'especially for Frodsham.') There are also a few indoor and outdoor tables where you can eat in. If the coffee and walnut brownie is on the counter, go for it – it's the perfect combination of crispy top and squidgy centre.

SHOPPING

Shops

Lady Heyes Crafts & Antiques Centre Kingsley Rd, WA6 6SU ⌇ 01928 788557 ⌇ ladyheyes.co.uk. Two miles southeast of Frodsham centre, this former working farm is now a magnet for anyone who likes browsing antiques and vintage stalls. Housed in a cluster of large buildings, you'll find dozens of dealers' units, their shelves crammed with a

REVEREND FRANCIS GASTRELL

Officially vicar of Frodsham from 1740 to 1772, the notorious Reverend Francis Gastrell somehow found time to live – and make himself deeply unpopular – in Stratford-upon-Avon, too. In 1756, he bought New Place, the site of Shakespeare's former home, where the garden contained a mulberry tree said to have been planted by the playwright himself – a point of pilgrimage for visiting Bard lovers. Eventually, infuriated by all the sightseers peering over his garden fence for a glimpse of the tree, Gastrell chopped it down and sold the wood. The townspeople duly smashed his windows but his role as a Shakespearian baddie didn't end there: after a subsequent row about taxes with the local authorities, he also destroyed the house itself in a fit of pique before fleeing the outraged citizens of Stratford and heading back up north. A byelaw was passed in Stratford forbidding Gastrell and any of his descendants from ever living there again. He's remembered rather more fondly in Frodsham, however, where he bequeathed a collection of 18th-century silverware to the church.

fascinating range of goodies: medals and model soldiers, comics and Corgi cars, travel trunks, teddies, typewriters and a whole lot more. Other attractions on site include craft workshops, a tea room, a great secondhand record shop and a playbarn for children.

Roy's Relics 112 Main St, WA6 7AR ⌕ 07876 170934. Don't let the tiny shop front fool you – owner Roy Adams (a mine of information on everything from Roman coins to Beatles albums) has a huge amount of stock crammed in here and even more squirrelled away elsewhere. Talking a million miles a minute, he points out 17th-century Japanese silks and a French secretaire, an old RAF uniform and a 12th-century monk's ring – proof that he will, as he says, 'buy anything that hasn't got a plug on it'.

Markets

Frodsham's weekly market (⊙ Thu) is a bustling, sociable affair, with stalls lining the north side of Main Street, and the old coaching inns and newer cafés doing a roaring trade.

ARTS & CULTURE

Castle Park Arts Centre Off Fountain Ln, WA6 6SE ⌕ 01928 735832. On the edge of Castle Park the old estate coach house and stables were converted into an arts centre in the 1980s and now host exhibitions that change every six weeks and showcase the work of artists (many of them from the northwest) working in a range of different media. Most of the work is for sale and prices are very reasonable. Units in the courtyard are also available to rent for use by local artists, societies and musicians – we wandered round to a very pleasant audio backdrop of banjo-playing from Blue Grass Seeds in Unit 3.

MERSEY & NORTHWEST CHESHIRE

16 HELSBY

If you think the view from Overton Hill in Frodsham is good, wait till you see the one from quieter **Helsby Hill**. It's a steep-in-parts climb from the little car park at Helsby Quarry in Alvanley but it only takes 15 to 20 minutes, heading up through lovely woodland, until you reach the trig point, out on the wide-open sandstone bluff, with a 360-degree vista. Yes, I'd love to press a magic button that would let me see it before the 20th and 21st centuries made their ugly marks, but the scale and drama of it still blows me away, looking out across the marshes and wide Mersey Basin, in towards the Cheshire plain and south to the Welsh mountains. Retrace your steps to take a stroll round the former **Helsby Quarry**, now a Local Nature Reserve, where an exposed rock face reveals layers of Triassic-era sandstone. At Helsby Post Office (215 Chester Rd, WA6 0AB) you can pick up a 'Helsby Parish Paths' leaflet (£1.50) detailing footpaths and bridleways throughout Helsby, Alvanley and nearby Manley.

FOOD & DRINK

JTO Vintage & The Old Bank Tea Rooms 213 Chester Rd, WA6 0DA ⌀ 01928 724846. Smiley owner Diane Ormrod has created a very popular little bunting-and-polka-dots kind of place where you can browse the gifts and crafty goodies on sale (many of them from local craftspeople) while you enjoy homemade cakes supplied each morning by local bakers. The menu includes generous salad plates and other savoury items, too.

LYMM TO GREAT BUDWORTH

This part of the northwest area is very different to the more industrial landscapes along the Mersey shores. The attractive town of Lymm may be technically in Warrington but from here down to Great Budworth everything feels much more quintessentially Cheshire. The landscape is gentler and more rural, with small villages surrounded by farmland and, at Arley Hall, one of the county's loveliest gardens.

17 LYMM

Broomedge Farm Cottages (page 294)

How many village centres have a pond, mill race, rocky ravine, canal, 17th-century cross, stocks *and* a dinosaur footprint all within a couple of hundred yards of each other? Just the one, I suspect. Lovely Lymm.

The pond, **Lower Dam**, is a pretty spot flanked by greenery and cottages, with a few wooden benches if you want to sit for a while and watch the mallards bobbing around. It's fed by a stream that runs down the ravine from **Lymm Dam** (see below) and then passes under the main road to splash noisily on into Slitten Gorge below. By the benches is where you'll find the famous fossil, unearthed in a nearby quarry in 1842. You can't miss it – a whacking great 'DINOSAUR FOOTPRINT' sign, visible from the other side of the road, marks the spot.

Nearby is **Lymm Cross**, a square stone structure topped with finials and a slightly wonky weathervane, all sitting on a chunky, pyramidal sandstone outcrop, cut in to steps. The restorers who spruced it up for Queen Victoria's Diamond Jubilee added bronze sundials on three sides, along with rather solemn inscriptions: 'We are a Shadow,' 'Save Time' and 'Think of the Last'.

Just north of the cross, winding east to west through the village, is the **Bridgewater Canal**, which opened in the late 18th century and helped boost the development of local industries including fustian cutting and nail making. When the railway followed in 1853, it brought wealthy Manchester merchants, who built their large Victorian villas here, far from the city smog, along Brookfield Road and Church Road. There are no trains any more – the line fell victim to Dr Beeching's cuts in 1962 – but the old rail route now forms part of the western section of the Trans Pennine Trail.

You'll find useful historical information boards marking key spots on the 3½-mile **Lymm Heritage Trail**, a self-guided route that can be broken into smaller sections. There's also a new heritage centre, hidden away on tiny Legh Street (⊙ noon–16.00 Thu–Sun) and run by volunteers.

Lymm Dam

A popular local beauty spot, Lymm Dam is a manmade lake created in 1824 when the turnpike road (now the A56) was built across the valley. A footpath leads right round it, sometimes down by the water's edge, sometimes threading through the surrounding woodland of oak, beech, ash and sycamore. There are always wildfowl cruising across the water, and herons keeping a beady eye out for the many resident fish; if you're lucky, you'll spot the kingfishers that nest here or see the great crested grebes performing their bobbing, balletic courtship display in spring.

On summer evenings there are bats on the wing (pipistrelles, noctules and Daubenton's); in winter, lovely clear views across the frosty lake to St Mary's church.

At the southern end of the lake is the broad, ornamental Crosfield Bridge. If it seems incongruously grand in its out-of-the-way setting, that's because it was originally intended to be part of a far larger scheme. In the early 20th century, Lymm Dam and the lands around it, which then formed the Beechwood Estate, were bought by William Hesketh Lever of Port Sunlight fame (page 49), who intended to create another garden village on the site. The plan was eventually abandoned but not before some of the early landscaping had been completed – this bridge; The Avenue, lined with Lombardy poplars, which runs off it; Lakeside Road on the west side of the water; and the bridleway on the east.

Spud Wood

Follow the Bridgewater Canal towpath a mile east from the centre of Lymm and you come to this Woodland Trust site on the southern bank. A pleasant area of meadow and broadleaf woodland and starting point for the 22-mile Mersey Valley Timberland Trail (page 255), it gets its name from the potato field that was here before the trees – a mix of oak, ash and silver birch – were planted in the late 1990s. On its southern edge it's bordered by the much older **Helsdale Wood**, a semi-natural ancient woodland, populated by mosses and lichens that have earned it a Site of Biological Importance (SBI) designation. There are no facilities on-site (bar a small car park, a few picnic tables and the odd bench) but it's not far to **The Barn Owl Inn** (Agden Wharf, Warrington Ln, WA13 0SW ⌁ 01925 752020 ⌁ thebarnowlinn.co.uk), a freehouse pub with a canalside terrace, half a dozen cask ales and a very popular lunch deal for senior citizens. In between the wood and the pub, near Burford Lane underbridge, look out for the early 19th-century warehouse and adjoining agent's house – rare survivors from the canal's early days, when goods were transferred to and from barges here.

FOOD & DRINK

The Brewery Tap 18 Bridgewater St, WA13 0AB ⌁ 01925 755451 ⌁ lymmbrewing.co.uk ⌁ noon–23.00 Mon–Thu, noon–midnight Fri–Sat, noon–22.30 Sun. The Costello family, who also own Dunham Massey Brewing Company (page 226) and a couple of bars in Altrincham and Stockton Heath, are behind this down-to-earth pub and micro-brewery

(Lymm Brewing Co), housed in the former post office. Two of the cask ales are brewed in the basement (you'll know when it's a brewing day by the sweet, hoppy smell that greets you as you walk in) and the rest come from Dunham Massey.

The Church Green Higher Ln, WA13 0AP 01925 752068 aidenbyrne.co.uk noon–21.00 Mon–Fri, 09.00–noon & 12.30–22.00 Sat, 09.00–noon & 12.30–19.00 Sun. Owned by Aiden Byrne, a familiar face to anyone who watches TV cookery programmes, this gastropub offers the choice of fine dining in the restaurant or more relaxed pub classics and sharing platters in the lounge. Either way, it's a great place to stop off before or after a walk round Lymm Dam and has a roomy outdoor decked area for sunny summer days.

Sextons 2 Eagle Brow, WA13 0AD 01925 753669 sextonsbakery.co.uk 08.30–17.00 Mon–Sat, 09.30–16.00 Sun. Every morning at 02.00 the hard-working staff at family-run Sextons set to in the basement bakery, whipping up the excellent breads, cakes and hand-raised pies on sale in the shop above. There's also a deli section selling fine preserves, pickles and the like, a good cheese counter and, to the left of the shop, a sizeable coffee shop so you can eat in as well as take out.

18 HIGH LEGH

Fir Tree Barn Cottages (page 294)

On the surface this is a small and unremarkable village but it has a long and complicated history, having spent much of its life divided between two confusingly named families, each with their own hall and chapel: the Leghs (later the Cornwall Leghs) of East Hall and the Leighs (aka the Egerton Leighs) of West Hall. The halls are long gone but both chapels remain. On Pheasant Walk, incongruously surrounded by a 1960s housing estate, is the 16th-century **Chapel of the Blessed Virgin Mary**, once a secluded place of worship for the East Hall residents, while the West Hall had **St John's**, a pretty 1893 mix of half-timbered walls and red-tiled roofs that's now the parish church.

In the 19th century a young Robert Moffat used to work as an estate gardener at West Hall, before going on to become a famous missionary in southern Africa and father-in-law of David Livingstone, who married Moffat's daughter Mary. He's remembered locally with one of the village roads named after him and the annual 10k Robert Moffat Memorial Race in March, which raises funds for the community.

SHOPPING

Abbey Leys Farm Peacock Ln, WA16 6NS 01925 753465 abbeyleys.co.uk 10.00–16.00 daily, closed bank hols. This Soil Association-certified farm, owned and run by the friendly and helpful Harrison family, produces organic potatoes and eggs, with speciality hens including Speckeldy, White Leghorn and Welsummer. Come at the right time of year and you can also get geese and turkey eggs – they only lay for about three months a year, starting around February. The farm shop is small but stuffed full of goodies, much of it from other local producers, including fruit, veg, dairy produce and honey. There are homemade pies and cakes, too – I can vouch for the deliciousness of Janet Harrison's almond slice and my other half is a big fan of her steak and ale pie. On the first Sunday of each month Abbey Leys hosts a Community Farmers Market, with stalls selling fresh produce and local handcrafts. As you leave, look out for Eric and Ernie in the field on your right – two pet male turkeys who'll come rushing up to the fence to chase you on your way.

19 ARLEY HALL

Arley CW9 6NA 01565 777353 arleyhallandgardens.com check website for details

It's a little beauty, Arley. Heaven knows, Cheshire isn't short of great country houses and gardens – but this is probably the one I've revisited more than any other over the years. It may not have the high profile of a Tatton or a Little Moreton but neither (unless you visit during one of the many special events) does it seem to have the same crowds. You can have real moments of peace here, hidden away in one of the many nooks and crannies of its glorious gardens.

The **hall** itself, standing on the site of an earlier incarnation, is a Victorian take on Elizabethan and Jacobean architecture and is definitely worth a look inside, with some particularly handsome ceilings, oak panelling and stained glass. It's the **gardens**, though, that deliver the wow factor, from the loveliest herbaceous borders you're ever likely to see to the surreal avenue of holm oaks, made up of 14 trees, all around

ELEVEN BOYS IN A TREE

In the course of researching this book I read many old books about Cheshire, all of them decades, if not centuries, out of date. They clearly weren't reliable guides to the county today but they made fascinating reading, providing wistful little glimpses into Cheshire past and telling interesting anecdotes about places and people. Occasionally, they also proved totally baffling. Take this little gem from Arthur Mee's 1938 book, *The King's England: Cheshire*. In the section on Arley, under the headline 'Eleven Boys in a Tree', he writes: 'Hereabouts are grand old trees, among them a gnarled oak into which a squire of Arley is said to have squeezed 11 boys, paying them a shilling each to be so discomfited.' And that's the lot – end of anecdote. So many questions...

30 foot tall, clipped into giant columns. There's a walled garden, a rose garden and a fish garden; a mountain dell area called the Rootery, a kitchen garden and a flag garden. And then, just when you think you must have seen it all, you realise there's a whole other area (behind the hall and the 19th-century chapel designed by Anthony Salvin): The Grove. It's lovely at any time of year, dotted with assorted sculptures but particularly beautiful in spring, when the rhododendrons and azaleas are a joy to behold.

20 GREAT BUDWORTH

Small but perfectly formed, this is one of the prettiest of Cheshire villages, with a church, stocks, old pump house and pub at its heart and chocolate-box cottages lining the surrounding streets. Its handsome appearance owes much to Rowland Egerton-Warburton, 19th-century squire of Arley Hall, who commissioned leading architects of the time to make the village more picturesque. This they duly did, restoring old houses and building new ones to blend in. The result is a lovely, harmonious whole: 17th-century black-and-white cottages and possibly 15th-century Old Hall sitting happily alongside Victorian houses with diaper brickwork and decorative chimneystacks. It's all very well kept, too, every hedge neatly trimmed (look for the topiary peacock), every window box and hanging basket overflowing with summer flowers, and the old red phone box transformed into a community library with everything from cookery books to crime novels, baby manuals to boating magazines. Although the village shops are long gone, you'll often find some of the locals selling off surplus produce from their gardens. On a sunny August afternoon, we picked up homemade jam and free-range eggs from the honesty stall in the porch of Cob Cottage on Church Street, plus a gorgeous bunch of scented sweet peas and a couple of pounds of fresh-from-the-ground potatoes from one of the High Street houses.

"Although the village shops are long gone, you'll often find some of the locals selling off surplus produce from their gardens."

The church, **St Mary & All Saints** (High St, CW9 6HF), dates back to the 14th and 15th centuries, though there's been a church on this site since at least the 11th. A leaflet inside lists the building's highlights, including the Georgian beadles' staves, medieval oak chest and alabaster effigy of Sir John Warburton, missing feet and hands and scratched with

MERSEY & NORTHWEST CHESHIRE

> ### JUST OVER THE BORDER
> **The Dream** Sutton Manor WA9 4BE. Jaume Plensa's 66-foot-tall white sculpture of a girl's head is a prominent landmark on the site of a former colliery.
> **Speke Hall** Speke L24 1XD ⌂ National Trust. A few miles west of Hale, in Merseyside, is one of Britain's finest examples of a Tudor manor house.

graffiti, but resplendent in Elizabethan costume. If you have trouble finding any of them, grab a copy of the booklet intended for children – it has illustrations to make things easier.

Hidden away behind the church is a peaceful little garden and a narrow avenue of lime trees, which leads nowhere in particular but is a pleasant stroll. At the other end of the village, on the corner of Warrington Road, you'll find the lower **pump house**, once the village water source. It's a tiny little building, adorned with a wrought iron gate, where water pours from a rusty tap into a big stone basin below, with another trough outside, presumably for thirsty horses.

FOOD & DRINK

George & Dragon High St, CW9 6HF ✆ 01606 892650 ⌂ georgeanddragonatgreatbudworth.co.uk. In the days when Great Budworth was a stopping point on the road to London, there were four inns in the village centre. Now this is the last man standing and a very popular spot for a pub lunch, with cosy, traditional interiors and pavement tables where you can sit out on a sunny day and enjoy the view of the ironwork pub sign and the church across the road.

Great Budworth Real Dairy Ice Cream Farm New Westage Farm, Heath Ln, CW9 6ND ✆ 01606 891211 ⌂ icecreamfarm.co.uk ⊙ Apr–Oct noon–18.00 daily, Mar & Nov–Dec 13.00–17.00 weekends only, closed Jan–Feb. 'From cow to cone' is the slogan of this family-run venture on the edge of the village, where the little tea room serves delicious ice cream, whipped up daily in the on-site dairy using milk from the farm's herd of Friesian cows.

> ### FOLLOW US
> Use **#cheshire** to share your adventures using this guide with us – we'd love to hear from you.
>
> Bradt Travel Guides
> @bradtguides (#cheshire)
> youtube.com/bradtguides
>
> @BradtGuides & @Traveltappers (#cheshire)
> pinterest.com/bradtguides

ACCOMMODATION

Our choice of accommodation has been based on a few simple Slow principles. We've searched out attractive places – after all you are taking a break – that are often set in an historic building or somewhere with an architectural story to tell. We've also prized independent accommodation, especially where local producers are championed in welcome hampers or at the breakfast table. But mostly we have gone for quality, because we know that you'll be exhausted from your daily explorations and deserve a good night's rest. The hotels, B&Bs and pubs with rooms here are indicated by 🏠 under the heading for the town or village in which they are located, while self-catering properties are indicated by 🏠 and campsites by ▲. For detailed listings, go to ⌕ bradtguides.com/cheshiresleeps.

1 CHESTER & WIRRAL

Hotels
The Chester Grosvenor Eastgate, Chester CH1 1LT ✆ 01244 324024 ⌕ chestergrosvenor.com
Edgar House 22 City Walls, Chester CH1 1SB ✆ 01244 347007 ⌕ edgarhouse.co.uk
Hillbark Hotel & Spa Royden Pk, Frankby CH48 1NP ✆ 0151 625 2400 ⌕ hillbarkhotel.co.uk
Oddfellows Hotel 20 Lower Bridge St, Chester CH1 1RS ✆ 01244 345454 ⌕ oddfellowschester.com; see ad, 4th colour section

B&Bs
42 Caldy Road 42 Caldy Rd, West Kirby CH48 2HQ ✆ 0151 625 8740 ⌕ 42caldyroad.co.uk
80 Watergate Street 80 Watergate St, Chester CH1 2LF ✆ 01244 314879 ⌕ 80watergatestreet.co.uk

Pubs with rooms
The Boathouse and Riverside Rooms 21 The Groves, Chester CH1 1SD ✆ 01244 328709 ⌕ theboathousechester.co.uk
The Ship The Parade, Parkgate CH64 6SA ✆ 0151 336 3931 ⌕ the-shiphotel.co.uk

Self-catering
The Book Keeper's Cottage Port Sunlight, Wirral CH62 5DX ✆ 0151 644 6466 ⌕ portsunlightvillage.com
Heritage View Chester Inside city walls ⌕ airbnb.co.uk
Inglenook Cottage Kelsall Rd, Ashton Hayes, nr Chester CH3 8BH ✆ 01829 752109 ⌕ inglenookcottages.com
The Little Tin Chapel Chester Outside city walls ⌕ holidaylettings.co.uk
The Outbuilding Oscroft, nr Tarvin ⌕ airbnb.co.uk

ACCOMMODATION

2 SOUTH CHESHIRE

Hotels
32 by The Hollies 32 High St, Tarporley CW9 0DY ⌂ theholliesfarmshop.co.uk
Peckforton Castle Stone House Ln, Peckforton CW6 9TN ☏ 01829 260930 ⌂ peckfortoncastle.co.uk

B&Bs
The North Wing Combermere Abbey, nr Whitchurch SY13 4AJ ☏ 01948 662880 ⌂ combermereabbey.co.uk

Pubs & restaurants with rooms
Allium by Mark Ellis Lynedale Hse, Tattenhall CH3 9PX ☏ 01829 771477 ⌂ theallium.co.uk
The Badger Inn Cross Ln, Church Minshull CW5 6DY ☏ 01270 522348 ⌂ badgerinn.co.uk
The Cholmondeley Arms Wrenbury Rd, Cholmondeley SY14 8HN ☏ 01829 720300 ⌂ cholmondeleyarms.co.uk
The Crown High St, Nantwich CW5 5AS ☏ 01270 625283 ⌂ crownhotelnantwich.com
The Pheasant Inn Higher Burdwardsley, Tattenhall CH3 9PF ☏ 01829 770434 ⌂ thepheasantinn.co.uk

Self-catering
Barton Bank Cottage Red Hs, Barton SY14 7HU ☏ 01829 782720 ⌂ bartonbank.com
Cheshire Boutique Barns Cholmondeley Rd, Wrenbury CW5 8HJ ☏ 07922 277292 ⌂ healdcountryhouse.co.uk
Combermere Abbey Cottages Combermere Abbey, nr Whitchurch SY13 4AJ ☏ 01948 660345 ⌂ combermereabbey.co.uk
Garden Cottage Bunbury ⌂ airbnb.co.uk
Manor Farm Holiday Cottages Manor Farm, Egerton Gn, Cholmondeley SY14 8AN ☏ 01829 720261 ⌂ egertonmanorfarm.co.uk
Millmoor Farm Cottages Millmoor Farm, Malpas SY14 8ED ☏ 01948 820304 ⌂ millmoorfarm.co.uk
Newton Hall Shepherd's Hut Tattenhall ⌂ airbnb.co.uk
Pillory House Loft Apartment Nantwich ⌂ airbnb.co.uk
Redwood Cottage Dorfold Hall, Nantwich CW5 8LD ☏ 01270 625245 ⌂ dorfoldhall.com
Sandstone Trail Cottages Sherrington Ln, Broxton CH3 9JU ☏ 01829 782169 ⌂ sandstonetrailcottages.co.uk
The Snuggery Nantwich ⌂ airbnb.co.uk
Victoria Apartments Tarporley ⌂ airbnb.co.uk

Camping & glamping
Broad Oak Farm Birds Ln, Tattenhall CH3 9NL ☏ 01829 770325 ⌂ broadoakfarmcamping.co.uk
Cheshire Farm Yurts The Croft, Newton Ln, Tattenhall CH3 9NE ☏ 07984 470333 ⌂ cheshirefarmyurts.co.uk

3 HEART OF THE PLAIN

Pubs with rooms
The Royal Oak Chester Rd, Kelsall CW6 0RR ☏ 01829 7512808 ⌂ theroyaloakkelsall.com
The White Bear Wheelock St, Middlewich CW10 9AG ☏ 01606 837666 ⌂ thewhitebearmiddlewich.co.uk

Self-catering
11 Bostock Green by Tatton Stays Bostock Green ⌂ airbnb.com
The Hollies Forest Lodges Tarporley Rd, Little Budworth CW6 9ES ☏ 01829 760761 ⌂ theholliesfarmshop.co.uk

Camping & glamping
Delamere Forest Camping & Caravanning Club Site Station Rd, Delamere CW8 2HZ ☏ 01606 889231 ⌂ campingandcaravanningclub.co.uk
Shays Farm Caravan & Camping Shays Ln, Little Budworth, nr Tarporley CW6 9EU ☏ 01829 760233 ⌂ shaysfarm.co.uk

4 CREWE & THE STAFFORDSHIRE BORDERS

B&Bs
The Alexandra Court Hotel 7 Newcastle Rd, Congleton CW12 4HN ✆ 01260 297871 🌐 thealexandracourthotel.com
Mere Cottage 118 Crewe Rd, Alsager ST7 2JA ✆ 01270 361743 🌐 merecottagealsager.co.uk

Pubs with rooms
The Bear's Paw School Ln, Warmingham, nr Sandbach CW11 3QN ✆ 01270 526317 🌐 thebearspaw.co.uk
The Wheatsheaf 1 Hightown, Sandbach CW11 1AG ✆ 01270 762013 🌐 wheatsheafsandbach.co.uk

Self-catering
Chequer Stable Sandbach 🌐 homeaway.co.uk
Dane Cottage Holidays Congleton ✆ 01260 276323 🌐 danecottageholidays.co.uk

Camping & glamping
Castle Camping Congleton Rd, Mow Cop ST7 3PL ✆ 07539 682202 🌐 castlecampingltd.co.uk

5 MACCLESFIELD & THE PEAK DISTRICT

B&Bs
Common Barn Farm Smith Ln, Rainow SK10 5XJ ✆ 01625 574878 🌐 cottages-with-a-view.co.uk
Hill Top Farm Wincle SK11 0QH ✆ 01260 227257 🌐 hill-top-farm.co.uk
Sleep, Eat, Repeat The Flat Above, 23c Church St, Macclesfield SK11 6LB ✆ 07474 102490 🌐 churchstreetcobbles.co.uk

Pubs with rooms
Legh Arms The Village, Prestbury SK10 4DG ✆ 01625 829130 🌐 legharmsprestbury.pub
Robin Hood Inn Church Ln, Rainow SK10 5XE ✆ 01625 574060 @RHRainow
The Ryles Arms Hollin Ln, Sutton SK11 0NN ✆ 01260 252244 🌐 rylesarms.com
Stanley Arms Bottom of the Oven, Macclesfield Forest SK11 0AR ✆ 01260 252414 🌐 stanleyarms.com

Self-catering
The Apartment at Bartomley Farm Wincle 🌐 airbnb.co.uk
Cheshire Hunt Holiday Cottages Hedge Rw, off Spuley Ln, Rainow SK10 5DA ✆ 01625 572034 🌐 cheshirehuntholidaycottages.co.uk
Clough Brook Cottage Allmeadows Farm, Wincle SK11 0QJ ✆ 01260 227209 🌐 peakcottages.com
Crag Hall Wildboarclough SK11 0BD ✆ 0845 200 4801 🌐 craghall.co.uk
Dane Cottage Wincle ✆ 01260 276323 🌐 danecottageholidays.co.uk
Disley Hall Disley Hall, Corks Ln SK12 2DA 🌐 sykescottages.co.uk
East Lodge Lyme Pk, Disley 🌐 National Trust
Kerridge End Cottages Kerridge End Hs, Rainow SK10 5TF ✆ 01625 424220 🌐 kerridgeendholidaycottages.co.uk
Otter's Retreat Mellor Knowl Farm, Wincle SK11 0QE ✆ 01260 277235 🌐 ottersretreat.co.uk
Swythamley Chapel Swythamley 🌐 airbnb.co.uk

Camping & glamping
Underbank Camping Barn Blaze Farm, Wildboarclough SK11 0BL ✆ 01260 227266 🌐 underbankcampingbarn.co.uk

6 STOCKPORT & THE CHESHIRE PANHANDLE

Hotels
Oddfellows on the Park Bruntwood Pk, Cheadle SK8 1HX ✆ 0161 697 3066 🌐 oddfellowsonthepark.com; see ad, 4th colour section

ACCOMMODATION

Pubs with rooms
The Red Bull 14 Middle Hillgate, Stockport SK1 3AY ℘ 0161 480 1286 ⌘ robinsonsbrewery.com
Ring O'Bells 130 Church Ln, Marple SK6 7AY ℘ 0161 427 2300 ⌘ robinsonsbrewery.com

Self-catering
Magpie Cottages Lower Dale Farm, Dale Rd, Marple SK6 6NL ℘ 07718 041193 ⌘ magpiecottages.co.uk

7 NORTHEAST CHESHIRE

Hotels
The Longview Hotel 51–55 Manchester Rd, Knutsford WA16 0LX ℘ l01565 632119 ⌘ longviewhotel.com
The Belle Epoque 60 King St, Knutsford WA16 6DT ℘ 01565 633060 ⌘ thebelleepoque.co.uk

B&Bs
Ash Farm Park Ln, Little Bollington WA14 4SU ℘ 0161 929 9290 ⌘ ashfarm.co.uk
Birtles Farm B&B Ashley Rd, Ashley, Altrincham WA14 3QH ℘ 0161 928 0458 ⌘ birtlesfarm.co.uk
Goose Green Farm Oak Rd, Mottram St Andrew SK10 4RA ℘ 01625 828814 ⌘ goosegreenfarm.com
The Hinton Guest House Town Ln, Mobberley WA16 7HH ℘ 01565 873484 ⌘ thehintonguesthouse.co.uk
Holly Tree Farm Holmes Chapel Rd, Lower Withington SK11 9DT ℘ 01477 571257 ⌘ hollytreefarm.org
Millbrook Cottage Guesthouse Congleton Rd, Nether Alderley SK10 4TW ℘ 01625 599390 ⌘ millbrookcottage.co.uk
Owen House Farm Wood Ln, Mobberley WA16 7NY ℘ 07754 370721 ⌘ owenhousefarm.co.uk
Wizards Thatch Macclesfield Rd, Alderley Edge SK9 7BG ℘ 01625 599909 ⌘ wizardsthatch.co.uk

Pubs with rooms
The Roebuck Mill Lane, Mobberley WA16 7HX ℘ 01565 873939 ⌘ roebuckinnmobberley.co.uk
The Vicarage Freehouse & Rooms Knutsford Rd, Cranage, Holmes Chapel CW4 8EF ℘ 01477 533393 ⌘ thevicaragecheshire.com

Self-catering
Cheshire Country Holidays Brookbank Farm, Bridge Ln, Blackden Heath, Holmes Chapel CW4 8BX ℘ 01477 518448 ⌘ cheshirecountryholidays.co.uk
Dairy Apartments Tatton Park, Knutsford WA16 6QL ℘ 01244 746104 ⌘ sykescottages.co.uk

Camping & glamping
Capesthorne Hall Caravan Park Capesthorne Hall, Congleton Rd, Siddington SK11 9JY ℘ 01625 861221 ⌘ capesthorne.com/caravan-park

8 MERSEY & NORTHWEST CHESHIRE

Hotels
The Partridge Tarporley Rd, Stretton WA4 4LX ℘ 01925 730848 ⌘ thepartridgestretton.co.uk

Self-catering
Beechlands Cottage Frodsham ⌘ sykescottages.co.uk
Broomedge Farm Cottages Broomedge Farm, Burford Ln, Lymm WA13 0SE ℘ 01925 752830 ⌘ www.broomedgefarm.co.uk
Childe of Hale Cottage Hale ⌘ homeaway.co.uk
Fir Tree Barn Cottages Fir Tree Farm, Pennypleck Ln, Crowley CW9 6NX ℘ 01565 777327 ⌘ firtreebarn.co.uk

Camping & glamping
Lady Heyes Holiday Park Kingsley Rd, Frodsham WA6 6SU ℘ 01928 788557 ⌘ ladyheyespark.com

NOTES

NOTES

NOTES

NOTES

INDEX

Entries in **bold** refer to major entries.

A

Abney Hall Park 199–200
accessibility 17, 24
accommodation 16, 291–4
Acton 88–9
Adlington Hall 178–9
Aethelflaed 25, **26**, 266
Aikin, J 216
Alcock, John 182
Alderley Edge 244–7
Aldford 38
Alsager 128–32
Altrincham 222–4
ancient sites
  archaeological excavations, Mellor 210
  Bowstones 185
  Bridestones 147
  Bullstones 185
  Clulow cross 185
  Greenway cross 185
  Iron Age hillforts 58, 111
  Kelsborrow Castle 117
  Maiden Castle 66, 67
  Old Man O'Mow 154
  Saxon crosses 133, 134, 163, 185
  Standing stones 185
Anderton Boat Lift 105–6
Anderton Nature Park 102
apple juice 145, 226
architecture 10–11
Arley Hall 288–9
Armitstead, Rev John 134
arts and culture 11, 30, 33–4, 37, 50, 60, 61, 75, 87, 99, 104, 123–4, 131, 143, 146, 153, 162, 167, 197, 204, 239–40, 257–8, 271, 283 *see also* festivals
Ashton's Flash 102
Astbury Mere Country Park 147–8
Aston by Sutton 279
Audlem 76–8

B

Bagshaw, Samuel 194
Bakewell, Robert 73
Barry, EM 126
Barthomley 127–8
Bateman, James 144
Beeston 60
Beeston Castle 58–9
Biddulph Valley Way 144
bike hire and repair 22, 57, 97, 160, 193, 222, 255–6
birdwatching 41, 59, 102–3, 107, 112, 197–8, 138, 138–9, 186, 232, 260–1, 263, 263–4, 269, 272–3
Birkenhead Park 46–9
Bisto kids 110
Blackden Trust 238–9
Blore, Edward 76, 250
Bolesworth Castle 62
Bollin Valley 172, 243
Bollington 173–8
bookshops 45, 87, 114, 131, 203, 206, 223, 270
Boothsdale 117
Bostock Green 106–7
Bourne, Hugh 127
Bower, Thomas 84, 127, 135
Bradshaw, Judge John 141, 206, 212
Bramall Hall 201–2
Brereton, Sir William 24
Brereton Heath Local Nature Reserve 137–8
breweries 10, 32, 173, 188, 226, 235
Bridgewater, Duke of 270
Brierley, Thomas 210
Brindley, James 15, 168, **270–1**
Broadbottom 211, **213–14**
Broadmills Heritage Site 213
Brocklehurst, Marianne 163
Brooke, Sir Richard 275
Broomheath Plantation Bushcraft Academy 40
Brown, Capability 38, 91, 126
Brown, Ford Madox 205
Brunner Mond 103
Brunner, John 103
Buckley, William 248
Budworth Mere 102
Buffalo Bill 129
Bulley, Arthur Kilpin 41
Bunbury 65–8
Bunbury Mill 65
Burne-Jones, Edward 205
Burrell, Paul 68
Burwardsley 60–1
Byrne, Aiden 287

Byron, Lord John 32, 79

C

canal-boat hire 57, 97, 121, 160, 256
canals 14–15
  Audlem locks 77
  Bridgewater Canal 267, **270–1**, 285
  Bunbury Staircase Locks 65
  Cheshire Ring 14, 98, 159, 192, 221, 255
  Chester Basin 31
  Chester Canal 31
  Macclesfield Canal 168, 169, 173, 203, 209
  Manchester Ship Canal 52, 262
  Marple aqueduct 203
  Marple locks 203
  Northgate locks 32
  Peak Forest Canal 181, 203, 204, 208, 209
  Sankey Canal 272
  Shropshire Union Canal 31, 52, 65, 74, 77, 85, 108
  Trent and Mersey Canal 102, 104, 108, 133
  Wardle Canal 108, 110
Capesthorne Hall 249–50
Carden Hall 69
Carroll, Lewis 262, 276–7
Celia Fiennes Waymark 72
Chadkirk Chapel and Country Estate 211–12
Chaplin, Charlie 124
Charles I 24
Charles II 75
Cheadle 198–201
cheese 9, 83
Cheshire Cat pubs and bars 234
Cheshire families 37, 39, 69, 70, 75, 102, 107, 110, 128, 132, 152, 153, 166, 167, 181, 231, 244, 245, 250, 264, 287
Cheshire Wildlife Trust 40, 102, 240
Chester 19–20, 22–37
  Chester Canal 31
  Chester Castle, Agricola Tower and Chapel of St Mary de Castro 32
  Chester Cathedral, Addleshaw Tower, Falconry and Nature Gardens 28–9
  Cheshire Military Museum 32

INDEX

Chester Mystery Plays 34
Chester Racecourse (Roodee) 25, 33
Chester Zoo 34–5
city tours 25, 26
city walls 24–6
Eastgate clock 25
ghosts 29
Grosvenor Museum 25, **33**
Grosvenor Park and Open Air Theatre 31
Minerva shrine 31
Moonlight Flicks 30
River Dee, The Groves and The Meadows 22, 30, 31
Roman amphitheatre 29
Roman Gardens 30
the Rows 26
St John the Baptist 27
Storyhouse 33
Winter Watch and Saturnalia parades 34
Within These Walls 25
Christie, Agatha 200, 206
Church Farm 44
churches
  All Saints, Odd Rode 153
  All Saints, Siddington 249
  Brook Street Chapel, Knutsford 227
  Cathedral Church of Christ and the Blessed Virgin Mary, Chester 28
  Christ Church, Alsager 130
  Christ Church, Weston Point 268
  Church of the Immaculate Conception, Broadbottom 211
  Jenkin Chapel (St John the Baptist), Saltersford 184
  Old Chad, Tushingham 72–3
  Primitive Methodist Memorial Chapel, Mow Cop 154
  St Andrew's, Tarvin 40
  St Bertoline's, Barthomley 127
  St Boniface, Bunbury 65
  St Catherine's, Birtles 165
  St Edith's, Shocklach 69
  St James, Audlem 76
  St James and St Paul, Marton 248
  St James the Great, Gawsworth 167
  St John the Baptist, Chester 27
  St John's, Adlington 179
  St John's, High Legh 287
  St Laurence, Frodsham 281
  St Luke Mission, Mow Cop 154
  St Luke's, Holmes Chapel 241
  St Margaret's, Wrenbury 74
  St Martin's, Marple 205
  St Mary and All Saints, Great Budworth 289
  St Mary's, Acton 88
  St Mary's, Astbury 148
  St Mary's, Cheadle 199
  St Mary's, Disley 182
  St Mary's, Eccleston 38
  St Mary's, Hale 273
  St Mary's, Halton 273
  St Mary's, Nantwich 80, **82–4**
  St Mary's, Nether Alderley 247
  St Mary's, Sandbach 134
  St Mary's in the Marketplace, Stockport 195
  St Michael and All Angels, Macclesfield 160, 161
  St Michael and All Angels, Middlewich 109
  St Michael and All Angels, Mottram in Longdendale 215
  St Michael's, Marbury 74
  St Michael's, Crewe Green 127
  St Oswald's, Lower Peover 236
  St Oswald's, Malpas 70
  St Oswald's, Winwick 258
  St Peter, Aston by Sutton 279
  St Peter, Prestbury 171
  St Peter's, Congleton 141
  St Philip's, Hassall Green 130
  St Saviour's, Wildboarclough 187
  St Stephen (Forest Chapel), Macclesfield Forest 186
  St Thomas, Mellor 210
  St Wilfrid's, Grappenhall 262
  St Wilfrid's, Mobberley **234–5**, 236
Clark, Edwin 105
Clonter Opera 239–40
Combermere Abbey **75–6**, 88
Congleton 139–46
corn dollies 249
Cotebrook Shire Horse Centre and Countryside Park 115
Craig, Sir Ernest 129
Crewe 121–6
Crewe Green 127
Crewe Hall 121, **126**
Crewe Heritage Centre 124
Crewe, Sir Randolph 126
Crocky Trail, The 39
Croston, James 245
Cuckooland 233–4
cycling 14, 21, 57, 97, 120, 159, 193, 221–2, 255

D

Dairy House Meadows 102
damson orchards 9
Dane Valley 187, 241
Danebridge Fisheries 188
Daresbury 276–7
d'Avranches, Hugh 23
De Quincey, Thomas 223
Dee Estuary 42, 43
Defoe, Daniel 260
Delamere Forest 112–14
Delves Hall 91
Delves, Sir John 91
Denzell Gardens and the Devisdale 222
Disley 181–3
distilleries 10, 49, 51
Dock Road Pumping Station 101
Doddington Hall 91
Dodgson, Charles Lutwidge *see* Carroll, Lewis
Dorfold Hall 81, 85, 87–8
Douglas, John 31
Dunge Valley Gardens 185
Dunham Massey 224–6
Dutton 278

E

Earnshaw, Lawrence 216
Eaton Hall and the Grosvenor villages 37–9
Eccleston 38
Edge, Joseph 182
Edward I 24, 32, 108
Edward the Elder 262
Egerton-Warburton, Rowland 289
Eisenhower, General 237
Elizabeth I 81
Ellerton, Rev John 127
Empress of Austria, Elizabeth 75
Engels, Friedrich 194
Engelsea Brook Chapel and Museum 127
English Civil War 24, 32, 59, 71, 79, 108, 128, 132, 149, 259, 274
English Heritage 59, 133

F

farm shops 44, 51, 62, 86, 114–15, 131, 138, 139, 148, 214, 226, 230, 236, 244, 259, 265, 287
Farndon 68–9
Fawcett, Eric 105
festivals
  Barnaby Festival, Macclesfield 165
  bluedot festival, Jodrell Bank 238
  Bollington Walking Festival 175
  FAB Festival, Middlewich 110
  Goostrey Gooseberry Show 239
  Holly Holy Day, Nantwich 79
  Just So Festival, Rode Hall 153

INDEX

Knutsford Royal May Day festivities 230
Marbury Merry Days 74
Quince and Apple Day, Norton Priory 276
Royal Cheshire County Show 233
Sandstone Ridge Festival 60
Transport Festival, Sandbach 133
Warrington Contemporary Arts Festival 258
Winter Watch and Saturnalia parades, Chester 34
Willaston World Worm Charming Championships 88
Wybunbury Fig Pie Roll 92
Yesteryear Rally, Malpas 71
Fildes, Mary 104
film, TV and radio 35, 65, 89, 180, 199
Fitton, Mary 166–7
Foden Brass Band 133
folklore 29, 31, 72, 84, 92, 142, 184, 186, 211, 226, 230, 246, 249, 258–9
Forestry Commission 112
Forrest, George 42
Frodsham 279–83
Fryer's Garden Centre 232
Furey Woods 102

G

gardens 11–12
Abbeywood Gardens 113
Adlington Hall 178–9
Arley Hall 288–9
Bluebell Cottage Gardens and Nursery 278
Cholmondeley Castle Gardens 73
Combermere Abbey 76
Denzell Gardens 222
Doddington Hall 91
Dorfold Hall 88
Dunge Valley Gardens 185
Dunham Massey 225
Eaton Hall 38
Gawsworth Hall 166–7
Grappenhall Heys Walled Garden 263
Jodrell Bank Garden and Arboretum 238
Little Moreton Hall 149
Lovell Quinta Arboretum 240
Lyme Park 181
Mount Pleasant Gardens 113
National Open Gardens Scheme 113
Ness Botanic Gardens 41
Norton Priory Museum and Gardens 275–6
Old Town Bloom, Runcorn 267
Pocket Parks, Congleton 144
Quarry Bank 242
Rode Hall 152
Roman Gardens, Chester 30
Stonyford Cottage Gardens 113
Swettenham lavender meadow 240
Tatton Park 231–2
Walton Hall 264
Garner, Alan 184, 238, 245, 248
Gaskell, Elizabeth 104, 219, 224–5, 227–8
Gastrell, Francis 281, 283
Gauntlet Birds of Prey 232
Gawsworth 166–8
Gawsworth Hall 166
Maggotty's Wood 167
Gee, Sir Henry 33
Gerard, John 85
Gibbons, Grinling 180
Gibbs, James 257
Gibson, Reginald 105
Godwin, E W 140
Goostrey Gooseberry Show 239
Grappenhall 261–3
Grappenhall Heys Walled Garden 263
Great Budworth 289–90
Greg, Samuel 241
Gritstone Trail, The **150–2**, 159, 169, 171, 173

H

Hack Green Secret Nuclear Bunker 90–1
Hale 273
Childe of Hale 273
Hale Duck Decoy 273
Halton 273–5
castle 273
Hamilton, Lady Emma 43
Handel 28, 178, 281
Hare Hill 246
Harrison, Thomas 24, 28, 32
Harthill 60–1
Hassall Green 130
Havannah 139
Heber, Reginald 70
Helsby 284
Helsdale Wood 286
Henbury Hall 165
Henry III 32, 58
heronry, Trentabank 186
Heswall 43
High Legh 287–8
Higher Walton 264–5
historic houses and stately homes
Adlington Hall 178–9
Arley Hall 288–9
Bolesworth Castle 62
Booth Mansion, Chester 27
Bramall Hall 201–2
Brereton Hall 137–8
Cholmondeley Castle 73
Churche's Mansion 81
Combermere Abbey 75–6
Crewe Hall 121, **126–7**
Doddington Hall 91
Dorfold Hall 83, **87**
Dunham Massey 224–5
Eaton Hall 37–8
Gawsworth Hall 166–7
Little Moreton Hall 149
Lyme Park 179–81
Milton House 129
Old Hall, Sandbach 134
Peckforton Castle 59–60
Port Sunlight 49–51
Tabley House 233
Tatton Park 231–2
Hockenhull Platts 40
Holinshed, Raphael 168
Holloway, Stanley 266
Holmes Chapel 241

I

ice-cream farms
Backford Belles 53
Blaze Farm 187
Daresbury Dairy 277
Great Budworth Real Dairy Ice Cream Farm 290
Ice Cream Farm, The 63
Seven Sisters 230
Snugbury's 89
industrial archaeology 213
Irvine, Andrew 236
Isherwood, Christopher 182, 212

J

James I 273
Jessop, William 52
Jodrell Bank Discovery Centre 237–8
John of Gaunt 274
Johnson, Samuel 'Maggoty' 168
John Turner stone 184

K

Kemp, Edward 31, 48, 124, 143, 280, 289
Kempe, Charles 76
Kendrick, James 261
Kerridge 173, 175
King Canute 227, 230

301

INDEX

King John 71, 274
Kingdon-Ward, Frank 42
Knutsford 227–31
    Knutsford Tapestry 228
    Watt, Richard Harding 227, **228–9**

L

Lady Lever Art Gallery 50
Laurel, Stan 124
Legh, Thomas 184
Lever, William Hesketh (Lord Leverhulme) 49, 286
Lindow Man 244
Lion Salt Works 103–5
Little Moreton Hall 149
Little Switzerland 115–17
Local Nature Reserves
    Abney Hall Park 200
    Brereton Heath 137–8
    Great Wood 214
    Helsby Quarry 284
    Lindow Common 243
    Risley Moss 260–1
    Pickerings Pasture 272
    Wigg Island 269
local produce 9–10
Longdendale 216–17
    Longdendale Lights 217
    Longdendale Trail 217
Lovell, Sir Bernard 238, 240
Lovell Quinta Arboretum 240
Lovell Telescope *see* Jodrell Bank Discovery Centre
Lower Peover and Over Peover 236–7
Lowry, L S 215
Lutyens, Sir Edwin 38, 50
Lyme Park 179–81
Lymm 284–7

M

Macclesfield 160–165
    Barnaby Festival 165
    museums 162–3
    Treacle Market 160, 161, 165
Macclesfield Forest 169, 185–6
    Trentabank heronry 186
Mallory, George 234, 235, 236
Malpas 70–2
maps 16–17
Marbury 74
Marbury Country Park 102
markets
    Abbey Leys 288
    Alsager 132
    Altrincham 224
    Bollington 174, 178
    Cheadle 199
    Chester 37
    Congleton 146
    Crewe, 126
    Frodsham, 283
    Knutsford 231
    Macclesfield 160, 161, 165
    Middlewich 110, 111
    Nantwich 87
    Northwich 101
    Rode Hall 152
    Sandbach 137
    Stockport 195, 198
    Tarporley 64
    Wilmslow 244
Marple 203–6
    Marple Hall 206, 212
    locks 203
    Marple Aqueduct 203
Marple Bridge 206–7
Marple, Miss 206
Marton 248
mazes 44, 76, 176, 179, 226, 231
Mee, Arthur 288
Mellor 207–10
    Mellor Mill 203, 208
    Roman Lakes 207
meres, mosses and flashes 112, **116**
Mersey Estuary 269, 279
Mersey Ferry 48
Mersey Valley Timberland Trail 255, 286
Mid-Cheshire Line 104
Middleton, John 273
Middlewich 107–11
Middlewood Way, The 173
Midshires Way 212
milk vending machines 9
Mobberley 234–6
Moffat, Robert 287
Mond, Ludwig 103
Moore Nature Reserve 263–4
Morris, William/Morris and Co 161, 205, 248
Mottershead, George 34
Mottram in Longdendale 214–6
mountaineers 236
Mow Cop 127, **153–4**
Murder stone 183
museums
    Anderton Boat Lift 105–6
    Catalyst, Widnes 272
    Cheshire Military Museum 32
    Congleton Museum 142–3
    Crewe Heritage Centre 122, 124
    Englesea Brook Chapel and Museum 127
    Grosvenor Museum 25, 33
    Hat Works 197
    Hack Green Secret Nuclear Bunker 90–1
    Lion Salt Works 103–5
    Middlewich Virtual Museum 109
    Nantwich Museum 82, 84
    National Waterways Museum 51–2
    The Old Sunday School 162
    Paradise Mill 162
    Penny Farthing Museum 230
    Port Sunlight Museum 50
    The Silk Museum 162
    Stockport Museum 195
    Weaver Hall Museum 100
    Warrington Museum and Art Gallery 257
    West Park Museum 163

N

Nab, The 175
Nantwich 78–87
Nantwich Show, The 83
national collections 42, 240, 276
National Trust 149, 153, 180, 225, 231, 241, 245, 246, 247, 277, 290
Nether Alderley 247–8
Nicholson, Archibald Keightley 205, 236, 281
Nield Chew, Ada 125
No Man's Heath 72
Normans 23, 55, 79, 112
Northwich 98–101
Northwich Woodlands 102–3
Norton Priory Museum and Gardens 275–6
Neumann's Flash 102

O

Oldknow, Samuel 203, 207
Orford, Emily 182
Ormerod, George 267, 279
Oswald, King 259
Over Peover *see* Lower Peover and Over Peover
Overton Hill 281
Owen, Wilfred 63

P

Panhandle 191
Parkgate 43
parks and country parks

INDEX

Abney Hall Park 199–200
Anderton Nature Park 102
Astbury Mere Country Park 147–8
Birkenhead Park 46–9
Congleton Park and Town Wood 123–4
Cotebrook Shire Horse Centre and Countryside Park 115
Grosvenor Park 31
Lyme Park 179–81
Marbury Country Park 102
Marple Memorial Park 204
Milton Park, Alsager 129
pocket parks, Congleton 144
Queen's Park, Crewe 124
Roman Lakes 207, 208
Runcorn Hill Nature Park 267
Sandbach Park 126
Tatton Park 231–2
Tegg's Nose Country Park 170–1
Werneth Low Country Park 213
Wirral Country Park 44
Parr, Thomas 263
Patton, General 237
Paxton, Joseph 47, 231
Peak District National Park 179–89, 217
Peckforton 60
Peckforton Castle 59–60
Penney, Edward 141, 248
Pennine Way 217
Peover Hall 237
Piggford Moor 186
Port Sunlight 49–51
Pott Shrigley 183–4
  Shrigley Abduction 183
Prestbury 171–2
Price's Village 51
Pugin, A W N 200

Q
Quarry Bank 241

R
RAF Burtonwood 258
Rainow 184–5
Ranulph, Earl of Chester 58
Reade, Shanaze 124
Reaseheath Zoo 89–90
Redesmere 249
Repton, Humphry 127, 152, 279
RHS Flower Show 231
Risley Moss Local Nature Reserve 260–1
rivers
  Bollin 160, 171, 241, 243
  Croco 108

Dane 108, 139, 143
Dee 22, 30, 38, 41
Etherow 213
Goyt 181, 203, 207
Mersey 52, 194, 272
Weaver 85, 100, 102
Wheelock 108
RNLI 77
Rode Hall 152–3
Roe, Charles 161
Romans 22, **24–5**, **29–30**, 70, 100, 102, 107, 108, 210
Rossetti, Dante Gabriel 205, 215
Rostherne Mere 226
Rowton Heath 24, 25, 29
Royal Cheshire County Show 233
RSPB 59
RSPB Burton Mere Wetlands 41
Runcorn 265–71
rushbearing ceremonies 72, 186

S
Saighton 38
salt 100, **102–3**, 108, 159, 216
Saltersford 184
Salvin, Anthony 250, 289
Sandbach 132–7
Sandbach Flashes 138
Sandstone Ridge 58
Sandstone Ridge Trust **58**, 66
Sandstone Trail 280
Saxons 23, 132, 133, 134, 163, 185
scarecrows 74, 184
Scott, Sir George Gilbert 28, 83, 127, 130, 134, 153, 172, 274, 280
Sedding, John Dando 205
Shakerley, Irene 248
Shakespeare, William 142, 166, 283
Shocklach 69–70
Shutlingsloe 186
Siddington 249
silk 139, **160–1**, 162
Slow movement 8
Spud Wood 286
St Werburgh 28, 68
Stanley, Lady Jane 229
Stockport 194–8
Stretton Mill 69
Styal 241–3
  Quarry Bank 241
Styles, Harry 241
Sutton 168–9
Swettenham 240

T
Tabley House 233
Tarporley 63–4
Tarvin 40
Tattenhall 61–2
Tatton Park 231–2
Taylor, A J P 182
Tegg's Nose Country Park 170–1
Telford, Thomas 52, 74, 85, 87
The Marches 70
Thelwall 261–3
Thomas, Dylan 182
Thor's Stone 44
Three Shire Heads 187
Thurstaston 43–4
Tollemache, Lord John 59
tourist information 21, 44, 57, 98, 121, 160, 193, 256
Trafford 222
Trans Pennine Trail 221, 255, 272, 285
transport 20, 56, 96, 120, 158, 192, 220, 254
Travellers' Rests 259, **260**
Tree of Imagination 237
Tunnicliffe, Charles 162, 163, 168
Turing, Alan 229
Turner, Ellen 183

U
United States Army Air Forces (USAAF) 258
US Third Army 237

V
Vale Royal Abbey **108**, 110
Vegetarian Society 223
Vikings 42, 139, 232

W
Wakefield, Edward Gibbon 183
Walk Mill 39
walking 13–4, 21, 30–2, 38, 40, 43–4, 56, 61, 85–6, 92, 96, 102–3, 104, 107, 112–4, 116–7, 120, 130–1, 137–8, 141, 144, 147–8, 158, 168–9, 170–1, 175, 185–6, 192–3, 212, 217, 220–1, 243–4, 254–5, 268, 284
Walkers Are Welcome 13, 175, 181
walks
  Bickerton Hill 66–7
  Dane-in-Shaw Pastures to Mow Cop 150–2
  In the footsteps of Samuel Oldknow (Mellor/Marple) 208–9

INDEX

Middlewood Way and Macclesfield Canal 176–7
West Kirby to Hilbre Island 46–7
Walton Hall 264
Walton Lea 264
Warrington 256–8
  RAF Burtonwood 258
Waterhouse, Alfred 37, 82
Watson, Joseph 182
Watt, Richard Harding 227, **228–9**
Weaver Navigation 105, 106
Webb, F W 124
Webb, Geoffrey 276
well dressing 182, 210, **211**, 212
Werneth Low Country Park 213
West Kirby 44
Weston/Weston Point 268
Whall, Christopher 161, 205
Wheelock Rail Trail 130
White Nancy 174, 175
White Peak Alpaca Farm 235
Whitegate Way, The 106
Widnes 271–3
Wigg Island 269
Wilbraham, Sir Roger 81, 87
wild swimming 187
Wildboarclough 186–7
Willaston World Worm Charming Championships 88
William the Conqueror 23, 31
William of Orange 75
Williams-Ellis, Clough 62
Willington 116
Wilmslow 243–4
Wilson, Henry 205
Wincle 188–9
Winsford flashes 107
Winterley Pool 138–9
Winwick 258–9
Wirral 20, 40–53
  Wirral Country Park 44
  Wirral Way, The 43
Wood, William 183
Woodland Trust 286
Woolston Eyes Nature Reserve 263
Wrenbury 74
Wyatt, Lewis 231
Wyatt, Samuel 91
Wybunbury 92
  Wybunbury Moss 92
  Wybunbury Tower 92

Z

zoos 34–5, 89–90

INDEX OF ADVERTISERS

Oddfellows Chester/Oddfellows on the Park   4th colour section
Visit Cheshire   4th colour section

VISITCHESHIRE.COM

Your official guide to Chester, Cheshire and Beyond...

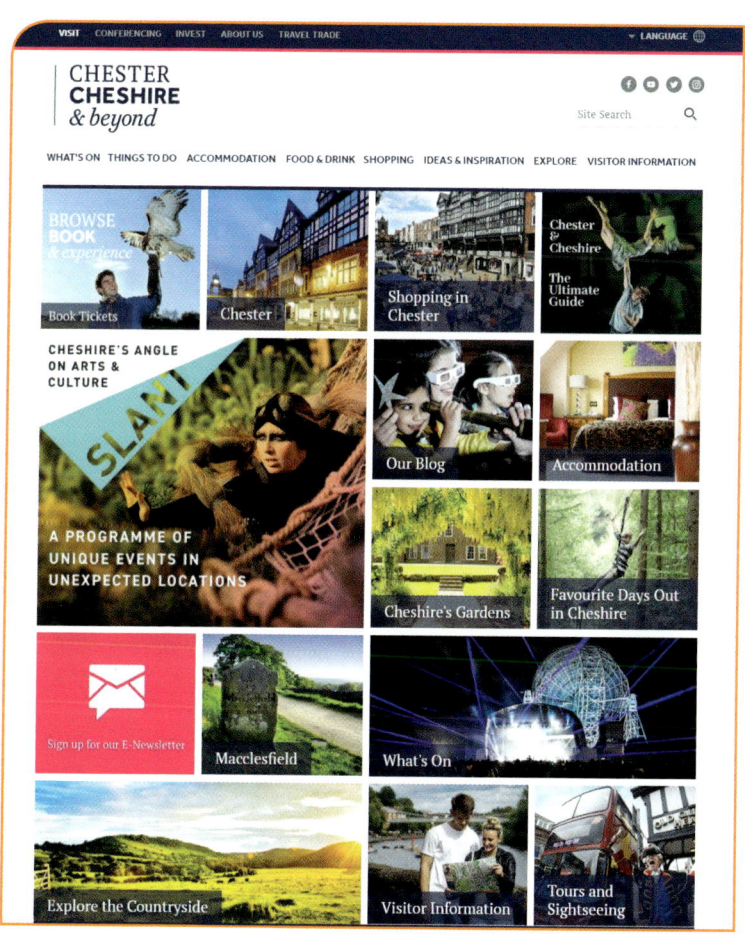

CHESTER CHESHIRE & beyond

Marketing Cheshire
1 Castle Drive
Chester

🖱 www.visitcheshire.com
📞 01244 405600
✉ info@marketingcheshire.co.uk

Hotels with character, charm and a little bit of 'Odd'.

ODDFELLOWS
Chester

01244 345454 |
reception@oddfellowschester.com |
www.oddfellowschester.com
20 Lower Bridge Street | CH1 1RS

ODDFELLOWS
On the Park

0161 697 3066 |
reception@oddfellowsonthepark.com |
www.oddfellowsonthepark.com
Bruntwood Park, Cheadle | SK8 1HX

A MEMBER OF **DESIGN HOTELS**™

"Slow guides take time to point the way."

Hugh Fearnley-Whittingstall

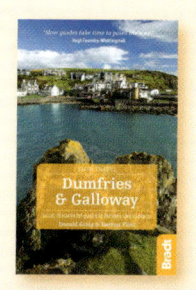

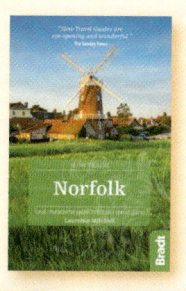

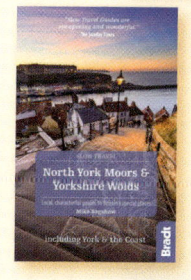

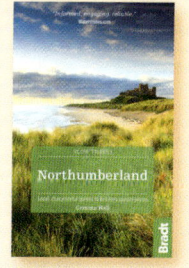

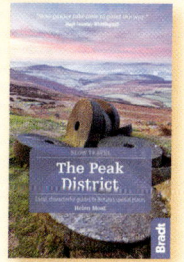

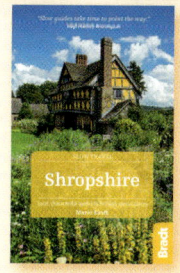

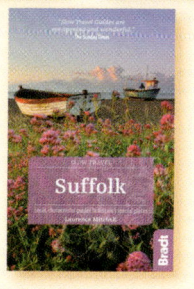

Dumfries & Galloway

Norfolk

North York Moors & Yorkshire Wolds

Northumberland

The Peak District

Shropshire

Suffolk

Local, characterful guides to Britain's special places

Bradt

Available from bookshops or www.bradtguides.com

Something different for the weekend

Whether wild camping or wildlife-watching, let us help you make the most of your weekends.

Bradt

Available to buy in all good bookshops or on www.bradtguides.com

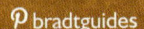

BradtTravelGuides @BradtGuides @bradtguides bradtguides